Assessing Knowledge

of

Retirement Behavior

Eric A. Hanushek and Nancy L. Maritato, Editors

Panel on Retirement Income Modeling

Committee on National Statistics

Commission on Behavioral and Social Sciences and Education

National Research Council

NATIONAL ACADEMY PRESS
Washington, D.C.   1996

NATIONAL ACADEMY PRESS • 2101 Constituion Avenue, N.W. • Washington, D.C. 20418

The project that is the subject of this report is supported by funds from the Pension and Welfare Benefits Administration of the U.S. Department of Labor, the National Institute on Aging of the U.S. Department of Health and Human Services, the Pension Benefit Guaranty Corporation, the Social Security Administration, and TIAA-CREF.

Library of Congress Catalog Card Number 96-69361

International Standard Book Number 0-309-05547-4

Additional copies of this report are available from National Academy Press, 2101 Constitution Avenue, N.W., Box 285, Washington, D.C. 20055 Call 800-624-6242 or 202-334-3313 (in Washington Metropolitan Area). Order electronically via Internet at http://www.nap.edu.

iii

Preface

The Panel on Retirement Income Modeling of the Committee on National Statistics was established to review the state of the art and make recommendations to inform policy making on retirement income security. The panel's work considers what data, research, and models exist and what are needed to estimate the short-run and long-run implications of current retirement-income-related policies and proposed changes to them. Support for the project was provided by the Pension and Welfare Benefits Administration in the U.S. Department of Labor, the National Institute on Aging, the Pension Benefit Guaranty Corporation, the Social Security Administration, and TIAA-CREF.

In order to inform its work, the panel commissioned the papers in this volume, which review the state of research on such topics as individual labor supply and savings behavior and employer behavior that is relevant to retirement income security. The papers were originally presented at a conference in September 1994; they were subsequently modified to incorporate the comments of discussants at the conference, panel members, and reviewers. The authors provide comprehensive assessments of their subject areas, and we thank them.

Our thanks go next to the discussants: Richard Burkhauser, Syracuse University; David Cutler, Harvard University; Marjorie Honig, Hunter College; Michael Hurd, State University of New York, Stony Brook; Marvin Kosters, American Enterprise Institute; Alicia Munnell, Council of Economic Advisors; Patricia Ruggles, Joint Economic Committee, U.S. Congress; John Rust, University of Wisconsin, Madison; Dallas Salisbury, Employee Benefit Research Institute; Eugene Steuerle, The Urban Institute; Lawrence Thompson, The Urban Institute; and Joshua Wiener, The Urban Institute

The panel also gratefully acknowledges the commitment and support of all those who worked collaboratively to organize the conference and prepare this volume. Constance Citro, the panel's study director, developed plans for the conference in collaboration with panel members. Nancy Maritato worked with the authors to shepherd their papers through revision and review and collaborated with me to draft the introduction. Agnes Gaskin facilitated the conference arrangements, and Candice Evans prepared the final manuscript.

Most important, the papers and the workshop discussion contributed significantly to the panel's work and our report, which will be published early next year.

Eric A. Hanushek, *Chair*
Panel on Retirement Income Modeling

Contents

Assessing Knowledge
of
Retirement Behavior

1

Introduction

Eric A. Hanushek and Nancy L. Maritato

Federal, state, and local governments are continually adopting or revising policies and programs that affect the economic well-being of the nation's citizens. Unfortunately, it is all too often true that the process of such policy development and implementation is not closely linked to scientific and analytic policy research. This situation became clear during the health care reform debates of 1993-1994. As task forces and policy makers attempted to develop legislation that would improve the provision of health care services in the United States, they found that key information was missing. The dearth of relevant information was most apparent when analysts attempted to estimate the cost of reform proposals: for each proposal, different analysts arrived at cost estimates that differed by a factor of two or three. Similar problems affect analyses of proposals in the area of retirement income security.

With the aging of the population, with increasing uncertainty about the solvency of the Social Security system, and with growing concern about the availability of adequate private pensions, retirement income policy is likely to be the focus of increasing attention. In some respects, the information necessary to formulate sound retirement income policy is more difficult to obtain than the information needed for health care reform. Economic, social, and demographic trends make the level of income security that future retirees can expect highly uncertain. In addition, long delays between the implementation of policies and the full realization of their effects add to the challenge of making informed decisions in this area. Without the appropriate information, decision makers run the risk that the proposals they adopt may be ineffective, or worse, counterproductive.

In order to improve this situation, the Pension and Welfare Benefits Administration in the U.S. Department of Labor, with support from the National Institute on Aging, the Pension Benefit Guaranty Corporation, the Social Security Administration, and TIAA-CREF, asked the Committee on National Statistics at the National Research Council to establish a Panel on Retirement Income Modeling. The charge to the panel was not to recommend changes in public or private policies that affect retirement income security. Instead, the charge was to consider a critical adjunct to the policy process—namely, the projection models, databases, and research findings that are needed to provide reliable information about the likely short- and long-term costs and benefits of today's retirement-income-related policies and proposed changes to them.

Modeling the likely future effects of any current policy or policy proposal is a difficult task at best. This is especially true when the policy pertains to retirement income security because of the need to project the effects of both current policy provisions and proposed changes to them over long periods of time. As just one example, to assess adequately the implications that tax law provisions to encourage contributions to 401(k) employer pension plans or Individual Retirement Accounts will have for post-retirement (and pre-retirement) living standards, the effects of those provisions on savings behavior must be projected over at least a generation. The long time horizon for many retirement-income-related policy projections greatly increases the uncertainty of the estimates compared with, say, the 5-year projections that are typically prepared for tax law and welfare policy proposals.

Further increasing the difficulty of the modeling task and the uncertainty of the estimates is the need to take account of all, or at least the main, sources of retirement income support (and the potentially major drain on income represented by health care costs). These income sources include Social Security, employer-provided pensions, personal savings, other transfers (e.g., public assistance and public and private disability payments), post-retirement earnings from part-time employment, and bequests and other transfers among family members. For some purposes, it may be appropriate—and challenging enough—to model one of the components in isolation, such as the effects of changes in Social Security payroll taxes or benefits on the solvency of the Social Security Trust Fund and on likely rates at which Social Security benefits will replace earnings. However, such an analysis cannot provide an adequate picture of overall retirement income security if the Social Security changes in turn affect other components of retirement income (e.g., levels of employer pension coverage and other savings). Moreover, to the extent that there is interaction among the components, such an analysis may not provide an adequate picture of the effects of the changes on the Social Security system itself.

Particularly when an analysis considers sources of retirement income other than Social Security, there is an added difficulty due to the heterogeneity among workers and employers. While almost all workers are covered by Social Security, there is wide variation in the extent to which workers are covered by employer-provided pensions and in the provisions of such coverage. There is also wide variation in personal savings behavior. For policy deliberations, this heterogeneity becomes very important. Much of the focus of government retirement policy is on ensuring some minimum living standard for the subset of elderly people who may have been unlucky or unwise in preparing for their retirement. It is thus important that projection models produce estimates of the likely numbers of such people, as well as estimates of the average experience.

Priorities for improving data, research knowledge, and models with which to inform debates about retirement income policies need to be motivated by a consideration of what is known and not known about relevant behaviors and the state of the art with respect to analytical and projection modeling. To learn from experts in the field, in September 1994 the panel sponsored the Conference on Modeling the Impact of Public and Private Policies on Retirement Behavior and Income: What Do We Know and What Do We Need to Know? Six papers were commissioned from knowledgeable researchers and policy analysts for presentation and discussion at the conference. This volume presents those papers as they were revised by the authors to incorporate the comments of discussants, panel members, and reviewers.

The paper authors were asked to review the issues, literature, and state of knowledge in six topic areas:

- projecting the distribution of income and wealth of retired workers and their families from all sources (Alan L. Gustman and F. Thomas Juster);
- labor supply behavior that is relevant to retirement decisions and, ultimately, retirement income (Robin L. Lumsdaine);
- microlevel savings behavior and substitution effects between public and personal savings vehicles and the implications for retirement income (James M. Poterba);
- the behavior of firms that is relevant to workers' retirement decisions and their retirement income (Donald O. Parsons);
- projecting the older population, the likely health care costs they face, and the implications for retirement income (Ronald D. Lee and Jonathan Skinner); and
- estimating the overall effects of policy changes on future retirement income security in a context that includes the macroeconomic effects of government tax and transfer policies (Gary Burtless).

The authors of the first five papers were asked to include the following: (1) an introduction about the relevant policy issues in the area; (2) a review of the current literature, focusing on why some questions have not yet been satisfactorily answered; (3) modeling approaches, both for improving research knowledge and for providing answers to policy questions; (4) an indication of the desired state of the art with regard to data, research, and modeling strategies; and (5) recommendations of research, modeling, and data collection priorities. The author of the final paper was asked to take a broader look at retirement income modeling, concentrating on an overall framework for policy analysis in this area.

The panel anticipates that the papers in this volume will serve as a useful reference for the research and policy communities as to what is known about retirement-income-related behaviors and the gaps and deficiencies in knowledge, data, and modeling techniques. The panel has drawn on the papers in its deliberations about priorities for developing an improved capability for assessing the short-term and long-term costs and benefits of retirement-income-related policy changes. The findings and conclusions of the panel will be provided in its final report.

INCOME AND WEALTH OF OLDER AMERICAN HOUSEHOLDS

The paper by Gustman and Juster focuses on the distribution and sources of income and wealth of households with retired workers. They report that income and wealth data show substantial disparities among elderly households, and the disparities appear to be greater for households whose members are age 70 and older than for other households. The available data also suggest that favorable economic circumstances tend to coexist: for example, people with higher levels of wealth tend also to have income from private pensions. Although there are some problems with income data, Gustman and Juster conclude that wealth data are much more problematic, especially for assets other than housing.

In order to more closely examine income and wealth at retirement, Gustman and Juster review separate behavioral models that address several relevant issues: earnings, lifetime savings, and pensions. Beginning with labor supply and retirement decision models, they argue that current models of labor force participation and earnings could be improved to better account for the trend toward early retirement. Although the literature suggests that the preferences of workers have shifted, the models attribute the shift to changing incentives. The primary savings models (e.g., the life-cycle model, the precautionary savings model, the bequest motive model) have not been successful in explaining why so many elderly reach retirement with little or no savings. This theme underscores the analysis of household savings behavior in the paper by Poterba.

A majority of research on private pensions approaches the issue in terms of individual behavior. On the employer side, Gustman and Juster do not find a model with sufficient structure that can be used to predict the effects of government policies on employers' decisions about pension benefit levels, other plan characteristics, insurance features, or other outcomes that would be useful in understanding how pension policies affect retirement incomes and wealth. Although Gustman and Juster attribute the lack of models largely to a lack of databases on employers that include detailed pension offering information along with employer characteristics, Parsons argues that more fundamental conceptual issues may also be important.

By focusing on the economic well-being of the elderly, Gustman and Juster are led to a key missing element in existing thinking and modeling: the extraordinarily important interaction of labor supply, savings, and pension decisions. Knowledge of the separate components is insufficient unless one makes the unrealistic assumption that they are independent or that part of the decisions is exogenously determined. This interaction issue clearly taxes available modeling abilities, but it cannot be ignored.

Gustman and Juster conclude that the new Health and Retirement Survey (HRS) and the Asset and Health Dynamics Among the Oldest Old (AHEAD) survey provide essential data for much of the modeling of individual behavior that is needed. As just one example, HRS will allow researchers to sort out the effects of earlier savings decisions on the retirement decision by providing panel data on detailed asset accumulation before retirement. Similarly, data from AHEAD will enable researchers to determine to what extent older households decumulate assets, particularly housing assets, to finance consumption after retirement.

LABOR SUPPLY BEHAVIOR

The paper by Lumsdaine considers the choices that workers make, and the factors influencing their choices, about when to retire. She reports trend data showing that the average retirement age is falling while life expectancies are increasing. Both of these trends suggest that retirement savings will need to be stretched over more years of life. However, a large proportion of the retirement-age population is reaching retirement with relatively low levels of savings.

Because most of the elderly population is affected by Social Security, Lumsdaine suggests that it is the obvious place to start in discussing broad-based policy changes that can influence retirement behavior and income. Although some changes to the program have been legislated over the past decade, much of the research on Social Security suggests that the effects of these changes will not be substantial. However, debate still continues as to the relative importance of Social Security on retirement decisions and retirement income.

Because Social Security may not provide enough income for many retirees, pensions are a source of additional retirement income that government policy has encouraged. Lumsdaine reports evidence that suggests, for those people who will receive pension benefits, the magnitude of the expected benefits can strongly influence their retirement behavior. However, it is difficult to make inferences about labor supply behavior with nationally representative data due to the lack of detailed pension plan information in most data sets.

There has been increasing discussion about the relationship between Social Security Disability Insurance and retirement and the possibility that a liberalization of disability benefits is partly responsible for earlier retirement decisions and declines in labor force participation generally. Lumsdaine reports that there is still considerable disagreement in the literature about the causal relationship between increased generosity of disability benefits and declining labor force participation, although there is a correlation. Understanding the link between disability and retirement is the first step to being able to predict how changes in Social Security policy may affect disability application.

Another important issue to address is workers' flexibility to choose hours of work. Although evidence suggests that workers would prefer to gradually reduce their amount of work hours rather than make an abrupt transition from full-time work to complete retirement, evidence also suggests that workers are in fact constrained in their choice of hours. One option they have is to retire from a career job but take a new job with fewer hours of work.

Overall, Lumsdaine provides a picture of a rich set of analyses addressing retirement decisions of individual workers, although she notes that the appropriate approach to best understand these decisions is not completely determined. Nonetheless, plentiful examples provide a sample of different approaches. By far the most important issue in Lumsdaine's view is better understanding of how individuals form expectations. Because expectations about retirement income and support are crucial to individual choices, fundamental research is needed. She also provides insight into alternative modeling approaches. While seeing the conceptual appeal of dynamic optimization models, Lumsdaine raises a note of caution about the feasibility of developing these very complex and computationally burdensome kinds of behavioral models much further in the near term.

Lumsdaine concludes that many of the shortcomings of the literature, as well as the failure to model adequately the multiple factors influencing the retirement decision, stem from insufficient data. HRS and AHEAD, according to Lumsdaine, show great promise for use by future researchers to model the complexities of the retirement decision and retirement income. For example, information on pension plan provisions collected from sample members' employers will make it possible to develop more sophisticated models of the retirement decision. Also, repeated measures of health status and employment and earnings for middle-aged workers as they age should help answer the question of whether poor health status reduces employment opportunities and earnings or whether poor job prospects and earnings impair health. Similarly, such data should help answer the question of whether poor health leads to early retirement or whether a report of poor health is a rationalization of a decision to retire early that would have been made in any case.

PERSONAL SAVING BEHAVIOR

The paper by Poterba examines the choices that workers make, at various stages in their work life, between types of public and private savings vehicles and about the level of their contributions to private pension plans (including decisions to withdraw contributions). Beginning with an examination of income and wealth holdings of the elderly, Poterba reports (as do Gustman and Juster) that there are wide disparities in wealth among the elderly and that the majority of them reach retirement age holding relatively low levels of liquid assets. The predominant model of savings behavior—the life-cycle/permanent income hypothesis model—fails to explain this phenomenon. Other savings models, such as the precautionary motive model and the bequest motive model, have the same shortcoming.

The failure to understand individual motives behind savings decisions is important. For example, individuals' reactions to different policies will differ due to their underlying motivation for saving. Moreover, while improved data will help in understanding savings, the underlying modeling questions cannot be ignored. An important issue, which is a recurring theme throughout the papers, is that individual heterogeneity is central to much of the analysis and policy debate, but appropriately incorporating such heterogeneity is a very difficult analytical task.

For those individuals managing to reach retirement age with a significant level of wealth, a lingering question in the literature is the rate of accumulation or decumulation of that wealth. Poterba reports that evidence in the literature is mixed and that this is an important area for future research.

Poterba also examines the research related to the question of whether individuals who participate in private pension plans adjust other aspects of their saving to offset their pensions. He suggests that this question is difficult to answer because of data problems. For example, few data sets combine information on the structure of private defined benefit pension plans and other components of household wealth.

For many of the important questions of interest with respect to private saving and the future financial status of the elderly, concludes Poterba, the existing research base does not provide detailed and convincing information on crucial parameter values and behavioral estimates. This problem will be partially remedied by HRS and AHEAD, but these surveys alone will not resolve all of the outstanding research questions.

EMPLOYER BEHAVIOR

The paper by Parsons examines the choices that employers make about their work forces, pension benefits, and financing of pension plans. An understanding of employers' decisions about hiring and retention of older workers and about whether to offer pension benefits (and, if so, what type to offer) is crucial to predicting the future well-being of the retired population. Parsons notes that as employers deal with a heterogenous population of aging workers, various attributes decline nonuniformly, making it difficult to adjust compensation to new productivity levels. In addition, workers are resistant to downward adjustments in pay, although they seem to more readily accept compensation cuts in the form of actuarially unfair adjustments in pension accruals.

Employers vary greatly in the types of pension plans they offer, if they offer one at all. Historically, employers most often offered defined benefit plans. The reasons for offering this type of plan range from forestalling union activity to decreasing voluntary job turnover and enhancing job performance. These types of plans can also be used to induce exit from a company or to provide the company a graceful way to reduce employee compensation. Lately, defined contribution plans, such as 401(k) plans, have been on the rise. These plans are advantageous to workers because they provide a vehicle for tax-deferred savings. At the same time, employers benefit from them because the plans permit the targeting of pension contributions to workers who value them.

The questions about employers' behavior are very similar to those about individuals. How do employers' decisions about retirement options and benefits interact with Social Security and other public programs and with individual retirement decisions? These questions, however, go to a deeper level that involves the fundamental underlying motivations of employers. Employers have incentives to encourage or discourage particular workers to stay because of productivity concerns, and these incentives interact with law, regulations, and individual contracts, but little is known about the strength of employer motivations and there are no well-developed models on this issue. Indeed, the contrast in knowledge, compared with modeling individual retirement decisions, is stark. Parsons describes some of the larger questions but without the means to evaluate alternative modeling approaches. Moreover, a basic message from Parsons' discussion is that some key prior questions, such as the pattern of age-productivity relationships, must be addressed before one can move to questions of individual employer or worker motivations and behavior.

The central issues in understanding employer behavior thus come down to defining better the key questions to be addressed and to developing basic research programs. Because this area is so underdeveloped, there are also fundamental questions about what kinds of data would be most useful to collect and how one should obtain those data. An implication is that the design of cost-effective data collection is much more important in this area than in others covered in this volume.

MORTALITY, HEALTH STATUS, AND HEALTH CARE COSTS

The paper by Lee and Skinner looks at the relationship of life expectancy and health issues to retirement behavior and income. To begin, Lee and Skinner examine mortality rates because it is important to have good forecasts of mortality to determine how long people are likely to draw Social Security or private pension benefits or how long their personal savings are likely to last. Lee and Skinner find that there are large differentials in mortality forecasts, which lead to very different forecasts in the number of elderly. Also problematic is that mortality data by race and ethnic group are of suspect quality.

Another issue involves the projection of health and disability status. Although current evidence suggests a trend toward lower levels of disability among the elderly population, Lee and Skinner note that accurate projection is difficult because no unique definition of disability exists in historical data. This problem will largely be corrected in the future by the continued collection of a variety of health and disability measures in HRS and AHEAD.

Improving forecasts of the general price of health care costs, in contrast, is not something that can be done simply by attaining more historical data on prices. The problem, according to Lee and Skinner, is that there is no good model of how health care costs are determined. Much work remains to be done to understand what factors are important in determining health care costs and how they might be expected to evolve over the next 30 years. Ultimately, because of shortcomings of existing modeling, progress in this area is very uncertain in the near term.

How will changing mortality, health, and health care costs affect retirement income security? Lee and Skinner suggest that projections about retirement income security often focus on average levels of health care expenditures within quite broad demographic groups. However, the design of appropriate public policy is more likely to be concerned with the retirement outcomes of a specific group of people, such as those at the bottom portion of the income distribution. Hence, the authors suggest that developing methods for predicting the future financial security of specified demographic groups may be beneficial for policy purposes.

A FRAMEWORK FOR ANALYZING
RETIREMENT INCOME SECURITY

The paper by Burtless outlines a broad framework for conducting analyses of retirement income security and projecting likely future effects of policy changes. His proposed analytical strategy rests on a microsimulation model that would project labor force status, job tenure and turnover, private pension and Social Security accrual, and household saving. Aggregate predictions from this model could be calibrated to predictions of the Social Security actuarial model. A macroeconomic model should also be created and linked to the microsimulation model to explain how savings are divided across alternative uses; to account for growth in capital stock, worker productivity, and wages; and to explain market rates of return on different classes of assets.

Burtless admits that the initial implementation of this modeling approach would probably produce relatively unrealistic results. However, he suggests that analysts could offer a range of possible outcomes, from very optimistic to very pessimistic. He also suggests that continuing work be done on improving the reliability of the linked micro and macro models through additional empirical research on key retirement-income-related topics.

Pursuing the use of an overall microsimulation strategy for modeling retirement income has two important justifications. First, such a formulation provides structure for separate analyses of behavioral components. An overall integrated model requires continual consideration of what behavioral interactions are most important, of which parameters are crucial for analysis and which are less important, and of how concepts and variables might be consistently defined and measured. Second, while various analytical models could play this integrative role, microsimulation models have distinct advantages in the context of retirement modeling because they are designed to explicitly incorporate the heterogeneity of the population. As noted above the central nature of individual heterogeneity is a recurring theme in all the papers. At the same time, the demands of microsimulation models for data and knowledge of individual behavior are truly great, suggesting that when and how to build a new microsimulation model are strategic questions for which there are no obvious or easy answers.

CONCLUSION

A clear message from the papers in this volume is that a number of questions about retirement income policy could be clarified with new data from HRS and AHEAD. The authors stress the importance of continuing to collect these data so that they provide sufficient observations to explain behavior patterns over time. In some cases, however, additional data are needed, not only through additional questions on current surveys and through links among existing surveys, but through the establishment of new surveys. It seems especially important to collect more employer-level information.

Additional work is also needed in modeling. The availability of new data will certainly help, but in some cases, much more conceptual thinking is needed. Currently, there is no consensus about such absolutely key questions as why individuals save. It is certainly true that good data and good models must work in conjunction to provide useful analysis.

2

Income and Wealth of Older American Households: Modeling Issues For Public Policy Analysis

Alan L. Gustman and F. Thomas Juster

This paper is concerned with the economic behavior determining the income and wealth of older American households, and with our capacity to analyze the effects of public policies determining their income and wealth. It begins by providing a structure for relating the outcomes of interest to leading behavioral models. This is followed by descriptive statistics indicating the relative importance of the major components of income and wealth. The paper then assesses the current state of models, describing what is known about the behavior of individuals and firms that affects income and wealth determination, what is not known, and what kinds of models and data are needed to do an adequate job of understanding income and wealth outcomes and the effects of policies meant to influence these outcomes. The final part of the paper considers an array of policy changes that might be expected to influence the income and wealth of older households.

CONCEPTUAL OVERVIEW

Figure 2-1 indicates the major components of income and wealth of the older population and the elements of behavior of individuals, of markets, and in the public sector that determine these income and wealth outcomes. Box A repre-

The authors are grateful to the National Institute on Aging for research support. Helpful comments by Gary Engelhardt, Anna Lusardi, Andrew Samwick, Jonathan Skinner, Tim Smeeding, and Steve Venti are very much appreciated.

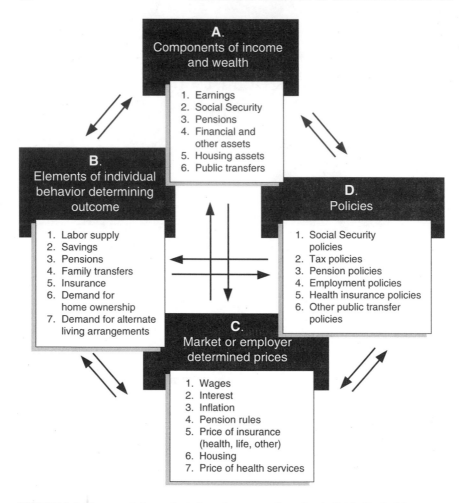

FIGURE 2-1 Framework for analysis from the perspective of an individual's decisions.

sents a matrix of income and wealth outcomes. The outcomes are delineated by type of income, but the matrix is meant to represent the full dimension of time and cohort effects, as well as the various sources of heterogeneity in outcomes. Box B lists the behavioral decisions. They include the basic decisions of labor supply and savings, as well as other behaviors that must receive attention for a full understanding of wealth and income. Below that in Box C is an array of market-determined outcomes that are taken as exogenous to the individual, such as the features of the pension plan, determined by the employer subject to market constraints. The right-hand box, D, lists some of the basic categories for the policies that will be discussed. The arrows indicate that each box helps to determine elements in other boxes.

A central focus of the paper is the behavior of individuals and the efforts of firms to accommodate the behavior and preferences of individuals. Our aim is to determine whether the analyses of the various dimensions of behavior indicated in Figure 2-1 are sufficiently reliable to support policy analysis, and if not, what additional research is required to improve the quality of the available behavioral models. As a result of our analysis, we conclude that among the key dimensions of behavior, we have greater confidence in the retirement models for use in policy analysis than in models of saving or pensions. Models of savings and pensions continue to wrestle with behavioral issues that remain unresolved at a more fundamental level than the questions that confront retirement modeling. But we also find that none of the models of behavior in any one area takes sufficient account of the behavior along other dimensions. These behaviors may interact in important ways, and most of the literature ignores these interactions.

COMPONENTS OF INCOME AND WEALTH OF OLDER HOUSEHOLDS

To measure the importance of the major components of income and wealth, we begin with descriptive data on income and wealth outcomes for recent cohorts. The relevant data include the Current Population Survey (CPS), where we use 1992 income data analyzed by Grad (1994); the Survey of Income and Program Participation (SIPP), where we use 1991 wealth data analyzed by Poterba, Venti, and Wise (1994); the Health and Retirement Survey (HRS), where we use income data from 1991 and wealth data from 1992; and the Asset and Health Dynamics Among the Oldest Old (AHEAD) survey, where we use income data from 1992 and wealth data from 1993.

These data sets are complementary. CPS covers the entire age range, as does SIPP, but the income and wealth data from these surveys, especially the wealth data, tend to be underestimates relative to either HRS or AHEAD; in both HRS and AHEAD, new survey technologies have been introduced that result in substantially smaller biases resulting from missing data components. But while HRS and AHEAD appear to have data of somewhat higher quality, they represent particular cohorts and do not include a full range of age distributions. HRS includes the birth cohorts of 1931 to 1941, while AHEAD includes the birth cohorts of 1923 and before.

The data in Table 2-1 provide a useful overview of the sources of income and wealth for households that are in a transition stage between work and retirement—those 65 to 69 years of age. For these households, earnings comprise a little under 30 percent of total income; Social Security comprises another 30 percent, while pensions and income from assets each comprise a bit under 20 percent. On the asset side, if both Social Security income flows and pension

TABLE 2-1   Sources of Money Income and Wealth for 65- to 69-Year Olds

Income and Wealth Source	Share of Aggregate Income of Aged Units (%)	Average Wealth From Indicated Source as a % of Total Net Worth
Earnings	28.9	
Social Security	29.9	31.9
Pensions	18.8	19.9
Financial and other assets	18.7	27.8
Public assistance	0.7	
Other income	3.1	
Housing		20.8
Total	100.1	100.4

SOURCE: Income percentages are from Grad (1994, Table VII.1). Grad's figures are based on the 1992 CPS. Wealth percentages are computed from Poterba, Venti, and Wise (1994, Table 1). Their data are from SIPP and are reported for 1991.

income flows are capitalized, the two make up a little over half of total wealth, with the other half coming from conventionally measured net worth—the sum of financial and other assets and housing equity.

From these data we can see the extent of the underestimation problem in the measurement of assets: Assets in Table 2-1 are based on data from SIPP, where conventionally defined net worth (the total of financial and other assets plus housing equity) for these 65- to 69-year-olds had a mean value of roughly $150,000 in 1991; SIPP households aged 55 to 64, a younger age group that typically has smaller net worth than the 65-to-69 group, had a mean 1991 total of about $140,000. In contrast, the HRS data on net worth for households between 51 and 61, where asset holdings would be expected to be smaller still, had a mean 1992 value of approximately $240,000—a figure that is approximately 60 percent larger than the Table 2-1 estimate. And the AHEAD net-worth data, for an age group much older than the SIPP 65- to 69-year-olds and one that would therefore be expected to have a much lower asset level, had a 1993 mean value for conventionally defined net worth of approximately $170,000—higher than the 65- to 69-year-olds in Table 2-1.

Note that the data in Table 2-1 are missing some components. For example, one would generally prefer to include imputed income from housing equity in the income definition and might well include imputed values for services provided by Medicare and Medicaid. The wealth data might include present discounted values for Supplemental Security Income, other welfare payments, and transfers. According to Hurd (1990b, Table 18), these are not negligible sources of income or wealth. It is also worth noting that although the capitalized value of future Social Security or pension benefits, which is included as part of wealth, appropriately reflects the consumption value of these assets, it represents a relatively

inflexible source of economic support. To some extent that is also true of housing equity, although here the inflexibility lies as much in consumer choice as in
legal or institutional constraints. But it is certainly clear that Social Security
wealth cannot be bought and sold, nor can pension wealth, and while housing
equity can be bought or sold, most households appear to treat housing equity as
an immutable fact of economic circumstances, not an asset that can be used to
smooth consumption flows in future years.

An important feature of both income and wealth is their heterogeneity among
households. Households are always heterogeneous in the types and amounts of
income and wealth that they own, but that heterogeneity is likely to grow as
households move into older age groups. And both distributions, especially the
wealth distributions, are highly skewed in that medians are small relative to mean
values.

The heterogeneity of the income sources received by older households is
documented in Tables 2-2 and 2-3. Table 2-2 shows the detailed structure of
income from HRS (for age groups in their 50s), and for AHEAD (for age groups

TABLE 2-2   Income Components, HRS and AHEAD, in Thousands of
Dollars

Income Source	Age of Household Head					
	51-55[a]	56-61[a]	70-74[b]	75-79[b]	80-84[b]	85+[b]
Earnings	40.6	32.4	4.0	1.5	1.0	0.2
Pensions	1.0	2.8	16.6	15.9	12.4	10.4
Social Security	0.1	0.2	10.2	10.4	9.4	8.2
Private pension	0.9	2.6	6.4	4.5	3.0	2.2
Capital Income	5.1	5.9	2.1	2.9	2.6	1.8
Disability	0.4	0.6				
Welfare	0.3	0.3	1.1	0.8	0.7	0.8
Unemployment	0.4	0.3				
Other	0.2	0.2				
Total	48.0	42.4	24.8[c]	21.9[c]	17.8[c]	15.7[c]
Household members other than respondent or spouse	4.9	4.7	3.0	2.8	3.7	5.0
Total	52.9	47.1	27.8	24.7	21.5	20.7

[a]1991 HRS data.

[b]1992 AHEAD data.

[c]Derived from an independent question, not from summing the components. The sum of components is generally lower than the above total for technical reasons (mainly the use of unfolding
brackets for the total income question).

SOURCE: 1991 HRS data for ages 51 to 61; 1992 AHEAD data for ages 70 to 85+.

TABLE 2-3   Components of Income, AHEAD Sample

Income Component and Age Group	Mean for Sample	Mean if Greater Than Zero ($)	Percentiles ($)				
			10	25	50	75	90
Wage Income							
70-74	4,059	18,989	0	0	0	0	8,000
75-79	1,463	14,934	0	0	0	0	0
80-84	1,013	15,586	0	0	0	0	0
85+	162	12,776	0	0	0	0	0
Capital Income							
70-74	2,089	6,923	0	0	0	240	4,620
75-79	2,941	9,396	0	0	0	318	4,800
80-84	2,605	9,182	0	0	0	300	5,000
85+	1,798	6,987	0	0	0	0	3,600
Social Security Income							
70-74	10,246	10,259	4,440	6,516	9,480	13,000	15,900
75-79	10,374	10,390	4,800	6,420	9,210	12,696	16,308
80-84	9,384	9,411	4,608	6,000	8,208	11,724	14,712
85+	8,248	8,276	4,236	5,550	7,578	9,492	12,000
Pension Income							
70-74	6,404	10,660	0	0	2,680	7,218	16,080
75-79	4,539	8,647	0	0	1,200	4,644	11,604
80-84	2,964	6,714	0	0	0	2,964	9,540
85+	2,247	6,366	0	0	0	2,247	6,900
Other Income							
70-74	1,109	6,126	0	0	0	0	2,400
75-79	773	4,652	0	0	0	0	1,861
80-84	740	4,076	0	0	0	0	1,861
85+	773	4,189	0	0	0	0	2,160
Other Family Members' Income							
70-74	3,026	19,870	0	0	0	0	13,162
75-79	2,839	19,719	0	0	0	0	13,162
80-84	3,689	22,379	0	0	0	0	13,162
85+	4,979	21,386	0	0	0	6,571	13,162
Total Family Income							
70-74	27,778		8,280	12,460	19,304	29,723	49,200
75-79	24,754		7,428	10,374	16,539	25,004	42,374
80-84	21,515		6,528	9,398	13,992	22,561	38,352
85+	20,723		6,564	8,400	13,000	20,476	35,064

in their 70s and 80s). Total household income is of course substantially larger for the HRS sample than for AHEAD, partly because of cohort differences in earnings but mainly because of age differences. The HRS households are about 30 years younger than the AHEAD households that are ages 80 and over, and thus there has been 30 years worth of economy-wide improvement for the HRS cohort compared with the AHEAD 80 and older cohort. In addition, the AHEAD data reflect the fact that the replacement of earnings by the sum of Social Security benefits and pensions is at much lower than a one-to-one ratio for most households.

The income component data in Table 2-2 do not contain any surprises. Earnings are the dominant source of income for the HRS cohorts in their 50s, while pensions, especially Social Security, are the dominant source of income for households in the AHEAD cohorts. Earnings are relatively unimportant for households in the AHEAD age range, and the pattern of private pension income, which is about three times as high among AHEAD cohorts in the 70- to 74-year-old group as in the 85 and older group, is explainable both by cohort differences and by the growing incidence of widowhood among older households in the AHEAD cohorts. Finally, earnings of household members other than the HRS or AHEAD survey respondent and spouse are an important source of family income, especially for the oldest AHEAD cohort (those 85 years of age or older).

The heterogeneity of income components for the AHEAD cohort shows up very clearly in Table 2-3, which contains sample means, means for households with positive income in a particular category, and percentile distributions. Not surprisingly, hardly any AHEAD age groups have wage income, all the way up to the 90th percentile. Equally surprising to some, capital income is zero for the entire lower half of the AHEAD distribution, is only a few hundred dollars for AHEAD cohorts up as high as the 75th percentile, and becomes a substantial sum only when we get around the 90th percentile, where the amounts are several thousand dollars rather than several hundred dollars. The only income sources that are at all widely distributed among AHEAD households are Social Security income, which virtually everyone receives, and pension income, which is received by the upper half of the distribution in the younger age cohorts and by the upper quarter in the older age cohorts. For each age category and percentile, pension income exceeds Social Security income in the AHEAD sample for only one age cohort and one of the percentiles shown—the 90th percentile for the 70- to 74-year-olds. As we note later, it looks as if this pattern will be a bit different when the HRS cohorts get to be in the AHEAD age range, although that will depend in part on changes over time in the proportion of jobs providing pensions and in the proportion of pensions that contain survivors' rights.

The heterogeneity in economic status among older households is even more pronounced when we examine the data on net worth. Tables 2-A1 to 2-A7 in the Appendix contain estimates of total net worth, net worth in the form of housing equity, and net worth less housing equity for various HRS and AHEAD classifications of households. For HRS, we divide the sample into couples, single men, and single women (Table 2-A1), by racial/ethnic groups (blacks, Hispanics, and all others including whites, Table 2-A2); and by 1991 income (Table 2-A3). For the AHEAD sample, we show data for couples and singles in Table 2-A4 (total net worth) and Table 2-A5 (net worth excluding home equity), as well as for racial/ethnic groups in Tables 2-A6 (total net worth) and 2-A7 (net worth excluding home equity). For the AHEAD data, we show separate estimates for four age groups: 70 to 74, 75 to 79, 80 to 84, and 85 and up.

The principal message from this set of net-worth tables is that wealth is highly unevenly distributed among the older population: both in the HRS and the AHEAD samples, married couples have substantially higher levels of wealth than single men or single women, even after implicit correction for household size; the disparities are substantially larger for net worth less housing equity than for total net worth, since housing equity itself is somewhat more evenly distributed than most other assets; minority households have substantially fewer assets than whites by an order of magnitude of 4 or 5 to 1 in mean values, and an order of magnitude more like 10 to 1 for net worth less housing equity.

For the AHEAD data, there are of course substantial differences by age group as well as by family composition and racial/ethnic group. In general, older households have smaller net worth, other things equal, although the differences by age are surprisingly small for couples up through the age of 80 to 84. The most striking disparities in the AHEAD data are those shown by the tabulations of net worth excluding home equity, both by family composition and by racial/ethnic group, divided according to age group. For the family composition data, fully half the single women had net financial assets excluding home equity of under $10,000 regardless of age—the 70-to-74 group and the 85 and older group have just about the same (minimal) assets. Single men are a little better off, but fully half of this group have under $20,000 of net worth excluding home equity. For couples, in contrast, the median net worth excluding home equity is a little over $55,000 for the 70-to-74 age group and is still about $20,000 for the 85 and older age group. As would be expected, there are some very wealthy subcategories of households in the sample: AHEAD households in the 90th percentile among couples have over $400,000 of net worth excluding home equity, and almost $600,000 net worth in total, for those with heads age 70 to 74. Even for couples age 85 and up, AHEAD households have over a quarter of a million dollars in net worth excluding home equity at the 90th percentile and over $400,000 of total net worth. For minority households in the AHEAD sample, it is essentially correct that fully half of all black and Hispanic households have close to zero net worth excluding home equity, regardless of age, and even at the 75th percentile, neither black nor Hispanic households have as much as $20,000 of net worth excluding home equity in any of the AHEAD age groups. To all intents and purposes, most minority households can be thought of as having negligible financial asset holdings in old age.

Income Distribution Issues

The income and wealth data show substantial disparity among households, and the disparities appear to be a bit greater for households 70 and over than for others. One way to look at issues of income distribution is to examine the economic circumstances associated with private pensions.

Two alternative models might be contrasted. In one model, the existence of a private pension, since it involves a cost to the employer, provided less current income during the working years. On that model, households with substantial pensions would have had less current income than other comparably situated households; during retirement, they would be expected to have more pension income than others, but less income from capital and from Social Security benefits.

In an alternative model, the market is such that jobs that carry pensions are also apt to carry higher current income than other jobs, perhaps because only those with high wage rates want pensions, given the tax advantages of pensions and the low Social Security replacement rate for high wage jobs. Hence households with pensions will have more favorable economic circumstances generally as they move toward retirement. On that model, households with substantial pension income would also be expected to have substantial capital income relative to other households (because of their higher current income while working) and to have higher Social Security benefits (again because of their more favorable current income while working). In short, an important issue is, do households with jobs that carry substantial pensions have offsetting differences in other sources of retirement income, or do the differences tend to cumulate—those with pensions having more of other forms of retirement income as well?

Tables 2-4 and 2-5 show comparisons for both the HRS and the AHEAD sample. For HRS (Table 2-4), we contrast households in which both respondent and spouse have jobs with pension rights, households where one has a job with pension rights and the other a nonpension job, and households where neither has

TABLE 2-4   Earnings and Capital Income by Pension Status, HRS Households Working for Pay and Not Self-Employed

Whether Pension Income	% of Cases	Mean Values ($000)		
		Earnings	Capital Income	Total Income
Singles				
Yes	66.8	29.0	2.4	37.1
No	33.2	14.9	1.3	23.3
Couples[a]				
Both Have	57.1	64.4	4.0	75.0
One Has	34.6	49.7	2.9	62.1
Neither Has	8.3	36.7	5.3	49.2

NOTE: All categories weighted by the HRS household population weight.

[a]Both spouses in the couple households are working.

TABLE 2-5   Pension, Social Security, and Capital Income by Whether
Pension Income and Age, AHEAD Households[a]

Whether Pension Income	% Having Pension Income	Mean Pension Income ($)	Mean Social Security Income ($)	% Having Capital Income	Mean Capital Income ($)	Mean Total Income ($)
All cases (N=5,457)						
Yes	50.6	8,915	10,981	39	2,869	25,908
No	49.4	0	8,532	20	1,722	15,507
Age 70-74 (N=1,818)						
Yes	58.3	10,340	10,964	37	2,290	28,237
No	41.7	0	8,815	20	1,979	18,053
Age 75-79 (N=1,415)						
Yes	50.0	8,504	11,385	43	3,727	26,626
No	50.0	0	9,041	19	1,795	16,047
Age 80-84 (N=1,120)						
Yes	42.3	6,803	10,404	39	3,443	21,092
No	57.7	0	8,200	20	1,866	14,011
Age 85+ (N=794)						
Yes	34.1	6,099	9,011	39	2,773	19,064
No	65.9	0	7,202	19	1,131	11,148

NOTE: All categories weighted by the AHEAD household population weight.

[a]All income is for respondent and spouse only.

a job with pension rights although both have jobs. We also show data for singles
who work, with and without pensions on their job. We tabulate current earnings
for these HRS households, and also tabulate capital income. For the AHEAD
households (Table 2-5), we divide the sample into households receiving some
pension income versus those receiving none, and tabulate pension income, Social
Security benefits, capital income, and total income for each of the AHEAD age
groups.

It is clear enough from the data, especially the AHEAD data, that favorable
economic circumstances cumulate rather than offset. Both for the HRS age range
and for the various AHEAD age ranges, households either expecting or receiving
pension income have substantially higher nonpension income (capital income
and job earnings in the case of HRS households, Social Security benefits and
capital income in the case of AHEAD households). For the AHEAD sample,
where the differences are clearest and the analysis is least ambiguous, households
receiving pension income have close to twice as much total income as other
households.

Finally, we show a mapping of the relationship between health status and
both income and wealth for HRS households (see Appendix, Figures 2-A1 to 2-

A4). Although these data come from a cross section and therefore are not helpful on questions of causality, the strength of the relationship between health and wealth or health and income is quite remarkable, whether measured by relationships involving means or medians. For the net-worth measure, couples where both spouses are in either excellent or very good health have net worth in the area of $400,000, while households where both spouses are in fair or poor health tend to have net worth of less than a quarter of that. These differences are even sharper for median net worth and are almost as large for either mean or median household income. Interestingly enough, if there is any difference in the relationship between household financial variables and health for the male or female spouse, it appears that the health of the female spouse is more systematically related to the household's financial well-being than the health of the male spouse.

MODELS OF INDIVIDUAL AND FIRM BEHAVIOR EXPLAINING RETIREMENT INCOME AND WEALTH

This section briefly considers what we know and do not know about the dimensions of behavior that are central to an understanding of how policies affect retirement incomes and retirement wealth. The discussion covers labor supply decisions, savings behavior, pension plan determination, and the determination of Social Security income at the level of the individual. Also discussed are the behaviors determining family structures and transfers, and the demand for housing.

Income From Earnings Based on Labor Supply Decisions

To project earnings, it is necessary to explain patterns of labor force participation among older workers on jobs offering different wage rates.[1] Thus, an important part of the approach to understanding the determination of the earnings of older individuals, and the effects of public policies on earnings, is to apply a conventional intertemporal model of labor supply and to use the labor supply outcome together with the wage to determine earnings.

The conventional model for explaining labor force behavior into retirement is dynamic. Subject to a series of constraints, including the wage offer for full-time work, the wage offer for part-time work, and the rate of pension accrual (including its option value), as well as the corresponding rate of accrual in Social Security benefits and other factors, the individual reaches a decision on whether to continue working full time, part time, or not at all. In this approach, the parameters of a utility function are estimated so as to maximize the likelihood of observing the sequence of outcomes realized for each individual, subject to the constraints created by the elements of the opportunity set (Fields and Mitchell, 1984; Burtless and Moffitt, 1984, 1985; Gustman and Steinmeier, 1986b;

Berkovec and Stern, 1991; Rust, 1990; Stock and Wise, 1990a, 1990b; Lumsdaine, Stock, and Wise, 1990, 1992a, 1992b).

Different versions of the model have proved capable of explaining some major features of data reflecting labor supply of older individuals and their retirement. These include the spikes in the retirement hazard, most commonly at age 65, but at 55 for some and 62 for others. The models also explain the fact that two thirds of retirees proceed directly from full-time work to retirement, the relatively short duration of partial retirement, the coincidence of retirement decisions by husbands and wives, and some (about a quarter) of that portion of the trend to earlier retirement observed from 1970 through the mid-1980s (see Gustman and Steinmeier, 1986b, 1994a; Anderson, Gustman and Steinmeier, 1994).

Recent contributions have been made on a number of dimensions, adding to the richness of the dynamic specification, considering reaction to risk as well as expected values, incorporating interdependence of decisions at the level of the family, entertaining the possibility of retirement behavior that is influenced by liquidity constraints, and enriching the array of nonfinancial considerations employed in the model.[2]

Despite all of this work, there are many basic questions about retirement behavior that have not yet been addressed. Although we have made important progress in improving the dynamic and stochastic structures of retirement models, considerable work remains before we incorporate in a single setting the full array of behaviors in relation to uncertainty, mistakes, revisions, surprises, and random shocks. For example, Rust (1990) and Berkovec and Stern (1991) omit any consideration of the relation of pension incentives to labor market outcomes, by either focusing on the portion of the sample without a pension or simply ignoring the existence of the pension. In estimating these models, it will be important to measure pension incentives using data collected from worker descriptions as well as from firms.[3]

Findings based on the HRS by Brown (1993) suggest that some workers who accept an offer of a retirement window from one employer actually continue working, sometimes accepting another full-time job. This implies that some elements of mobility models (e.g., as in Allen, Clark, and McDermed, 1993; Gustman and Steinmeier, 1993) will have to be incorporated within retirement models that, to date, have analyzed the departure from a full-time job as if it always involved a substantial cessation of economic activity. Brown's findings are especially troublesome for studies that define retirement as exit from the payroll of a single firm. What is required for the models of Lumsdaine, Stock, and Wise (1992a, 1992b), for example, is to incorporate wages from work after retirement, as in the study of retirement from the Air Force by Ausink and Wise (1993), but allowing for the joint choices of work or retirement after leaving the job.

One test that is natural to impose on available studies is whether a model satisfactorily explains major social trends and policy outcomes. The weakness of available labor supply and retirement models is reflected in the limited ability of such models to explain the trend to earlier retirement satisfactorily. For example, for the period from 1970 through the mid-1980s, simple decomposition analyses that would explain the trend on the basis of changes in the composition of workers' demographic characteristics or employment cannot successfully explain the trend to earlier retirement (Ruhm, 1992; Anderson, Gustman, and Steinmeier, 1994). With the use of structural retirement models, some of the trend (about a quarter of the trend in the 1970s and 1980s) can be explained by the changes in pensions and Social Security.[4] We still do not have enough confidence in the implied substitution and income effects from these models to have a firm handle on the causes of these trends.[5] Also disturbing in this context are the strong implications of the pension literature that pensions are designed to meet the preferences of covered workers (Gustman, Mitchell, and Steinmeier, 1994), so that even those portions of the trend to earlier retirement that are associated with changing Social Security and pension benefit formulas may reflect the effects of changing tastes, rather than the changing incentives in the opportunity set.

Cohort-specific characteristics may be important determinants of retirement and of retirement trends. Some potential candidates for cohort effects include the change associated with the increasing participation of women throughout their lifetime, the changing structure of the division of labor in the household (more male hours, fewer female hours; see Juster and Stafford, 1991), and the changes in employer attitudes induced by the different histories and expectations about labor force commitment of the members of different cohorts. The literature does not, however, do a very good job of isolating cohort effects when explaining trends in retirement. Only time will tell whether these changes are adequately represented by differences in measurable characteristics among families or whether behavior will differ among subsequent cohorts because of cohort-specific effects.

Efforts are just beginning to expand the methodology available for examining the interdependence of family retirement decisions in a structural model, for incorporating measures reflecting job conditions or difficulty of work, and more generally for understanding the relation of financial measures, and of imperfections in capital markets, to retirement outcomes (see the discussion in Hurd, 1993, and Rust and Phelan, 1993, for example).

The roles of imperfect information, complex calculations, and responses to uncertainty remain to be sorted out and satisfactorily modeled for inclusion in behavioral analyses of relevant policies. An extensive set of questions in HRS on expectations and attitudes about risky choices has been used to analyze relevant aspects of decision making in the context of the complex choices facing the potential retiree (Barsky et al., 1993), but this information has not been incorporated in a structural retirement model.

Many questions also remain about the relation of behavior to expectations. Formal models of the retirement decision assume that workers make decisions in each period to maximize utility over their remaining lifetime. While some theoretical progress has been made in modeling such decisions in the presence of uncertainty, empirical work inevitably pretends that workers either know the value of future income streams associated with various choices or make rational expectations forecasts, and that they also know the "length of the planning horizon"—that is, how long they will live. The analysis of the relation of retirement expectations to incentives is encouraging (Hurd and McGarry, 1993a), but many questions remain unanswered. Previous research has suggested that there will be some whose expectations are unreasonable (Mitchell, 1988; Gustman and Steinmeier, 1989; Bernheim, 1988, 1989). In particular, there is a tail of the distribution with individuals who expect their benefits to be larger than is called for by their firm's pension plan, given their work and earnings history. More generally, we need to know how expectations are formed, how they are revised, and what differences there are in the formation of expectations and behavior for those who correctly report their constraints and for those who do not.

When the role of health status is measured in structural retirement models, it is measured by relatively direct questions about whether the individual suffers from health problems that impede work or other activities.[6] Researchers are aware that reported health status may involve an ex post rationalization, with an individual reporting he retired owing to ill health when that was not the motivating factor. This problem will be substantially remedied once panel data become available for estimating structural retirement models with HRS. The medical information is sufficiently detailed that it will be possible to isolate the effect of poor physical health from that of self-rationalization in the health measures used.

Savings and Wealth Determination

Savings and consumption analysis are major areas of economic research in both microeconomics and macroeconomics. From the perspective of aging research, analyses pertaining to life cycle, precautionary, and bequest motives are of particular interest.[7] Sophisticated econometric models have been estimated with microdata on the basis of equations derived with each of these behavioral motivations in mind, and recent work has attempted to explain wealth and savings outcomes on the basis of more than one of these behavioral motivations. There has also been useful empirical research that imposes somewhat less structure but focuses on major features of the data related to cohort and age effects. In addition, there is a line of research that questions whether savers can make the sophisticated calculations called for by dynamic stochastic models of savings.

Life-Cycle Analysis

A basic prediction of the simple life-cycle model is that with a rising mortality hazard, once the sum of the time preference and the mortality hazard exceed the interest rate, consumption and wealth will fall with increasing age. A good deal of relevant evidence has been collected and is presented in Hurd (1990b), who argues that if panel data are used and are corrected for the effects of mortality, profiles of bequeathable wealth do turn down at plausible ages and are consistent with the life-cycle model.[8]

A number of anomalies have encouraged researchers to expand the model of savings beyond a perfect capital market/life-cycle specification. Nevertheless, the forward-looking consumer continues to characterize the central agent of many models of savings behavior.

Precautionary Models of Savings

The individual faces a wide range of risks that might promote saving. If there are liquidity constraints or other factors creating incomplete markets for insurance, then a precautionary motive for saving may be important. If there are high rates of time preference, then the precautionary motive may dominate savings behavior even if the capital market is perfect. In precautionary models where agents display prudence, a precautionary motive may lead them to choose not to borrow, so they appear to be credit constrained.

A basic fact puzzling researchers of savings is why such a large number of individuals reach retirement with little or no savings. This raises the question of whether the predominance of an alternative motivation for saving beside the life-cycle model, and in particular precautionary saving, might account for the wide heterogeneity in observed outcomes. Other researchers have been motivated by evidence that suggests to them that the young don't borrow, the old don't decumulate, and consumption growth is positive even when the interest rate is low or negative in a certain period (see Zeldes, 1989a). An analysis of precautionary motives must explain both how expectations are formed and what the reaction is to risk. In microlevel studies there have been analyses of the properties of some of the major risks facing the individual, including pensions, earnings, length of life, and ill health (Skinner, 1988; Carroll, 1992; Guiso, Jappelli, and Terlizzese, 1992; Samwick, 1993b, 1994; Hubbard, Skinner, and Zeldes, 1994b). In the context of these analyses, it is also hoped that it will be possible to solve such puzzles as why consumption tracks income so closely (see Hall and Mishkin, 1982; Carroll and Summers, 1991), a phenomenon that suggests the importance of liquidity constraints (Zeldes, 1989a), and perhaps also to better understand how the saving motivation is affected by the availability of insurance (Hubbard, Skinner, and Zeldes, 1995).

Researchers are investigating the best way to categorize and measure the effects of and the reactions to risk, distinguishing risk aversion from prudence, analyzing their properties, and exploring the impact of these different features of preferences (Kimball, 1990, 1993).[9]

Bequest Motive

An alternative motivation for saving is to provide a bequest for one's heirs. The bequest motivation may be simple, as in dividing a fixed sum among one's heirs, or it may be complex, as in leaving a benefit in accordance with need or specifying a strategic arrangement in exchange for certain services from one's children (see, e.g., Becker, 1991; Bernheim, 1991; and Bernheim, Shleifer, and Summers, 1985). The fact that one leaves a bequest does not mean the bequest was intended or that it was the amount that would have been delivered in a world with perfect foresight. In the absence of efficient annuity markets or insurance by families, individuals may be forced to underconsume to avoid outliving their assets (Kotlikoff and Spivak, 1981; Davies, 1981; Abel, 1985). Nor is it optimal for everyone to want to leave a bequest—for example, children may be better off than their parents. Also, it is possible that consumption declines with age and bequests follow because, for some, the capacity to consume declines with age (Borsch-Supan and Stahl, 1991).

The evidence on the operation of a bequest motive is very mixed. The question is how important the bequest motive is relative to other motives for saving, including the basic life-cycle motivation. Consider the contradictory findings in a recent paper by Smith (1994). On the one hand, he finds that HRS respondents who believe that leaving an inheritance is very important have accumulated significantly more wealth ($85,000) than those who do not think that bequests are important.[10] On the other hand, using panel data from the Panel Study of Income Dynamics (PSID), he finds, consistent with Hurd (1987),[11] no linkage between savings and number of children ever born. Kotlikoff and Summers (1981) suggest that the bequest motive accounts for the bulk of observed wealth, while Modigliani (1988) disagrees (see, however, Kotlikoff's, 1988, reply).

Although the life-cycle model considers the calculations of the individual or couple in isolation, research on bequest motives involves adopting intergenerational or family-based models for analyzing consumption and savings. There is interest not only in the extent to which bequests are a motivation for savings, but also in what determines the amounts of bequests and the division of bequests among children and others. (Analysis of the effects of intergenerational linkages include Becker's analyses collected in Becker, 1991; Barro, 1974; and Bernheim, 1991.)

Research Integrating These Motives

Efforts at integrating these various explanations for savings do not yet involve estimating full structural models. One approach is to create simulation models on the basis of parameters obtained from original estimation as well as from other independent sources and to use the models to simulate the paths of asset accumulation. For example, Hubbard, Skinner, and Zeldes (1995) attempt to integrate a precautionary model of savings with a life-cycle model, while including the effects of asset-based means testing in social insurance programs. A related approach assumes that high rates of discounting govern the life-cycle motivation, but there also is a precautionary motive operating in the context of a model with liquidity constraints, and creating the need for buffer stocks against adverse events (see Carroll, 1992; Carroll and Samwick, 1994; Samwick, 1994). The relative weight given in these models to life-cycle retirement savings and precautionary savings varies. Nevertheless, the models do incorporate responses to risks such as those from earnings variation, health outcomes, and uncertain length of life. These models do seem capable of reproducing important features of the data, in particular, low levels of savings in early years, differences in savings among income groups, and savings and then dissaving through the life cycle.

Research That Imposes Only Limited Structure

Some empirical analyses of asset composition rely on specifications that impose as little structure to the underlying model and error terms as possible, employing considerably less structure than some formal empirical models of life cycle and precautionary savings. (See, e.g., the models of Venti and Wise, 1987, 1990, and Poterba, Venti, and Wise, 1993, for studies that attempt to separate cohort and age effects on savings.) When not much structure is imposed, that limits the ability to predict the effects of policy changes; if the structure that would otherwise be assumed is incorrect, this limitation is appropriate. The alternative is to impose a specific functional form, a process that will reveal more of the key parameters required for policy analysis, on the assumption that the structure that is imposed is correct. Otherwise, the imposition of too much structure will create bias in the estimated coefficients and will foster misleading policy analysis. Because of the continuing debate about the behavior underlying the savings decision, the extent to which these models should impose a particular structure continues to be a subject of disagreement (Venti and Wise, 1993; Engen and Gale, 1993).

In some sense those who do not impose a great deal of structure on their empirical estimates have a different methodological perspective. Especially when investigating the effects of well-defined policy changes, they are applying a quasi-experimental approach in which their major aim is to distinguish the effects of that policy, such as the adoption of rules permitting Individual Retirement Accounts (IRAs) or 401(k) savings plans. They are not, however, attempting to isolate the effects of the components of the policy. Often those who have a tight structural model in mind do not estimate the full structural model but a reduced form of one type or another. When that is the case, the parameter estimates obtained may be subject to a number of interpretations. Nevertheless, they may provide useful information even if the full structural model is incorrectly specified.

Research Arguing That Full Optimization Is Unlikely

Thaler (1994) argues that a number of findings in the savings literature are inconsistent with the predictions from leading models (see also Deaton, 1991; Zeldes, 1989a, 1989b). This in turn leads him to suggest that the leading models are probably not accurately describing behavior. Among the reasons is the difficulty of the assumed optimization. The assumed optimization requires the solution to a dynamic programming problem that when specified to include the array of risks that are encountered, requires a supercomputer to solve and is too hard even for *as if* behavior, especially because the behavior is not repeated but occurs only once in the lifetime. Moreover, because the problem is so complex, easy rules of thumb do not bring us close to the right answer. Bounded rationality and lack of self-control lead Thaler to suggest an approach to savings based on mental accounts, in which substitution among types of savings meant for different purposes is highly imperfect. Bernheim (1993) expresses doubts that the population is sufficiently economically literate, and he has discussed the importance of providing adequate information through the Social Security system. There is not sufficient understanding of the limitations in our computational abilities to predict the effects of providing potential retirees with increased information, as the new Social Security Administration initiative to inform individuals as to their entitlements will do.

Continuing Controversy in the Savings Literature

A major question in the savings area is how to reconcile the findings and models that have been developed with different behavioral motivations in mind. A number of the approaches to retirement savings summarized above are fundamentally inconsistent with one another. In addition, the relevant facts remain in dispute.[12] When policy innovations arise, such as the availability of IRAs and 401(k)s, either new savings is generated or it is not. (For discussion of the continuing debate on this topic, see Venti and Wise, 1987; Poterba, Venti, and Wise, 1993, 1994; Gale and Scholz, 1994; Engen, Gale, and Scholz, 1994. For a critique of the last study, see Bernheim, 1994.) Either those with pension or housing wealth reduce their holdings of financial assets proportionately, or they do not.[13] Without resolving these questions, which requires resolving ongoing controversies in the literature, we are in no position to judge the effects of a number of important policies that will affect savings.

The difficulties that modelers have faced in explaining these facts are widely appreciated. Some argue that it is a matter of integrating the various motivations and constraints into a single framework (see Hubbard, Skinner, and Zeldes, 1994a,

1994b). Some suggest that many of the outcome differences may be due to unmeasurable differences in taste and that selection issues will be difficult to unravel (Bernheim, 1994). Others suggest that in analyzing savings behavior, we are at the limits of the usefulness of a model that assumes full information and complete and rational decision making (Thaler, 1994). The question of the importance of each of these motivations for savings has yet to be resolved.

With regard to the analysis of savings, a fundamental task is to reconcile the competing explanations for the observed behavior. The puzzling differences in savings outcomes within the population, the failure to explain low savings rates and the counterintuitive findings on the substitution among different types of non-tax favored savings, tax-favored savings vehicles such as IRAs, 401(k)s, and pensions, and other savings vehicles, provide an opportunity to reconcile these results. A basic question in the savings literature is whether it will be possible to explain observed behavior with a significantly modified life-cycle model that integrates some of the other leading explanations for savings behavior. The weights given to these various motivations are unclear and at times appear inconsistent. It is possible that a different mix of theories may be required at different points in the income distribution to explain the variety of behaviors observed for those with different incomes. Alternatively, it may be necessary to pay much greater attention to the difficulties of making life-cycle calculations, incorporating rules of thumb and importing ad hoc or nonconventional explanations for imperfect substitutability among various types of savings instruments, the very high apparent rate of time preference among younger workers, the wide heterogeneity in savings, and the high frequency of zero savers.

Pensions and Social Security

At the Level of the Individual

At the level of the individual's decision, Social Security and pension income are the result of joint choices determining labor supply and benefit acceptance. The provisions of Social Security and pensions are taken as exogenous to the choices the individual will make. The pension benefit coverage, pension formulas, and earnings histories of each individual determine potential pension incomes in retirement, conditional on the choice of retirement date and on the timing of pension and Social Security acceptance (see Burkhauser, 1979, and Rust and Phelan, 1993, among others).

It is a straightforward procedure to apply retirement models to explain the effects of changes in Social Security and pension policies on retirement outcomes and on incomes from pensions and Social Security in retirement.[14] However, there are some questions that arise from findings that suggest both that individuals may not fully understand the rules governing Social Security and that they may be liquidity constrained; the second possibility has been recognized but is not incorporated in most dynamic life-cycle models of labor supply.[15]

Analysis of the incentives from pension plans suggests that if the pension formula is not actuarially fair, this may have a significant effect on the ultimate level of pension wealth. Changes in pensions and Social Security may induce further changes in savings behavior. But to predict the second-order effects of these changes will require a greater understanding of savings behavior than we now have.

Pension Plan Determination at the Level of the Firm

A basic building block in the conventional model explaining the demand for private pensions is the tax-favored status of the pension. Even the simplest models of why firms adopt pensions predict that workers like to substitute the tax-favored savings available under pension plans for private savings and that it is in the interest of firms to accommodate this demand (see, e.g., Woodbury, 1983; Woodbury and Huang, 1991). Early studies of the reaction between pensions and savings suggested greater savings by those who were covered by pensions (Cagan, 1965; Katona, 1965). A survey by Munnell and Yohn (1992) of studies conducted in the 1970s and 1980s suggests that there is substitution but that it is imperfect. More recent studies using actual rather than expected pension amounts or coverage suggest that the substitution is weak or nonexistent. If lifetime income is controlled for, those with higher employer-provided pension assets do not exhibit lower personal retirement saving.[16]

There is a substantial literature arguing that the firm has other motivations for pensions. Given its goal of maximizing profits subject to constraints from the production technology and factor supply curves, and operating within the implicit contract, the firm is hypothesized to choose parameters of pension plans to allocate compensation optimally among wages, pensions, and other fringes to influence employment, worker productivity, and other dimensions of costs.

Undoubtedly the tax-favored status of pensions contributed importantly to their spread in the post-World War II period (Ippolito, 1986). It is therefore quite surprising that the evidence is ambiguous that those with pensions reduce their savings in other forms. There are other questions about the behavioral mechanisms driving the determination of the coverage, terms, and amounts of pension savings, choice of plan types, explanations for pension backloading, and relationships of pensions to wages, turnover, and other dimensions of labor quality. Many of the human resource motivations that are said to underlie or buttress the demand for pensions are not consistent with the data.

Consider the questions that may be raised about the elaborate models of implicit contracts in which pensions are used as a tool of human resource policy to screen workers on the basis of unmeasured ability and to prevent shirking. Elements of these models that are not consistent with the data include the presumption that pensions provide a strong incentive against mobility in the years following hire and initial training (the incentive is really quite weak), that mobility is lower from pension-covered jobs because of pension backloading (mobility is lower from pension-covered jobs whether the pension is defined benefit and backloaded or defined contribution and not significantly backloaded), and that workers are inhibited from shirking because they are afraid they will lose their backloaded benefits if fired from a job offering a defined benefit plan (workers have only a modest understanding, if that, of the incentives in their pension plans). (For discussions of these and related predictions from conventional models of pensions that attribute the attraction of firms to pensions to their human resource properties, see Gustman and Steinmeier, 1989; Gustman and Mitchell, 1992; Gustman, Mitchell, and Steinmeier, 1994; and Gustman and Steinmeier, 1995a.)

Anomalies appear in studies with overidentifying restrictions. In turnover models we find that constraints requiring identical coefficients for wage and pension terms are violated and that the estimated coefficients differ by orders of magnitude. Within models of compensating wage differentials for pensions, the findings are not robust. And it is apparent from examining empirical work that identification has sometimes been forced, for example, by instrumenting on what are clearly endogenous variables—using some pension characteristics as instruments in a model that is designed to explain pension and wage outcomes (for details, see Gustman, Mitchell, and Steinmeier, 1994).

The conventional models also generate other predictions that do not accord with the data, raising concern for our ability to predict how private pensions will respond to changes in pension policies, in tax policies, or in the Social Security system.

Among the empirical regularities that pension studies attempt to explain are the basic result that compensation accrual and productivity do not correspond in each year of attachment and the existence of other unique labor market institutions, such as mandatory retirement provisions, which were commonplace before they were banished by law. Researchers have also tried to understand why defined benefit pensions are backloaded (that is accrue more in later than in earlier years), why union pensions are underfunded relative to nonunion pensions, why workers are less likely to leave pension-covered jobs than jobs without pensions, why firms grant post-retirement benefit increases, and other puzzles (see, e.g., Lazear, 1979, 1983; Ippolito, 1983, 1985a, 1985b, 1986, 1987). They have also attempted to generate predictions from models of long-term worker attachment and to test those predictions (see, e.g., Hutchens, 1986, 1987; Stern and Todd, 1993). Other efforts have described the differences in pension outcomes among demographic, firm, and industry groups and by unionization and other factors. Among the major differences in pension outcomes are differences in plan types, that is, whether the plan is defined benefit or defined contribution.[17] Still other studies have focused on documenting the trends in pension outcomes and explaining the reasons for these trends. (Relevant studies are reviewed in Gustman, Mitchell and Steinmeier, 1994.) After rising during the 1960s and 1970s, pension coverage ceased to grow in the middle 1980s. Now there is evidence that the upward trend in coverage, especially for defined contribution plans, may have resumed in just the last year or two (Employee Benefit Research Institute, 1993).[18]

Despite all of the efforts to explain the regularities in pension-related outcomes, most testing looks for partial relationships in the context of multivariate single-equation models. There has been no structural analysis of firms analogous to that available for analyzing behavior and policies from the perspective of the individual. This greatly limits our ability to use the available empirical work on pensions to predict the effects of pension regulations and policies on income and wealth outcomes. A basic reason there has been no structural analysis of firms is that the data are not available at the level of the firm. (For a discussion of the data that are available, the shortcomings in the data, and what would be required to support policy analysis, see Gustman and Mitchell, 1992.) And with all of the remaining questions about the importance of the competing motivations determining pension design, it is premature to impose a comprehensive model.

In sum, the pension literature is very far from generating empirical estimates of a reliable behavioral model. We certainly have no model with sufficient structure that it can be used to predict the effects of pension policies on the basic pension outcomes, including pension amounts, plan characteristics, insurance features, or other outcomes that would be useful in understanding how pension policies will affect retirement incomes and wealth. Nor can we predict the effects of these policies on wages.

Research on Family Structures and Transfers

There is some research linking earnings, wealth, and savings behavior to family structure. Earnings equations consistently find that earnings are higher among married individuals. With regard to savings and wealth, Smith (1994), for example, finds that married couples have higher assets and savings than unmarried individuals, even after standardizing for differences in incomes and using longitudinal data to distinguish the effects of selectivity of marital state, in which lower income families are more likely to dissolve. Thus, the need for help in old age is likely to be affected by the history of marital status. And, of course, the availability of help in old age is going to depend on whether unmarried individuals were ever married and whether they had children.

Living arrangements in old age are different from those at younger ages, reflecting not only the course of the life cycle as children leave home, but also the effects of mortality. Women are more likely to survive than men, so older households are more likely to include a single woman than a single man. When the survivor is a woman, however, the household is likely to be poorer. (See

Hurd and Wise, 1989, and Burkhauser, Holden, and Feaster, 1988, for studies addressing the economic status of widows.) Nevertheless, increases in real income over time have resulted in a halving of the fraction of older women living with relatives (Hurd, 1990b).

Work on family structure and transfers analyzes a range of decisions by families to transfer assets among members, from bequests through transfers from children or siblings to their parents. Moreover, decisions for multiple generations to live together affect decisions about the need to purchase (and save or insure for) different types of care outside the home, such as nursing home care. The basic structure of behavioral models ranges from Becker's seminal work (1991), including matching models that underlie the decision to form and leave a family and intergenerational models of transfers that have been used to explain bequests and caregiving to parents, to econometric models of household dissolution (Borsch-Supan, 1989, 1990; and Borsch-Supan, McFadden, and Schnabel, 1993), to analysis of housing demand by the elderly (Feinstein and McFadden, 1989), to models of demand for nursing homes (Garber and MacCurdy, 1990).

Integrated structural models have not yet been estimated. (For reduced form analyses using the HRS and PSID, see McGarry and Schoeni, 1994). HRS and AHEAD are going to provide excellent data for testing the integrated models of family relationships that are currently being refined. (For summaries and recent research, see Soldo and Hill, 1993.) These data are going to tightly constrain explanations, forcing researchers to integrate explanations based on intergenerational insurance, altruism, and bargaining models. But researchers have a considerable way to go before we have structural models of the type needed to simulate the effects of changes in tax policies, income and wealth testing of benefits, or health benefit policies, on the full array of outcomes that may be generated, including not only living arrangements but an understanding of the feedback on the income and wealth of the older family unit.

We are only beginning to explore the questions related to family structure and transfers, and their linkage to labor supply, savings, and pension determination. Living arrangements are a first outcome that will be investigated with more sophisticated models. We have mentioned the rising interest in models of joint labor supply behavior. Structurally, this is going to involve the introduction of bargaining models. Bargaining models are also a natural for trying to understand savings behavior. But to learn a lot more about the relation of family prospects to these dimensions of behavior is going to require specification of a credible mechanism and careful measurement of the threat price. These models will need to be extended to an intergenerational setting to resolve some of the continuing controversy about the motivations for bequests. We have yet to determine the motivation for dividing bequests and whether bequests are treated as a form of insurance. Analogous issues also arise about the transfer of time and money from children to parents, including the issue of how and why responsibilities get divided among children.

It appears that intergenerational linkages may be important in explaining the differences in savings behavior among countries (see Poterba, 1994). Where appropriate credit markets are not well developed, generations are more likely to be living together, and intergenerational transfers will be more of an everyday occurrence. There are models of the family as annuity market (Kotlikoff and Spivak, 1981). These behavioral models and changes in behavior with the rise of Social Security suggest that intergenerational linkages are no longer as important as they once were, but that family linkages should nevertheless be explicitly considered when analyzing the determination of labor market and savings behavior.

Research on Housing

Housing wealth peaks for older households between 55 and 70. About four out of five older households own a home. At least until they reach their early 70s, home owners do not draw down on their housing wealth. Although it may be argued that stickiness in housing wealth reflects the fixed costs of location, older home owners do not adjust housing equity even when they move (Venti and Wise, 1989). There is some evidence that individuals over 70 do draw down on their housing wealth, but not at a rate that would be suggested by life-cycle consumption (Sheiner and Weil, 1992). This suggests that housing wealth may be useful for a bequest motive or that it is an asset that is held to meet precautionary motives in old age. In the latter case we may find that the median older person is not downsizing, but that a person in the bottom of the income distribution who is in a bad state is. Still, it does not appear that housing wealth is a close substitute for other forms of wealth, which are presumably held to meet similar goals.[19] Moreover, while people do spend a portion of windfall gains to their housing assets, they incorporate changes in housing wealth in their other asset holdings only when housing assets decline in value (Engelhardt, 1994). Nor are the elderly enthusiastic about accepting reverse mortgages. In fact, Venti and Wise (1990) calculate that drawing down housing wealth through reverse mortgages would supplement the incomes of older families by only 10 percent. This suggests that housing equity could not substantially supplement the incomes of older Americans.

Large transaction costs make it difficult to isolate the relation of housing wealth to models of savings discussed above. Hurd (1990b) cites evidence on changes in housing wealth among those who turn over their housing that he feels is consistent with the life-cycle model. Nevertheless, he prefers testing the life-cycle model by using wealth data that exclude housing wealth. All of these findings leave us with a collection of facts, but raise a number of questions about how housing demand fits in with other dimensions of savings and wealth behavior.

RECONCILING RESEARCH ON LABOR SUPPLY, SAVINGS, AND PENSIONS

At least as disturbing as the formidable array of questions about our leading models within each of the separate areas of inquiry—labor supply, savings, and pension determination—is the inconsistency among these three areas of inquiry. Research in each area of behavior ignores findings from the other areas of behavior. For example, many models of savings assume that retirement is fixed, so insurance against unexpected earnings risk afforded by a flexible retirement date is ignored. Even when related behavior is not ignored, it is oversimplified. In structural retirement models, for example, savings is assumed either to be motivated by life-cycle savings, with savings choices made in the context of a perfectly operating capital market, or to occur in a world where income and consumption are assumed to be identical.[20]

Mechanically, with three major behavioral models, there are six linkages that we would like to understand. We would like to understand the linkages from labor supply to savings behavior and pension plan determination, from savings behavior to labor supply and pension plan determination, and from pension plan determination to labor supply and savings.

We are not talking here about effects that have a secondary impact on the mode of behavior under examination. Thus, for example, consider the consequence when most structural retirement models greatly oversimplify the motivations for savings and assume either that earnings are being reallocated to finance consumption in accordance with a simple life-cycle motivation in a perfectly operating capital market[21] or that lending and borrowing is not at all possible (see, e.g., Rust and Phelan, 1993). As is well known, if those approaching retirement with no liquid assets are overannuitized, they may time their retirement decision to regulate not only the amount of leisure, but also the path of consumption over time.[22] If that is the case, then parameters estimated in models that assume perfectly operating capital markets may be misleading, perhaps significantly so. On the other hand, we know that savings behavior is heterogeneous. Certainly those who approach the retirement date with some liquid assets are less likely to be overannuitized, and thus should not be influenced by the age 62 early retirement provisions of Social Security. Thus, the assumption that all retirees in a certain class are liquidity constrained is also likely to lead to bias, perhaps significantly so.

Moreover, policy changes that are viewed as benign in standard retirement models may have significant behavioral consequences if liquidity constraints play an important role, as they do in some models of precautionary savings. For example, according to most structural retirement work, moving the early retirement age under Social Security from 62 to 65 should have little effect, so long as the present values are not disturbed. Under the current system, benefits adjustments for work after 62 are actuarially fair. Even if liquidity constraints would normally inhibit borrowing, there should be little effect from having to wait for Social Security benefits that late in the life cycle, since all life cycle savings should have been completed. Yet if significant numbers of people enter retirement lacking financial wealth, as appears to be the case, then as suggested by Rust and Phelan's work, moving the retirement age from 62 to 65 will indeed have the effect of raising the retirement age. Consequently, the effects of certain policies will be misunderstood in retirement models that do not incorporate the effects of savings behavior.

The difficulties in understanding savings behavior thus have implications not only for the determination of income from nonpension savings, but also for understanding retirement behavior and thus for the path of income from earnings.

Consider next the implications of retirement research for the models of savings behavior. From the perspective of the precautionary model of savings, certain motivations cannot be insured by changing labor supply behavior. But certainly some variations in wages can be insured against by postponing retirement. Indeed, over the life cycle, it may also be possible to adjust to certain shocks by changing the allocation of work within the family or changing hours of work once the shock is resolved. Nevertheless, most savings models, even models of precautionary demand, take labor supply and retirement behavior as fixed (see, however, Samwick, 1994). Assuming fixed retirement dates can have adverse consequences for savings research for other reasons. As pointed out early in the savings literature, those who have preferences that favor early retirement, or who are working for firms that encourage early retirement, may be observed to have higher savings rates. To the extent that these considerations are ignored, it will appear that they will have higher life-cycle savings. In fact, the amount of life-cycle savings may be lower for early retirees once their shorter period of attachment to the labor force is taken into account.

Pension research also has implications both for retirement research and for savings research. With regard to retirement research, the issue of the possible endogeneity of pensions may be raised. Pensions are determined by the firm with the preferences of covered workers in mind. This raises the question of whether the effects of pension incentives on retirement are exaggerated. It is possible to argue that those now approaching retirement age could not have foreseen the sharp changes in pensions over the past two decades and thus did not select their jobs on the basis of a taste for early retirement.[23] Nevertheless, it still is in the firm's interest to shape the pension to accord with worker preferences. Thus a relationship between early retirement provisions in pension plans and retirement outcomes may to some extent reflect the firm's efforts to accord with their own workers' tastes, leading to an overstatement of the effect of pension incentives on retirement.

With regard to savings research, one cannot help but be puzzled by recent findings that those with pensions do not reduce their saving correspondingly. If we correctly hold constant factors associated with differences in tastes and standardize for incomes, it is hard to conceive of a model in which pensions should not substitute for financial savings, or at least for that portion of financial savings meant to finance retirement. Not only are pensions a tax-favored form of savings, but the defined benefit plans carry one of the few opportunities to purchase an annuity with a price that is not substantially increased by the effects of adverse selection. Moreover, the penalties are small enough that many forms of pension savings can meet the demands for other types of savings, such as saving to pay for the children's college educations. Somewhere in the process, one suspects that preferences are being changed as firms and unions provide information about the importance of retirement savings or for other reasons. This information must in turn be affecting the demand for financial savings, creating an unmeasured linkage between pensions and financial savings.

We have already seen that savings research has implications for pension research. The recent evidence that substitution between pensions and savings is weak or nonexistent is not consistent with the standard tax-based explanation for pensions.[24] It is not that we doubt that the favorable tax treatment of pensions underlies much of the growth of pensions (Ippolito, 1986). It does appear, however, that any effort to fit a model of pension demand must go beyond the mechanical substitution of pension for nonpension savings and provide an explanation for the empirical findings in available studies of pensions.

There are no simple fixes for these problems. But they do provide an important agenda for future research.

MODELS AND DATA NEEDED TO UNDERSTAND THE INCOMES AND WEALTH OF OLDER AMERICANS

In each of the separate areas of behavior, the direction that research is taking is appropriate. The basic outlines of dynamic retirement models are established. The models of savings behavior require further integration of competing motivations into a single framework. Models of pensions will require a further understanding of the motivation of the demand for pensions by workers as well as the behavior underlying human resource policies of the firm and their importance in shaping pensions. The question is how long it will take and how much progress will be required before we are in good enough shape to analyze the effects of the detailed policies specified in the next section.

The question facing those who would wish to use structural modeling as a basis for policy analysis in the more immediate future is, do we know enough about behavior to be comfortable imposing a model with sufficient structure to allow analysis of the effects of detailed changes in policy? A basic test of any model, and of the structure it imposes, is whether the model can explain major features of the data. If the structure is wrong in some fundamental way, we should be able to find important characteristics of the data that the model cannot explain. In the case of models of savings, retirement, and pensions that would be used for policy analysis, there are much data that could and should be brought to bear before policy analysis based on the model is taken seriously. Approaches that create complex models by borrowing parameters from various sources face significant problems. Presumably to avoid the kind of specification error that occurs when parameters are estimated in the context of a partially specified set of behavioral equations, we should eventually expect structural equations of more complex models to be estimated directly from data. Only in the area of retirement modeling have we come close to meeting this criterion.

There may be classes of models that achieve a balance, providing sufficient structure to analyze effects of complex policies while resisting any temptation to overparameterize, thus avoiding potential errors of the type we have been discussing. To the extent that the investigator has sufficiently good intuition, the policy analysis that emerges may not be badly biased by the failure to specify all dimensions of behavior fully. It is difficult to determine exactly when this goal has been achieved, but there are sufficient data to put any model through its paces.

To the extent that the three dimensions of behavior we have focused on most strongly, labor force participation, savings, and pensions, are separable, this careful balancing act is likely to be most successful. Otherwise, structural models incorporating the three types of behavior will be required to analyze the array of policies affecting incentives to retire, to save, and to form pensions with different characteristics. Even if behavior in each of the three areas were separable, the task ahead is formidable. Our descriptions of the motivations governing retirement, savings, and pensions must accurately depict the relevant behaviors, and as the discussion has indicated, a great deal of work is required before we reach that goal.

If retirement, savings, and pension plan determination are not separable modes of behavior, then before we can generate a set of equations useful for analyzing the types of structural changes that major policy innovations create, it will be necessary to make progress on all three fronts. Available models fail to consider the relation between the behavior being analyzed and the other leading modes of behavior that have been noted here. This leaves open the possibility that the parameters we have are biased and will provide misleading predictions about the likely effects of major policy initiatives.

Thus, in deciding on priorities for future research, we must answer questions such as the following: If the motivation for savings takes us well beyond the simple life-cycle model, what are the implications for parameter estimates obtained in most of our life-cycle labor supply models? If pensions are designed to meet the preferences of the work force, how serious is endogeneity of the pension incentives for our measurement of worker preferences? If the motivation for pensions is more complicated than the simple substitution of a tax-favored form of savings for one that is not (and many human resource explanations for pension characteristics are inconsistent with the data), then how can we integrate the findings from savings and pension theory to better understand what is driving pension coverage and the choice and structure of pension plans?

These efforts will be aided by the availability of data from HRS and AHEAD. HRS was designed with dynamic, structural retirement models in mind and provides the depth of information that will help us to improve our understanding of retirement behavior at the level of the individual.[25] HRS and AHEAD were designed to provide the basic information needed to model retirement and savings behavior. Special efforts were made to reduce measurement error. Where possible, data have been matched from administrative records and employer documents. For each individual we will have a record of Social Security earnings history and thus an objective record of employment that is not subject to recall bias. Incentives from pensions will be measured from pension data provided by the employer. As we have described, innovations are being employed to reduce bias in measuring wealth. Moreover, there will be unique data for measuring the experiences of those with disabilities and of those with health problems in general, and for measuring the financial and nonfinancial support provided by family structures. Once the panel data are in, we will have two related sources of data that are capable of supporting the next generation of behavioral research. Having the data in these surveys is not sufficient to overcome the serious difficulties we face in isolating the true model, but these data will be a significant help.

What we do not have are comparable data for improving our understanding of the behavior of the firm that determines pensions and their characteristics. There are some efforts under way at the Bureau of Labor Statistics to make available establishment data collected in the Employee Benefit Survey and the Employment Cost Index, but we are a long way from meeting the requirements for release of a data set that can support the types of behavioral models that are required for policy analysis.

SELECTED POLICIES AFFECTING
RETIREMENT INCOMES AND WEALTH

To conclude the paper, we return to the box labeled D in Figure 2-1, and briefly outline an array of policies changes that have the potential of significantly affecting the incomes and wealth of older Americans. These policies, if adopted, would change the incentives for retirement, savings, and pensions.

A wide variety of Social Security reforms have been recommended in the past and may be considered again in the future. One suggestion pertains to accelerating the reforms already scheduled under the 1983 Social Security amendments. Under an accelerated schedule, the normal retirement age would be raised to 67 and the delayed retirement credit increased to 8 percent immediately. The effect would be to decrease Social Security benefits for the transition generation (as they will be for all cohorts that face an age 67 retirement age under current law) and to increase the incentive to delay retirement age. A related suggestion is to abolish the retirement earnings test immediately.[26] After the recent increase in the portion of Social Security benefits subject to income tax, there have been suggestions to means-test Social Security benefits. It has also been continually suggested that changes be made in the treatment of spouse benefits under Social Security.

A more sweeping recommendation that continues to surface would allow some sort of privatization of the Social Security system. One possibility is to allow those who save in a tax-favored vehicle to opt out of the system, as is now possible in Britain. (For an analysis of potential enrollments in a privatized United States Social Security system, see Gustman and Steinmeier, 1995b.) Here the likely effects would incorporate fundamental reactions based on dimensions of behavior affecting labor supply, savings, and pensions. Such a program, for example, would probably encourage firms and workers to cash out defined benefit pensions to provide benefits in a form that would allow covered workers who found it to their advantage to opt out of the Social Security system to do so.[27]

We have recently witnessed a major health care reform debate. The role of retiree health insurance has received a good deal of attention in the course of that debate. The debate on policies that are required to balance the budget also may have major effects on health insurance. Resulting policies may change the age of eligibility for Medicare or otherwise break the linkage between work and health insurance. (For conflicting analyses of the effects of retiree health insurance on retirement, see Gustman and Steinmeier, 1994a, and Karoly and Rogowski, 1994.) With further pressure on the Medicare system, proposals are also surfacing for means-testing Medicare benefits.

Potential pension reforms continue to be formulated with at least five goals in mind: to increase coverage, to reduce revenue losses through tax deductibility, to protect the implicit pension contract, to increase the incentive to postpone retirement, and to level the distribution of benefits among high- and low-income employees.[28] Potential changes in policies could change the tax treatment of pensions, mandate the availability of pensions, alter a variety of eligibility and vesting rules, further change treatment of spouses under pensions, further change funding rules including minimum and maximum funding levels, change treatment of retiree health benefits, change acceptable actuarial assumptions and procedures, alter discrimination rules (including further regulation of matching provisions under 401(k)s), change rules governing Social Security offsets, change the rules governing pensions of highly paid employees, regulate the backloading of pensions, require that payments to terminated vested employees be based on projected earnings or some related mechanism rather than on the last few years of nominal earnings, adjust rules affecting the returns to invested pension assets by further regulating these investments or mandating certain types of investment, change rules governing asset investments for defined contribution plans, regulate or mandate post-retirement benefit increases, regulate rollovers from pension plans, and introduce an array of policies that would affect the terms of Pension

Benefit Guaranty Corporation insurance. (For further discussions of pension policies, see Congressional Budget Office, 1987, and Ippolito, 1983, 1986.)

One of the more controversial proposals that would reduce taxes on the income from savings is to resurrect the IRA in its initial form, as favored in the past by Treasury Secretary Bentsen. Such a reform would again allow full initial deductibility of IRA contributions up to specified limits, with eligibility not contingent on lack of pension coverage. On the other hand, proposals are now floating to reduce the eligibility for what is left of IRAs. Among the more sweeping tax reforms that would have major effects on incentives to save is adoption of a consumption tax.

A variety of training, employment, and regulatory programs in the labor market have also been suggested to foster increased employment of older individuals and to raise the reward to work.

To fully understand the effects of these policies, we will need a more complete understanding of behavior than we currently have. We will need a better understanding not only of the behaviors of labor supply, savings, and pension plan determination, but of the relationships among these modes of behavior.

APPENDIX TABLES AND FIGURES

The tables and figures begin on page 42.

TABLE 2-A1   Net Worth by Family Composition, HRS Data

Family Composition	Sample Size	Mean Value ($000)	Percentiles ($000)				
			10	25	50	75	90
Net Worth Less Housing Equity							
Couples	5,229	197.9	2.0	13.0	53.0	166.0	426.0
Single men	741	124.9	0	1.0	16.0	81.8	229.0
Single women	1,632	55.0	−0.7	0	7.0	45.0	140.0
Total	7,602	163.0	0	6.1	37.1	130.0	355.0
Housing Equity							
Couples	5,229	90.9	0	27.0	60.5	110.0	197.0
Single men	741	42.0	0	0	6.0	56.0	126.0
Single women	1,632	42.4	0	0	16.5	58.0	122.0
Total	7,602	76.9	0	10.0	50.0	100.0	177.5
Total Net Worth							
Couples	5,229	288.8	15.0	56.0	132.8	285.0	602.0
Single men	741	166.9	0	4.0	43.0	157.0	320.5
Single women	1,632	97.5	0	1.2	36.4	115.5	259.3
Total	7,602	239.9	1.1	32.4	101.0	239.0	512.0

TABLE 2-A2   Net Worth by Ethnicity, HRS Data

Ethnicity	Sample Size	Mean Value ($000)	Percentiles ($000)				
			10	25	50	75	90
Net Worth Less Housing Equity							
Black	1,424	45.4	−0.9	0	5.0	29.0	91.0
Hispanic	716	59.2	0	0.1	4.5	29.0	95.0
Other	5,462	189.7	1.3	11.7	50.0	160.0	415.9
Total	7,602	163.0	0	6.1	37.1	130.0	355.0
Housing Equity							
Black	1,424	38.6	0	0	17.0	50.0	89.0
Hispanic	716	45.2	0	0	22.0	59.0	129.0
Other	5,462	85.4	0	20.0	58.0	107.0	191.0
Total	7,602	76.9 '	0	10.0	50.0	100.0	177.5
Total Net Worth							
Black	1,424	84.1	0	0.4	30.5	86.5	170.1
Hispanic	716	104.4	0	1.7	34.0	95.5	224.5
Other	5,462	275.1	7.5	48.3	129.9	275.0	586.0
Total	7,602	239.9	1.1	32.4	101.0	239.0	512.0

TABLE 2-A3   Net Worth by Income Group, HRS Data

Income	Sample Size	Mean Value ($000)	Percentiles ($000)				
			10	25	50	75	90
Net Worth Less Housing Equity							
< 10K	854	48.6	–0.7	0	0.4	15.0	48.8
10-25K	1,696	66.2	–0.3	0.9	8.2	46.0	148.0
25-50K	2,405	96.7	1.2	9.5	34.0	97.0	224.2
50-100K	2,077	195.4	7.5	25.5	72.4	193.6	423.0
> 100K	570	665.4	32.0	90.0	240.0	695.0	1,792.2
Total	7,602	163.0	0	6.1	37.1	130.0	355.0
Housing Equity							
< 10K	854	29.3	0	0	0	35.0	80.0
10-25K	1,696	50.3	0	0	27.0	65.0	120.0
25-50K	2,405	65.3	0	17.0	48.0	85.0	150.0
50-100K	2,077	93.3	1.0	37.0	70.0	120.0	197.0
> 100K	570	181.7	29.0	67.0	125.0	225.0	393.0
Total	7,602	76.9	0	10.0	50.0	100.0	177.5
Total Net Worth							
< 10K	854	78.8	–0.5	0	5.8	54.0	169.6
10-25K	1,696	116.5	0	7.3	43.5	120.8	269.0
25-50K	2,405	162.0	8.0	39.0	92.0	188.0	350.0
50-100K	2,077	288.6	35.0	83.7	165.0	313.1	590.0
> 100K	570	847.1	100.3	198.0	405.0	923.4	2,166.0
Total	7,602	239.9	1.1	32.4	101.0	239.0	512.0

TABLE 2-A4 Total Net Worth by Family Composition and Age, AHEAD
Data

Family Composition	Sample Size	Mean Value ($000)	Percentiles ($000)				
			10	25	50	75	90
Age 70-74							
Couples	946	276.3	17.0	57.0	140.9	309.0	578.8
Single men	233	201.7	0	10.0	65.0	167.0	367.8
Single women	825	178.1	0	4.1	51.4	132.5	295.0
Total	2,004	209.2	0.3	26.6	90.6	315.0	462.5
Age 75-79							
Couples	581	274.1	11.0	50.7	118.0	264.0	610.0
Single men	203	164.3	1.0	14.0	71.0	171.0	319.0
Single women	812	105.1	0	3.7	47.8	116.0	236.0
Total	1,596	177.0	0.1	16.2	71.0	168.8	364.0
Age 80-84							
Couples	371	242.2	10.0	43.5	114.2	236.0	495.3
Single men	154	148.6	0.5	10.0	51.0	132.0	289.0
Single women	702	87.5	0	3.5	40.5	101.5	188.5
Total	1,227	142.7	0.1	10.2	60.0	143.0	290.0
Age 85+							
Couples	155	162.1	1.0	21.0	75.6	216.0	415.0
Single men	145	121.5	0	1.0	25.9	101.0	287.6
Single women	595	85.8	0	1.5	30.0	100.0	203.0
Total	895	104.7	0	2.0	37.0	111.0	247.0

TABLE 2-A5   Net Worth Excluding Home Equity by Family Composition and Age, AHEAD Data

Family Composition	Sample Size	Mean Value ($000)	Percentiles ($000)				
			10	25	50	75	90
Age 70-74							
Couples	946	176.6	1.0	11.0	55.7	190.0	420.0
Single men	233	140.3	0	2.1	17.0	89.0	255.4
Single women	825	68.3	0	0.1	7.5	50.0	160.5
Total	2,004	129.6	0	2.2	25.9	109.2	323.0
Age 75-79							
Couples	581	176.8	0.8	10.0	38.0	150.0	417.0
Single men	203	80.2	0	2.0	15.5	83.0	205.0
Single women	812	53.0	0	0.2	7.0	39.5	125.0
Total	1,596	103.6	0	1.3	15.8	76.3	247.0
Age 80-84							
Couples	371	161.3	1.0	8.0	37.0	139.0	370.3
Single men	154	107.5	0.1	1.2	19.5	66.8	224.0
Single women	702	42.7	0	0.2	5.1	40.0	112.0
Total	1,227	87.2	0	1.0	12.2	64.1	191.0
Age 85+							
Couples	155	104.8	0	2.0	20.0	125.0	271.0
Single men	145	74.8	0	0.4	7.0	45.0	114.3
Single women	595	48.1	0	0	5.0	33.2	113.0
Total	895	62.2	0	0.2	6.7	50.0	140.0

TABLE 2-A6   Total Net Worth by Ethnicity and Age, AHEAD Data

Ethnicity	Sample Size	Mean Value ($000)	Percentiles ($000)				
			10	25	50	75	90
Age 70-74							
Black	309	50.4	0	0	25.0	69.0	152.0
Hispanic	130	72.8	0	0	25.5	67.0	181.2
White plus other	1,565	238.5	5.5	45.5	116.2	262.2	522.0
Total	2,004	209.2	0.3	26.6	90.6	215.0	462.5
Age 75-79							
Black	241	51.6	0	0.8	25.0	56.2	113.0
Hispanic	90	42.6	0	0	1.0	43.0	99.0
White plus other	1,265	200.1	2.0	33.2	94.0	202.0	409.0
Total	1,596	177.0	0.1	16.2	71.0	168.8	364.0
Age 80-84							
Black	184	61.7	0	0.6	31.0	62.0	130.0
Hispanic	71	64.5	0	0	15.0	50.0	101.5
White plus other	972	159.0	0.8	20.0	77.7	166.5	332.0
Total	1,227	142.7	0.1	10.2	60.0	143.0	290.0
Age 85+							
Black	126	39.5	0	0	5.0	45.0	122.0
Hispanic	44	31.9	0	0	0.3	62.8	75.0
White plus other	725	116.4	0	5.5	46.2	131.0	270.0
Total	895	104.7	0	2.0	37.0	111.0	247.0

TABLE 2-A7 Net Worth Excluding Home Equity by Ethnicity and Age, AHEAD Data

Ethnicity	Sample Size	Mean Value ($000)	Percentiles ($000)				
			10	25	50	75	90
Age 70-74							
Black	309	20.3	0	0	1.0	16.0	60.0
Hispanic	130	25.5	0	0	0.5	8.0	48.8
White plus other	1,565	150.3	0.5	7.0	41.2	150.0	365.0
Total	2,004	129.6	0	2.2	25.9	109.2	323.0
Age 75-79							
Black	241	20.9	−0.5	0	0.8	10.0	40.0
Hispanic	90	11.9	−0.6	0	0	2.0	20.3
White plus other	1,265	119.0	0.3	5.3	26.0	101.0	297.0
Total	1,596	103.6	0	1.3	15.8	76.3	247.0
Age 80-84							
Black	184	23.0	0	0	1.0	13.1	45.5
Hispanic	71	27.7	0	0	0.3	5.2	35.0
White plus other	972	99.9	0	2.4	20.4	83.3	224.0
Total	1,227	87.2	0	1.0	12.2	64.1	191.0
Age 85+							
Black	126	14.9	0	0	0.2	9.5	40.0
Hispanic	44	7.9	0	0	0	2.5	30.0
White plus other	725	70.8	0	1.0	10.5	61.0	179.0
Total	895	62.2	0	0.2	6.7	50.0	140.0

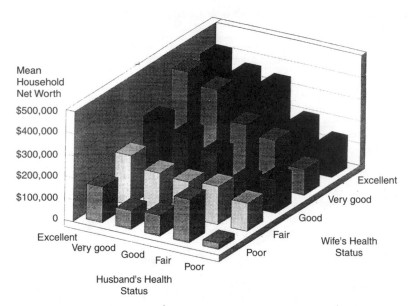

FIGURE 2-A1 Relationship of health status and mean net worth for married-couple households. NOTE: Health status is respondent's subjective rating. SOURCE: Tabulations of the Health and Retirement Survey.

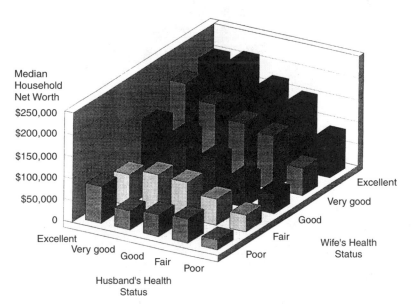

FIGURE 2-A2 Relationship of health status and median net worth for married-couple households. NOTE: Health status is respondent's subjective rating. SOURCE: Tabulations of the Health and Retirement Survey.

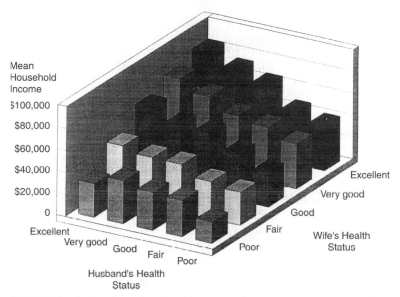

FIGURE 2-A3 Relationship of health status and mean income for married-couple households. NOTE: Health status is respondent's subjective rating. SOURCE: Tabulations of the Health and Retirement Survey.

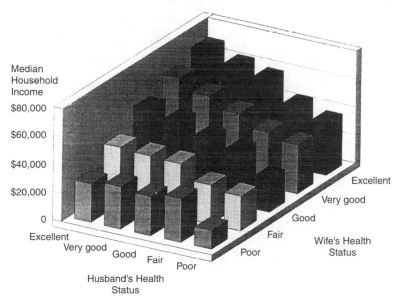

FIGURE 2-A4 Relationship of health status and median income for married-couple households. NOTE: Health status is respondent's subjective rating. SOURCE: Tabulations of the Health and Retirement Survey.

NOTES

1. In examining behavior from the perspective of the individual, we will take the wage offer at a given age and tenure as exogenous to the individual's decision in older age.

2. For recent studies elaborating on the dynamic structure of the dependent variable, see Blau (1994) and Peracchi and Welch (1994). For models of retirement using a rich set of dynamic flows in the context of a dynamic programming model, see, for example, Rust (1990) and Berkovec and Stern (1991). For an analysis that incorporates the effects of incomplete annuity markets, borrowing constraints, and incomplete markets for health insurance on labor market behavior, see Rust and Phelan (1993). For inclusion in the opportunity set of the discontinuities from the option value of the pension, see Stock and Wise (1990a, 1990b) and Lumsdaine, Stock, and Wise (1990). For family retirement models, see Hurd (1990a) and Gustman and Steinmeier (1994b). For models that include further information on nonwage aspects of employment, see Gustman and Steinmeier (1986a) and Hurd and McGarry (1993a).

3. In order to make estimation tractable, researchers have made a number of simplifications reducing the complexity of the dependent variable specification, the detail of the opportunity set, the complexity of the dynamic decisions allowed, and the richness of the econometric specification. Some inadequacies in models estimated to date have reflected limitations in the available data sets. One fundamental choice has been between nationally representative data sets that include only re-spondent-provided descriptions of a few elements of the pension plan, such as studies based on data from the Retirement History Study or the National Longitudinal Study of Older Men, and data sets with highly detailed employer-provided descriptions of pensions, but with very narrow samples, including the employees of only a few firms. Thus, studies using employer-provided plan descrip-tions have been confined to analyzing the decision to leave the firm from which the pension data had been obtained; subsequent employment experience was not observed and could not be analyzed. Nor in the studies focusing on the analysis of behavior in a few firms have there been data on family characteristics and labor market activity or detailed information on the health status of the worker. Health is simply included under the random term. Only recently have we begun to see retirement analysis based on nationally representative data that include information from employer-provided pension plan descriptions (Samwick, 1993a). But the model specification remains highly simplified compared with some of the structural analyses now available in the literature.

4. Anderson, Gustman, and Steinmeier (1994) attribute about a quarter of the trend to the sharp lowering of early and normal retirement dates for pension eligibility and to the reduced effect of continued work on the Social Security benefit in the 1980s as compared with the incentives in the early 1970s. This type of analysis does not answer why the pension incentives were changed as they were and leaves unexplained the other three-fourths of the change in retirement behavior.

5. One issue that has recently been subject to disagreement is the question of whether the trends in retirement are due to trends in incentives and unexpected wealth effects from the start-up and revisions of pension plans and Social Security, as implied by the work of Ippolito (1990) and others, or to trends in wages differentials and the forces underlying these trends, as implied by Peracchi and Welch (1994). If trends in retirement among older cohorts may be attributed to the effects of *unexpected* changes in Social Security wealth, then this raises a question. Shouldn't we expect to see the trend cease, as we did, and then strongly reverse itself as the Social Security system matured and Congress ceased granting important benefit increases after the 1970s? (Perhaps the flattening of the trend in recent years is just the beginning of a strong reversal; however, it has been 8 years since the trend ceased and no strong reversal is yet apparent.) Moreover, if changes in the wage structure due to the decline in relative and real wages of the unskilled account for the trend to earlier retirement, as Peracchi and Welch (1994) argue, why do we see the same trend to earlier retirement in the last two decades in Britain, where despite a decline in relative wages for the unskilled, real wages for the unskilled continued to increase? If higher wages are responsible for the trend to earlier retirement, why did the trend begin only after the 1930s in the United States? And more generally, why aren't these wage effects picked up by structural retirement models?

6   The studies with the best pension measures, those obtained directly from firm-provided data, have no information on health status, for example, Fields and Mitchell (1984), Stock and Wise (1990a, 1990b), and Lumsdaine, Stock and Wise (1990, 1992a, 1992b).

7.   Savers may also be motivated by the need to finance various expenditures, such as their children's college education or the purchase of a home, or by other motivations.

8.   Hurd (1990b) also argues that consumption paths are consistent with the life-cycle model.

9.   HRS is designed to permit direct measurement of individuals' attitudes toward risk as well as their time preference and expectations regarding particular risks to, among other, the economy and to Social Security and to provide the opportunity to explore heterogeneity in these measures within the population. For a study based on the new HRS data, see Barsky et al. (1993).

10.   Smith (1994) also finds that the bequest motive is more likely to be operating among those with higher incomes. He finds much smaller effects of a belief in a bequest motive when using median regressions than when using mean regressions.

11.   As a test of the importance of the bequest motive, Hurd examines the wealth path of families with and without children and concludes that the higher rate of decumulation of wealth by those with children is evidence against the importance of the bequest motive.

12.   Hamermesh (1984) argues that asset decumulation is too rapid to sustain consumption after retirement. On the other hand, it has frequently been argued that decumulation is too slow for life-cycle motivations and that bequests will result (see Kotlikoff and Summers, 1981).

13.   Those with a pension save less than those without a pension (Smith, 1994), but there is a question about the rates at which these assets are substituted. See, for example, Bernheim and Scholz (1993) and Samwick (1994) on the relation between pension holding and nonpension wealth. See Hoynes and McFadden (1994) for evidence on the nonhousing wealth of those who do and do not own houses.

14.   One set of results suggests that although Social Security benefit changes adopted in 1983 will reduce retirement incomes by about 14 percent by the time they are fully phased in, half of the reduction will be offset by induced increases in earnings as retirement is postponed in response to the change in incentives (Gustman and Steinmeier, 1985). Another set of results suggests that accelerating the 1983 Social Security reforms to eliminate penalties from continuing work after reaching Social Security normal retirement age, or equivalently abolishing the retirement earnings test, will have only a small effect on retirement in the affected cohorts (Gustman and Steinmeier, 1991). Simulations with models fit to payroll data from selected firms (Stock and Wise, 1990a, 1990b; Lumsdaine and Wise, 1994; Wise and Woodbury, 1994) suggest that retirement incentives from Social Security are much weaker than are incentives from pensions. Other recent work focuses on the proper modeling of Social Security effects on retirement (Reimers and Honig, 1993a, 1993b; Rust and Phelan, 1993). These studies suggest that simple, mechanical models of a response to the benefit formula and earnings test are unsatisfactory, and that liquidity constraints, knowledge of the earnings test, and the nonwage characteristics of jobs (Hurd and McGarry, 1993b; Gustman, Mitchell, and Steinmeier, 1994) are important.

15.   The suggestion that workers may not fully understand the Social Security rules comes from a finding of a spike in the participation rate at the disregard amount of the Social Security earnings test (Burtless and Moffitt, 1984). The rules allow any benefit that is lost to the earnings test by someone between the ages of 62 and 65 to be recovered in future years on a roughly actuarially fair basis, so that the spike at the disregard amount would not make sense for those under 65 if they understood the rules. Analogously, incentives from Social Security should not create a spike in the retirement hazard at age 62, in that any loss to the earnings test can be recovered in future years (Hurd, 1990a). Nevertheless, in some studies there is a suggestion at age 62 of a spike in the retirement hazard that seems to be associated with Social Security. Specifically, while findings in Gustman and Steinmeier (1986b) suggest that spikes in retirement hazards can be completely attributed to actuarial incentives of pensions, Social Security, and mandatory retirement, without considering any effects of liquidity constraints, Hurd (1990b), using data from Kotlikoff and Wise (1985, 1987), finds a spike in the

retirement hazard at age 62 for workers with a pension plan that does not generate any retirement incentive at age 62. This leads Hurd to infer that liquidity effects associated with Social Security are responsible, a finding confirmed in subsequent analysis by Wise and his colleagues. Nalebuff and Zeckhauser (1985) explain why liquidity effects may also arise from pension plans that are designed for a heterogeneous work force.

16. See Venti and Wise (1993) for a discussion and evidence of imperfect substitution between personal retirement savings and a number of other savings instruments. Venti and Wise include assets in 401(k) plans under the heading of personal targeted retirement assets, as opposed to employer-provided pension assets. See also the evidence in Samwick (1994).

17. Studies of pension outcomes discuss the effects of certain plan differences; for example, Green (1985) and Bodie (1990) analyze the differential risk of defined benefit and defined contribution plans. Most of the empirical studies of the choices of pension outcomes are descriptive, relating pension outcomes to demographic and employment characteristics.

18. Recent articles examining trends in pension coverage include Parsons (1991, 1993), Bloom and Freeman (1992), Turner and Beller (1992), and Even and Macpherson (1994). Other studies have tried to describe and explain trends in plan type (Clark and McDermed, 1990; Gustman and Steinmeier, 1992; Ippolito, 1995; Kruse, 1995) and to understand the forces shaping the trends in provision of pensions (Mitchell and Luzadis, 1988; Luzadis and Mitchell, 1991; Mitchell, 1992).

19. Skinner (1993) found a negative association between housing wealth and nonhousing savings in the PSID, measuring housing values by the individual's self-report of the housing value in two periods. Hoynes and McFadden (1994) used data on housing prices in metropolitan areas and found either a very small positive association between changes in housing prices and the savings rate, or a larger one, depending on specification. When Engelhardt (1994) reestimated the results in Hoynes and McFadden using median regression, reducing the weight on outliers, he found a negative and significant effect of housing wealth on savings about the same size as the effect found by Skinner.

20. In either case such phenomena as the bunching of retirees at the Social Security earnings test maximum are difficult to explain (see Burtless and Moffitt, 1984).

21. Rust (1989, 1990) developed an influential model of the joint determination of savings and retirement, but that model has not been estimated. Otherwise, all of the structural models mentioned above are estimated using procedures that ignore information about savings behavior.

22. Nalebuff and Zeckhauser (1985), Hurd (1990b), Rust and Phelan (1993), and others note that in the absence of assets, liquidity-constrained individuals will retire at 62 to obtain access to their Social Security benefits.

23. The normal retirement age for pension covered workers in the Retirement History Study averaged 64.2. The early retirement age averaged 61. According to 1989 Survey of Consumer Finances data, the normal retirement age averaged 61.7 and the early retirement age averaged 54.3 (Anderson, Gustman, and Steinmeier, 1994). For data on the changes in early retirement provisions of pension plans over the past two decades, see Ippolito (1990) and Mitchell (1992).

24. Venti and Wise (1993) find no evidence of any offset at all between pension wealth and personal financial assets, with the coefficient on the relationship being positive but insignificant. See also Bernheim and Scholz (1993), who relate savings to a qualitative indicator of pension coverage and find an indication of some substitution for those with college degrees. The analysis of the relation between pensions and savings is at an earlier stage than some other lines of research. Nevertheless, the work to date raises important questions about the substitutability between pensions and other forms of savings.

25. These data sets and their potential use in research on retirement, savings, health, family linkages, and related issues are described in detail in a forthcoming issue of the *Journal of Human Resources*.

26. These suggestions were made by Dorcas Hardy, the former head of the Social Security Administration, and continue to be made by others. For an analysis, see Gustman and Steinmeier (1991).

27. We have not emphasized the disability system, but clearly changes in disability rules will affect incentives to save for precautionary reasons. Moreover, disability provisions may interact with early retirement provisions of pension programs affecting retirement incentives. Because the roll of the disability system has grown rapidly in recent years and the finances of that system have deteriorated, there have been a number of suggestions for change. Such changes might, for example, include tightening eligibility requirements, reducing benefits, and limiting the duration of benefits.

28. Pension discrimination rules attempt to equalize benefits within firms. Special pension regulations pertaining to high-income employees limit the absolute size of benefits.

REFERENCES

Abel, A.B.
  1985 Precautionary savings and accidental bequests. *American Economic Review* 75(4):777-791.
Allen, S.G., R.L. Clark, and A.A. McDermed
  1993 Pensions, bonding and lifetime jobs. *Journal of Human Resources* 28(3):463-481.
Anderson, P.M., A.L. Gustman, and T.L. Steinmeier
  1994 The Trend to Earlier Retirement Among Males. Report to the Social Security Administration.
Ausink, J.A., and D.A. Wise
  1993 *The Military Pension, Compensation, and Retirement of U.S. Air Force Pilots.* NBER Working Paper #4593. Cambridge, Mass.: National Bureau of Economic Research.
Barro, R.J.
  1974 Are government bonds net wealth? *Journal of Political Economy* 82(6):1095-1117.
Barsky, R., M. Kimball, M. Shapiro, and F.T. Juster
  1993 Experimental Measures of Preferences in the HRS. Paper presented at Health and Retirement Survey Early Results Workshop, Survey Research Center, University of Michigan.
Becker, G.S.
  1991 *A Treatise on the Family.* Cambridge, Mass.: Harvard University Press.
Berkovec, J.C., and S. Stern
  1991 Job exit behavior of older men. *Econometrica* 59(1):189-210.
Bernheim, B.D.
  1988 Social Security benefits: An empirical study of expectations and realizations. Pp. 312-345 in R.R. Campbell and E. Lazear, eds., *Issues in Contemporary Retirement.* Stanford, Calif.: Hoover Institution.
  1989 The timing of retirement: A comparison of expectations and realizations. Pp. 335-355 in D.A. Wise, ed., *The Economics of Aging.* Chicago, Ill.: University of Chicago Press.
  1991 How strong are bequest motives? *Journal of Political Economy* 99(5):899-927.
  1993 Personal Saving, Information, and Economic Literacy: New Directions for Public Policy. Unpublished manuscript. Department of Economics, Princeton University.
  1994 Do saving incentives work?: A discussion of Engen, Gale and Scholz. *Brookings Papers on Economic Activity* 1994(1):152-156.
Bernheim, B.D., and J.K. Scholz
  1993 Private saving and public policy. Pp. 73-110 in J. Poterba, ed., *Tax Policy and the Economy* Vol. 7. Cambridge, Mass.: MIT Press.
Bernheim, B.D., A. Shleifer, and L.H. Summers
  1985 The strategic bequest motive. *Journal of Political Economy* 96(6):1045-1076.
Blau, D.M.
  1994 Labor force dynamics of older men. *Econometrica* 62(1):117-156.

Bloom, D.E., and R.B. Freeman
  1992 The fall in private pension coverage in the United States *American Economic Review,
        Papers and Proceedings* 82(2):539-545.
Bodie, Z.
  1990 Pensions as retirement income insurance. *Journal of Economic Literature* 28(1):28-49.
Borsch-Supan, A.
  1989 Household dissolution and the choice of alternative living arrangements among elderly
        Americans. Pp. 119-146 in D.A. Wise, ed., *The Economics of Aging.* Chicago, Ill.:
        University of Chicago Press.
  1990 A dynamic analysis of household dissolution and living arrangement transitions by eld-
        erly Americans. Pp. 89-114 in D.A. Wise, ed., *Issues in the Economics of Aging.* Chi-
        cago, Ill.: University of Chicago Press.
Borsch-Supan, A., D. McFadden, and R. Schnabel
  1993 Living Arrangements: Health and Wealth Effects. Unpublished paper. Department of
        Economics, University of California, Berkeley.
Borsch-Supan, A., and K. Stahl
  1991 Life cycle savings and consumption constraints: Theory, empirical evidence and fiscal
        implications. *Journal of Population Economics* 86:3-27.
Brown, C.
  1993 Early Retirement Windows: Windows of Opportunity? Defenestrations? (and Even
        Refenestrations. . .). Paper presented at Health and Retirement Survey Early Results
        Workshop, Survey Research Center, University of Michigan.
Burkhauser, R.V.
  1979 The pension acceptance decision of older workers. *Journal of Human Resources* 14(1):63-
        75.
Burkhauser, R.V., K.C. Holden, and D. Feaster
  1988 Incidence, timing, and events associated with poverty: A dynamic view of poverty in
        retirement. *Journal of Gerontology* 43(2):S46-S52.
Burtless, G., and R.A. Moffitt
  1984 The effect of Social Security benefits on the labor supply of the aged. Pp. 135-174 in H.J.
        Aaron and G. Burtless, eds., *Retirement and Economic Behavior.* Washington, D.C.:
        Brookings Institution.
  1985 The joint choice of retirement age and postretirement hours of work. *Journal of Labor
        Economics* 3(2):209-236.
Cagan, P.
  1965 *The Effect of Pension Plans on Aggregate Saving: Evidence from a Sample Survey.*
        National Bureau of Economic Research Occasional Paper 95. New York: Columbia
        University Press.
Carroll, C.D.
  1992 The buffer-stock theory of saving: Some macroeconomic evidence. *Brookings Papers
        on Economic Activity* 2:61-135.
Carroll, C.D., and A.A. Samwick
  1994 The Nature of Precautionary Wealth. Manuscript, National Bureau of Economic Re-
        search, Cambridge, Mass.
Carroll, C.D., and L.H. Summers
  1991 Consumption growth parallels income growth: Some new evidence. Pp. 305-343 in D.B.
        Bernheim and J.B. Shoven, eds., *National Saving and Economic Performance.* Chicago,
        Ill.: University of Chicago Press.
Clark, R.L., and A.A. McDermed
  1990 *The Choice of Pension Plans in a Changing Regulatory Environment.* Washington, D.C.:
        American Enterprise Institute.

Congressional Budget Office
    1987   *Tax Policy for Pensions and Retirement Savings.* Washington, D.C.: U.S. Government
           Printing Office.
Davies, J.B.
    1981   Uncertain lifetime, consumption, and dissaving in retirement. *Journal of Political
           Economy* 89(3):561-576.
Deaton, A.
    1991   Savings and liquidity constraints. *Econometrica* 59(5):1221-1248.
Employee Benefit Research Institute
    1993   Pension coverage and participation growth: A new look at primary and supplemental
           plans. *EBRI Issue Brief* No. 144. Washington, D.C.: Employee Benefit Research Insti-
           tute.
Engelhardt, G.V.
    1994   House Prices and Home Owner Saving Behavior. Unpublished manuscript. Dartmouth
           College.
Engen, E.M., and W. Gale
    1993   IRAs and Saving in a Stochastic Life-Cycle Model. Unpublished manuscript. University
           of California, Los Angeles.
Engen, E.M., W.G. Gale, and J.K. Scholz
    1994   Do saving incentives work? *Brookings Papers on Economic Activity* 1994(1):85-180..
Even, W.E., and D.A. Macpherson
    1994   The pension coverage of young and mature workers. Report to the U.S. Department of
           Labor. Pp. 85-106 in *Pension Coverage Issues for the 90's.* U.S. Department of Labor,
           Pension and Welfare Benefits Administration.
Feinstein, J., and D. McFadden
    1989   The dynamics of housing demand by the elderly: Wealth, cash flow and demographic
           effects. Pp. 55-86 in D.A. Wise, ed., *The Economics of Aging.* Chicago, Ill.: University
           of Chicago Press.
Fields, G.S., and O.S. Mitchell
    1984   *Retirement, Pensions and Social Security.* Cambridge, Mass.: MIT Press.
Gale, W.G., and J.K. Scholz
    1994   IRAs and household saving. *American Economic Review* 84(5):1233-1260.
Garber, A.M., and T.E. MacCurdy
    1990   Predicting nursing home utilization by high risk elderly. Pp. 173-200 in D.A. Wise, ed.,
           Issues in the Economics of Aging. Chicago, Ill.: University of Chicago Press.
Grad, S.
    1994   *Income of the Population 55 or Older, 1992.* Washington, D.C.: U.S. Department of
           Health and Human Services, Social Security Administration.
Green, J.
    1985   The riskiness of private pensions. Pp. 357-375 in D.A. Wise, ed., *Pensions, Labor, and
           Individual Choice.* Chicago, Ill.: University of Chicago Press.
Guiso, L., T. Jappelli, and D. Terlizzese
    1992   Earnings uncertainty and precautionary saving. *Journal of Monetary Economics* 30:307-
           337.
Gustman, A.L., and O.S. Mitchell
    1992   Pensions and labor market activity: Behavior and data requirements. Pp. 39-87 in Z.
           Bodie and A.H. Munnell, eds., *Pensions and the Economy: Sources, Uses, and Limita-
           tions of Data.* Philadelphia, Pa.: Pension Research Council Publications and University
           of Pennsylvania Press..

Gustman, A.L., O.S. Mitchell, and T.L. Steinmeier
    1994   The role of pensions in the labor market. *Industrial and Labor Relations Review* 47(3):417-438.
Gustman, A.L., and T.L. Steinmeier
    1985   The 1983 Social Security reforms and labor supply adjustments of older individuals in the long run. *Journal of Labor Economics* 3:237-253.
    1986a   A disaggregated structural analysis of retirement by race, difficulty of work and health. *Review of Economics and Statistics* 67(3):509-513.
    1986b   A structural retirement model. *Econometrica* 54(3):555-584.
    1989   An analysis of pension benefit formulas, pension wealth and incentives from pensions. Pp. 53-106 in R. Ehrenberg, ed., *Research in Labor Economics* 10. Greenwich, Conn.: JAI Press.
    1991   Changing the Social Security rules for work after 65. *Industrial and Labor Relations Review* 44(4):733-745.
    1992   The stampede towards defined contribution pension plans: Fact or fiction? *Industrial Relations* 31(2):361-369.
    1993   Pension portability and labor mobility: Evidence from the survey of income and program participation. *Journal of Public Economics* 50:299-323.
    1994a   Employer-provided health insurance and retirement behavior. *Industrial and Labor Relations Review* 48(1):124-140.
    1994b   *Retirement in a Family Context: A Structural Model for Husbands and Wives.* NBER Working Paper #4629. Cambridge, Mass.: National Bureau of Economic Research.
    1995a   *Pension Incentives and Job Mobility.* Kalamazoo, Mich.: W.E. Upjohn Institute for Employment Research.
    1995b   *Privatizing Social Security: First Round Effects of a Generic, Voluntary, Privatized U.S. Social Security System.* NBER Working Paper #5362. Cambridge, Mass.: National Bureau of Economic Research.
Hall, R.E., and F.S. Mishkin
    1982   The sensitivity of consumption to transitory income: Estimates from panel data on households. *Econometrica* 50(2):461-482.
Hamermesh, D.S.
    1984   Consumption during retirement: The missing link in the life cycle. *Review of Economics and Statistics* 66(1):1-7.
Hoynes, H., and D. McFadden
    1994   *The Impact of Demographics on Housing and Non-Housing Wealth in the United States.* NBER Working Paper #4666. Cambridge, Mass.: National Bureau of Economic Research.
Hubbard, R.G., J. Skinner, and S.P. Zeldes
    1994a   Expanding the life-cycle model: Precautionary saving and public policy. *The American Economic Review, Papers and Proceedings* 84(2):174-179.
    1994b   The importance of precautionary motives in explaining individual and aggregate saving. *Carnegie-Rochester Conference Series on Public Policy* 40(June):59-126.
    1995   Precautionary saving and social insurance. *Journal of Political Economy* 103(2):360-399.
Hurd, M.
    1987   Savings of the elderly and desired bequests. *American Economic Review* 77(3):298-312.
    1990a   The joint retirement decisions of husbands and wives. Pp. 231-254 in D.A. Wise, ed., *Issues in the Economics of Aging.* Chicago, Ill.: University of Chicago Press.
    1990b   Research on the elderly: Economic status, retirement and consumption and saving. *Journal of Economic Literature* 28(2):565-637.

1993   *The Effect of Labor Market Rigidities on the Labor Force Behavior of Older Workers.*
        NBER Working Paper #4462. Cambridge, Mass.: National Bureau of Economic Re-
        search.
Hurd, M., and K. McGarry
    1993a *Evaluation of Subjective Probability Distributions in the HRS.* NBER Working Paper
          #4560. Cambridge, Mass.: National Bureau of Economic Research.
    1993b *The Relationship Between Job Characteristics and Retirement.* NBER Working Paper
          #4558. Cambridge, Mass.: National Bureau of Economic Research.
Hurd, M., and D.A. Wise
    1989 The wealth and poverty of widows: Assets before and after the husband's death. Pp.
          177-200 in D. Wise, ed., *The Economics of Aging.* Chicago, Ill.: University of Chicago
          Press.
Hutchens, R.
    1986 Delayed payment contracts and a firm's propensity to hire older workers. *Journal of
          Labor Economics* 4(4):439-457.
    1987 A test of Lazear's theory of delayed payment contract. *Journal of Labor Economics*
          5(4)Part 2:S153-S170.
Ippolito, R.A.
    1983 Public policy toward private pensions. *Contemporary Policy Issues*, a supplement to
          Economic Inquiry 3:53-76.
    1985a The economic function of underfunded pension plans. *The Journal of Law and Econom-
          ics* 28(3):611-651.
    1985b The labor contract and true economic pension liabilities. *American Economic Review*
          75(5):1031-1043.
    1986 *Pensions, Economics and Public Policy.* Homewood, Ill.: Dow Jones-Irwin.
    1987 The implicit pension contract: Developments and new directions. *Journal of Human
          Resources* 22(3):441-467.
    1990 Toward explaining earlier retirement after 1970. *Industrial and Labor Relations Review*
          43(5):556-569.
    1995 Toward explaining the growth of defined contribution pension plans. *Industrial Relations*
          34(1):1-20.
Juster, F.T., and F.P. Stafford
    1991 The allocation of time: Empirical findings, behavioral models, and problems of measure-
          ment. *Journal of Economic Literature* 29:471-522.
Karoly, L.A., and J.A. Rogowski
    1994 The effects of health insurance on the decision to retire. *Industrial and Labor Relations
          Review* 48(1):103-123.
Katona, G.
    1965 *Private Pensions and Individual Saving.* Ann Arbor, Mich.: Survey Research Center,
          University of Michigan.
Kimball, M.S.
    1990 Precautionary saving in the small and in the large. *Econometrica* 58(1):53-73.
    1993 Standard risk aversion. *Econometrica* 61(3):589-611.
Kotlikoff, L.J.
    1988 Intergenerational transfers and savings. *The Journal of Economic Perspectives* 2(2):41-
          58.
Kotlikoff, L.J., and A. Spivak
    1981 The family as an incomplete annuities market. *Journal of Political Economy* 89(2):372-
          391.
Kotlikoff, L.J., and L. Summers
    1981 The role of intergenerational transfers in capital accumulation. *Journal of Political
          Economy* 89(4):706-732.

Kotlikoff, L.J., and D.A. Wise
    1985   Labor compensation and the structure of private pension plans: Evidence for contractual
           vs. spot labor markets. Pp. 55-85 in D.A. Wise, ed., *Pensions, Labor, and Individual
           Choice*. Chicago, Ill.: University of Chicago Press.
    1987   The incentive effects of private pension plans. Pp. 283-336 in Z. Bodie, J.B. Shoven, and
           D.A. Wise, eds., *Issues in Pension Economics*. Chicago, Ill.: University of Chicago
           Press.
Kruse, D.L.
    1995   Pension substitution in the 1980's: Why the shift toward defined contribution pension
           plans? *Industrial Relations* 34(2):218-241.
Lazear, E.P.
    1979   Why is there mandatory retirement? *Journal of Political Economy* 87(6):1261-1284.
    1983   Pensions as severance pay. Pp. 57-89 in Z. Bodie and J.B. Shoven, eds., *Financial
           Aspects of the United States Pension System*. Chicago, Ill.: University of Chicago Press.
Lumsdaine, R., J. Stock, and D.A. Wise
    1990   Efficient windows and labor force reduction. *Journal of Public Economics* 43:131-159.
    1992a *Pension Plan Provisions and Retirement: Men & Women, Medicare, and Models*. NBER
           Working Paper #4201. Cambridge, Mass.: National Bureau of Economic Research.
    1992b Three models of retirement: Computational complexity versus predictive validity. Pp.
           19-57 in D. Wise, ed., *Topics in the Economics of Aging*. Chicago, Ill.: University of
           Chicago Press.
Lumsdaine, R., and D.A. Wise
    1994   Aging and labor force participation: A review of trends and explanations. Pp. 7-41 in D.
           Wise, ed., *Aging in the United States and Japan: Economic Trends*. Chicago, Ill.:
           University of Chicago Press.
Luzadis, R.A., and O.S. Mitchell
    1991   Explaining pension dynamics. *Journal of Human Resources* 26(4):679-703.
McGarry, K., and R.F. Schoeni
    1994   Transfer Behavior: Measurement and the Redistribution of Resources Within the Family.
           Paper presented at Health and Retirement Survey Early Results Workshop, Survey Re-
           search Center, University of Michigan. Revised.
Mitchell, O.S.
    1988   Worker knowledge of pension provisions. *Journal of Labor Economics* 6(1):28-39.
    1992   Trends in pension benefit formulas and retirement provisions. Pp. 177-216 in J.A. Turner
           and D.J. Beller, eds., *Trends in Pensions 1992*. Washington, D.C.: U.S. Department of
           Labor, Pension and Welfare Benefits Administration.
Mitchell, O.S., and R.A. Luzadis
    1988   Changes in pension incentives through time. *Industrial and Labor Relations Review*
           42(1):100-108.
Modigliani, F.
    1988   The role of intergenerational transfers and life cycle saving in the accumulation of wealth.
           The Journal of Economic Perspectives 2(2):15-40.
Munnell, A.H., and F.O. Yohn
    1992   What is the impact of pensions on savings? Pp. 115-139 in Z. Bodie and A.H. Munnell,
           eds., *Pensions and the Economy: Sources, Uses, and Limitations of Data*. Philadelphia,
           Pa.: Pension Research Council Publications and University of Pennsylvania Press.
Nalebuff, B., and R.J. Zeckhauser
    1985   Pensions and the retirement decision. Pp. 283-316 in D.A. Wise, ed., *Pensions, Labor,
           and Individual Choice*. Chicago, Ill.: University of Chicago Press.
Parsons, D.O.
    1991   The decline in private pension coverage in the United States. *Economics Letters* 36:419-
           423.

1993   The Contraction in Pension Coverage. Unpublished manuscript. Ohio State University.

Peracchi, F., and F. Welch
1994   Trends in labor force transitions of older men and women. *Journal of Labor Economics* 12(2):210-242.

Poterba, J.M., ed.
1994   *Public Policies and Household Savings.* Chicago, Ill.: University of Chicago Press.

Poterba. J.M., S.F. Venti, and D.A. Wise
1993   *Do 401(k) Plans Crowd Out Other Retirement Savings?* NBER Working Paper #4391. Cambridge, Mass.: National Bureau of Economic Research.
1994   Targeted retirement saving and the net worth of elderly Americans. *American Economic Review* 84(2):180-185.

Reimers, C., and M. Honig
1993a   The perceived budget constraint under Social Security: Evidence from reentry behavior. *Journal of Labor Economics* 11(1)Part 1:184-204.
1993b   Responses to Social Security by Men and Women: Myopic and Far-Sighted Behavior. Paper presented at the 1993 meeting of the Association for Public Policy Analysis and Management.

Ruhm, C.J.
1992   Secular Changes in the Work and Retirement Patterns of Older Men. Unpublished manuscript. University of North Carolina, Greensboro.

Rust, J.
1989   A dynamic programming model of retirement behavior. Pp. 359-398 in D.A. Wise, ed., *The Economics of Aging.* Chicago, Ill.: University of Chicago Press.
1990   Behavior of male workers at the end of the life cycle: An empirical analysis of states and controls. Pp. 317-379 in D.A. Wise, ed., *Issues in the Economics of Aging.* Chicago, Ill.: University of Chicago Press.

Rust, J., and C. Phelan
1993   How Social Security and Medicare Affect Retirement Behavior in a World of Incomplete Markets. Unpublished manuscript. Department of Economics, University of Wisconsin.

Samwick, A.A.
1993a   The Joint Effect of Social Security and Pensions on the Timing of Retirement: Some New Evidence. Unpublished manuscript. Dartmouth College.
1993b   Wage Risk Compensation Through Employer-Provided Pensions. Unpublished manuscript. Dartmouth College.
1994   The Limited Offset Between Pension Wealth and Other Private Wealth: Implications of Buffer Stock Saving. Unpublished manuscript. Dartmouth College.

Sheiner, L., and D.N. Weil
1992   *The Housing Wealth of the Aged.* NBER Working Paper #4115. Cambridge, Mass.: National Bureau of Economic Research.

Skinner, J.
1988   Risky income, life-cycle consumption and precautionary savings. *Journal of Monetary Economics* 22:237-255.
1993   *Is Housing Wealth a Sideshow?* NBER Working Paper #4552. Cambridge, Mass.: National Bureau of Economic Research.

Smith, J.P.
1994   Marriage, Assets, and Savings. Unpublished manuscript. The RAND Corporation, Santa Monica, Calif..

Soldo, B.J., and M.S. Hill
1993   Family Structure and Transfer Measures in the HRS: Background and Overview. Paper presented at Health and Retirement Survey Early Results Workshop, Survey Research Center, University of Michigan.

Stern, S., and P. Todd
    1993   A Test of Lazear's Mandatory Retirement Model. Unpublished manuscript. University of
            Virginia.
Stock, J.H., and D.A. Wise
    1990a   The pension inducement to retire: An option value analysis. Pp. 205-224 in D.A. Wise,
            ed., *Issues in the Economics of Aging.* Chicago, Ill.: University of Chicago Press.
    1990b   Pensions, the option value of work, and retirement. *Econometrica* 58(5):1151-1180.
Thaler, R.H.
    1994   Psychology and savings policies. *American Economic Review* 84(2):186-192.
Turner, J.A., and D.J. Beller, eds.
    1992   *Trends in Pensions 1992.* Washington, D.C.: U.S. Department of Labor, Pension and
            Welfare Benefits Administration.
Venti, S.F., and D.A. Wise
    1987   IRAs and saving. Pp. 7-52 in M. Feldstein, ed., *The Effects of Taxation on Capital
            Accumulation.* Chicago, Ill.: University of Chicago Press.
    1989   Aging, moving and housing wealth. Pp. 9-48 in D.A. Wise, ed., *The Economics of Aging.*
            Chicago, Ill.: University of Chicago Press.
    1990   But they don't want to reduce housing equity. Pp. 13-29 in D.A. Wise, ed., *Issues in the
            Economics of Aging.* Chicago, Ill.: University of Chicago Press.
    1993   *The Wealth of Cohorts and the Changing Assets of Older Americans.* NBER Working
            Paper #4600. Cambridge, Mass.: National Bureau of Economic Research.
Wise, D.A., and R.G. Woodbury
    1994   Policy toward the aged. Pp. 741-780 in M. Feldstein, ed., *American Economic Policy in
            the 1980s.* Chicago, Ill.: University of Chicago Press.
Woodbury, S.A.
    1983   Substitution between wage and nonwage benefits. *American Economic Review* 73(1):166-
            182.
Woodbury, S.A., and W. Huang
    1991   *The Tax Treatment of Fringe Benefits.* Kalamazoo, Mich.: W.E. Upjohn Institute for
            Employment Research..
Zeldes, S.P.
    1989a   Consumption and liquidity constraints: An empirical investigation. *Journal of Political
            Economy* 97(2):305-346.
    1989b   Optimal consumption with stochastic income: Deviations from certainty equivalence.
            Quarterly Journal of Economics 104:275-298.

3

Factors Affecting Labor Supply Decisions and Retirement Income

Robin L. Lumsdaine

Recent retirement research has focused on factors affecting the retirement *decision*, reflecting the notion that retirement has become voluntary (Quinn, Burkhauser, and Myers, 1990, document the transition over the last four decades from "involuntary" retirement due to health reasons to the current situation in which most people *choose* to retire). Leonesio (1993a) cites the "life-cycle view of work, saving, and consumption" as the motivating influence behind the behavioral focus of the retirement literature, particularly with regard to decisions about Social Security, pensions, leaving a career job, and accepting post-retirement work. Recognizing the life-cycle view, economists have concentrated not just on the final decision to retire but on the individual's whole history of labor force participation decisions.

Owing to both the projected shortfall in Social Security and an overall anticipated labor shortage, recent policy has focused on ways to alter these labor supply decisions, particularly with regard to affecting retirement behavior and income. Gustman, Mitchell, and Steinmeier (1994) and Hurd (1993) identify some of the factors that influence the retirement decision. Gustman, Mitchell, and Steinmeier consider factors affecting the individual, such as health status, retirement status of spouse, additional family needs, and the individual's savings

Financial support for this paper from the National Institute on Aging, grant number R37-AG00146, and the Center for Economic Policy Research at Princeton University is gratefully acknowledged. This paper has benefited substantially from comments on earlier drafts by Constance Citro, Marjorie Honig, John Rust, and participants at the panel conference.

and consumption patterns, while Hurd surveys some of the institutional causes that lead individuals to retire at different ages, such as fixed employment costs, the Social Security earnings test, and pre-existing condition clauses in health insurance. In addition, the perceived financial condition of the employer may play a role in an individual's decision to leave a firm.

This paper examines the determinants of some of the key labor supply decisions and their relationship to retirement behavior and retirement income. In order to determine which policies will have the most desirable effects at the lowest cost, we need to assess the relationships and interactions among direct and indirect influences. Some of the questions that have been debated are the following: Will increasing the Social Security early and normal retirement ages create a substitution toward increased disability applications? Have increasing life expectancies resulted in more productive years of life or just prolonged years of nonwork life? Is the relationship between longevity and the ability to work becoming weaker as labor-intensive jobs are a smaller proportion of available jobs? How do individuals formulate expectations about the future and how do they incorporate uncertainty into their decisions? What would be the impact of universal health coverage on labor force participation?

This paper will investigate the data and research methodology needed to answer questions such as these. The first section summarizes some of the trends in factors affecting labor force participation decisions and retirement income. The ability to predict future trends is critical to forecasting the success of proposed changes in policy aimed at ensuring adequate retirement income. The next five sections focus on specific key areas that potentially affect the labor supply decision, the transition to retirement, and associated retirement income: Social Security, pensions and early retirement "window" plans, disability, Medicare and other forms of health insurance, and job characteristics. Each of these sections begins with a summary of questions and currently available techniques for addressing them. I then identify future research priorities, focusing on data and methods necessary to understand the extent of the interaction among these areas and how policies aimed at specific areas will ultimately affect retirement behavior and income. I present conclusions in the final section.

SUMMARY OF TRENDS

While legislation over the last few decades has aimed to reduce the incidence of poverty among the elderly, the threat of poverty has not been eradicated, as shown in Figure 3-1. As individuals age, the probability of being at or near the poverty line increases substantially. One group of elderly particularly at risk are the nearly one-third of Americans over age 65 that live alone, most often women:

> For the millions of elderly people who live alone, the threats of impoverishment, loss of independence, loneliness and isolation are very real. Many have serious health and economic problems that our society and our governments are

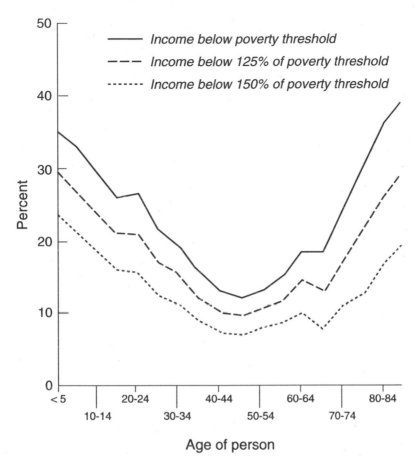

FIGURE 3-1 Percentage of persons below poverty and near poverty thresholds, by age, 1990. SOURCE: Radner (1993a).

neglecting. These conditions persist despite the substantial improvements that Social Security and health and income assistance programs have made in the lives of most older Americans over the past 20 years (Kasper, 1988).

Women currently account for more than four-fifths of the elderly living alone, as seen in Figure 3-2. Poverty rates for the elderly are also expected to be concentrated on single women in the future, despite expectations that the elderly as a group will have higher standards of living than previous cohorts (Kingson, 1992). Radner (1993b) considers income, wealth, and combined income-wealth measures and finds that the economic status of widows living alone is significantly worse than that of other groups of elderly.

Across all ages, uncertainty about Social Security is increasing. Concerns

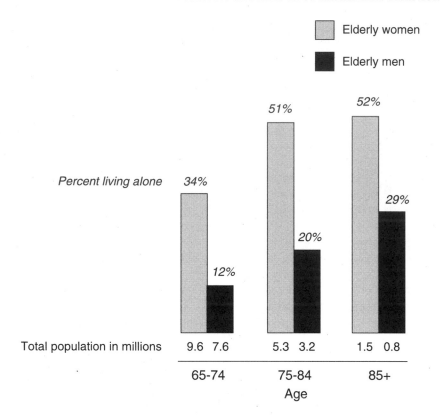

FIGURE 3-2 Percentage of elderly women and men living alone. SOURCE: Kasper (1988).

over the budget deficit have threatened the current levels of Social Security benefits. Even if benefits are held at their current levels, the aging of the baby boom population poses an additional strain on the Social Security Trust Fund. Combined, these two concerns have undermined confidence regarding adequate income for future generations of elderly.

Despite concerns over the adequacy of Social Security retirement income, the wealth of the elderly remains surprisingly low. The typical American family with a household head age 60 to 65 has very little retirement saving, with median liquid wealth equal to about $6,600 (Venti and Wise, 1992). Lumsdaine and Wise (1994) document various components of elderly wealth and labor force participation and discuss their interaction. Auerbach, Kotlikoff, and Weil (1992) note that the incomes of the elderly are becoming increasingly annuitized as a result of increases in pension benefits and Social Security during the early 1980s. They note that the fraction of elderly income attributable to these two sources rose from 40 percent in 1967 to 55 percent in 1988, a 37 percent increase. Increased annuitization could make retirement income planning easier by reducing future uncertainty. However, it is not the fraction of annuitization that is important for the adequacy of retirement income, but the amount.

There is additional evidence that the elderly will continue to find themselves with inadequate income to carry them through retirement. The American Society of Pension Actuaries (ASPA) found that employees receive only limited investment advice when it comes to retirement planning. What advice is given often occurs within 1 or 2 years of retirement. ASPA recommends four vehicles for improving one's retirement income. At the individual level, income is expected to come from personal savings, Social Security, pension, and supplemental work after retirement. At the macro level, they emphasize a need for universal coverage and replacement rates targeted as high as 85 percent of final pay for low-income workers and 73 percent for higher income workers. In 1990, average replacement rates for Social Security varied from 28 percent for maximum earners to 56 percent for low wage earners. Currently only 12 percent of employers surveyed have pension plans that are designed around specific replacement rate goals. Of those that do have specific replacement rate goals, the target replacement rate falls far short of those recommended by ASPA (Employee Benefit Plan Review, 1994a). Figure 3-3 shows average replacement rates for defined benefit plan participants in 1989. Evidence in Mitchell (1992) concurs; for representative workers in defined benefit plans with 30 years of service, replacement rates ranged from 34.6 percent for individuals with final earnings of $15,000 to 29.8 percent for individuals with final earnings of $40,000. Fewer years of service substantially lowered replacement rates at all levels; for example, a worker with only 10 years of service could expect a maximum replacement rate of 12.1 percent. According to reports in Employee Benefit Plan Review (1994b), using the Consumer Expenditure Survey, replacement rates for lower income individuals in 1993 were nearly the same as in 1988; the replacement rates for higher income individuals had gone up dramatically.

Of particular concern is the adequacy of retirement income for women (for a review of the literature, see Weaver, 1994). Although the proportion of elderly living alone is expected to remain constant in the future, the percentage that are women is projected to increase, as seen in Figure 3-4. In addition to having longer life expectancies, women have traditionally been more likely to experience gaps in service, leading to reduced Social Security and pension benefits. As more women enter the labor force, concern over adequacy of retirement income for women may decrease. In 1959, 40 percent of women above age 16 were in the labor force, compared with 60 percent in 1989 (U.S. Department of Labor, 1992). Additional evidence suggests improvements in earnings that will lead to higher Social Security benefits. Over roughly the same time period, the percentage of women over 62 receiving Social Security benefits on the basis of their own work history has increased from 43.3 percent to 59.7 percent (see Table 3-1). It

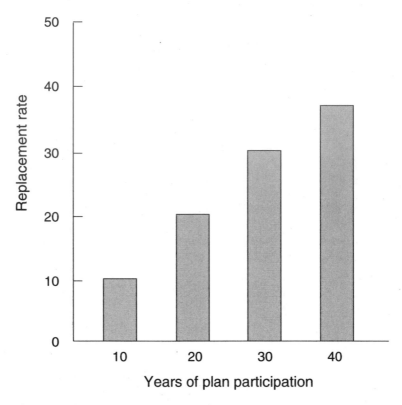

FIGURE 3-3 Average replacement rate for defined benefit pension plan participants, medium and large private establishments, 1989. NOTE: Calculations based on retirement at age 65 with annual salary of $35,000 in final year. SOURCE: U.S. Department of Labor (1992:Chart 20).

is not clear that there have been similar improvements in pension benefits. Even and MacPherson (1994) note that "pension coverage for women is less likely to convert into pension receipt at retirement" (p. 562). In addition, the average level of benefits for women is between 55 percent and 62 percent of the average level of benefits for men. Even and Macpherson estimate that one-third of the gap in coverage between men and women is attributable to women's absence from the labor force (their work history). Some of the policies that have been proposed to address this disparity are earnings sharing, homemaker credits, and caregiving credits (Employee Benefit Plan Review, 1994a, from Ferber, 1993).

While an obvious solution to the threat of inadequate retirement income is a shortened retirement phase (through either prolonged work, delayed retirement, or earlier mortality), trends both in labor force participation and life expectancies suggest that retirement savings will need to be stretched over more years of life

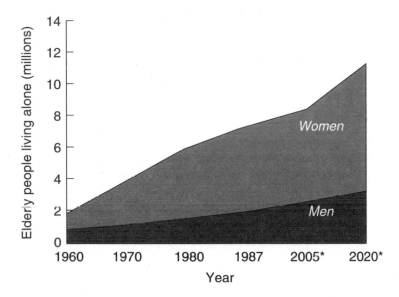

FIGURE 3-4 Composition of elderly people living alone. NOTE: Asterisked years are projections. SOURCE: Kasper (1988).

rather than fewer. Labor force participation rates of the elderly are decreasing, particularly among men. Table 3-2 compares labor force participation rates of men and women at various ages between 1970 and 1990. While male labor force participation rates have decreased dramatically, corresponding rates for women have increased in the first three groups but have declined in the 62-to-64 and 65+ age groups. As a result, the gap between male and female labor force participation has narrowed over the last two decades, by about 15 percentage points for those aged 50 to 62 (Peracchi and Welch, 1994). In addition, the modal labor

TABLE 3-1 Percentage of Women Over Age 62 Receiving Social Security on the Basis of Their Own Work History

Year	Percent
1960	43.3
1970	50.6
1980	56.9
1988	59.7

SOURCE: U.S. Department of Labor (1994) and Lingg (1990) (primary source).

TABLE 3-2   Labor Force Participation Rates (percent)

Gender and Year	Age				
	45-54	55-59	60-61	62-64	65+
Men					
1970	94.3	89.5	82.6	69.4	26.8
1990	90.7	79.8	68.8	46.4	16.4
Women					
1970	54.4	50.4	41.4	32.3	9.7
1990	71.2	55.3	42.9	30.7	8.7

SOURCE: Bureau of the Census (1992, Table 622).

TABLE 3-3   Life Expectancy and Projections Among White Men and Women, Age 65 (in years)

Gender and Scenario	Actual		Projected	
	1980	1990	2000	2020
Men	14.2	15.2		
I			15.3	15.6
II			15.9	16.7
III			16.4	18.0
Women	18.4	19.1		
I			18.9	19.1
II			19.6	20.4
III			20.2	21.9

SOURCE: U.S. National Center for Health Statistics (1990) (actual) and Hurd (1994b) (projections).

force participation transition age moved from 65 in 1968 to 62 in 1991 (Quinn and Burkhauser, 1992; Peracchi and Welch, 1994).

In addition to declining labor force participation trends, life expectancies are also increasing. Table 3-3 shows life expectancies and projections for white men and women under three different demographic scenarios (these are described in Hurd, 1994b). In the last decade, the life expectancy for men has increased by 1 year. Depending on the projection used, even scheduled increases in the Social Security eligibility age, aimed at encouraging later retirement, will not keep up with the increasing life expectancies. The elderly population is itself aging. In 1980, 40 percent of individuals 65+ were over age 75. It is expected that by 2000,

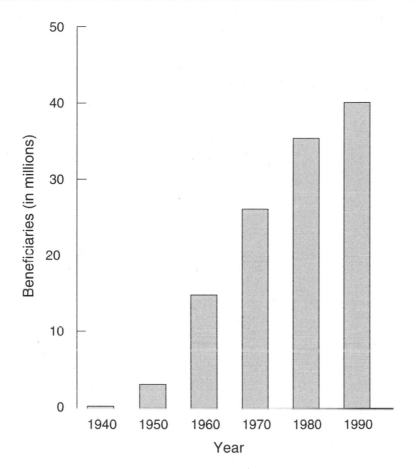

FIGURE 3-5 Recipients of Social Security payments, 1940-1990. SOURCE: U.S. Department of Labor (1992:Chart 25).

this proportion will rise to 50 percent. As individuals age, the threat of poverty rises substantially. In 1990, one-fifth of persons age 85 or older had income levels at or below the poverty threshold (Radner, 1993b).

Because of these trends, the ratio of the retired population to the working population is expected to rise from 0.21 in 1990 to 0.27 in 2020 to 0.37 in 2035 (Congressional Budget Office, 1993). The number of Social Security beneficiaries has also increased dramatically, as shown in Figure 3-5. To remain solvent, the current Social Security system will have to impose an increasingly large tax burden on the shrinking working population in order to support the growing elderly population.

SOCIAL SECURITY

In 1990, nearly 40 percent of the income of the elderly (65+) was from Social Security (Congressional Budget Office, 1993). In addition, 57 percent of the elderly obtained more than half their income from Social Security; 24 percent obtained more than 90 percent from this source (Hurd, 1994a). Almost 95 percent of elderly households reported receiving Social Security benefits (Hurd, 1994a; Congressional Budget Office, 1993); these benefits are an especially important component of income for households in the lower income brackets and are the largest single source of income for all but the highest income quintile of the elderly (Reno, 1993). It is projected that for retirees in the bottom half of the income distribution in 2019, 60 percent to 70 percent of retirement income will come from Social Security (Kingson, 1992). As a result of pressures on the Social Security system and rising health care costs, concern that the income of the elderly will be inadequate has created debate over how to increase retirement income, accompanied by legislation aimed at effecting such an increase.

Because Social Security affects so much of the elderly population, it is the obvious place to start in discussing broad-based policy changes that influence retirement behavior and income. Previous research considering the effects of changes in Social Security policy on retirement and labor force participation includes Gustman and Steinmeier (1991) and Feldstein and Samwick (1992). As Table 3-2 showed, it is clear that labor force participation rates decline precipitously among individuals that have reached the Social Security early and normal retirement ages (62 and 65, respectively). Using aggregate time series data, Stewart (1995) provides further evidence of the influence of Social Security, demonstrating that ratios of primary insurance amount (PIA) to earnings closely mirror the nonparticipation rate of men ages 65 and older, as shown in Figure 3-6. However, evidence in Bondar (1993) suggests that individuals with high pre-retirement earnings (as estimated based on PIA amount) are most likely to continue to work and earn high post-retirement earnings. In addition, replacement rates (PIA/earnings) are higher for low wage individuals, suggesting that the labor force participation decline is being driven by precisely the individuals for whom concerns over retirement income adequacy are the largest. Therefore, discussions about the government's role in ensuring adequacy of retirement income have focused on the Social Security program and its ability to meet the needs of a growing elderly population.

Researchers have also become increasingly aware of the Social Security system's inability to adequately provide for many women in their retirement. This is due partly to the societal norms under which the system was designed (i.e., around the "traditional" one-earner family) and to differences in men's and women's labor force history and attachment. Ferber (1993) provides evidence that the earnings gap, along with male/female differences in labor force participation and tenure, has declined, but not disappeared.

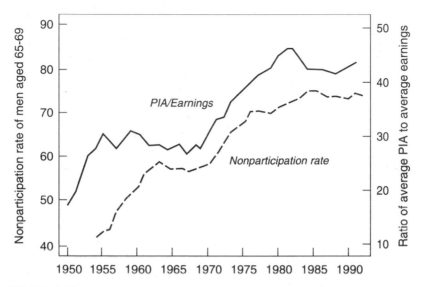

FIGURE 3-6 The PIA/earnings ratio and the nonparticipation rate of men aged 65-69 in the labor force. NOTE: PIA is the primary insurance amount. SOURCE: Stewart (1995).

In order to increase labor force participation and decrease the burden on the Social Security system, current Social Security policy dictates an increase in the normal retirement age from 65 to 67. Those born in 1937 will be the last group with a normal retirement age of 65. Those born in 1960 will be the first with a normal retirement age of 67. Many believe that this increase is too gradual. In addition, the level of benefit reduction at age 62 will gradually increase from 20 percent to 30 percent. The earnings test will be liberalized; it currently affects only individuals below age 70. To try to reduce some of the perceived inadequacies of the Social Security system, an earnings-sharing proposal (where the Social Security benefit is based on the earnings of the household, not just on individuals) and a two-part payment system have also been suggested. The latter is an attempt to meet the dual roles of the Social Security system—to provide a basic amount of coverage to all elderly (not just wage earners and their spouses) and to provide an additional payment proportional to wages. As mentioned earlier, additional proposals include caregiving and homemaker credits, but the current design (of supporting *wage earners* in retirement based on revenues from current wage earners) does not suggest an obvious answer to the question of who will pay for such credits.[1]

The earnings test component of Social Security, which applies to individuals below age 70 (the age limit was 72 prior to 1983), is viewed as a significant barrier to continued work. In addition, the earnings test is more liberal for Social

Security recipients above age 65 than for those aged 62 to 64. In 1990, the benefit reduction rate was decreased for individuals 65 and over from one-half to one-third. That is, for individuals aged 62 to 64, for every $2 of earnings above the maximum allowable limit, an individual's Social Security benefit is reduced by $1, while the same reduction is applied to every $3 of earnings for those age 65 and over.

Bondar (1993) studies individuals affected by the earnings test in 1989. Among Social Security beneficiaries, 75 percent were retired workers; 36 percent of these had their entire benefit withheld. He notes that in addition to Social Security beneficiaries, there is a potentially large group of individuals who are discouraged from applying for Social Security benefits because they know their benefits will be withheld. This group is unobservable and their existence therefore limits the accuracy with which predictions about potential policy changes can be made. It is estimated that approximately 40 percent of insured men and women age 62-64 do not file for benefits and that about 5 percent of men and 15 percent of women age 65 and older do not.

Honig and Reimers (1989) argue that the returns to eliminating the earnings test are decreasing with the proliferation of private pensions, which often encourage individuals to withdraw completely from the labor force. This suggests that in modeling the impact of Social Security policy, it is important to include private pensions; omitting this crucial interaction may prove misleading. Evidence of this is also given in Stock and Wise (1990a) and Lumsdaine, Stock, and Wise (1996a), who demonstrate via simulation, using data from two individual Fortune 500 firms, that for individuals with pension plan availability, changes in Social Security policy will have very little effect. They attribute this to the relative magnitudes of pension versus Social Security benefits. However, for individuals who rely solely on Social Security, changes will have a much larger effect. In addition, Lumsdaine, Stock, and Wise (1996a) show that even for individuals who have access to both a pension plan and Social Security, the complete elimination of Social Security would have a significant impact on labor supply behavior.

Leonesio (1993a:54), in summarizing the literature and findings regarding the Social Security earnings test, concludes:

> . . . research suggests that retirement decisions are influenced by the availability and generosity of Social Security and private pensions, health status, job characteristics, wage offers, family circumstances, and personal preferences for work versus leisure time. These other contributing factors that encourage or enable retirement appear to be dominant.

In order to promote continued work and to partially offset the effect of the earnings test for *workers* age 65 to 69, the delayed retirement credit (the amount added to one's annual Social Security benefit to take into account nonreceipt in previous months, due either to the earnings test or to postponement of application) has increased over the last decade, from 1 percent to 3 percent in 1983 and to 4 percent in 1989. It will continue to increase by 0.5 percent every other year until reaching a maximum of 8 percent in 2010, with the age past which it is applied increasing as the normal retirement age increases. This is designed to be approximately actuarially fair using current mortality probabilities. Although this is an alternative to the relaxation of the earnings test, it may achieve similar results, aiding those with higher benefits (earnings) more. In terms of behavioral impact, however, the two may differ substantially depending on the structure of individual preferences (see Honig and Reimers, 1989:endnote 1). Whether or not this policy will succeed in its goal of eliminating the cost associated with continuing to work depends on assumptions about the future, both at a macroeconomic level (e.g., the stability of tax rates) and at a microeconomic level (e.g., individual earnings profiles).

Research seems to suggest that the labor supply impact of these liberalizations will not be substantial (Gustman and Steinmeier, 1991; Leonesio, 1990). Gustman and Steinmeier (1991) conduct a simulation study using the Survey of Consumer Finances (SCF) to assess the impact of changing the delayed retirement credit from 3 percent to 8 percent and of eliminating the earnings test. The SCF has the advantage of also containing information about pension plans. Gustman and Steinmeier incorporate many details such as pensions that other studies omit and include a number of stochastic terms representing such things as health status. Their results suggest that the impact on labor supply would be modest, increasing labor force participation by about 3.5 percent per year for individuals age 65 to 69. In particular, the average date of retirement would increase by about 3 weeks. They argue that this is because individuals will adjust to policy changes by altering their time of application for benefits rather than modifying their labor supply behavior. In addition, they argue that no single delayed retirement credit is appropriate for all individuals.

Mitchell (1991) considers four changes in the Social Security benefit formulas: (1) raising the normal retirement age, (2) delaying the cost-of-living adjustment, (3) increasing the delayed retirement credit, and (4) increasing the penalty for early retirement. All are intended to increase labor force participation and delay retirement and are representative of policy currently being implemented. Mitchell (1991) simulates the retirement response to these changes via a logit model. Despite drastic changes in benefit amounts, the predicted impact of an increased penalty for early retirement is modest; retirement for men is delayed by 3 months. The other simulations yield smaller results; these findings are consistent with those of Gustman and Steinmeier (1991) and Lumsdaine, Stock, and Wise (1992, 1996b). For women, the impacts are even less pronounced. Using time series data, Stewart (1995) predicts a much larger effect than previous studies based on microdata of changes in Social Security provisions. In particular, he attributes nearly 40 percent of the decline in labor force participation rates to Social Security. Of the four changes considered, Mitchell finds it is the final change that contains the most powerful financial incentives to alter labor supply behavior. Stewart (1995) concurs, citing liquidity constraints as the reason many individuals wait for the Social Security early retirement age to exit the labor force. Increasing the penalty for early retirement will cause more individuals to be liquidity constrained and therefore unable to finance an exit from the labor force. In particular, there is evidence that such changes will have a substantial effect on the fraction of elderly families at or near the poverty level, precisely those that are likely to be liquidity constrained. In 1988, 68 percent of new retired worker Social Security awards for men (74% for women) were made prior to the normal retirement age (Kingson, 1992); it is therefore unlikely that changes to this later age would have substantial effects on retirement behavior.

Leonesio (1993b) describes other Social Security policies that have been proposed in an attempt to encourage prolonged work by the elderly. His conclusion is that "changes in Social Security programs of the type and magnitude that are politically feasible in the foreseeable future are unlikely to produce large changes in retirement patterns" (p. 47). This brings into question the expenditure invested in examining Social Security policy. Perhaps the focus should be in areas thought to have greater effects. In documenting previous results by a variety of researchers (e.g., Burtless and Moffitt, 1984, 1985; Fields and Mitchell, 1984), he notes that the effects of increases in monthly benefit levels tend to be modest; a 10 percent increase (decrease) is associated with a corresponding increase (decrease) of the retirement age by about 1 month. In fact, the effects of all policy changes he reviews are described in terms of months, not years. He argues, however, that this is because it is also necessary to examine the effects of Social Security policy changes on related decisions that may affect the retirement decision.

While much of the literature on Social Security (and retirement behavior more generally) has used reduced-form models, which can document correlations and explanatory power, structural models are important for assessing potential policy impacts. As noted by Rust (1989), early research on Social Security used a life-cycle consumption model, which, in its simplest form, predicts that individuals will decumulate their wealth towards the end of their lives. This is contrary to observations on savings behavior of the elderly. However, a more general life-cycle model, with rigidities such as liquidity constraints or a bequest motive, provides a dynamic context in which to model behavior. Rust formulates a dynamic programming model in which workers use an optimal decision rule to choose their retirement date. The control variables are consumption expenditures and the decision regarding retirement; the model allows for uncertainty in the state variables, which are things like life expectancy, health status, and retirement earnings. One of the elements missing from Rust's (1989) model is pension benefits. This is due to data limitations in the Retirement History Survey (RHS); such limitations will be less apparent in the new Health and Retirement Survey (HRS).

Despite significant research devoted to the impact of Social Security provisions, debate still continues as to the relative importance of Social Security on the retirement decision and retirement income. Part of the difficulty lies in attempts to predict responses in a heterogeneous population. Inferences depend crucially on the sample studied and on additional factors and sources of income. There is also disagreement about the validity and accuracy of using reduced-form models to predict the effects of policy changes; even among structural models, static and dynamic approaches can result in very different predictions.

PENSIONS AND WINDOW PLANS

What can be done to alleviate the projected shortfall in Social Security? One solution is to rely on pensions for supplemental income. Income from pensions accounts for about 18 percent of all income of elderly (65+). The proportion of elderly households receiving income from all types of pensions in 1990 was 44 percent (Congressional Budget Office, 1993). This proportion and its relative importance vary considerably along demographic lines. For example, while 57 percent of elderly couples age 65 and older report receiving a pension, only 32 percent of unmarried women do (Reno, 1993). It is projected that for those in the upper half of the retirement income distribution in 2019, 30 percent to 40 percent of cash income will come from private pension benefits (Kingson, 1992, citing a Congressional Budget Office projection). Two-thirds of individuals in the HRS report having pension coverage (Gustman, Mitchell, and Steinmeier, 1994). Of these, 42 percent have only defined benefit plans, while 16 percent have only defined contribution plans. It is becoming increasingly common for employees to face a number of choices regarding pension plan and saving for retirement. According to a survey by Merrill Lynch, as reported in the Employee Benefit Plan Review (1994b), "only 61% of preretirees have savings and investments apart from an employer-sponsored pension plan."

Reimers and Honig (1992) cite difficulties in inference on labor supply behavior with nationally representative data owing to a lack of detailed pension plan information. This is particularly important when analyzing the behavior of men, for whom pension benefits are a greater proportion of retirement income. "The lack of pension information means not only that one cannot estimate the effect of pensions, but also that one cannot obtain unbiased estimates of the effects of other variables" (p. 3).

It has also been shown that for firms, pension plans can be a useful tool for affecting workers' behavior. Clark, Gohmann, and McDermed (1988) note that defined benefit plans in particular provide incentives for employees to remain at a specific firm and to refrain from behavior that might lead to their dismissal. They note that "firms with high costs of hiring and high monitoring costs also will tend to use defined benefit plans" (p. 11). In addition, firms can use defined benefit plans to alter retirement behavior. Ruhm (1994) provides evidence that pension coverage is associated with increased attachment to the labor force through certain ages, followed by decreased probability of attachment at later ages.

Lumsdaine, Stock, and Wise (1992) use data from a single Fortune 500 firm to illustrate the dangers of drawing inferences without pension information for individuals that, in fact, have access to a pension plan. In simulating the effects of eliminating Social Security early retirement using information on both types of retirement income, they estimate between a 9 percent and a 15 percent reduction in retirement rates of individuals ages 62 to 65; if pension information is not incorporated, the reduction is estimated to be between 43 percent and 72 percent. In addition, the interaction between Social Security and pension plan provisions is well documented—the General Accounting Office (1989) estimates that 42 percent of pension plans used some method of integration in computing benefits.

While pension coverage rates have remained reasonably stable over the last 20 years (Table 3-4; see U.S. Department of Labor, 1994), the percentage of pension-covered workers enrolled in primary defined benefit plans has declined dramatically, from 87 percent in 1975 to 68 percent in 1987 (Ruhm, 1994, citing Beller and Lawrence, 1992). Clark, Gohmann, and McDermed (1988) argue that in response to increased pension regulation and to legislation, the 1980s have seen a shift from defined benefit to defined contribution pension plans. Reno (1993) notes that this shift accounts for only 10 percent of the growth in primary defined contribution coverage; the majority of the growth is due to new plans, both primary and supplemental. Defined benefit plans are often based on final salary (or an average of the final few years) and take the responsibility of saving for retirement away from the individual. To the extent that individuals fail to save adequately for their retirement, this may not be a negative characteristic. In a survey of 944 major U.S. employers, 96 percent of defined benefit plans did not require employee contributions (Hewitt Associates, 1990). Even firms that have a defined benefit plan as their primary plan often offer a defined contribution plan to supplement the primary plan. Defined contribution plans often allow for more mobility than defined benefit plans. Particularly popular are 401(k) plans, where the employee shares in the responsibility for his/her retirement income by contributing jointly with the employer. By 1987, they were primary plans for 8 percent of private plan participants—supplemental for an additional 23 percent (Reno, 1993, citing Beller and Lawrence, 1992). An additional attractive feature is that the employee can make supplemental voluntary tax-deferred contributions (Reno, 1993). The observed increase in defined contribution plans means increased portability. "Without portability, the average private pension participant receives benefits 15% lower than if all benefits were fully portable" (Marks and Seefer, 1992:57). However, there is also evidence that portable benefits are often received as a lump sum; this option undermines the security such plans are intended to provide. Prior to receipt of the pension distribution, the risk of investment performance of the pension funds in defined contribution plans is

TABLE 3-4   Coverage Rates, Employer-Provided Pensions, 1979-1987 (percent)

Panel	1979	1980	1981	1982	1983	1984	1985	1986	1987
Panel A[a]									
Total	44.9	44.9	44.3	43.8	43.4	42.4	42.8	42.6	40.8
Male	51.5	51.0	50.1	48.9	48.3	47.1	47.5	47.0	45.1
Female	37.0	37.5	37.3	37.7	37.7	37.0	37.4	37.6	36.0
Panel B[b]									
Total	47.1	46.5	45.6	44.7	44.1	43.7	44.1	44.2	42.2

SOURCE: U.S. Department of Labor (1994) and Parsons (1991a).

[a]Civilian wage and salary workers covered by pension plans.
[b]Households with one or more members covered by employer-provided pension plans.

borne by the employee. In addition, recipients are able to use distributions for other purposes (Woods, 1993). Reno (1993) notes that in 1988, only 11 percent of workers with previous lump-sum distributions reported rolling it all into a tax-deferred retirement account.

Policy changes in private pension plan provisions have occurred in a variety of ways, from the extreme form of liquidation of the existing company plan[2] to special "window" (incentive) plans targeted at a particular group of workers. Such plans have sometimes accompanied a restructuring or downsizing of the firm and have tended to be fairly generous. As a result, these plans, which often target a specific group of workers and provide special incentives to retire (leave the firm), have a profound effect on the labor force participation rates of the target group.

Literature Review and Previous Methodology

Much of the literature on pension plans and retirement is based on results using static models. These include least squares models as well as limited dependent variable specifications (e.g., Clark, Gohmann, and McDermed, 1988, using plan choice (DB or DC) as the dependent variable, Lumsdaine, Stock, and Wise (1992) and Samwick (1994), using retirement as the dichotomous dependent variable, Even and Macpherson (1994), using coverage as the dependent variable, Haveman, deJong, and Wolfe (1991), using labor market participation as the dependent variable, Gustman and Steinmeier (1993b), using job separation as the dependent variable), median regression (Samwick, 1994), and proportional hazard models. These different types of models have systematically documented the effects of pension plan provisions on the retirement decision and retirement income. They have been less successful in predicting the effects of a change in policy.

Gustman and Steinmeier (1993b) address the notion that pension plans reduce labor mobility (create "job lock"). Using separation as the dependent variable in a reduced-form probit model, they find that pension plans are not a substitute for wage compensation; instead compensation in pension-covered jobs is higher. The "compensation premium"—rather than the nonportability of pension plans—accounts for increased attachment to the firm. Defined contribution plans, which are more portable, exhibit similar effects on mobility.

Allen, Clark, and McDermed (1993) note that the observed lower mobility among pension-covered workers may be due to both a bonding effect (as noted by Gustman and Steinmeier, 1993b) and a sorting effect, that is, that workers with certain observable characteristics prefer pension jobs.[3] They find evidence of "self-selection of workers with low odds of turnover into jobs covered by pensions" (p. 476). Understanding and modeling such selection issues is critical to interpreting and predicting the impact of changes to pension plans.

A careful review of pension legislation over the last decade is in Clark, Gohmann, and McDermed (1988), who use a probit model with plan choice as the dependent variable to consider the impact of regulation on a firm's choice of pension plan type. They find that the probability of a firm's offering at least one defined benefit plan has declined throughout the last decade. The shift towards defined contribution plans as a result of favorable tax treatments and anti-age-discrimination regulation is indicative of the way that firms can respond to government legislation. This casts doubt on the efficacy of government plans to alter the labor force composition via Social Security changes; Lumsdaine, Stock, and Wise and others have argued that firms may well offset potential effects via their pension plans.

Luzadis and Mitchell (1991) also find that the regulatory environment has significant impact on employer-sponsored pension incentives, most noticeably with regard to Social Security policy changes. There is also evidence that the observed dynamics pertain to the "buyout" hypothesis, that is, that firms encourage certain individuals to leave. Both of these findings emphasize that response to pension plan provisions should be modeled in a dynamic context, which acknowledges the flexibility employers have to manipulate plan characteristics and incentives.

A number of models have been used to capture more of the dynamic decision process of individuals. Such dynamic models are critical to understanding actual behavior. The benefit of dynamic behavioral models is the potential for policy analysis. The model's parameters can be estimated under a base-case scenario, and a variety of dynamic policies can be assessed. Unfortunately, exactly modeling such dynamics in a way that mirrors reality is difficult, if not impossible. It is therefore necessary to make simplifying assumptions in order to achieve tractability. In addition, there is debate as to what the goal of mirroring reality seeks to accomplish—do we want to imitate the decision-making process, or are we satisfied with achieving similar outcomes and the ability to predict future outcomes accurately?

Gustman and Steinmeier (1986) ignore uncertainty and assume perfect markets in constructing a life-cycle model of retirement. Their model specifies reduced wages for diminished work effort. They use the RHS data set and maximum likelihood estimation. They note that the peaks in retirement rates at ages 62 and 65 are completely attributable to Social Security, pension provisions, and mandatory retirement. Simulations implementing the shift of the Social Security normal retirement age to 67 produce a corresponding shift in the latter peak in retirement rates.

Stock and Wise (1990a, 1990b) proposed the "option value" model, where individuals retire at the age that achieves the maximum gain from the choice of postponing retirement versus retiring in the current period. The motivation for their model is from Lazear (1979), which suggests that by delaying retirement, individuals retain the option to retire at a later date, under potentially more advantageous terms. In the Stock-Wise model, individuals reassess their options at each new time period. The model is fairly flexible in that it allows for correlated individual-specific errors and features a parsimonious specification. Correlated errors in a dynamic setting are difficult to model analytically, as the model would involve high orders of integration. The tractable simplification, in this case, is that individuals maximize the present discounted value of expected wealth.[4] In addition, a parameter is included to take into account the possibility that an individual values a dollar associated with work differently from a dollar associated with leisure. Stock and Wise use data from a single Fortune 500 firm. These data consist of a panel of individual earnings histories over a number of years. In addition, the data are well suited for analyzing the validity of the model; parameter estimates can be obtained from data from one year and used to predict behavior in subsequent years. The results of such an analysis, as well as the incorporation of individual-specific errors that follow an AR(1) process, are in Stock and Wise (1990b).

Stock and Wise (1990a) also consider a number of simulations to assess the effects of potential policy changes. Using the parameters obtained under the base specification, they simulate the effects of increasing the firm's early retirement age, increasing the Social Security early retirement reduction factor, and increasing the Social Security early retirement age. Subsequent papers by Lumsdaine, Stock, and Wise (1990, 1994) have considered modifications to the base model.

Lumsdaine, Stock, and Wise (1992) compare a simpler, static model (probit), two dynamic programming models with uncorrelated individual-specific errors, and the option value model. They find that the three dynamic models perform significantly better in terms of fit and prediction than do static probit models. A separate issue, raised by Lumsdaine, Stock, and Wise (1992), is what the goal should be with these increasingly complex models (see also Burtless, 1989).

There are clear gains in inference from using dynamic models over the static ones. If the goal is to mirror the observed pattern of behavior, these models do quite well. However, it may also be desirable to mimic the actual decision-making process that an individual undergoes. In this case, it is hardly plausible that the average individual will utilize the level of complexity specified in these dynamic models. In addition, usually the more complicated the model, the more simplifying assumptions necessary to retain tractability. It is therefore necessary to ensure that models are robust to misspecification and to determine the impact of these assumptions and their relation to actual behavior.

Lumsdaine, Stock, and Wise (1994) compare the behavior of men and women. Contrary to common belief, for individuals in the specific firm they consider, the actual behavior is quite similar; this is also reflected in the parameter estimates and the predicted behavior. Because there are only two transition states, maximum likelihood is feasible; a modified simulated annealing (random search method, not requiring second or even first derivatives of the relevant function) is at times employed in estimation. Dynamic models that allow for multiple choices (transition states) usually need to employ integral approximation techniques to retain tractability.

Window plans, when analyzed with the corresponding individual firm's pension details, provide a convenient way to test a model out of sample; the model is estimated under the normal pension provisions, and the estimates are then used to predict the effects of the window plan. Lumsdaine, Stock, and Wise (1990, 1991) evaluate the effect of a window plan in the same Fortune 500 firm that Stock and Wise (1990a, 1990b) considered. Lumsdaine, Stock, and Wise (1991) find that the predicted effects typically match the actual effects well, the notable exception being at age 65, when the models always underpredict the retirement effect. Lumsdaine, Stock, and Wise (1990) use a beta distribution to approximate the firm's pension plan in order to investigate whether the firm could have achieved its potential goals more efficiently. A beta distribution provides a parsimonious flexible functional form that allows the pension schedule to vary continuously (thus providing determination of exact schedules without being bound by discretization). Lumsdaine, Stock, and Wise then consider potential motivations that the firm may have had for offering a window plan, based on economic theory, and investigate whether the firm could have structured its plan more efficiently, subject to the budgetary restrictions that it faced. If the main motivation was to reduce the current size of its labor force immediately, the firm acted close to optimally.

In a more recent paper, Lumsdaine, Stock, and Wise (1996a) simulate the effects of a number of different policy changes, using data from another Fortune 500 firm. Besides confirming their earlier results using this alternative data set, they investigate the effects on labor force participation of changes in the Social Security early and normal retirement ages, the private pension plan provisions, the interaction of changes in both Social Security and pensions, retiree health insurance, forced reductions in workload, and other policies.

The evidence associated with this body of literature is relatively clear. For those people who will receive pension benefits, the magnitude of the expected benefit is such that pension plan provisions can strongly influence their retirement decision.

What We Would Like to Know

An important aspect of modeling the determinants of retirement behavior and retirement income is understanding how Social Security and pensions interact with other forms of retirement savings. In particular, do they provide additional savings or are they substitutes for alternative forms? Much of the research has focused on shortfalls in retirement income or benefit levels for individual retirees. From a macroeconomic perspective, it is important (Day, 1993) to assess the trade-off between generations as part of the cost/benefit analysis. Day cites overwhelming support across all ages for maintaining or increasing Social Security benefit levels, but suggests that younger workers may not completely understand how these levels would be raised. Attitudes towards taxes and attitudes towards benefits are only weakly correlated. Day claims this is because attitudes towards taxes are more likely to be driven by self-interest whereas attitudes towards benefits are more ideological in nature.

Another significant source of uncertainty is how firms will react to changing labor force participation and needs. Will they support government policy to encourage older workers to continue working, or will they try to counterbalance the Social Security effects via manipulation of their pension plan provisions? The upward-sloping wage curve makes it difficult for firms to retain older workers in a cost-effective way. In addition, anecdotal evidence of firms' rehiring retirees who have opted for a window plan, often at higher consulting wages, suggests that firms have difficulty convincing the "right" (less productive) people to retire; a more systematic assessment of firm behavior would provide insight as to the frequency with which this occurs. Note that economic theory would predict that workers with a high opportunity cost of leaving (those that would have difficulty finding an equivalent job) would be less likely to accept a window plan. The results of Lumsdaine, Stock, and Wise (1991) are not inconsistent with this theory and anecdotal evidence; they do, however, suggest that firms may be operating under rather myopic, short-term objectives (such as paring down the size of their labor force, without regard to overall productivity or future productivity) when offering window plans.

It is also clear that individuals do not always have an accurate perception of the components of their expected retirement income. A study by Merrill Lynch (as reported in Employee Benefit Plan Review, 1994b) found that of individuals ages 45 to 64, 36 percent cited pensions as their expected most important source of retirement income. In reality, only 10 percent of income comes from pensions, according to a U.S. Department of Health and Human Services report (Radner, 1993a). A poll by the Employee Benefit Research Institute found that nearly half of all respondents believed that $150,000 or less was what they needed in order to fund their retirement. In addition, only one-third of individuals correctly chose the range of dollar amounts that included the maximum Social Security benefit when given four choices. Additional evidence of inaccurate understanding of the Social Security earnings test rules by the elderly is found in Leonesio (1993b).

While much of the literature on pensions has focused on coverage, in considering individuals most at risk in terms of potential future income inadequacy, it is important to consider pension receipt, not pension coverage. Gender differences in pension coverage become even more pronounced when measuring receipt; women are much more likely to experience interruptions in labor force attachment and are thus less likely to meet vesting requirements in a pension plan than men.[5] In 1992, median income from private pensions for male recipients was approximately twice that of female recipients, at all 5-year age intervals for individuals above age 65 (Grad, 1994). When tenure is controlled for, coverage rates are fairly similar, as shown in Table 3-5. Another reason that women are particularly at risk is the earnings gap. The coverage rates for men and women

TABLE 3-5   Job Tenure and Pension Coverage of
Full-Time Private Sector Workers, by Gender,
1988 (percent)

Years With Primary Employer	Women	Men
Job Tenure		
All tenures	100	100
Less than 1 year	19	17
1 to 4 years	37	33
5 to 9 years	18	17
10 to 14 years	10	11
15 to 19 years	6	7
20 years or more	5	11
Pension Coverage		
All tenures	43	50
Less than 1 year	13	18
1 to 4 years	37	39
5 to 9 years	63	62
10 to 14 years	70	73
15 to 19 years	72	77
20 years or more	75	82

SOURCE: Korczyk (1992, Table 6.11).

TABLE 3-6   Earnings Distribution and Pension Coverage Rates Among Full-Time Private Sector Workers, by Gender, 1988 (percent)

Earnings	Women	Men
Earnings distribution		
Total	100	100
Less than $10,000	23	10
$10,000 to $19,999	47	31
$20,000 to $29,999	21	25
$30,000 to $49,999	9	27
$50,000 and over	1	8
Pension coverage rate		
All earnings	43	50
Less than $10,000	13	13
$10,000 to $19,999	46	36
$20,000 to $29,999	64	63
$30,000 to $49,999	75	74
$50,000 and over	77	79

SOURCE: Korczyk (1992, Table 6.6).

are very similar at similar earnings levels; disparity arises owing to the concentration of women in the lower part of the earnings distribution, as shown in Table 3-6. Multiple vesting further increases the gender gap. Among men age 50 to 59 who were working full time in 1988, 15 percent were vested in a previous job (24% of workers age 60 and older) while among women in both age groups only 5 percent to 6 percent were so vested (Woods, 1993).

There is some evidence that for women, pension coverage is associated with increased attachment to the labor force in later life (Pienta, Burr, and Mutchler, 1993). Possible explanations for this counterintuitive observation include a selection effect and the need to make up for an earlier discontinuous work history in terms of vesting and the earnings gap. This explanation is supported by evidence in Ruhm (1994), who finds that for men in the RHS, late entry into a pension-covered job is associated with increased attachment to the labor force, even more than for non-pension-covered individuals.

In addition, pension coverage may be leveling off (recall Table 3-4). Quinn, Burkhauser, and Myers (1990) suggest that if increasing pension coverage is responsible for the observed trend towards early retirement, a leveling off of coverage may signal a corresponding increase in average retirement ages relative to current projections. Defined contribution participants seem to compose one-third of all pension participants, as compared with one-sixth 15 years earlier. In addition, more employers are offering supplementary coverage; this is most often in the form of a defined contribution plan. The proliferation of these plans also suggests that the incentives to retire early, usually associated with defined benefit plans, are weakening. However, defined benefit plans are relaxing their requirements for receipt of benefits; see the sources cited in Quinn and Burkhauser (1992) for evidence that this promotes early retirement.

Much of the literature has used large aggregate data sets to investigate the influence of pension plans on the retirement decision. The advantage of using large data sets is that they may be more representative of the population and therefore more useful for policy evaluation. The disadvantage is the loss of heterogeneity, which typically arises from the absence of details for each individual pension plan. In order to control for some of this loss of heterogeneity, Stock and Wise (1990a, 1990b) use data from one particular Fortune 500 firm. The size of the firm allows for an adequate sample while providing a level of detail regarding the pension plan provisions that is not found in more aggregate data sets.

The obvious benefit of using data from a single firm is the use of detailed pension plan information and earnings records. However, such an approach is not necessarily representative of the aggregate population. An important research priority should be obtaining better earnings records, in a more timely manner, while still maintaining confidentiality. Data on Social Security earnings records would provide an entire wage history for each individual; tax data from the Internal Revenue Service would supplement this with information on additional assets, which are critical for evaluating the adequacy of retirement income and savings. While some information would still have to be imputed (e.g., expected future levels), the level of imputation would be much more accurate than what is currently available; imputations from aggregate data do not effectively capture the heterogeneity in the population.

More recent data sets, such as the HRS, link extensive survey responses on work history, health status, and assets to pension plan detail from the individual's specific firm. This provides hope of estimating more dynamic models using broader based studies that are more representative of the population. In addition, evidence in Hurd and McGarry (1993a) suggests that workers' subjective probabilities of working past ages 62 and 65 reflect details of their pension plan provisions. In particular, the probability of working past age 65 for individuals with no pension plan is more than double the corresponding probability among workers with pension plans that allow for full benefits by age 62. Additional subjective questions, such as how large benefits are expected to be, will, in future years, be matched with actual receipt in order to draw inferences about expectations. The HRS also asks what form the benefit is expected to be received in (e.g., lump sum, annuity). Many other subjective questions about work and perceptions of and interactions with areas related to work are also asked, and additional information regarding early retirement window plans is also requested.

While many researchers have noted the significant effect of pension plan provisions and have estimated it to be much larger than the effect of changes in

Social Security provisions, it is important to emphasize that for the fraction of the population that relies solely on Social Security benefits, changes to Social Security will have a profound effect. This is discussed in Hurd (1994b) and Lumsdaine, Stock, and Wise (1996a). Pension benefits are thought to be of more importance when the relative magnitudes of actual benefits for individuals that have them are considered; Social Security benefits may be more important when the aggregate (or even the median) impact of policy changes is assessed.

It has been documented (Kotlikoff and Wise, 1985, 1987) that pension plans, particularly defined benefit plans, have incentive effects that firms can use to manipulate the composition of their employees. Federal regulations have sought to limit these incentive effects (Clark, Gohmann, and McDermed, 1988). For example, the Age Discrimination in Employment Act protects older workers from the threat of mandatory retirement. Quadagno and Hardy (1991) argue that "private firms developed extensive early retirement packages that provided incentives for early retirement and disincentives for continued employment" (p. 471).

The recessions of 1973-1974 and 1981-1982 provided additional inducements for firms to offer early retirement programs; window plans allowed firms to target a specific group of workers for attrition without resorting to layoffs. Window plans were perceived as being highly lucrative and beneficial to the employee; firms meanwhile were able to limit future pension liability (Quadagno and Hardy, 1991).

Ironically, while legislation has sought to limit the incentive effects of pension plans, window plans have fallen under less regulation and therefore remain a powerful tool by which firms can seek to influence workers' participation decisions. As the relation between window and pension plans would suggest, the existence of a window plan, along with to whom it is offered, varies considerably across demographic lines. As antidiscrimination legislation has increased, window plans remain one of the few ways that employers can legally discriminate among workers (in targeting a specific subset of workers) and over time (historically, as mentioned above, window plans have been prevalent during periods of downsizing). As a result, window plans should continue to be a major policy focus for the next decade.

As we learn more about individual responses to window plans and how they affect labor force participation decisions, it will be equally important to model firm response and consider whether firms have increased utilization of window plans in light of the more favorable regulatory environment (relative to pensions) or decreased it (perhaps because the wrong people are leaving). Detailed questions about window plans should be included in surveys of firms such as the SCF's Pension Provider Supplement and the Bureau of Labor Statistics' Employee Benefits Survey.

Because window plans can vary considerably, studies documenting their effects have focused on a single window plan. Data on window plans are difficult to obtain, as they must be gathered directly from the firm. The HRS is the first survey to contain detailed questions about window plans. It is hoped that analysis of the responses to these questions will lead to a broader understanding of the magnitude of the individual incentive effects and the potential implications for aggregate impacts on labor force participation.

From a modeling perspective, window plans have offered a unique type of "natural experiment" in the literature of the previous decade. Because there had been no historical precedent for such alterations to pension plans, initially they were unanticipated. Therefore models could be estimated using pre-window-plan provisions and then used to predict the effects of the window plan, in effect creating an out-of-sample test of model predictability. With the current proliferation of window plans among firms and even within the same firm, research methodology requires a change of focus. Models that study the effects of window plans will need to consider how expectations are formulated and incorporated into an individual's retirement decision. Just as the existence of a window plan can induce additional retirements, the absence of one may inhibit retirements if employees expect one to be offered in the near future. Smith (1994) provides further caveats regarding the interpretation of window plans as an out-of-sample test of the model, citing endogeneity of other factors influencing departure rates, such as the perceived financial condition of the firm. This endogeneity could result in a change in the model parameters, a change that is not captured by the current form of policy simulation.

With focus shifting to issues of solvency of government programs, private sources of retirement income, such as pension plans, as well as individual savings, will become increasingly important. As discussed earlier, Auerbach, Kotlikoff, and Weil (1992) note that the income of the elderly is becoming increasingly annuitized; shifts from defined benefit to defined contribution plans suggest that this trend may not continue. Future research needs to focus not only on the availability of outside sources of retirement income but also on the form of the distribution of this income. With the increase in popularity of defined contribution plans, individuals have more options regarding their distributions and a substantial fraction of individuals elect a lump-sum payment.

Policy in recent years has begun to focus on "preservation" of retirement benefits (Woods, 1993) by enacting legislation that imposes stiff penalties for failing to roll pre-retirement distributions into a qualified retirement plan.[6] Woods (1993) finds that many pre-retirement lump-sum distributions went to individuals who were either vested in or covered by but not vested in another pension plan. He argues that there should be less concern about potential consumption of a lump-sum distribution for these individuals, especially as such distributions tend to be of fairly small magnitude (the median amount is $2,830). Of the individuals who show no source of additional pension income, Woods finds that many saved or invested the entire distribution, concluding that concern over choice of distribution is of secondary importance to more general concerns over how to increase coverage.

Much of the previous literature has focused on *pre-retirement* lump-sum distributions; caution should be exercised in using such results to draw inferences on the adequacy and preservation of post-retirement analogs. Analysis of the HRS will reveal whether pre-retirement patterns of distribution choice and savings reflect post-retirement behavior. The obvious concern is that lump-sum distributions return too much responsibility for retirement saving to the individual; legislation has attempted to enforce the need for adequate retirement-related savings vehicles. Additional research on post-retirement distribution choices is clearly needed.

In terms of modeling, as Gustman and Steinmeier (1986) point out, the use of life-cycle models requires computation of earnings histories. These are often imputed either from self-reported recollections or, in the case of individual firm records, from company records. In the latter case, transitions between jobs are not documented. Stock and Wise (1990a, 1990b) use a log linear autoregressive wage equation to impute earnings histories and forecast future earnings. Because the time dimension of the panel in their firm was substantially shorter than that used by Stock and Wise, Lumsdaine, Stock, and Wise (1994, 1996a) use a fixed effects model. In addition, in most of the dynamic models, future wage uncertainty is not allowed. Thus, the potential accuracy of our models and our ability to predict the effects of policy changes are limited by our earnings forecasts. Furthermore, other types of uncertainty (such as demand by firms for future labor) and individuals' expectations about them (such as inferences about a firm's financial condition or the probability of a layoff after the announcement of a window plan) may significantly contribute to an individual's uncertainty. This suggests that future dynamic models may need to incorporate beliefs about changes in the system itself. Such "macro" risks may contribute far greater uncertainty than "idiosyncratic" risks (such as wage uncertainty or health risks). Accurate forecasts of firm response and behavior are critical to understanding what workers will be doing on the supply side of the labor market.

While the models of Lumsdaine, Stock, and Wise fit retirement rates well at most ages, they systematically fail to capture the magnitude of the retirement rate at age 65. They attribute this underprediction to "social custom," an interpretation criticized by Rust and Phelan (1993), who argue instead that the cause is the omission of other key considerations, most noticeably, Medicare.

DISABILITY

There is increasing discussion about the relation between Social Security disability insurance and retirement and about the possibility that liberalization of disability benefits is partially responsible for declines in labor force participation (see discussion in Rust, 1989; Lewin-VHI, 1994). In addition to the link with retirement, there is also evidence that policy variables influence applications for disability. There is a positive correlation between disability applications and unemployment rates. Others have cited a negative correlation between labor force participation and the generosity of benefits as measured by the replacement ratio (benefits to wages). It seems (Quinn and Burkhauser, 1992; Bound and Waidmann, 1992; Waidmann, Bound, and Schoenbaum, 1995) that applications for disability increased over the 1970s and declined in the 1980s. Measuring disability is difficult, however, because some people who are disabled will just choose to retire (or some people will leave when eligible for retirement when, if they were completely healthy, they would have continued working). Further-more, disability may result not in complete exit from the labor force but in a reduction in the number of hours worked.

Another indication of the link between disability and retirement is that to the extent that individuals are likely to exaggerate their disability conditions, only about half of the rejected applicants return to work (Bound, 1989). One potential reason is that workers filing a disability claim must wait 5 months from the time they leave their jobs to receive benefits. In addition, disability benefits, like Social Security benefits, are subject to an earnings test at $500 per month. Both of these features inhibit subsequent labor force participation. Some of the litera-ture on this subject suggests an equivalency between the decision to apply for disability benefits and a decision to withdraw from the labor force (i.e., disability is a substitute form of retirement). Indeed, disability benefits convert to retire-ment benefits at age 65. If policy is aimed at keeping individuals in the work force, the findings of Bound (1989) and Burkhauser et al. (1992) suggest that such efforts should target individuals before they begin the application process.

As mentioned above, the timing of application for disability benefits seems to be correlated with the replacement rate; a higher rate means earlier application on aggregate. In addition, a higher rate is associated with a shorter waiting time before applying after the onset of a health condition (Burkhauser et al., 1992). Other variables that affect the timing of application include savings and the extent to which the employer could accommodate the disability.

The prevalence of disability among working age persons in the United States is estimated to be between 7 percent and 14 percent (Lewin-VHI, 1994). This rate has fluctuated over the last three decades, as Table 3-7 partially illustrates. Recent trends in disability insurance have seen a growth in both applications and awards. Much of this is attributable to changes in aggregate macroeconomic variables, such as unemployment. In addition, qualifying rules were liberalized in 1984; this has contributed to the observed growth in awards (Lewin-VHI, 1994). From 1988 to 1992, applications increased by 29 percent (40% using the redefined measure of applications, which excludes technical denials and dupli-cate applicants). Although gender-specific data on applications are not available before 1988, in 1992 60.9 percent of applicants were male. It is argued that some of the recent growth in application (and resulting awards) may be due to demo-

TABLE 3-7   Percentage of Working-Age Population Disabled, by Sex, 1962-1984, Various Years and Sample Sizes

Year	Percentage			Actual Number of Observations	
	Male	Female	Total	Male	Female
1962	9.5	4.8	7.0	218	120
1968	13.0	8.2	10.5	911	746
1973	12.8	9.3	11.0	1434	
1976	14.6	7.5	10.9	491	304
1980	11.9	9.6	10.7	501	416
1982	10.6	9.1	9.6	441	380
1984	10.5	8.6	9.5	461	454

NOTE: Calculations by the authors from Current Population Survey data for various years; see text.

SOURCE. Haveman and Wolfe (1989: Table 1).

graphic trends (e.g., the increase in female labor force participation, the aging of the baby boom cohort). The number of awards over the same time period rose 54 percent. Similar dramatic growth spurts occurred in the early 1970s. The fraction of Social Security disability-insurance awards to women has risen, most likely as a result of rising applications (in 1992, this fraction was 37%). The ratio of awards to applications (the "allowance rate") has fluctuated, in recent years ranging from 0.29 in 1982 to 0.49 in 1992. In addition, toward the late 1980s, more individuals were applying concurrently for Social Security disability insurance and supplemental security income. These applications accounted for between 60 percent and 69 percent of the growth in applications in 1992; they accounted for about 48 percent in 1988. Lewin-VHI (1994) document substantial variation across states in the growth of applications from 1988 to 1992. For example, North Dakota had a 4 percent increase in concurrent applications; for Rhode Island, the increase was 134 percent.

The size of the disability-insured population has increased as well. "From 1970 to 1992, the average annual growth rate was 1.48 percent for men and a much larger 3.91 percent for women" (Lewin-VHI, 1994:IV.2). The growth appears to be slowing. The award rate for women is below (roughly 80% of) the award rate for men. The age-distribution of the adult disability-insured population declines with age past age 35, as seen in Figure 3-7. The percentage of men age 55 to 64 receiving Social Security disability-insurance benefits has grown from 5.3 percent in 1965 to 10.5 percent in 1985 (Bound, 1989; Lewin-VHI, 1994). Because award rates are correlated with age (see Figure 3-8), an increasing elderly population suggests an increased burden in the future on Social Security disability insurance.

In contrast to Social Security and pensions, replacement rates for new Social

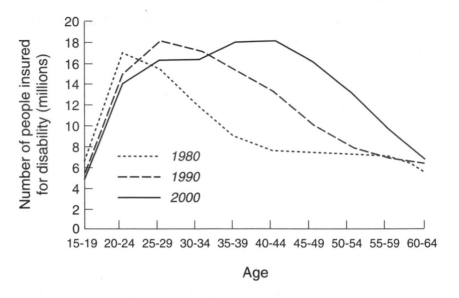

FIGURE 3-7 Age distribution of the people insured for disability, by 5-year age cohort, 1980, 1990, 2000. SOURCE: Lewin-VHI (1994:Exhibit IV.A.3).

Security disability-insurance beneficiaries are generous. At the first quartile, replacement rates over the last decade have been approximately 55 percent for men; for women they have been close to 85 percent. At the median, replacement rates are 46 percent for men and 61 percent for women. Nevertheless, it is apparent that individuals should not rely on disability payments as their primary source of retirement income before age 65. While the Social Security trust fund is projected to have a surplus through 2015 and become exhausted in 2044, the disability insurance trust fund is expected to become insolvent in 1995 (Congressional Budget Office, 1993). In 1977, the denial rate on disability applications was increased owing to financial pressures (Lewin-VHI, 1994). During subsequent years, evidence suggests that the increased denial rate was responsible for a decrease in applications (Parsons, 1991c; Lewin-VHI, 1994). This episode in history may provide useful insight into projections of future disability determination and receipt of award. Over the last decade, the prevalence of disability in the United States among working age persons has remained constant, as shown in Figure 3-9.

Literature Review and Previous Methodology

Common static models for investigating disability insurance include least squares and instrumental variables (because of correlation using self-reported

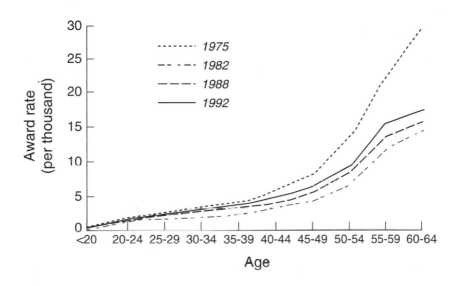

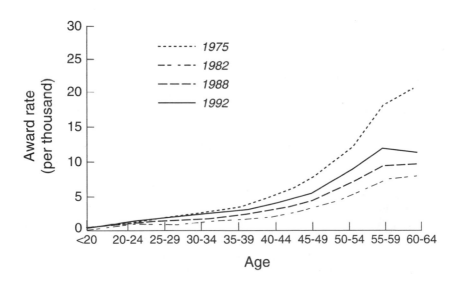

FIGURE 3-8 Social Security disability insurance award rates for men and women, selected years, 1975-1992. NOTE: Award rates for men (women) are calculated as the number of awards to men (women) divided by thousands of men (women) insured for disability. SOURCE: Lewin-VHI (1994:Exhibits IV.A.4, IV.A.5).

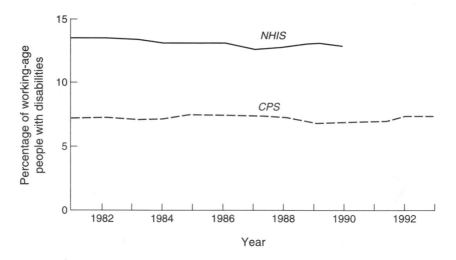

FIGURE 3-9 The prevalence of disability in the United States among working age persons from 1981 to 1990 as measured by the Current Population Survey and the National Health Interview Survey. NOTE: NHIS data available only to 1990. SOURCE: Lewin-VHI (1994:Exhibit IV.D.1).

health). Relatively few studies have employed pure time series data to investigate the relationship between macroeconomic events and applications for disability insurance (such as an increase in the unemployment rate). This is in part due to the implausibility of a stable relationship accurately describing application rates in light of institutional changes over the relevant time period. For example, Lewin-VHI (1994) cites Hambor (1992), who finds a negligible effect of a 1 percentage point increase in unemployment, once dummy variables for changes in the law are included. Other studies have used cross-sectional data and variation across states to address the relation between unemployment and disability-insurance applications. Bound and Waidmann (1992) use pooled data to incorporate both time series and cross-sectional features in their model.

There have also been a number of models that have attempted to capture the dynamic nature of the disability-application decision using pooled individual-level data. Such data have often been used to characterize other decision processes such as the labor force participation decision and the Social Security application decision. Dynamic modeling of disability-insurance applications and awards is more complicated, owing to uncertainty about the receipt of benefits and the cost (social stigma?) associated with applying. Haveman, DeJong, and Wolfe (1991) use a switching regression model to mimic the decision process of a worker choosing between working at the offered wage versus receiving disability. In their data set, about two-thirds of the sample receive disability benefits

(Social Security disability insurance); of these 90 percent do not work. They predict that a 20 percent increase in expected Social Security disability-insurance benefits would decrease the labor force participation rate by 0.3 percent. Thus they conclude that the increase of 43 percent in benefits per recipient could not have been responsible for the 12 percent decrease in labor force participation of 55- to 64-year-old males between 1968 and 1978.

Burkhauser et al. (1992) use a multistate, continuous time hazard model and choice-based sampling to model the application for disability. They consider the decision process as one in which the individual is choosing how long after the onset of a health condition to wait to apply for disability benefits. Some of the justification for waiting comes from the uncertainty of actual receipt of benefits. They modify a dynamic retirement model to estimate the optimal age at which an individual should apply for benefits, assuming perfect capital markets and uncertainty regarding program acceptance. The key assumption is that the individual will not return to work once deciding to apply, regardless of the outcome of the application.

Stern (1988) characterizes the endogeneity between the disability application and labor force participation decisions using a simultaneous equations framework. With a two-step estimation procedure, he finds that while disability (as measured by a number of physician-diagnosed or self-reported conditions) affects the labor force participation rate, participation does not seem to affect disability directly. Maximum-likelihood estimates suggest some effect of participation on disability, but the sign of the coefficient on participation suggests that it diminishes health status. While the results imply that disability is a reasonable measure with which to predict labor force participation, there is no measure of disability benefits in the model (as noted by Stern). The methodology (of correcting for potential endogeneity) should be employed in related contexts, such as in comparing the relationship between labor force participation and the *application* for disability insurance.

Bound (1989) also cautions about potential endogeneity. In particular, the magnitude of the disincentive effect will vary across individuals and will be a function of past labor force behavior. Comparison of alternative decisions is difficult at the individual level because wages of those individuals out of the work force and disability benefits for those at work are not observed. To address this issue of endogeneity, Bound (1989) examines rejected disability applicants, claiming that this group forms a "control" comparison group. His key assumption is that individuals in this control group are healthier and more capable of work than those receiving disability benefits. In addition to finding (as noted above) that the majority of rejected applicants do not return to work, Bound notes that among those that do return, earnings are substantially below both their pre-application levels and the earnings of nonapplicant comparison groups.

In a response to Bound's (1989) results, Parsons (1991b) re-emphasizes the endogeneity of the rejection on future labor force participation. In particular, he notes that after the 5-month waiting period and a denied application, individuals are likely to encounter difficulty returning to work; furthermore, they may opt to stay out of the labor force in order to appeal or reapply. Parsons argues that even after application denial, the disability system plays a significant role in individuals' future labor force participation decisions.

In Rust's (1989) model, a disabled individual is still allowed the full range of transition states; potentially this allows assessment of how receipt of Social Security disability insurance inhibits or encourages reentry into the labor force. Unlike models that incorporate Social Security, in models that include disability it is important to capture the uncertainty surrounding receipt of benefits conditional on application. Rust and Phelan (1993) are working on incorporating the disability-insurance application process into their dynamic specification. It will be important to think about the correlation structure between these decisions.

Before we propose policy aimed at effecting a particular response, it is important to establish whether there is a causal link (and what is the magnitude of any potential effect) between increased generosity of benefits and declining labor force participation. Unfortunately, there is still considerable disagreement in the literature about the relationship. Earlier work by Parsons (1980) attributed the rise of the labor force nonparticipation rate of older men since 1946 to the expansion of the disability program. Haveman and Wolfe (1984) criticized Parsons' results, citing potential endogeneity, multicollinearity, and sample selection problems with his estimation. Although they use a different data set, they sequentially correct for each of these cited problems and conclude that doing so results in an insignificant elasticity of nonparticipation with respect to benefits. Parsons (1984) takes issue with their arguments; perhaps most convincing is a graph (see Figure 3-10) of the relationship between the nonparticipation rate of men 45 to 54 and the recipiency rate of Social Security disability benefits. While such graphical evidence does not designate causality, it does suggest existence of a correlation between the two rates.[7]

What We Would Like to Know

A fairly comprehensive discussion of the problems in econometric modeling of Social Security disability-insurance applications and awards is found in Lewin-VHI (1994). Most studies have used cross-sectional data for modeling disability. Among the problems with time series data, they cite the lagged response of disability-insurance applications to shifts in macroeconomic variables. Modeling the lag structure is nontrivial; however, analysis of impulse response functions or other spectral techniques could be useful in this regard. Lewin-VHI (1994) also cites low frequency of data; indeed the Hambor (1992) study contained only 22 observations. State space-filtering algorithms would allow mixed frequency data to be used in modeling.

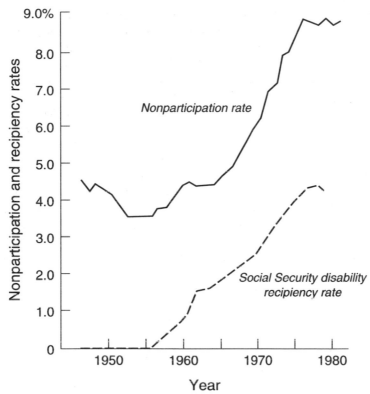

FIGURE 3-10 Nonparticipation in the labor force and Social Security disability recipiency, males aged 45-54, 1947-1982. SOURCE: Parsons (1984).

Lewin-VHI (1994) suggests separate analysis of time series data for subgroups of the population. However, it does not seem that data are currently available to enable such an analysis. The pooled data across states could be useful for this. Multivariate structural break models (see, e.g., Bai, Lumsdaine, and Stock, 1994) allow endogenous determination of structural change and would therefore control for key institutional changes as discussed above. By precisely estimating the date of change, one could draw inferences about the lag structure and the propagation mechanism of shocks.

As with the decision to accept a pension-covered job, selection occurs among disability applicants as individuals assess their probability of acceptance. In order to control and correct for selection, a data priority should be to collect more accurate applicant surveys. Some use of subjective probability questions may prove valuable for evaluating how an applicant (as well as a nonapplicant) assesses the probability of an award. Detailed data recommendations are contained in Lewin-VHI (1994). Lewin-VHI identifies the need for a pooled data source and, in addition, suspects that concurrent applications (for both Social Security disability insurance and supplemental security income) are highly sensitive to changes in the labor market or the macroeconomy. A pooled data source may provide a means of distinguishing such trend components in disability.

Understanding the link between disability and retirement is the first step to being able to predict how changes in Social Security policy will affect disability applications. To the extent that Social Security and disability benefits are complements, an increase in the Social Security retirement age may induce more individuals to apply for disability. To verify this, we must first ascertain the direction of causality—are people applying because they are ready to leave the labor force or does the very act of applying cause individuals to drop out of labor force (due to stigma, the long waiting period, or other reasons)?

An additional uninvestigated research topic is the interaction between window plans and Social Security disability insurance. Lewin-VHI (1994) suggests that windows are more likely to be attractive to those who are eligible for Social Security disability insurance. This contradicts other evidence on window plans that suggests that the "wrong" individuals (i.e., those with attractive alternative employment opportunities) leave. Particularly with regard to disability insurance, where there is uncertainty about acceptance of the application (as opposed to Social Security, pensions, and Medicare, where acceptance depends solely on quantifiable characteristics such as age and years of service), selection issues are likely to play a key role in inference. Parsons (1991c) models self-screening in Social Security disability insurance—the extent to which individuals pre-assess their probability of acceptance and condition their decision to apply on this preliminary analysis. Parsons investigates self-screening efficiency, that is, the accuracy of this selection mechanism.

MEDICARE AND HEALTH INSURANCE

Much of the concern about the adequacy of retirement income is due to the uncertainty surrounding future events and needs, particularly health status and health care costs. Elderly individuals over age 65 are covered by Medicare and/ or Medicaid, so that very few are uninsured. In 1990, 99 percent of those 65+ were insured (Congressional Budget Office, 1993) while 10 percent of men and 13 percent of women between ages 55 and 64 did not have insurance. In 1987, 94 percent of people 65+ incurred medical expenses (not including long-term care). Individuals 65+, as well as those that have been receiving disability for over 2 years, regardless of age, are eligible for Medicare. Among those 55 to 64 in 1987, 85 percent incurred some medical expense (not including long-term care). Of those that were retired in 1987, 70 percent held employment-related coverage. Post-retirement coverage is more prevalent in large firms; in 1990, 90 percent of the largest firms provided post-retirement coverage (Hewitt Associates, 1990), 83 percent for individuals both before and after age 65. Of these, approximately 20 percent required no contributions, an additional 8 percent required contributions for spouse coverage only. For post-65 coverage, 31 percent of these firms did not require any employee contributions. Most post-65 retirement plans (97%) are integrated in some way with Medicare. However, even with Medicare coverage, individuals are facing increased out-of-pocket expenses. The percentage of Medicare enrollees' per capita income needed to cover such costs increased from 4.2 percent in 1975 to approximately 5.7 percent in 1990 (Kingson, 1992). Rising medical costs and costs of insurance may result in a decrease of pension benefits or a decline in retiree health benefits (Congressional Budget Office, 1993). In the 1960s, Medicare disbursements were estimated to be approximately 0.6 percent of gross national product; in 1991 their share of gross national product had doubled to 1.2 percent (Hurd, 1994b); this share is projected to be 2.7 percent by 2020 (also Hurd, 1994b).

Like Social Security and disability insurance, Medicare is not adequately financed to meet the anticipated increase in health care needs. Under moderate projections, Medicare funds are expected to be depleted by 2001. In order to sustain the program, therefore, a combination of tax increases, benefit reductions, and cost containment will be necessary (Kingson, 1992). As a result, retiree health insurance is increasing in importance. Like other fringe benefits such as pensions, retiree health insurance may have powerful incentive effects. In particular, the existence of retiree health insurance should reduce job mobility to the extent that it represents an implicit contract between employer and employee. An implication of this, Macpherson (1992) argues, is that women should be covered less frequently than men, owing to less attachment to the labor force. In addition, large firms, which presumably have high monitoring and training costs, are more likely to offer retiree health insurance (creating a "bonding" effect, similar to that for pensions, as argued by Allen, Clark, and McDermed, 1993, and Gustman and Steinmeier, 1993b). Per capita costs of retiree health insurance will also be lower at larger firms. Barron and Fraedrich (1994) take a similar view, focusing on employer heterogeneity to explain differences in fringe benefit offerings, particularly with respect to retiree health insurance and leave policies.

Another reason it is important to include Medicare in a model of retirement behavior is that an individual is eligible for Medicare due to disability if he or she is entitled to Social Security on the basis of a disability, that is, has been receiving Social Security for this reason for at least 2 years, under age 65. It is estimated that approximately 80 percent of Social Security disability-insurance beneficiaries receive Medicare coverage (Lewin-VHI, 1994). If the individual goes off disability and goes back on again for the same disability, the 2-year waiting period is waived. In addition, there is a continuation allowance if the individual returns to work (a 9-month trial period and up to 15 months afterwards, Commerce Clearing House, Inc., 1993). As with non-disability-related cases, if the individual is covered by an employer-sponsored plan, Medicare is the secondary payer.

Besides Medicare, government influence in health benefits to the elderly has occurred via legislation, such as passage of the Consolidated Omnibus Budget Reconciliation Act of 1985 (COBRA), which mandated continued health care benefits to retired employees for up to 18 months. While provisions of COBRA allow employers to charge up to 102 percent of premium costs, many plans pay the entire cost of this continuation coverage (Barron and Fraedrich, 1994). For individuals that remain attached to the labor force solely because of the availability of health insurance until eligibility for Medicare at age 65, this effectively lowers the feasible retirement age to 63-1/2.

Literature Review and Previous Methodology

As noted earlier, papers by Lumsdaine, Stock, and Wise have systematically underpredicted retirement rates at age 65, despite reasonable predictions at other ages. Lumsdaine, Stock, and Wise (1996b) address this issue directly, focusing on two selected samples from a specific firm: a balanced sample of individuals (the same number from each age group; random samples tended to have relatively few individuals at the older ages) and a sample of 65-year-olds. Standard economic variables do not seem to explain the large retirement rates at this age. Discussion by Rust (1989) and Rust and Phelan (1993) suggests that this underprediction may be due to the absence of health benefits in the model specification. The specific firm that Lumsdaine, Stock, and Wise (1996b) study offers continued post-retirement medical coverage, leading the authors to argue that the incentive to stay employed to retain health insurance should not apply to individuals in this firm. Nonetheless, the spike in the hazard rates at age 65 is still noticeably pronounced. In addition, Madrian (1993) has computed hazard rates using three aggregate data sets for individuals with and without retiree health insurance; the difference between the two groups is not statistically significant, and in one case, the hazard rate is actually lower for those with retiree health insurance than for those without it.

Gustman and Steinmeier (1993a) note that "Retirement incentives from health benefits for retirees are analogous to those created by defined benefit pensions" (p. 32). In particular, it is advantageous to remain with the firm until the age of eligibility for such benefits. In considering the interaction between employer-provided health insurance and retirement behavior, they predict a minor effect on labor supply; the magnitude of the effect is considerably less than a year. Gustman and Steinmeier simulate the effects of a variety of retiree health insurance assumptions. Because no data set contains all the important information for such a simulation, they estimate a life-cycle model using the RHS and embed the resultant estimated utility function into a simulation model using data from the SCF. In doing this, they are able to both model the key elements of the retirement decision and incorporate detailed features of pension plan provisions. The measure of health insurance used in their simulation is an imputed amount of employer contribution. Post-retirement health insurance is a fraction of the value of this contribution, based on national averages. As with their (1991) study on the impact of policy changes to Social Security, Gustman and Steinmeier measure the effect of providing retiree health insurance to be a change (in this case a decrease) in the average date of retirement of roughly the same magnitude; individuals would retire approximately 3 weeks earlier. They attribute this modest effect to the magnitude of the value of health insurance relative to other forms of compensation.

Lumsdaine, Stock, and Wise (1994) incorporate Medicare into the base retirement model, valuing medical insurance at its cost and treating it as comparable to wage compensation. The addition of this measure of the value of medical insurance does nothing to explain the departure rate at 65. In principle, other things such as savings also could be incorporated in this way.

It is puzzling that some structural models such as those of Lumsdaine, Stock, and Wise (1994) or Gustman and Steinmeier (1993a) fail to capture a significant Medicare/health insurance effect, as anecdotal evidence and media attention suggest that concern over health insurance is on the minds of many individuals nearing retirement. Reduced-form models have been more successful at capturing a larger effect, at the expense of policy inference. Using a probit model, Gruber and Madrian (1993b) find a significant effect of post-retirement health insurance on retirement, exploiting state cross-sectional variation in continuation of coverage laws. They find that 1 year of continuation benefits raises retirement rates by 20 percent. In addition, the effect is not clustered near the age of Medicare eligibility but is similar at all ages. Their results suggest that individuals value continuation benefits at a much higher level than at actual employer cost. Subsequent work by Gruber and Madrian (1993a) finds that continuation mandates have a large effect on increasing insurance coverage, but a relatively small effect on increasing retirement. Karoly and Rogowski (1994) also use a probit model and find significant effects of health insurance on retirement. Because they use the Survey of Income and Program Participation (SIPP), which has no information on retiree health benefits, they use an imputed measure of benefits, based on firm size, industry, and region.

Rust and Phelan (1993) use dynamic programming as in Rust (1989) to model jointly the labor supply decision and the decision to apply for Social Security using the RHS dataset. They cite the liberalization of Social Security and Medicare benefits as a significant contributing factor in the decline of labor force participation. They also review some of the earlier techniques used to study this question. Regarding the impact of health insurance, they criticize the use by earlier studies (in particular, Gustman and Steinmeier, 1993a; and Lumsdaine, Stock, and Wise, 1994) of the expected value of Medicare reimbursements and employer contributions, arguing that risk-averse individuals respond asymmetrically to the probability of a catastrophic event. Thus, "the certainty equivalent value of Medicare coverage will be substantially greater than the expected value of Medicare reimbursements and retiree health insurance premiums" (pp. 26-27).

They found that the Pareto distribution provides a very close fit to the long, thin upper tail of the distribution of annual health care expenditures. The large influence that Social Security exerts over labor force participation at age 65 is attributed to incomplete annuities markets. Additional responsibility for the large peak in retirements at this age is due to incomplete health insurance markets. In the dynamic programming model they use, Social Security is basically the only annuity available to the individual. In particular, the data are limited to men who do not have access to a pension plan. An obvious desirable extension to their model would be to relax this constraint. The model also assumes no savings (total borrowing constraints). The results justify retirements at ages 62 and 65 (and mirror the peaks extremely well), with those at 65 being attributed to Social Security and those at 62 attributed to the presence of retiree health insurance or some other form of health insurance. Without health insurance, individuals typically postpone their retirement until they are also eligible for Medicare. The delayed retirement credit is blamed for the magnitude of the sharp peak at 65 (virtually no one will work after 65); this suggests a reduction in the peak in the future due to scheduled increases in the delayed retirement credit. Rust and Phelan predict that high-income workers will continue to work but will still apply for Social Security (and thus be eligible for Medicare) at 65 as a costless way of obtaining supplementary health insurance, despite the limitation imposed by the earnings test.

What We Would Like to Know

One of the hottest topics of debate in the 1992 election was universal health care coverage, which is likely to continue to be a key issue. Opponents cite unsurmountable costs while proponents argue that lack of universal coverage reduces labor mobility and stifles entrepreneurship (by discouraging self-employment) because employer-provided health insurance, like defined benefit pensions, are typically not portable and often contain pre-existing condition clauses. Holtz-Eakin, Penrod, and Rosen (1994) investigate the latter claim. They find little evidence to support the idea that universal coverage will increase entrepreneurship, noting instead that the significant negative impact of an employer-provided health insurance plan on the probability of a transition into self-employment is due to heterogeneity based on other observable characteristics.

While selection issues are likely to be important in analyzing the effects of retiree health insurance, they are less important in Medicare analysis since (as noted above) virtually everyone over age 65 is covered by Medicare. Barron and Fraedrich (1994) assume that employers offer fringe benefits to induce self-selection; this assumption arises in a model of labor contracting where certain types of firms need to reduce mobility of their employees, perhaps due to costly training, which represents a long-term investment.

Holtz-Eakin, Penrod, and Rosen (1994) also raise the important point of determining a reliable measure of expected health costs. They define 12 different proxies, including previous medical expenses associated with hospital stays, the number of doctor visits, and the number of people in the family covered by the plan, incorporating each one separately. It is likely that a weighted combination of many proxies would be the most accurate in determining the influence of retiree health insurance.

Because Medicare provides near-universal coverage for the elderly over age 65, policy related to it is likely to focus on issues of cost containment. Two approaches that have been discussed are (1) capping expenditures or rationing of services and (2) raising the Medicare eligibility age. To the extent that some of the observed retirement at age 65 is due to Social Security and some is due to Medicare eligibility, attempts to increase labor force participation by raising the Social Security normal retirement age, increasing the Social Security early retirement penalty, and increasing the delayed retirement credit will be offset. As life expectancies increase and the population ages, the Medicare trust fund in its current state will be expected to support greater numbers of elderly.

It is equally critical, in light of the above-mentioned policy experiments, to be able to assess the direction of causality between Medicare and retirement. Although the 1983 Social Security amendments raise the normal retirement age and application of the delayed retirement credit from 65 to 67 (as noted in the section on Social Security), a commensurate increase in the age of Medicare receipt has not been legislated. It is therefore possible (as, e.g., the Rust-Phelan, 1993, model suggests) that the intended impact of these amendments will be dampened if individuals are health-insurance constrained and the retirement peak may well remain at 65. To the extent that Medicare influences the retirement decision, increasing the Medicare eligibility age may be another way policy makers can increase labor force participation. If, instead, Medicare application occurs because other sources of health insurance are limited at age 65, increasing the eligibility age may have the undesirable effect of raising the proportion of uninsured individuals.

Besides documenting the relationship between Medicare and health insurance on labor force participation and retirement, future research should focus on the policy implications of such relationships. Holtz-Eakin, Penrod, and Rosen (1994), for example, find that for a subsample of individuals who were continuously employed, the number of doctor visits over the last 4 months is a significant predictor of a transition to self-employment. They note, however, that the quantitative relevance of this significance is limited, predicting an increase in the transition probability of 0.35 percent for this part of the population. This is consistent with findings of Gustman and Steinmeier (1993a) and Lumsdaine, Stock, and Wise (1996b) that despite significant coefficients on employer-provided health insurance in their structural retirement models, the quantitative effects of a change in coverage would be small in magnitude.

Most of the dynamic models used in examining retirement behavior arise from a life-cycle framework. Just as current labor force participation decisions depend on the individual's entire work history, attitudes toward the importance of health insurance and the valuation of health benefits can be inferred in a life-cycle manner. These attitudes are likely to differ substantially across individuals and depend on observable characteristics such as those mentioned in Holtz-Eakin, Penrod, and Rosen (1994). Lumsdaine, Stock, and Wise include expected premium as a proxy for medical expenditures in a base specification (1994) and in simulations (1996a). They find little effect of medical benefits on retirement. As noted by Rust and Phelan (1993), this limited allowance for heterogeneity may not adequately capture the manner in which individuals assess such benefits. While it is clear that individual-specific effects (such as highly correlated error terms that capture unobserved persistent heterogeneity such as individual health status) are important to dynamic models, it is also important in this context to model uncertainty, as there is substantial evidence that individuals are highly risk averse and that their demand is driven not by considering a certainty equivalent but in adequately insuring against the probability of a catastrophic event.

One of the ways in which dynamic specifications could be improved is by including an estimate of the individual's expected present discounted value of medical expenses, using either combined premiums and out-of-pocket expenditures or total expenditures including insurance payments. These could be imputed in a manner similar to predictions of future wages, based on observable demographic characteristics and a data set (such as the National Medical Expenditure Survey) that contains detailed information on health care expenditures. Another way to allow for more heterogeneity in models is to incorporate individual-specific life expectancies (also imputed from observable characteristics). Such imputations still would enable use of data sets with details on pensions and earnings.

Ideally, individual heterogeneity can be included by incorporating self-assessed health status. A limitation of the firm-specific data sets of Lumsdaine, Stock, and Wise, for example, is that information on health status is missing. The HRS combines detailed questions on health with specific pension plan information and will allow researchers to model a richer set of dynamics than was previously possible.

HOURS FLEXIBILITY AND CAREER JOBS

In their models of retirement behavior, Gordon and Blinder (1980) and Reimers and Honig (1993) assume that workers can work any number of hours they choose at a constant hourly wage. However, there is much evidence that workers are constrained in their choice of hours. Hurd and McGarry (1993b), using the HRS, find that 24.1 percent of respondents can decrease their hours; another 13.6 percent want to but cannot. In terms of increasing hours, 36 percent of respondents report being able to, and an additional 15.1 percent want to but are unable. Over half of all respondents claim their job has no flexibility with respect to hours. Those who cannot decrease their hours but want to have a significantly greater probability of retiring at ages 62 and 65. Those who cannot increase their hours but want to have a greater probability of working full time at ages 62 and age 65. Hill, Soldo, and Li (1993) find that having access to flexible work hours is positively correlated with total work hours.

There is evidence that hours flexibility will become an increasingly important job characteristic. "With the growing complexity of family structure and resulting caregiving demands, flexible work strategies will be required to keep both young and old workers in the labor force" (Marks and Seefer, 1992:56). Modeling hours flexibility is especially important when studying the labor supply behavior of women. Currently 74 percent of women aged 25 to 54 are in the labor force; this is expected to rise to 82 percent by 2005 (Kingson, 1992). In addition, "about 40 percent of full-time private sector wage and salary workers are women," (Korczyk, 1992:119). Pienta, Burr, and Mutchler (1993) suggest that a woman's employment status in later life is determined by the work history pattern over the course of her lifetime, concluding that "labor force behavior in later life is often a continuation of earlier adult decisions and behavior" (p. 15). In terms of concerns over income inadequacy, a reduction in income will translate into less Social Security and pension income, placing women potentially at even greater risk. Korczyk (1992) concurs, noting that gender differences in pension coverage arise from different employment patterns (recall Table 3-5). Blank (1994) also provides evidence of such gender differences. Looking at working age women, she finds that 40.5 percent of women in her sample had been in all three states of labor force participation (full time, part time, out of the labor force) during a 14-year period, as opposed to just 6.3 percent of men.

One reason to investigate more flexible hours in the workplace is increasing evidence that individuals would prefer to gradually reduce their amount of hours worked, as opposed to making an abrupt transition from full time to completely retired. Reimers and Honig (1993) and Hurd (1993) argue that institutional rigidities impede an individual's ability to do this. Because of this, retirement has often been modeled as a dichotomous decision as opposed to a continuous choice (of how many hours to supply).

Literature Review and Previous Methodology

Hurd (1993) summarizes some of the institutional rigidities that impede complete flexibility in hours determination. Some of these are due to fixed employment costs and requirements of team production. Impediments to job change arise from loss of job-specific skills, making employers unwilling to invest in training for an older worker. Other rigidities are due to regulation and policy towards factors affecting retirement; some of these, such as the Social

Security earnings test, defined benefit pension plans, and health insurance, have already been discussed.

As evidence of a gradual transition toward retirement, Quinn and Burkhauser (1992) find that "the importance of part-time work rises dramatically with age" (p. 6). Using data from the U.S. Bureau of Labor Statistics, they note that 16 percent of men aged 60 to 64 work part time (less than 35 hours a week), while a full 50 percent of men over 65 do. For women, these percentages are 33 percent and 60 percent, respectively. The proportion of individuals working part time has grown steadily. Therefore, Quinn and Burkhauser conclude, individuals are still exhibiting a tendency towards early retirement, but through a reduction in hours. Of those who switch employers, Quinn, Burkhauser, and Myers (1990) find that 75 percent were still on the job after a year, almost 60 percent after 2 years. Departures from career jobs tended to be characterized by a decrease in wage, with many transitions associated with a complete change of industry and/or occupation (Ruhm, 1990; Parnes and Sommers, 1994). Gustman and Steinmeier (1986) incorporate wage reduction into a model of leaving full-time work.

Ruhm (1990) also finds substantial evidence for a gradual transition, noting that in the RHS, "only 36% of household heads retire immediately on the end of their career positions, and nearly half remain in the labor force for at least 5 additional years" (p. 486). This is even more pronounced at the younger ages; of those aged 55 to 59, only 11.6 percent retire completely. In addition, there are often financial reasons why an individual might want to exit a career job, thus becoming eligible to receive a pension benefit, and then may want to continue to work (the opportunity to earn additional wages, combined with health coverage until eligibility for Medicare at age 65). These incentives usually decline upon receipt of Social Security, however, owing to the earnings test. Ruhm (1990) finds that 47.7 percent of workers eligible for a pension continue to work after leaving their career job. The observation that partial retirement occurs mainly between ages 62 and 67 indicates the influence of the Social Security earnings test. Nearly 25 percent of retirees reenter the labor force, with almost one-third choosing full labor force participation.

While some people define retirement as "receiving retirement income" or "no longer working," a gradual transition suggests a phase-in toward the retirement state that begins when one leaves a "career job." But even the definition of career job is ambiguous—Reimers and Honig (1993) use "a job an individual had held since before age 55, provided he does not describe himself as either partially or fully retired." Ruhm (1990) uses "the longest spell of employment with a single firm, up to and including the position held at the beginning of" the RHS. Defining career job as a job that has lasted for 10 or more years, Ruhm (1994) shows that many elderly (individuals above age 58) who work full time are not in a career job.

Over the past few decades, an increasing proportion of individuals claim to have retired voluntarily (that is, because they wanted to, not, as in the past, owing to health constraints or being laid off). Some of this may be attributable to the earlier ages of retirement (before health problems emerge), as well as to publicity presenting retirement in a positive light. Others may argue that the generosity of retirement benefits has made retirement more feasible; Hardy (1991) suggests that it is still important to distinguish between workers who choose retirement owing to a perceived lack of alternative employment opportunities versus those who anxiously await a time of leisure. Parnes and Sommers (1994), using the National Longitudinal Survey of Mature Men (NLS-MM 1990), report that health problems were a considerably less important reason offered by nonworkers as to why they had no interest in working than a general preference for leisure. Less than 40 percent cited health reasons as a cause.

Some research has used discrete choice models to capture the retirement decision. The simplest of these is a binomial probit or logit; these models treat retirement as an all-or-nothing decision. It is clear, however, that employment (and, correspondingly, retirement) can no longer be modeled as a dichotomous variable. Individuals often face a wider range of choices along the labor/leisure frontier. Other research has used a multinomial logit model (e.g., Hardy, 1991, with retiree, reentrant, and available worker, or Anderson, Burkhauser, and Quinn, 1986, with early, on-time, and late retirement). Additionally, one could consider an ordered choice model (make retirement choice, then decide what to do— nothing, work part time or take a new full-time job). Which model is most appropriate is linked to perceptions of behavior and dynamic decision making.

Reimers and Honig (1993) use the RHS and consider reentry into the labor force after leaving a "career job" using a hazard model. They find that the Social Security earnings test affects reentry; a 10 percent increase in the level of exempt earnings is associated with a 5 percent increased probability of reentry. Hayward, Hardy, and Chiang (1990) use the NLS-MM in a similar fashion. They note that the risk of reentry declines precipitously after 2 years out of the labor force. In addition, more than twice as many reentrants move back to full-time versus part-time jobs and wage and salaried jobs verus self-employment. Unfortunately, neither of these data sets contains substantial detail on pension coverage or receipt, so it is impossible to determine the extent to which reentry is a means of supplementing a pension benefit or obtaining health insurance. They do find, however, that the number of previous retirements is negatively correlated with reentry into a full-time job; this is attributed to barriers that exist for those who exhibit labor force mobility late in life. Scott, Berger, and Garen (1992) suggest firms that offer generous (defined benefit) pension or health benefits are less likely to hire elderly (ages 55 to 64) workers. In contrast, the hiring practices of firms offering defined contribution plans appears to be age neutral. In terms of encouraging more elderly labor force reentry, Hayward, Hardy, and Chiang (1990) conclude that policies aimed at job training will have little effect as skill levels seem adequate. Reimers and Honig (1993) concur, citing an inadequate supply of part-time jobs.

Reimers and Honig (1992) consider gender differences in reentry behavior by modeling a reentry hazard function. They conclude that men behave "myopically" with regard to Social Security, considering only their current level of benefits, while women are "far-sighted," responding more to varying levels of Social Security wealth. They argue that older women's labor force participation is not affected by the earnings limit, as older women are likely to be in lower wage jobs. In addition, the amount of private pension influences the reentry decision of men, but not women. Such gender differences suggest a differential impact of proposed policy changes.

Blank (1994) compares three dynamic discrete choice models of labor force behavior: a 3-lag model that allows for complex dependence of the current decision on a short history of past labor force participation decisions, a 13-lag model that has a simplified dependence structure but allows influence of a longer history, and a random effects logit model that ignores previous history but allows for unmeasured heterogeneity. All three models perform fairly well in predicting aggregate behavior. In terms of individual behavior, however, the two models that account for previous decisions are substantially better (more than 10 times so) at predicting actual behavior.

Daula and Moffitt (1991) and Berkovec and Stern (1991) estimate dynamic programming models of job transition. Daula and Moffitt considered military retirement, where at each period an individual decides whether to stay or leave the service; Berkovec and Stern allowed for four transition states from full-time work—continuation, switching to a new full-time job, partially retiring, and fully retiring. Both models specify a value function, which depends on age, years of service, and other exogenous variables. There are individual-specific error terms; Berkovec and Stern (p. 191) take these to be "random components of the wage which are independent across time, matches, and individuals" and assume that they have an extreme value distribution in order to obtain analytic solutions via the method of simulated moments. Daula and Moffitt also allow for heterogeneity, assuming that their errors are uncorrelated over time and normally distributed.

Ausink (1991) considers retirement from the military of a sample of Air Force pilots. Although the military pension has cliff vesting at 20 years of service, many individuals leave, either voluntarily or involuntarily, before this time; even among those that stay, eligibility for military pension typically occurs when individuals are in their 40s. Thus the choice for most military individuals is not one of retirement but of exiting a career job. Two items of particular importance for a model of such behavior are the determination of the following:

• The date of exit. Since the individual is expected to enter a new full-time job, it is important to evaluate the expected wage trajectory. For example, as noted by Ausink, civilian pilots typically have greater earnings potential than military pilots although starting salaries are lower. However, most airlines compensate based on years of experience *at their specific firm* and do not reward based on total years of flying experience. A dynamic decision process therefore involves determining the optimal time of retirement, evaluating the tradeoff among pension receipt, compensation, and the present discounted value of future compensation in an alternative employment setting.

• The form of the pension benefit. Many plans offer a wide array of distribution choices upon electing to receive a pension benefit, from a lump sum to a fixed term to an annuity payment. Often the present discounted values of various options differ substantially. In addition, there is evidence that such distributions (especially in cases where individuals continue to work) are often not applied to retirement saving but are used for other purposes. Of particular note is an individual who takes a lump-sum distribution from a pension at a career job and uses it to start a business.

Ausink and Wise (1993) consider the effects of changes to the Air Force pension plan, reflecting some of the actual changes that have been implemented in the last decade. In addition, they compare the Stock-Wise "option value" model to the Air Force's "Annualized Cost of Leaving" models as well as to dynamic programming specifications similar to those of Lumsdaine, Stock, and Wise (1992).

Rust (1989) proposes incorporating partial retirement and multiple labor force transitions into a dynamic retirement model. The difficulty in capturing multiple labor force decisions in behavioral models used for prediction is numerical; every combination of transitions must be considered. In addition, the decision tree involves an exponential number of nodes; if the alternatives are working or not working (retired) over n future periods, 2^n transitions are involved. Adding the possibility of part-time work increases the number of transitions to 3^n. The computational burden associated with such a model is formidable.

According to the Congressional Budget Office (1993:39), "As long-term employment for a single firm is becoming less common, the risks of defined benefit plans are rising." This is due to the lack of portability in defined benefit pension plans. The link between pensions and the career job, as well as implications for retirement and retirement income, has been documented in the literature. Mehdizadeh and Luzadis (1994) simulate the effects of a number of different combinations of job mobility and type of pension plan to analyze the potential impact of such choices on retirement income. In particular, they find that pension plans that are integrated with Social Security tend to hurt the financial well-being of their recipients relative to an equally generous plan without such a provision. These simulations are illustrative, but far from comprehensive. It would be interesting to simulate a retirement from a career job followed by a series of shorter jobs, all with pension plans. In particular, it is possible, because of shorter vesting periods and the incentive effects in defined benefit plans to retire early, that such a strategy may increase retirement income. As pensions become an increasing source of retirement income, attention will focus on the adequacy of retirement income from the primary employer (Mitchell, 1992; Hurd, 1993; Ruhm, 1990; Peracchi and Welch, 1994). However, it is argued that pension incentives encourage retirement from one's primary job. If perceptions regarding retirement income are inaccurate, retirees will be forced to return to work.

What We Would Like to Know

As institutional barriers to flexible hours break down, we will need to know how to model the continuous transition into retirement. Reimers and Honig (1992) attribute exit and reentry behavior to worker response in an environment in which hours cannot be smoothly adjusted to accommodate an increasing preference for leisure. In addition, Pavalko, Elder, and Clipp (1993) note a link between work history and mortality. They recommend improvements in modeling work lives and incorporating entire work histories. One possible reason they offer for increased mortality risk associated with multiple transitions between unrelated jobs is due to inadequate pension and health insurance benefits, which may cause increased stress surrounding retirement.

Because of the evidence that labor force decisions, particularly those of women, depend on both economic and noneconomic considerations, Pozzebon and Mitchell (1989) argue that women's retirement behavior should ideally be modeled in a life-cycle framework. As a simplification, they model the wife's decision to retire conditional on the husband's decision, using the RHS. As they note, a joint-decision model would be more general. In order to project future income streams, they designate a planning date. Others (e.g., Lumsdaine, Stock, and Wise) have imputed income streams at each future decision date.

A potentially fruitful way to model transitions in and out of the labor force is via the duration method used in Klerman (1992). In a different context (considering spells with and without health insurance using SIPP data), Klerman considered each combination of runs. For example, over seven periods, the number of combinations would be 2^7. He then related these runs to a variety of explanatory variables. To the extent that individuals' labor supply behavior is determined over the life cycle, such a model provides a useful framework for examining the dynamic decision process. The computational burden, being exponential, quickly becomes formidable owing to loss of degrees of freedom. This method would be computationally cumbersome for investigating employment decisions over the course of one's adult life. It is well suited for considering exit and reentry patterns of the elderly, particularly after exiting a career job.

As noted above, many individuals return to work after retirement from a career job. This must be modeled explicitly; Rust (1994) suggests failure to do so attaches undue uncertainty to the retirement decision. It is also important to consider how labor force transitions, particularly reentry, are correlated with other factors influencing the retirement decision, particularly pension benefit receipt. While much of the literature has focused on a job transition resulting in a decline in pension wealth, for some individuals, such as those in Ausink's (1991) military data set, it is expected that individuals will collect pension benefits from multiple sources (double- or triple-dipping).

Besides hours flexibility, other job characteristics will similarly affect transition decisions. Hurd and McGarry (1993b) consider a number of these, such as physical strain and attitudes of co-workers. Individual perceptions and self-selection are likely to play a key role in understanding labor force transitions and the effects of job characteristics, both for individuals on the verge of retirement and throughout their work histories. For example, in deciding whether to leave a career job, a worker may evaluate the probability of losing the current job or finding another job. Questions in the HRS are intended to capture these subjective assessments, which may or may not reflect actual probabilities. Even without misperceptions, subjective probability assessments may allow researchers to capture otherwise unobserved heterogeneities. Identifying misperceptions will improve the way in which an econometrician can model the decision process, particularly when many existing models do not incorporate such uncertainties.

CONCLUSIONS

What determines retirement and retirement income? Often the definition depends on the research question being addressed. It is also clear, however, that over time our definitions have changed fundamentally as, for example, labor force exit becomes more of a voluntary decision rather than stemming from necessity. It is possible, too, that some definitions are becoming less pronounced, such as that of a career job. In this section I summarize the key ingredients to a richer model of retirement behavior and income.

Expectations

Why are retirement rates so high at age 65? The work by Lumsdaine, Stock, and Wise consistently underpredicts retirement at this age, despite being able to accurately capture retirement behavior at other ages. They attribute much of the peak to "social custom," via either influence from co-workers or general social norms. How these norms are formulated is not addressed, but they could be due to indirect influences of Social Security and Medicare, which cause certain ages to be associated with retirement. That modal retirement ages may be determined by social custom is echoed in Leonesio (1993a, 1993b). In addition, he cautions that policy analysis must consider endogenously determined expectations and how a proposed policy may affect future expectations. He thus speculates that policies to encourage later retirement may generate the desired response and that, as expectations and perceptions about working longer become more positive, the observed effect will be greater than initially estimated.

Responses to questions in the HRS about why individuals retired and how much they knew, planned, or discussed with others before retirement will shed light on whether or not there has been (as put forth by a number of authors) a trend towards more voluntary retirements. If this is the case, policy should focus on how to improve public perception to allow individuals to properly assess factors influencing their retirement decision. We do not yet have aggregate evidence on the extent of misperception, but based on evidence in Bernheim (1994), using a sample of baby boom individuals, households save well below their self-perceived target level. According to the General Accounting Office (1990), of 25 million workers who were in defined benefit pension plans, 18 million (72%) were incorrect about, or did not know, when they could retire with full benefits (16% said they did not know). Of these individuals, 22 million (88%) were in plans with an early retirement option. Of these, almost 14 percent did not know whether or not they were eligible for such an option; an additional 27 percent were incorrect in assessing their eligibility. This points to a need for increased public awareness, counseling, and guidance. Leonesio (1993a) discusses misperception about Social Security provisions, saying, "This raises a number of interesting questions about the accuracy of predicting the behavioral consequences of changing a provision that is poorly understood" (p. 54).

Evidence from a military "window plan" suggests inadequate understanding or perception of the variety of distributional options offered; in the particular case examined, the lump-sum choice of distribution is far from actuarially fair (amounting to between 40 percent and 55 percent of the annuity when compared in present discounted value terms, using a discount rate of 0.95), yet this form was preferred almost 10 to 1 over the annuity among the enlisted populations, with an almost even split among officers. According to a sample of individuals who opted for the program, the reason for taking the lump-sum option was primarily to pay off debts or to have a cash reserve while seeking employment, while majors reported choosing the annuity because of the perceived greater overall value and the guarantee of long-term income.[8]

In addition to Social Security and private pension plans, which are aimed directly at the timing of retirement, there are many indirect influences. These include policies designed to increase savings (such as the introduction of individual retirement accounts (IRAs), 401(k)s and their tax-advantaged status; see, e.g., Venti and Wise, 1992) and publicity about the benefits of working after exiting a career job (Day, 1993; Bernheim, 1994; Employee Benefit Plan Review, 1994b). In general, there is evidence that the public responds to such campaigns; Venti and Wise (1992) note that "Several aspects of the public response to IRAs in the 1982 to 1986 period suggest to us that the fanfare accompanying IRAs was an important ingredient of their success" (p. 33).

What are expectations about future window plans? Anderson, Burkhauser, and Quinn (1986) considered male workers in the RHS and found that actual departures were within a year of the predicted date for 60 percent. Instead of focusing on the determinants of the retirement decision, they were interested in the relation of actual to expected retirement. Of those that did not retire on their predicted date, more retired earlier than expected. In contrast, Bernheim (1989), using the same data set, finds little relationship between the expected date of retirement and the mean date (the average over all individuals that report the same expected date). However, he finds evidence that individuals respond to the question of when they expect to retire with the modal value (he terms this "the Modal Value Hypothesis"). In fact, the modal date of retirement corresponds with the expected date in 75 percent of the groups. What kind of options do elderly workers face and is this set of choices narrowing with age? Answers to these questions may or may not match perceptions about the probability of a new job.

How do we model expectations? What is the accuracy with which we can model them or with which individuals can evaluate their own expectations? These questions are difficult to answer because, as noted earlier, the dimensionality of individual beliefs is very large. Bernheim and Levin (1989) analyze expected Social Security benefits and their effect on individual savings levels. Hurd and McGarry (1993a) provide evidence that individual assessments regarding probability are remarkably close to population averages. In addition, these assessments vary along demographic lines, in ways analogous to actual probabilities. This provides optimism for using such survey responses for prediction and forecasting, although current expectations reflect the current state of the world and will not necessarily agree with future probabilities. Because they at most incorporate all current and past information, they obviously are unable to capture significant legislative or health changes in the future. Adequately modeling expectations and uncertainty surrounding future changes, which perhaps represent the biggest threat to retirement income security, is crucial to understanding the factors influencing labor force participation decisions and represents a substantial challenge for research.

Endogeneity

This paper has documented a number of forms of endogeneity in assessing retirement behavior and income. The first form emphasizes the need for models that specify a dynamic system of equations that incorporate the interactions between decisions about retirement, from leaving a career job to applying for social benefits such as Social Security, Medicare, and disability. Leonesio (1993a) notes that these interactions between decisions are consistent with a life-cycle model of economic behavior; such observations emphasize the importance of dynamic decision processes.

One impediment to fully modeling all the interactions between these many factors in the past has been computational limitation. However, computers are becoming increasingly faster, and with this, models are increasing in complexity.

With improved technology comes an ability to accommodate the proliferation of choices in our economic models. Besides choosing a retirement date, many individuals are faced with having to decide how to receive a pre- or post-retirement distribution (annuity or some other form); these decisions might be modeled in a simultaneous decision framework.

Virtually the only attempt to model *all* interactions is Rust (1989), where an astounding quantity of (admittedly discrete) transitions are modeled. Given that data are often in discrete units, however, this does not seem like an unrealistic approximation, even though behavioral decisions are more accurately modeled as continuous processes. In addition, Rust specifies dynamic processes for marital status, employment, health status, wealth, and so forth. The problem is the computational burden involved. This is a problem with dynamic programming models in general, where, without simplifying assumptions, the number of nodes in the decision tree increases exponentially with the number of time periods (i.e., nodes = C^T, where C is the number of choices and T is the number of time periods). Future models, therefore, must focus on adequately modeling transitional behavior and conditional probabilities, where the conditioning information set incorporates the complete history of choices available to the individual. The emphasis should be on this as a means of reducing computational time and more closely approximating actual behavior.

Still, there are a number of limitations to the model in Rust (1989); these are recognized by Rust himself and also outlined in Burtless (1989) and Rust and Phelan (1993). Many modeling limitations are the fault of data limitations; in Rust's case, the limitation is inadequate information on pensions and caregiving responsibilities and computational burden. Burtless (1989) notes that most studies examine a single issue; more advanced ones consider a subset of the determinants, allowing for some interaction. Rust (1989) has laid out a comprehensive framework that, in principle, allows assessment of all determinants at once. Of course, it too is limited by data, computational burden, and assumptions about stochastic processes that describe the evolution of these factors over time. However, it defines the state of the art in terms of what models should, it is hoped, ultimately achieve—a way of mimicking behavior and mirroring the dynamic nature of decision making.

Another form of endogeneity arises when one tries to draw inferences about policy changes. To the extent that policy and behavior are jointly determined, parameter estimates obtained from a base model under the current policy regime will not accurately reflect effects in an alternative policy state (see Lucas, 1981, and discussion therein).

A final form of endogeneity is sample selection. As discussed in each of the sections above, heterogeneity between a sample population and a reference population will render inferences useless. It is important, therefore, to assess the extent of sample selection and its role in affecting inferences and, if necessary, to attempt to correct biases that may arise.

Uncertainty

Few models of retirement behavior have allowed for uncertainty in the specification. Even dynamic models such as Gustman and Steinmeier (1986) assume perfect markets, and Stock and Wise (1990a, 1990b) assume perfect foresight in imputed earnings computations. Capturing individual uncertainty (including, but not limited to, modeling expectations, as discussed above), such as the probability of finding a new job or of qualifying for disability insurance, is crucial to understanding and modeling behavior. It is also important in dynamic models to control for aggregate uncertainty; in the case of pension plans this could include the financial condition of the firm or the termination of the plan. At more macroeconomic levels, this includes concerns over solvency of public programs such as Social Security, disability insurance, and Medicare.

One way to incorporate uncertainty into dynamic models is by simulation methods such as those in Keane and Wolpin (1994). This usually requires specifying an error distribution. When individual-specific correlation is introduced into a dynamic programming specification, a multidimensional integral results, often rendering the model intractable.[9] Keane and Wolpin use Monte Carlo integration to approximate the integral and suggest that such approximations perform well, both in being able to mimic behavior and in terms of providing plausible structural parameter estimates.

Data Issues

Rust (1989:371) raises the issue of approximating continuous processes with discrete variables, distinguishing between the discrete employment state and the continuous employment decision. Similarly, application for disability benefits (like Social Security) is dichotomous, but the decision process is not. It is therefore important to consider how to model the transition to disability, perhaps an even more continuous process than the transition to retirement. Discretizing health status is equally tricky. In general, models need to accommodate both decision variables, which are continuous, and associated behavioral states, which are discrete. Current research still does not adequately model both jointly.

Many of the shortcomings of previous literature, as well as the failure to adequately model the multiple factors influencing the retirement decision, stem from insufficient data sets. Two of the most promising data sets for future researchers are the HRS and the Asset and Health Dynamics Among the Oldest Old (AHEAD) survey.

Improving data accuracy and eliminating systematic biases should be a top priority. Evidence in Parsons (1991c) suggests that workers are reluctant to admit they have applied for disability insurance; similarly, virtually all surveys of income exhibit signs of underreporting of income by respondents. Linkages across data sets improve the ability to check responses for consistency and accuracy.

New techniques were employed to improve the response rate for the HRS. Besides asking the same questions a number of times with slightly different phrasing, interviewers also used unfolding brackets and card brackets to encourage responses. Juster and Smith (1994) argue that these techniques provide significantly more accurate imputations of financial variables, such as nonhousing wealth. They also propose using an "optimal brackets" method of threshold determination, where the optimality criterion is to maximize the between-group sum of squares. They find that asset imputations "are almost twice as large as those currently being obtained in SIPP"; this suggests that previous studies that have used SIPP's imputations have understated nonhousing wealth by 22 percent. Extending the bracketing techniques of Juster and Smith (1994) to other survey data sets still in progress is another way in which we can improve the quality of data for studying questions related to retirement and retirement income.

Other Concerns

As noted in the Introduction, concerns exist over income inadequacy of the elderly and projected funding inadequacy among government programs such as Social Security, Medicare, and disability insurance. The interactions among decisions related to retirement behavior and income suggest that inadequacy may affect an increasingly concentrated proportion of the population. If current demographic trends continue and policy emphasis does not address their needs, this population will most likely be elderly women living alone. Correlations among the variates considered in this paper point to the development of a bimodal distribution of elderly (Reno, 1993)—those who were high wage earners in their work lives and who therefore have adequate retirement income (in the form of pension benefits, a post-retirement job, low medical expenditures, and high levels of savings) and those who were not (having less attachment to the labor force, lower probability of a pension, and being in poorer health). In terms of policy directed at alleviating poverty among the elderly, as well as targeting public assistance to where scarce resources are most needed, the focus should be on this lower cluster of the distribution.

NOTES

1. For more discussion on these topics, see Ferber (1993).

2. From 1985 to 1988, there were 3.3 million participants in defined benefit plans that were terminated (Beller and Lawrence, 1992).

3. Or the workers agree to engage in the implicit labor contract that is offered. For theories of pension plans, see, for example, Ippolito (1985), Kotlikoff and Wise (1985), Viscusi (1985), and Lazear and Moore (1988).

4. In a true dynamic programming framework, individuals choose the expected maximum given a variety of choices in each time period. Thus the approximation in the Stock-Wise model induces a bias towards early retirement (Emax > maxE from Jensen's Inequality).

5. Woods (1993:6) notes that "while the gender gap is relatively small among workers under the age of 40, it diverges sharply among older workers."

6. In 1986, a 10 percent penalty tax was imposed; this tax was increased to 20 percent in 1993. For this and more details on lump-sum distributions, see Woods (1993).

7. In fact, the correlation in Parsons' data from 1947 to 1979 is 0.91.

8. I am grateful to John Ausink for providing the numbers and information in this paragraph.

9. A multidimensional integral will also arise with a multichotomous decision variable. Keane and Wolpin provide a four-dimensional example, where an individual's labor force participation decision is between two occupations, schooling, and staying home.

REFERENCES

Allen, S.G., R.L. Clark, and A.A. McDermed
  1993 Pensions, bonding and lifetime jobs. *Journal of Human Resources* 28(3):463-481.
Anderson, K.H., R.V. Burkhauser, and J.F. Quinn
  1986 Do retirement dreams come true? The effect of unanticipated events on retirement plans. *International Labor Relations Review* 39:518-526.
Auerbach, A.J., L.J. Kotlikoff, and D.N. Weil
  1992 *The Increasing Annuitization of the Elderly—Estimates and Implications for Intergenerational Transfers, Inequality, and National Saving.* NBER Working Paper #4182. Cambridge, Mass.: National Bureau of Economic Research.
Ausink, J.A.
  1991 The Effect of Changes in Compensation on a Pilot's Decision to Leave the Air Force. Unpublished Ph.D. dissertation. Harvard University.
Ausink, J.A., and D.A. Wise
  1993 *The Military Pension, Compensation, and Retirement of U.S. Air Force Pilots.* NBER Working Paper #4593. Cambridge, Mass.: National Bureau of Economic Research.
Bai, J., R.L. Lumsdaine, and J.H. Stock
  1994 Testing for and Dating Breaks in Integrated and Cointegrated Time Series. Unpublished manuscript. Department of Economics, Massachusetts Institute of Technology.
Barron, J.M., and A. Fraedrich
  1994 The implications of job matching for retirement health insurance and leave benefits. *Applied Economics* 26:425-435.
Beller, D.J., and H.H. Lawrence
  1992 Trends in private pension plan coverage. Pp. 59-96 in J.A. Turner and D.J. Beller, eds., *Trends in Pensions 1992.* Washington, D.C.: U.S. Department of Labor, Pension and Welfare Benefits Administration.
Berkovec, J.C., and S. Stern
  1991 Job exit behavior of older men. *Econometrica* 59(1):189-210.
Bernheim, B.D.
  1989 The timing of retirement: A comparison of expectations and realizations. Pp. 335-355 in D.A. Wise, ed., *The Economics of Aging.* Chicago, Ill.: University of Chicago Press.
  1994 Do Households Appreciate Their Financial Vulnerabilities? An Analysis of Actions, Perceptions, and Public Policy. Unpublished manuscript. Department of Economics, Stanford University.
Bernheim, B.D., and L. Levin
  1989 Social Security and personal saving: An analysis of expectations. *AEA Papers and Proceedings* 79(2):97-102.

Blank, R.M.
    1994   *The Dynamics of Part-Time Work.* NBER Working Paper #4911. Cambridge, Mass.:
           National Bureau of Economic Research.
Bondar, J.
    1993   Beneficiaries affected by the annual earnings test, 1989. *Social Security Bulletin* 56(1):20-
           28.
Bound, J.
    1989   The health and savings of rejected disability insurance applicants. *American Economic
           Review* 79:482-503.
Bound, J., and T. Waidmann
    1992   Disability transfers, self-reported health and the labor force attachment of older men:
           Evidence from the historical record. *Quarterly Journal of Economics* 107:1393-1419.
Bureau of the Census
    1992   *Statistical Abstract of the United States: 1992.* Washington, D.C.: U.S. Department of
           Commerce.
Burkhauser, R.V., J.S. Butler, Y.W. Kim, and G.A. Slotsve
    1992   *Modeling Application for Disability Insurance as a Retirement Decision: A Hazard
           Model Approach Using Choice-Based Sampling.* Policy Series Paper No. 3. Syracuse,
           N.Y.: The Maxwell School of Citizenship and Public Affairs, Syracuse University.
Burtless, G.
    1989   Comment. Pp. 398-403 in D.A. Wise, ed., *The Economics of Aging.* Chicago, Ill.:
           University of Chicago Press.
Burtless, G., and R.A. Moffitt
    1984   The effect of Social Security benefits on the labor supply of the aged. Pp. 135-174 in H.J.
           Aaron and G. Burtless, eds., *Retirement and Economic Behavior.* Washington, D.C.:
           Brookings Institution.
    1985   The joint choice of retirement age and postretirement hours of work. *Journal of Labor
           Economics* 3(2):209-236.
Clark, R.L., S.F. Gohmann, and A.A. McDermed
    1988   Declining Use of Defined Benefit Pension Plans: Is Federal Regulation the Reason?
           Unpublished manuscript. Department of Economics and Business, North Carolina State
           University, Raleigh.
Commerce Clearing House, Inc.
    1993   *1993 Medicare Explained.* Chicago, Ill.: Commerce Clearing House, Inc.
Congressional Budget Office
    1993   *Baby Boomers in Retirement: An Early Perspective.* Washington, D.C.: U.S. Govern-
           ment Printing Office.
Daula, T.V., and R.A. Moffitt
    1991   Estimating a dynamic programming model of army reenlistment behavior. Pp. 181-201
           in C.L. Gilroy, D.K. Horne, and D.A. Smith, eds., *Military Compensation and Personnel
           Retention: Models and Evidence.* Alexandria, Va.: U.S. Army Research Institute for the
           Behavioral and Social Sciences.
Day, C.L.
    1993   Public opinion toward costs and benefits of Social Security and Medicare. *Research on
           Aging* 15(3):279-298.
Employee Benefit Plan Review
    1994a March, 36-49.
    1994b June, 44-59.
Even, W.E., and D.A. Macpherson
    1994   Gender differences in pensions. *Journal of Human Resources* 29(2):555-587.

Feldstein, M., and A. Samwick
  1992   *Social Security Rules and Marginal Tax Rates.* NBER Working Paper #3962. Cambridge, Mass.: National Bureau of Economic Research.
Ferber, M.A.
  1993   Women's employment and the Social Security system. *Social Security Bulletin* 56(3):33-55.
Fields, G.S., and O.S. Mitchell
  1984   *Retirement, Pensions and Social Security.* Cambridge, Mass.: MIT Press.
Gordon, R., and A. Blinder
  1980   Market wages, reservation wages, and retirement decisions. *Journal of Public Economics* 14(2):277-308.
Grad, S.
  1994   *Income of the Population 55 or Older, 1992.* Washington, D.C.: U.S. Department of Health and Human Services, Social Security Administration.
Gruber, J., and B.C. Madrian
  1993a *Health Insurance and Early Retirement: Evidence From the Availability of Continuation Coverage.* NBER Working Paper #4594. Cambridge, Mass.: National Bureau of Economic Research.
  1993b *Health Insurance Availability and the Retirement Decision.* NBER Working Paper #4469. Cambridge, Mass.: National Bureau of Economic Research.
Gustman, A.L., O.S. Mitchell, and T.L. Steinmeier
  1994   *Retirement Research Using the Health and Retirement Survey.* NBER Working Paper #4813. Cambridge, Mass.: National Bureau of Economic Research.
Gustman, A.L., and T.L. Steinmeier
  1986   A structural retirement model. *Econometrica* 54(3):555-584.
  1991   Changing the Social Security rules for work after 65. *Industrial and Labor Relations Review* 44(4):733-745.
  1993a *Employer Provided Health Insurance and Retirement Behavior.* NBER Working Paper #4307. Cambridge, Mass.: National Bureau of Economic Research.
  1993b Pension portability and labor mobility: Evidence from the survey of income and program participation. *Journal of Public Economics* 50:299-323.
Hambor, J.C.
  1992   *The Role of Economic Factors in the Decline of the DI Trust Fund.* Washington, D.C.: U.S. Department of the Treasury.
Hardy, M.A.
  1991   Employment after retirement: Who gets back in? *Research on Aging* 13(3):267-288.
Haveman, R., P. DeJong, and B.L. Wolfe
  1991   Disability transfers and the work decision of older men. *Quarterly Journal of Economics* 106:939-949.
Haveman, R., and B.L. Wolfe
  1984   The decline in male labor force participation: Comment. *Journal of Political Economy* 92(3):532-541.
  1989   The economic well-being of the disabled: 1962-1984. *Journal of Human Resources* 25(1):32-54.
Hayward, M.D., M.A. Hardy, and M. Chiang
  1990   Work After Retirement: The Experiences of Older Men in the U.S. Unpublished manuscript. Department of Sociology and Population Research Institute, The Penn State University.
Hewitt Associates
  1990   *Salaried Employee Benefits Provided by Major U.S. Employers in 1990.* Lincolnshire, Ill.: Hewitt Associates.

Hill, M.S., B.J. Soldo, and W. Li
   1993   *Intergenerational Transfers and Labor Supply: Preliminary Evidence From the HRS.*
          Health and Retirement Survey working paper series, #94-009. Ann Arbor, Mich.: Insti-
          tute for Social Research, University of Michigan.
Holtz-Eakin, D., J.R. Penrod, and H.S. Rosen
   1994   *Health Insurance and the Supply of Entrepreneurs.* NBER Working Paper #4880. Cam-
          bridge, Mass.: National Bureau of Economic Research.
Honig, M., and C. Reimers
   1989   Is it worth eliminating the retirement test? *American Economic Review* 79(2):103-107.
Hurd, M.
   1993   *The Effect of Labor Market Rigidities on the Labor Force Behavior of Older Workers.*
          NBER Working Paper #4462. Cambridge, Mass.: National Bureau of Economic Re-
          search.
   1994a The economic status of the elderly in the United States. Pp. 63-83 in D. Wise, ed., *Aging
          in the United States and Japan: Economic Trends.* Chicago, Ill.: University of Chicago
          Press.
   1994b The Effects of Demographic Trends on Consumption, Saving and Government Expendi-
          tures in the U.S. Unpublished manuscript. Department of Economics, The State Univer-
          sity of New York.
Hurd, M., and K. McGarry
   1993a *Evaluation of Subjective Probability Distributions in the HRS.* NBER Working Paper
          #4560. Cambridge, Mass.: National Bureau of Economic Research.
   1993b *The Relationship Between Job Characteristics and Retirement.* NBER Working Paper
          #4558. Cambridge, Mass.: National Bureau of Economic Research.
Ippolito, R.
   1985   The labor contract and true economic pension liabilities. *American Economic Review*
          75(5):1031-1043.
Juster, F.T., and J.P. Smith
   1994   Improving the Quality of Economic Data: Lessons From the HRS. Unpublished manu-
          script. Institute for Social Research, University of Michigan.
Karoly, L.A., and J.A. Rogowski
   1994   The effects of health insurance on the decision to retire. *Industrial and Labor Relations
          Review* 48(1):103-123.
Kasper, J.D.
   1988   *Aging Alone: Profiles and Projections.* Baltimore, Md.: The Commonwealth Fund
          Commission on Elderly People Living Alone.
Keane, M.P., and K.I. Wolpin
   1994   *The Solution and Estimation of Discrete Choice Dynamic Programming Models by Simu-
          lation and Interpolation: Monte Carlo Evidence.* Staff report 181. Minneapolis, Minn.:
          Federal Reserve Bank of Minneapolis.
Kingson, E.
   1992   *The Diversity of the Baby Boom Generation: Implications for Their Retirement Years.*
          Washington, D.C.: American Association of Retired Persons.
Klerman, J.A.
   1992   How Long Is a Spell Without Health Insurance? Unpublished manuscript. The RAND
          Corporation, Santa Monica, Calif..
Korczyk, S.M.
   1992   Gender and pension coverage. Pp. 119-133 in J.A. Turner and D.J. Beller, eds., *Trends in
          Pensions 1992.* Washington, D.C.: U.S. Department of Labor, Pension and Welfare
          Benefits Administration.

Kotlikoff, L.J., and D.A. Wise
    1985   Labor compensation and the structure of private pension plans: Evidence for contractual vs. spot labor markets. Pp. 55-85 in D.A. Wise, ed., *Pensions, Labor, and Individual Choice*. Chicago, Ill.: University of Chicago Press.
    1987   The incentive effects of private pension plans. Pp. 283-336 in Z. Bodie, J.B. Shoven, and D.A. Wise, eds., *Issues in Pension Economics*. Chicago, Ill.: University of Chicago Press.

Lazear, E.P.
    1979   Why is there mandatory retirement? *Journal of Political Economy* 87(6):1261-1284.

Lazear, E.P., and R.L. Moore
    1988   Pensions and turnover. Pp. 163-188 in Z. Bodie, J.B. Shoven, and D.A. Wise, eds., *Pensions in the U.S. Economy*. Chicago, Ill.: University of Chicago Press.

Leonesio, M.V.
    1990   The effects of the Social Security earnings test on the labor-market activity of older Americans: A review of the evidence. *Social Security Bulletin* 53(5):2-21.
    1993a Social Security and older workers. *Social Security Bulletin* 56(2):47-57.
    1993b Social Security and older workers. Pp. 183-204 in O. Mitchell, ed., *As the Workforce Ages*. Ithaca, N.Y.: ILR Press.

Lewin-VHI
    1994   *Labor Market Conditions, Socioeconomic Factors and the Growth of Applications and Awards for SSDI and SSI Disability Benefits*. Fairfax, Va.: Lewin-VHI.

Lingg, B.A.
    1990   Women beneficiaries aged 62 or older, 1960-1988. *Social Security Bulletin* 53(7):4.

Lucas, R.E., Jr.
    1981   *Studies in Business Cycle Theory*. Cambridge, Mass.: MIT Press.

Lumsdaine, R., J. Stock, and D.A. Wise
    1990   Efficient windows and labor force reduction. *Journal of Public Economics* 43:131-159.
    1991   Windows and retirement. *Annales d'Économie et de Statistique* 20/21:219-242.
    1992   Three models of retirement: Computational complexity versus predictive validity. Pp. 19-57 in D. Wise, ed., *Topics in the Economics of Aging*. Chicago, Ill.: University of Chicago Press.
    1994   Pension plan provisions and retirement: Men and women, Medicare and models. Pp. 183-212 in D. Wise, ed., *Studies in the Economics of Aging*. Chicago, Ill.: University of Chicago Press.
    1996a Retirement incentives: The interaction between employer-provided pensions, Social Security, and retiree health benefits. In M. Hurd and N. Yashiro, eds., *The Economics of Aging in the United States and Japan*. Chicago, Ill.: University of Chicago Press.
    1996b Why are retirement rates so high at age 65? In D. Wise, ed., *Advances in the Economics of Aging*. Chicago, Ill.: University of Chicago Press.

Lumsdaine, R., and D.A. Wise
    1994   Aging and labor force participation: A review of trends and explanations. Pp. 7-41 in D. Wise, ed., *Aging in the United States and Japan: Economic Trends*. Chicago, Ill.: University of Chicago Press.

Luzadis, R.A., and O.S. Mitchell
    1990   Explaining pension dynamics. *Journal of Human Resources* 26(4):679-703.

Macpherson, D.A.
    1992   Employer-provided retiree health insurance: Who is covered? *Economics Letters* 39:95-99.

Madrian, B.C.
    1993   Post-Retirement Health Insurance and the Decision to Retire. Unpublished manuscript. Graduate School of Business, University of Chicago.

Marks, L.H., and R.G. Seefer
  1992   Afterword: Looking toward the future. Comment. Pp. 53-58 in *The Diversity of the Baby Boom Generation: Implications for Their Retirement Years*. Washington, D.C.: American Association of Retired Persons.
Mehdizadeh, S.A., and R.A. Luzadis
  1994   The effect of job mobility on pension wealth. *The Gerontologist* 34(2):173-179.
Mitchell, O.S.
  1991   Social Security reforms and poverty among older dual-earner couples. *Journal of Population Economics* 4:281-293.
  1992   Trends in pension benefit formulas and retirement provisions. Pp. 177-216 in J.A. Turner and D.J. Beller, eds., *Trends in Pensions 1992*. Washington, D.C.: U.S. Department of Labor, Pension and Welfare Benefits Administration.
Parnes, H.S., and D.G. Sommers
  1994   Shunning retirement: Work experience of men in their seventies and early eighties. *Journal of Gerontology* 49(3):S117-S124.
Parsons, D.O.
  1980   The decline in male labor force participation. *Journal of Political Economy* 88(1):117-134.
  1984   Disability insurance and male labor force participation: A response to Haveman and Wolfe. *Journal of Political Economy* 92(3):542-549.
  1991a The decline in private pension coverage in the United States. *Economics Letters* 36:419-423.
  1991b The health and earnings of rejected disability insurance applicants: Comment. *American Economic Review* 81:1419-1426.
  1991c Self-screening in targeted public transfer programs. *Journal of Political Economy* 99(4):859-876.
Pavalko, E.K., G.H. Elder, Jr., and E.C. Clipp
  1993   Worklives and longevity: Insights from a life course perspective. *Journal of Health and Social Behavior* 34:363-380.
Peracchi, F., and F. Welch
  1994   Trends in labor force transitions of older men and women. *Journal of Labor Economics* 12(2):210-242.
Pienta, A.M., J.A. Burr, and J.E. Mutchler
  1993   Women's Labor Force Participation in Later Life: The Effects of Early Work and Family Experiences. Unpublished manuscript. Department of Sociology, The State University of New York, Buffalo.
Pozzebon, S., and O.S. Mitchell
  1989   Married women's retirement behavior. *Journal of Population Economics* 2:39-53.
Quadagno, J.S., and M. Hardy
  1991   Regulating retirement through the Age Discrimination in Employment Act. *Research on Aging* 13(4):470-475.
Quinn, J.F., and R.V. Burkhauser
  1992   Retirement and the Labor Force Behavior of the Elderly. Unpublished manuscript. Department of Economics, Boston College.
Quinn, J.F., R.V. Burkhauser, and D.A. Myers
  1990   *Passing the Torch: The Influence of Financial Incentives on Work and Retirement*. Kalamazoo, Mich.: W.E. Upjohn Institute for Employment Research.
Radner, D.B.
  1993a An assessment of the economics status of the aged. In *Studies in Income Distribution, No. 16*. Washington, D.C.: U.S. Department of Health and Human Services.

1993b Economic well-being of the old old: Family unit income and household wealth. *Social Security Bulletin* 56(1):3-19.

Reimers, C., and M. Honig
1992 Labor Supply Differences Between Older Men and Women: Evidence From Re-entry Behavior. Unpublished manuscript. Graduate School, The City University of New York.
1993 The perceived budget constraint under Social Security: Evidence from reentry behavior. *Journal of Labor Economics* 11(1)Part 1:184-204.

Reno, V.P.
1993 The role of pensions in retirement income: Trends and questions. *Social Security Bulletin* 56(1):29-43.

Ruhm, C.J.
1990 Bridge jobs and partial retirement. *Journal of Labor Economics* 8(4):482-501.
1994 *Do Pensions Increase the Labor Supply of Older Men?* NBER Working Paper #4925. Cambridge, Mass.: National Bureau of Economic Research.

Rust, J.
1989 A dynamic programming model of retirement behavior. Pp. 359-398 in D.A. Wise, ed., *The Economics of Aging.* Chicago, Ill.: University of Chicago Press.
1994 Comment. Pp. 213-220 in D. Wise, ed., *Studies in the Economics of Aging.* Chicago, Ill.: University of Chicago Press.

Rust, J., and C. Phelan
1993 How Social Security and Medicare Affect Retirement Behavior in a World of Incomplete Markets. Unpublished manuscript. Department of Economics, University of Wisconsin.

Samwick, A.A.
1994 The Joint Effect of Social Security and Pensions on the Timing of Retirement: Some New Evidence. Unpublished manuscript. Department of Economics, Dartmouth College.

Scott, F.A., M.C. Berger, and J.E. Garen
1992 Do Health Insurance Costs and Non-Discrimination Policies Reduce the Job Opportunities of Older Workers? Unpublished manuscript. Department of Economics, University of Kentucky.

Smith, J.P.
1994 Comment. Pp. 220-222 in D. Wise, ed., *Studies in the Economics of Aging.* Chicago, Ill.: University of Chicago Press.

Stern, S.
1988 Measuring the effect of disability on labor force participation. *Journal of Human Resources* 24(3):361-395.

Stewart, J.
1995 Do Older Workers Respond to Changes in Social Security Benefits? A Look at the Time Series Evidence. Unpublished manuscript. Bureau of Labor Statistics, U.S. Department of Labor.

Stock, J.H., and D.A. Wise
1990a The pension inducement to retire: An option value analysis. Pp. 205-224 in D.A. Wise, ed., *Issues in the Economics of Aging.* Chicago, Ill.: University of Chicago Press.
1990b Pensions, the option value of work, and retirement. *Econometrica* 58(5):1151-1180.

U.S. Department of Labor
1992 *Employee Benefits in a Changing Economy: A BLS Chartbook.* Washington, D.C.: U.S. Department of Labor.
1994 *Pension Coverage Issues for the '90s.* Washington, D.C.: U.S. Department of Labor.

U.S. General Accounting Office
1989 *Private Pensions: Plan Provisions Differ Between Large and Small Employers.* GAO/HRD-89-105BR. Washington, D.C.: U.S. Government Printing Office.

1990   Equity Issues in a Changing Retirement System. Presentation at the Boston Geronto-
        logical Society of America Annual Meetings.
U.S. National Center for Health Statistics
1990   *Vital Statistics of the United States, 1990.* Hyattsville, Md.: U.S. Department of Health
        and Human Services.
Venti, S.F., and D.A. Wise
1992   Government policy and personal retirement saving. Pp. 1-41 in J.M. Poterba, ed., *Tax
        Policy and the Economy 6.* Cambridge, Mass.: MIT Press.
Viscusi, W.K.
1985   The structure of uncertainty and the use of nontransferable pensions as a mobility-reduc-
        tion device. Pp. 223-248 in D. Wise, ed., *Pensions, Labor, and Individual Choice.* Chi-
        cago, Ill.: University of Chicago Press.
Waidmann, T., J. Bound, and M. Schoenbaum
1995   *The Illusion of Failure: Trends in the Self-Reported Health of the U.S. Elderly.* NBER
        Working Paper #5017. Cambridge, Mass.: National Bureau of Economic Research.
Weaver, D.A.
1994   The work and retirement decisions of older women: A literature review. *Social Security
        Bulletin* 57(1):3-24.
Woods, J.R.
1993   Pension vesting and preretirement lump sums among full-time private sector employees.
        Social Security Bulletin 56(3):3-21.

4

Personal Saving Behavior and Retirement Income Modeling: A Research Assessment

James M. Poterba

Two of the central tasks in the design of retirement income policy are forecasting the future financial status of elderly households under the present system of government policies and estimating the likely effects of changes in such policies. Both of these tasks depend critically on the assumptions maintained about the determinants of personal saving, subjects of perennial controversy in both theoretical and empirical economics.

This background paper identifies several aspects of personal saving behavior that bear on projecting the future financial status of elderly households, with a particular focus on the effects of Social Security, pensions, and other government policies that affect personal saving. This paper does not attempt to follow Kotlikoff (1984), Hurd (1990a), or the Organization for Economic Cooperation and Development (1994) in presenting a systematic survey of existing research on saving behavior. Rather, it explores why it has been difficult to achieve a research consensus on a number of important aspects of personal saving behavior and how future study and data collection can contribute to developing such a consensus.

The paper is divided into seven sections. The first two are concerned with forecasting future financial status assuming the continuation of current government policies. The first section sketches a simple accounting framework for

I am grateful to Peter Diamond, William Gale, Michael Hurd, Lawrence Thompson, and members of the panel for helpful comments, and to the National Institute on Aging, the National Science Foundation, and the Center for Advanced Study in the Behavioral Sciences for research support.

assessing the financial status of households at various future dates. It also presents a brief overview of the financial status of households currently reaching retirement age in the United States, including the assets these households own and the typical level of such holdings. The subsequent section discusses three prominent models of saving behavior, the life-cycle model, the "precautionary saving" model, and the bequest model, and examines the degree to which each model appears to be supported by available data. It also considers the central implications of each model for predicting future financial status.

The next three sections are concerned with the effect of various policies on personal saving behavior. The third section discusses the interaction between Social Security and private saving, reporting on time series as well as cross-sectional studies of the Social Security offset. The fourth section presents a parallel discussion focusing on private pensions and other personal saving. The fifth section explores the recent increase in the popularity of targeted retirement saving vehicles, such as Individual Retirement Accounts (IRAs) and 401(k) plans, and how they are likely to affect the future financial status of the elderly.

The sixth section examines one form of wealth accumulation that is particularly widespread: housing wealth accumulation. It considers patterns of home equity accumulation, the role of housing wealth in financing retirement income needs, and the existing body of research on housing decisions of elderly households. A brief concluding section outlines a number of unresolved research questions. It also describes how some of these questions may be addressed using available data sets and notes why others may be difficult to resolve even with additional data.

FORECASTING FINANCIAL STATUS: AN ORGANIZING FRAMEWORK

If the average wealth in 1994 of individuals born in year a is $W_{a,1994}$, then the average wealth of individuals in this cohort in year $t > 1994$ can be forecast by

$$W_{a,t} = W_{a,1994} * (1+r)^{t-1994} + \sum_{j=0}^{t-1994} S_{a,t-j} * (1+r)^j$$

where $S_{a,k}$ is the forecast net saving in a year k by those born in year a, $k > 1994$, and r is the projected annual after-tax rate of return on savings. Because cohort averages conceal important differences in the wealth positions of households in a given cohort, and because retirement income policy is often concerned with the financial status of the least well-off groups in the population, a forecasting equation similar to the one above can be applied separately to different segments of a given cohort. Bernheim and Scholz (1993) follow such a strategy in separately forecasting wealth at retirement for those with college degrees, some college, and only high school education. Hurd (1992) describes a number of the more sophisticated microsimulation models that have been used to forecast retirement income and also raises a number of other important issues that occur in actual forecasting contexts, such as the treatment of married versus single individuals and the modeling of programs such as Medicare and Medicaid that may alter private consumption expenditures.

There are three important inputs to the simple forecasting equation presented above: the current wealth holdings of various cohorts, the prospective rate of return on different assets, and the age-specific pattern of net saving rates. Each of these inputs will be discussed in turn.

Patterns of Wealth Holding for Pre-Retirement Cohorts

The starting point for any projection of a cohort's future wealth holding is an estimate of its *current* wealth. For the majority of households over most of their lifetimes, financial asset holdings are relatively small. Principal assets are home equity, the present discounted value of employer-provided pension benefits, and net Social Security wealth. Each of these wealth components is subject to substantial measurement error.

For financial assets, there are substantial rates of nonresponse in most surveys, and these problems are most severe among households with higher wealth levels. Juster and Smith (1994) discuss such problems of nonresponse and possible ways of improving survey performance when collecting asset information. Reconciling estimates of total wealth stocks from households surveys and aggregate data sources, such as the Flow of Funds, has also proven difficult with many existing data sets.

For pension wealth, the data problem is not measurement error but the rarity of detailed data. Only a few surveys, such as the Survey of Consumer Finances Pension Provider Survey and the Health and Retirement Survey (HRS), provide sufficiently detailed information about the structure of employer-provided defined benefit pension plans and the employee's work history to permit accurate estimates of the present discounted value of pension wealth. Given the complexity of most defined benefit pension plans, another important issue is whether individuals understand the structure of their pension plan and its associated incentives.

Some of the same problems arise in estimating Social Security wealth, but they are less severe because the current benefit formulas that apply to individuals are known, and an estimate of future benefits can be made given information on an individual's earnings history. The HRS in particular will provide Social Security earnings histories for many respondents, and this will make it possible to compute precise estimates of prospective Social Security benefits.

To illustrate the current level of wealth holding and the relative importance of different assets in household portfolios, Table 4-1 summarizes the asset holdings of households that included individuals between the ages of 55 and 64, and between 65 and 69, in 1991. Mean and median asset holdings differ substantially

TABLE 4-1   Mean and Median Wealth Holdings, 1991, in Thousands of
Dollars

Wealth Holdings by Age and Type of Asset	Mean	Median
Household heads age 65-69		
Total financial assets	$52.9	$14.0
Targeted retirement assets	10.9	0.0
Other financial assets	42.0	7.4
Home equity	65.0	50.0
Equity in other property	33.9	6.0
Employer-provided pensions	62.3	16.0
Social Security wealth	99.7	99.2
Net worth	312.3	261.4
Net worth excluding pension and	150.3	96.6
Social Security wealth		
Household heads age 55-64		
Total financial assets	$42.0	$8.3
Targeted retirement assets	12.9	0.0
Other financial assets	29.1	3.0
Home equity	57.8	36.0
Equity in other property	44.3	8.2
Net worth excluding pension and	140.5	74.9
Social Security wealth		

SOURCE: Poterba, Venti, and Wise (1994a). Tabulations are based on the Survey of Income and
Program Participation, Wave 4, 1990 Panel. Sample size is 2,799 for the 55-to-64 age group and
1,525 for the 65-to-69 age group.

in both age groups, reflecting the concentration of financial assets among a small
group of households. For those approaching retirement age, the 55-to-64 age
group, home equity is the single largest asset category that can be evaluated;
neither pension wealth nor Social Security wealth can be estimated with any
precision for this pre-retirement group. Mean (median) holdings of all financial
assets for 55- to 64-year-olds total $42,000 ($8,300), with $12,900 (0) of this
amount in targeted retirement saving accounts such as IRAs and 401(k)s.

The Table 4-1 entries for 65- to 69-year-olds include information on the
present value of both publicly provided and private pensions. These data show
that Social Security wealth is the single most important asset for households in
this age group. The mean value of employer-provided pensions is comparable to
the mean value of home equity, but the median for private pensions is much
lower, reflecting the fact that more households own homes than are covered by
private pensions. Targeted saving accounts are less important for this group than
for the 55- to 64-year-olds, in part because they may have been cashed out and in
part because this cohort was eligible to accumulate funds in these accounts for a

shorter part of their working life than the younger cohort. A conclusion not illustrated in Table 4-1 comes from Auerbach, Kotlikoff, and Weil (1992), who suggest that one important pattern in the postwar period has been the increasing importance of annuitized wealth in the portfolios of elderly Americans. Except for households at the top of the income and wealth distribution, annuitized wealth, which includes private pension wealth and Social Security wealth, has become a much greater fraction of the household portfolio in the last three decades.

One of the central statistical patterns illustrated in Table 4-1 is the relatively low level of liquid assets held by the majority of households reaching retirement age. This finding may in part reflect the use of data from the Survey of Income and Program Participation (SIPP). The SIPP tends to yield lower estimates of mean wealth than other data sets, as a result of low response rates among high-income households. This problem should not substantially affect estimated medians, however, and more generally, the SIPP patterns of low wealth holdings at advanced ages are confirmed in other data sets.

Only a small fraction of households reaching retirement age have accumulated assets worth more than twice their pre-retirement annual income. The prevalence of households that save very little for retirement is an important consideration in evaluating how various policy interventions may affect the private saving rate. The current asset accumulation profiles of many households provide very limited opportunities to reduce financial wealth in response to initiatives that encourage new forms of wealth accumulation. The wide disparity in patterns of wealth accumulation also suggests the value of analyzing how potential policy shifts affect both those who currently accumulate substantial levels of financial assets in preparation for retirement and those who do not.

Why so many households save so little for retirement is an unresolved issue. Some households may be myopic and fail to accumulate assets because they do not recognize the value of providing for their future. Some may be unlucky and experience lower earnings or higher expenses than they expected before reaching retirement. Others may have high discount rates and therefore choose to consume a high fraction of income while working at the expense of lower consumption when retired. Still others may have incorrect expectations about their retirement income from Social Security, private pensions, and other sources, or about life expectancy and post-retirement consumption needs. Further work on the relative importance of these and other explanations would be helpful in guiding public policies that are designed to influence private saving behavior.

Rates of Return

A second critical input to the forecasting model, and one that is particularly important for forecasting the future wealth of those individuals who actually accumulate assets on their own account, is the long-term average rate of return on these assets. This involves two distinct issues: which assets are individuals likely to invest in, and what rates of returns are different types of assets likely to deliver?

There is some evidence suggesting that individuals are very conservative in their portfolio choices. In spite of the well-documented superior performance of equities relative to fixed-income investments over long time horizons, data from the 1989 Survey of Consumer Finances show only 28 percent of households with heads aged 45 to 54 hold any corporate stock either directly or through a stock mutual fund. A similar pattern emerges with respect to investment of self-directed retirement assets. VanDerhei's (1992) analysis of 1989 Form 5500 filings shows that common stock accounts for 21 percent of the asset value in 401(k) plan accounts, while insurance company products such as Guaranteed Investment Contracts account for 41 percent of value. These investment patterns are important because the increasing importance of self-directed defined contribution pension plans makes financial status at retirement substantially dependent on individual investment decisions. In spite of this, the determinants of household portfolio composition are neglected in research on wealth accumulation.

A related issue, and one that is largely beyond this paper, concerns the expected rate of return on different types of assets. The usual approach to projecting returns assumes that historical patterns of returns will persist into the future. A number of recent studies, however, have questioned this assumption. Schieber and Shoven (1994) argue that the coincident aging of the populations in most developed economies will raise the demand for assets in the short run and lower it several decades hence, thereby depressing rates of return on bonds and stocks over the financial planning horizon of the baby boom generation. This argument depends critically on the degree of integration of world capital markets and the absence of rapid growth in asset demand from currently less developed nations. Others, including Blanchard (1993) and Siegel (1994), argue that the prospective excess return of stocks over bonds is smaller than its historical value for a variety of reasons related to the financial market conditions of the last half century as well as to prospective conditions. Evaluating these arguments is an important part of long-term financial status forecasting.

Age-Specific Patterns of Net Saving

The third component of the forecasting equation is projection of the net saving behavior of households as they age. This projection involves several parts, such as the rate of saving out of earnings during the years when the household is working, the date of retirement and associated decline in earnings, and the rate at which the household decumulates or accumulates assets after retirement.

Pre-retirement saving behavior is central for predicting the wealth that households will have when they retire, and this will be discussed in the next section. The rising number of years that households spend in retirement and the substantially greater incidence of poverty and other measures of financial hardship among the oldest old, however, have drawn increased attention to the financial behavior of retired households. The question of whether retired households decumulate assets has been a subject of substantial empirical controversy. The first generation of research on this question, illustrated by Mirer (1979), suggested positive saving rates for retired households. A second wave of research, incorporating more careful definitions of saving and cohort rather than cross-sectional data on saving behavior, has found evidence of decumulation after retirement. Studies in this spirit include Bernheim (1987a), Hurd (1987, 1990b), and Attanasio (1992). Tests of whether households dissave after retirement have featured prominently in discussions of the life-cycle hypothesis. For forecasting the future retirement status of the elderly, however, the knife-edge question of whether retirees decumulate is less important than the rate at which accumulation or decumulation takes place.

Forecasting the future saving behavior of currently young cohorts is complicated by the need to separate age and cohort effects in observed saving patterns. Will today's 45-year-old save as much as today's 55-year-old when he or she reaches age 55, or will the *change* in this person's saving over the next 10 years be the same as the *change* in saving between ages 45 and 55 was for the currently 55-year-old, or will neither of these modeling assumptions suffice? A number of studies, including Shorrocks (1975) and Attanasio (1993), have shown that the age-saving pattern for a *cohort* can be very different from the cross-sectional age-saving pattern. This suggests the need for cohort data for studying saving and also indicates the potential value of a formal model of household behavior for predicting the financial status of future elderly households.

The difficulty of extrapolating age-specific saving rates across cohorts is illustrated in the Bosworth, Burtless, and Sabelhaus (1991) comparison of personal saving behavior in the 1960s and 1980s. This study shows that most age-specific saving rates fell between the early 1960s and late 1980s. Falling age-specific saving rates and shifting demographics have significantly affected the overall personal saving rate in the United States, which declined from an average of 6.7 percent of disposable income in the 1960s and 7.8 percent in the 1970s to 6.5 percent in the 1980s and only 4.5 percent in the 1990-1993 period. Explaining this decline represents one of the most important challenges to research on personal saving, and one important test of the potential value of a predictive model should be whether it would have tracked this decline. Explaining the decline in age-specific saving rates is also a priority research topic because information on the source of this decline will prove valuable in trying to project the future course of saving rates.

The simple wealth-forecasting equation at the beginning of this section illustrates the wide range of ways in which personal saving may respond to a change in government policy. For example, a reduction in the accruing value of Social Security benefits for an individual in cohort a at time t could lead to a change in contemporaneous saving ($S_{a,t}$), to a change in one or many *future* saving decisions ($S_{a,t+j}$), and potentially to changes in rates of return if individuals alter their investment behavior or if there are general equilibrium effects associated with the policy reform.

MOTIVES FOR AND MODELS OF PRIVATE SAVING: WHAT DO WE KNOW?

Projecting the future age-specific saving rates of cohorts that are currently not retired requires an economic model of saving decisions. Simple models of saving behavior, which yield strong predictions about the age-specific structure of saving rates, tend to be rejected by the data. More complex models are highly dependent upon parameter choices and yield results that are not conducive to simple presentation.

For the last four decades, the life-cycle/permanent income hypothesis has been the dominant economic model for analyzing saving behavior. The central insight of this model is that individuals save during periods when labor income is high to avoid reductions in consumption when labor income is low. In its simplest form, without uncertainty, bequests, or distinctions between different types of assets, this model yields strong predictions about the age-specific pattern of saving and the link between saving rates and employment. For some simple parameterizations of household utility functions, it is possible to characterize the shape of the lifetime consumption profile, as in Summers (1981). Given estimates of a household's future income path, calculating the optimal, and hence predicted, level of saving in each year until retirement is a straightforward procedure.

Researchers have used the stark predictions of the simple life-cycle hypothesis as "straw men" to motivate various empirical research projects on individual and aggregate consumption behavior. Existing household-level data provide very limited support for these predictions. As was noted in the last section, many households reach retirement age with virtually no financial assets, and there is substantial controversy as to whether or not households decumulate assets after retirement. These findings are not particular to the United States; data from six country studies in Poterba (1994) suggest that decumulation of household financial assets after retirement is the exception, rather than the rule, in developed nations. In addition, many individuals leave bequests, a finding that is difficult to reconcile with simple versions of the life-cycle model.

The simple life-cycle model also appears incapable of explaining a variety of stylized facts about aggregate consumption fluctuations. Carroll (1992) outlines the difficulties: the strong positive correlation between aggregate consumption growth and income growth, the apparent link between consumption fluctuations and forecastable changes in income, and sketchy evidence suggesting a link between measures of income uncertainty and the level of consumption spending. Some recent studies such as Attanasio and Weber (1995) suggest that the statistical failures of the lifecycle hypothesis may be due to data aggregation. A larger set of studies, however, have accepted the failures, and tried to develop more complex theoretical models that could explain the findings. Recent research has emphasized the role of uncertainty and potential capital market constraints in affecting household consumption choices. A number of studies, notably Hubbard, Skinner, and Zeldes (1994) and Carroll and Samwick (1993), have developed numerical algorithms for finding the optimal consumption rules of households facing different types of uncertainty and various constraints on consumption.

These models emphasize the existence of a precautionary motive for asset accumulation and suggest that the comparative statistics of saving behavior may be substantially different from the comparative statistics suggested by the life-cycle model. For example, if part of the stock of household wealth is accumulated to guard against future consumption downturns, wealth holdings may be relatively insensitive to changes in real rates of return. This may explain why empirical work on the intertemporal elasticity of substitution, such as Hall (1988), has suggested generally small effects of expected return fluctuations on the rate of consumption growth, even though simulations of life-cycle models with plausible parameter values suggest that much larger elasticities should be observed. Since expected return fluctuations as well as other exogenous shocks may have different effects on precautionary wealth and on wealth being held for retirement, recognizing precautionary motives for saving makes it more difficult to predict what should be observed in the data.

Models that incorporate precautionary motives for asset holding suggest that it may be appropriate to focus on several aspects of the economic environment and the saving process that the standard lifecycle model does not recognize as relevant. Precautionary saving models show that various aspects of the social safety net, such as the availability of unemployment insurance and disability insurance, the nature of health insurance, and other factors that influence the chance that a household will experience a prolonged period of low income relative to expenditure needs, have an important influence on asset accumulation decisions. The Hubbard, Skinner, and Zeldes (1994) computational model can be potentially used to assess how various policy changes affect pre-retirement saving. One of the general research needs on private saving is further exploration of expanded life-cycle models, with realistic parameterizations of uncertainty, to better understand the characteristics of optimal saving behavior in these models.

The precautionary saving model is not the only alternative to the life-cycle model. One strand of modeling concerns the role of bequest motives in explaining saving decisions. In the simplest life-cycle model, with a certain date of death and no altruistic links between generations, optimizing individuals would not leave bequests. Yet bequests are not only observed, but appear to account for a substantial share of the stock of household wealth; Kotlikoff (1988) and Modigliani (1988) disagree over the precise importance of bequest flows. Several explanations for bequests have been proposed. Andreoni (1989) considers the possibility that donors enjoy giving for its own sake; Barro (1974) focuses on intergenerational altruism; Bernheim, Shleifer, and Summers (1985) stress the potential role of bequeathable wealth in improving the lifestyle of elderly individuals. Another explanation for bequests is simply that with uncertainty about the date of death, some individuals will die unexpectedly, thereby leaving to their heirs assets that they had planned to consume. Because these explanations of bequest behavior are not mutually exclusive, it has proven difficult to design and implement tests of how bequest considerations affect saving decisions.

A third alternative to the standard life-cycle model, and one that has attracted substantial attention in the last decade, is the "behavioral approach to saving." Sheffrin and Thaler (1988; also Thaler, 1994) emphasize differences in the way households perceive different types of saving instruments and argue that different assets are held in distinct "mental accounts." A key implication of this view is that changes in the level of one asset may have relatively small substitution effects on holdings of other assets. This stands in contrast to the simple prediction of standard life-cycle models, in which different assets are perfect substitutes and total wealth at a given age is a summary statistic for the household's financial situation. Laibson (1994) presents a particularly intriguing justification for something like mental accounts by suggesting that consumers use hyperbolic rather than exponential discount factors to evaluate future events.

While the mental accounts model seems to resonate well with intuitions about how individuals save, there is little empirical evidence that directly supports this model. In part, this reflects the lack of a well-articulated model that can be estimated or tested with data. A natural avenue for further research lies in drawing out the implications of alternative models of saving behavior and exploring how these models would modify life-cycle-based predictions of pre-retirement saving behavior.

The possibility that individuals use rules of thumb or other simple heuristics in deciding how much to save is implicit in many behavioral discussions of personal saving. If such rules are relatively insensitive to prospective rates of return, then changes in such returns can have particularly large effects on the wealth of individuals at retirement. To illustrate this possibility, consider an individual who saves 5 percent of annual labor income each year between ages 35 and 65, regardless of the expected return on saving. If this person's real labor income is constant over this period, and the real rate of return is 3 percent per year, he or she will accumulate assets worth 2.43 times his or her annual labor income by age 65. If the annual rate of return is 6 percent, however, wealth at retirement will be 4.21 times annual labor income. Thus, if the *flow* of saving is insensitive to the expected return, the *stock* of wealth at retirement will be especially sensitive.

The mental accounts framework may be particularly relevant to the current debate on whether households in the baby boom generation are saving enough to provide for themselves in retirement. Bernheim (1993) argues that baby boomers are undersaving, and he bases this conclusion on an analysis of their projected nonhousing net worth at retirement. The Congressional Budget Office (1993) takes issue with this conclusion, pointing out that if housing wealth is included in net worth, then baby boomers are much closer to a wealth accumulation trajectory that will sustain pre-retirement levels of consumption after retirement. A key point of controversy between these studies involves the degree to which elderly households are prepared to decumulate net housing wealth during retirement. Bernheim (1993) implicitly assumes that elderly households are unable or unwilling to draw down their net housing equity to finance consumption during retirement, while the Congressional Budget Office, which focuses on net worth including housing assets, implicitly views housing wealth as fungible and equivalent to holdings of financial assets. Available evidence, discussed in greater detail below, suggests that the elderly may view housing as in a different mental account than other assets, and that they may be reluctant to downsize their homes or borrow against them to finance consumption needs.

SOCIAL SECURITY AND PRIVATE SAVING

Social Security is the government policy that most directly affects the financial status of elderly households. Benefit payments may not increase the financial status of the elderly by the full amount of the transfer, however, because households may anticipate such benefits and adjust their pre-retirement saving in response. The degree to which such offset occurs depends on many factors, including whether or not households correctly perceive the future value of their benefits, how retirement decisions are affected by Social Security, and whether individuals have operative bequest motives that link their utility to that of their children, who will be called upon to finance Social Security payouts. Although the net saving effect of the Social Security program is a first-order question for evaluating government policies toward retirement saving, the existing empirical literature in this area is weak and there is relatively limited prospect for improvement.

The first wave of empirical research on the Social Security offset question involved time series estimates of how aggregate consumption responded to changes in the value of aggregate Social Security wealth. Studies in this vein include Feldstein (1974, 1982), Barro (1978), Barro and MacDonald (1979), and Leimer and Lesnoy (1982). Aaron (1982) surveyed the then-extant literature, but the limited research since the early 1980s makes his survey still current. It is extremely difficult to disentangle the effects of Social Security wealth, a time series with a strong trend, from other trending variables and other shocks in a relatively short time series. Auerbach and Kotlikoff (1983) present simulation evidence showing that reduced form equations relating aggregate consumption to aggregate income, wealth, and Social Security wealth are extremely sensitive to specification changes and to other factors in the economic environment.

A separate strand of research has used household-level data to explore the degree of offset between Social Security wealth and other private wealth. Examples of studies in this tradition include Feldstein and Pellechio (1979), Blinder, Gordon, and Wise (1983), Hubbard (1986), and Bernheim (1987b). The point estimates of the degree of offset vary substantially across studies. More generally, this literature suffers from a difficult problem of identification. The cross-sectional variation in Social Security wealth stems largely from differences in lifetime income since benefit formulas are tied to an individual's earnings history. Since lifetime income may be correlated with an individual's saving propensity in a variety of ways, it is difficult to isolate the effect of Social Security wealth on the accumulation of non-Social Security wealth. Moreover, since all households of a given age face the same Social Security benefit schedule, it is not possible to compare otherwise identical households that face different benefits.

This identification problem can be addressed to some degree by using cohort-to-cohort variation in the structure of Social Security benefits, or by focusing on cross-sectional differences in benefits associated with the maximum and minimum benefit rules. Krueger and Pischke (1992) used the change in Social Security benefits for the "notch babies," currently-elderly individuals who received less generous Social Security benefits than those born only a few months earlier, to investigate the effects of Social Security benefits on retirement decisions. Their results suggest much smaller effects of the Social Security program on labor market decisions than do other studies with arguably less convincing identification strategies, and they raise questions about the findings on both labor supply and saving responses in earlier studies.

A central issue concerning Social Security and other private saving is the extent to which individuals are aware of the benefits they are eligible to receive and their degree of confidence in whether or not they will receive benefits. Many households in the baby boom generation have little confidence in the future of the Social Security system and do not expect to receive benefits. Bernheim (1994) presents survey evidence suggesting that those households with the *least* confidence in the future of the system exhibit the highest personal saving rates.

Heterogeneity in perceptions of expected benefits, unrelated to the actual structure of the Social Security system, raises a difficult problem for empirical research on Social Security wealth and its effect on private saving. There is no completely acceptable way for a researcher to calculate the expected present value of Social Security wealth for a household. Using current rules runs the risk of substantially mismeasuring the benefits that an individual is counting on when making saving decisions, while any alternative necessarily relies on difficult-to-justify assumptions about individual perceptions. Data from the HRS will permit some comparison of alternative measures, since the survey includes a question about Social Security benefit expectations, and for many respondents, data on Social Security earnings histories will also be available. Even with this detailed information on expected benefits, there remain difficult issues associated with discounting expected benefits. For example, should sex-specific and wealth-specific life tables be applied to the prospective benefit stream, or do individuals recognize that individual characteristics have significant effects on mortality rates?

Public perceptions of the Social Security system are related to a policy issue involving the imminent public information campaign to acquaint households with their prospective Social Security benefits. Bernheim (1994) argues that such information may discourage saving if households discover that the benefits they are slated to receive are larger than the benefits they expected. Little empirical evidence, however, is available to support or contradict this view.

A second important policy issue that is closely related to the Social Security offset issue concerns proposals for means-testing Social Security benefits. Such a plan would impose a tax burden on households that save for their retirement, and these higher taxes could discourage saving in pre-retirement years. Means-tested benefits would alter the rate of return to asset accumulation, just as means-tested scholarship programs alter the rate of return to households with pre-college-age children. Feldstein (1995) uses data from the Survey of Consumer Finances to suggest that households that face high educational tax rates tend to have lower levels of accumulated wealth than those with lower implicit tax rates. Edlin (1993) speculates that observing current behavior underestimates the potential effect of means-testing rules, because many parents with children currently approaching college age were not aware of the nature of the scholarship rules. Further work on the economic effects of means testing should be a high priority for the research program on forecasting the financial status of future elderly households.

PRIVATE PENSIONS AND SAVING

Most of the difficulties with measuring the effect of Social Security on personal saving also arise in studies that investigate whether individuals who participate in private pension plans adjust other aspects of their saving to offset their pension saving. There are additional difficulties in analyzing this "pension offset" issue, some of which stem from data problems, others of which are conceptual. Gale (1995) surveys some of these difficulties.

The paucity of data sets that combine detailed information on the structure of private defined benefit pension plans and other components of household net worth has resulted in fewer studies of private pension wealth offset than of Social Security wealth offset. Cagan (1965) found a positive correlation between pension wealth and other asset holdings, but Munnell's (1982) reanalysis of his data showed that after controlling for various individual characteristics, this positive correlation vanished.

A number of subsequent studies have found small, and typically negative, effects. Blinder, Gordon, and Wise (1983), in a very careful analysis of the cross-sectional pattern, find evidence of a positive correlation between pension and other wealth. Hubbard (1986) examines one of the better data sets for this purpose, a data set collected by the President's Commission on Pension Policy. His point estimates suggest that each dollar of private pension wealth reduces other net worth by 15 cents, while each dollar of Social Security wealth is estimated to have an 18-cent offset. Diamond and Hausman (1984) used the National Longitudinal Survey of Mature Men for the 1966-1975 period to consider the pension offset question. They predicted pension income for those who were still in the labor force and found evidence that both expected Social Security and expected pension benefits reduced personal saving. Both effects were estimated to provide less than dollar-for-dollar offset, and the estimated effect of Social Security was much larger than that of private pensions. King and Dicks-Mireaux (1982) explore pension and Social Security wealth offset in a Canadian data set similar to the Survey of Consumer Finances, and estimate offsets of between –0.10 and –0.25 for both Social Security wealth and private pension wealth, with larger effects for Social Security wealth. Venti and Wise (1996) show that the present discounted value of expected private pension benefits for those between ages 65 and 69 is essentially uncorrelated with the level of other financial wealth, after controlling for lifetime income. The central tendency of these results is that there is relatively little offset between private pensions and other forms of wealth.

Various theoretical predictions have been developed to explain the *potential* offset between pensions and other forms of wealth. In the life-cycle model, offset should be dollar for dollar. In a mental accounts setting, there could be relatively little offset; precautionary saving models suggest less offset as well. Cagan (1965) even developed an argument for positive effects, suggesting that individuals who participate in private pension plans become more aware of their retirement income needs and therefore save on own account.

One potential explanation for a positive correlation between pension assets and other wealth, and one that does not rely on the recognition effect, is that individuals with a taste for saving sort themselves into jobs with generous pension plans, and they also save a substantial amount on own account. The problem of endogenous matching of workers to jobs, and the possibility that worker characteristics are correlated with the nature of their benefit package, is a difficult empirical problem to resolve and one that besets essentially all research on the link between pensions and other household decisions. Convincing empirical evidence on the offset between pensions and other types of net worth must address the problem of saver heterogeneity, as some of the work discussed below on 401(k) plans have done. An important direction for future research is exploring how individual characteristics that may affect saving affect an individual's decision of what type of firm to work for.

The interaction between pensions and other wealth accumulation is a natural application of precautionary saving models. Pension assets, particularly the present discounted value of the benefits from a defined benefit pension plan, are poor substitutes for liquid assets if households face near-term financial emergencies. Samwick (1994) develops a model to illustrate this; he shows that for plausible calibration values, there is relatively little offset between accumulation of pension wealth and other nonpension components of household net worth. Models with precautionary saving effects are subject to some ambiguities, however. Leimer and Richardson (1992) use a model with elements similar to Samwick's to analyze the offset effects associated with Social Security, and they conclude that reductions in Social Security wealth should have a substantial effect on private asset accumulation. Their findings are driven by Social Security's role in providing a consumption floor in retirement, and precautionary considerations therefore drive households to accumulate private wealth if this floor is removed.

Recent trends in the structure of pension arrangements in the United States also raise new issues about pensions and saving. Beller and Lawrence (1992) document the shift from defined benefit to defined contribution pension plans since the late 1970s. The recent but continuing trend away from pension plans that provide recipients with a nominal annuity, toward plans that are self-directed and that allow individuals the option of decumulating their plan balance in the early stages of retirement, could have significant effects on the financial condition of elderly households. Identifying these effects from existing data sources is difficult for the same reasons that confound the measurement of the saving offset from private pension plans. If individual characteristics affect choices of whether to work for firms that offer defined benefit or defined contribution pension plans, then simple comparisons between the decumulation behavior of those with defined benefit and defined contribution pension plans may not provide a valid basis for assessing the current spread of defined contribution plans. There is relatively little consensus, however, on how the diffusion of defined contribution as opposed to defined benefit pension plans will affect the financial status of households as they approach retirement or how it will affect the evolution of their financial status during retirement.

TARGETED RETIREMENT SAVING ACCOUNTS AND PERSONAL SAVING

One of the most significant changes in the pattern of personal saving during the last decade has been the growing importance of saving through targeted retirement saving accounts, primarily IRAs and 401(k) and 403(b) accounts. These plans provide individuals with opportunities to invest at pretax rates of return, often with generous employer contributions, and to defer taxes on their current labor income. A detailed description of the provisions of these plans may be found in Poterba, Venti, and Wise (1995a). Participation in Individual Retirement Accounts rose rapidly between their introduction in 1981 and their limitation in the Tax Reform Act of 1986. Since 401(k) plans first became available in the early 1980s, they have grown in popularity, and in 1993, the Census Bureau estimated that 39 million employees were eligible to participate in such plans. More than 25 million have participated. Poterba, Venti, and Wise (1994b) present tabulations of age- and income-specific participation rates in these plans and show that eligibility for a 401(k) increases with income, but is not strongly related to age. For those eligible, participation is unrelated to age and is above 60 percent for all income groups.

The growing importance of.these targeted retirement saving vehicles raises at least three important questions for the analysis of prospective saving behavior. First, how much are individuals who are currently contributing to these accounts likely to accumulate between now and the time they reach retirement? Second, how does the accumulation of balances in these accounts affect other forms of personal saving and wealth accumulation? Finally, how are these account balances likely to affect the evolution of wealth during retirement?

Prospective Accumulation in Targeted Saving Accounts

The first important issue concerns the asset balances that individuals with targeted retirement saving accounts are likely to accumulate by retirement age. Forecasting future contributions to these accounts raises many of the same problems of separating age effects from cohort effects that arise with respect to saving behavior more generally. Nevertheless, Poterba (1996) and Venti and Wise (1996) present some evidence on this question, using somewhat different approaches to impute future asset growth in targeted saving accounts. Poterba (1996) assumes that the age-specific changes in average 401(k) balances, computed from the 1987 and 1991 SIPP, will apply to the currently youngest cohorts as they age. Venti and Wise (1996) fit a polynomial in age to contributions and then use the fitted values from this equation to predict future contributions. In both cases the results suggest that if currently middle-aged 401(k) contributors behave like the older 401(k) contributors in earlier cohorts, they will accumulate very substantial balances in targeted retirement saving accounts.

Forecasts in Poterba (1996) suggest that if a 3 percent annual real return on plan assets is assumed, households between the ages of 35 and 39 in 1991 could expect to reach age 60 to 64 with a pretax value of $26,025 (1991 dollars) in 401(k) plan assets. The after-tax value of the account is somewhat smaller and depends on the marginal federal and state/local income tax rate that the household would face when withdrawing assets. The reported average combines the roughly three-quarters of all households without targeted retirement saving accounts with the one-quarter with such accounts. The account balances for those with these accounts would average roughly $100,000 (1991 dollars). These average balances are an order of magnitude larger than those of households reaching retirement in the early 1990s. They also omit possible saving through other forms of targeted retirement saving accounts, such as IRAs.

One of the particularly difficult issues in modeling the long-run evolution of balances in targeted retirement saving accounts is that a substantial number of such accounts are terminated each year, and the assets are withdrawn as lump sums. In the March 1993 Employee Benefit Supplement to the Current Population Survey, 12.4 million individuals reported that they had received a lump-sum distribution from a retirement plan at some point. The median (mean) distribution was $3,500 ($10,800). Less than a quarter of these respondents indicated that they had rolled over all of their distribution into another tax-deferred retirement account, while 42 percent reported some rollover activity. Salisbury (1993) notes that recent changes in the tax treatment of lump-sum distributions are likely to affect the disposition of these payments. Further research on the link between individual characteristics, the incidence of 401(k) lump-sum distributions, and the disposition of these distributions is one of the top priorities for research on this aspect of the retirement saving system.

Net Saving Effects

A second critical issue related to the growing importance of assets in targeted retirement saving accounts concerns the interaction between rising balances in these accounts and other forms of personal saving. This is a topic of active research and controversy. A number of studies, prominently Venti and Wise (1987, 1990b) and Gale and Scholz (1994), have examined the net saving effect of contributions to IRAs. They reach very different conclusions: the former study suggests that most IRA saving offsets other saving, while the latter study suggests most IRA contributions are "net saving." Several more recent studies, including Engen, Gale, and Scholz (1994), Gale and Engen (1995), Poterba, Venti, and Wise (1995a, 1996), and Venti and Wise (1996), have focused on 401(k) accounts.

Analyzing the net saving effects of targeted saving vehicles is complicated by the absence of any controlled experiments and the presence of substantial heterogeneity in household saving propensities. Since households with higher saving propensities may contribute to targeted retirement saving plans and also accumulate other assets more quickly, cross-sectional comparisons of the net worth of targeted retirement saving plan participants and nonparticipants can be an unreliable way to assess the net saving effects of these plans. This argument applies with particular force to comparisons of IRA savers and nonsavers, since there are no exogenous factors that determine eligibility for these plans. It is weaker as an objection to studies of 401(k) saving that use employer-determined eligibility for such plans as the source of variation in household saving opportunities although it is, at least in principle, possible for such variation to be related to worker attributes and therefore to underlying saving propensities. Poterba, Venti, and Wise (1996) and Gale and Engen (1995) discuss the saver heterogeneity problem at some length. Because most households hold relatively low balances of other financial assets, there is limited prospect that contributions to targeted retirement saving accounts will be offset on an ongoing basis by reductions in other asset balances. For some high-income households, however, the prospects are likely to be much greater.

One margin on which targeted retirement saving plans *may* substitute for other saving is by replacing traditional pension plans. The 401(k) plans that were started in the early and mid-1980s do not appear to have replaced more traditional pension arrangements; in many cases they were converted thrift plans. Papke, Petersen, and Poterba (1996) present some evidence on these transitions. Venti and Wise (1996) find virtually no offset between private pension wealth and balances in 401(k) and similar targeted retirement saving accounts.

The more recent growth of 401(k) plans *may* involve some displacement of alternative pension assets. Yakoboski and Reilly (1994) report that nearly three-quarters of current participants in salary reduction plans view these plans as their primary pension plan, a substantial increase from 1988 when 49.1 percent of participants viewed these as primary plans. Whether this change is due to a changing perception of a given set of retirement plans by the participants, to changes in the nature of the plans, or to changes in the set of workers who are covered by these plans, should be explored.

Another unresolved aspect of the net saving debate is the degree to which IRA and 401(k) plan contributions are financed by increased borrowing. Poterba, Venti, and Wise (1995a) report median nonhousing household indebtedness for households without IRAs, but with 401(k) plan accounts, of $1,240 (1987 dollars) in 1991. Moreover, the median (mean) household debt levels for 401(k) participants without IRAs, measured in 1987 dollars, were $1,153 ($3,261) in 1984, $1,247 ($3,071) in 1987, and $1,240 ($3,223) in 1991. For those with both IRAs and 401(k) plan accounts, the pattern is similar.

The low level of household indebtedness suggests that debt-for-401(k) swaps are unlikely to be a substantial factor in the run-up of 401(k) balances. The statistics presented above do not include mortgage debt, which could provide one channel for household borrowing against rising 401(k) and IRA wealth. This issue is not yet resolved. Gale and Engen (1995) present evidence suggesting substantial offet, while Poterba, Venti and Wise (1996) present data that support smaller offset effects. The phaseout of tax deductibility for interest on unsecured consumer debt during the years since the Tax Reform Act of 1986 has made home equity loans a particularly attractive way for households to borrow. Mortgage borrowing has risen, but the interaction with 401(k) contributions remains unclear.

A further question related to the net saving effects of targeted retirement saving accounts involves the relationship between contributions to these accounts and aggregate statistics on personal saving. At precisely the same time that individual contributions to various targeted retirement saving became substantial, the National Income and Product Accounts measure of personal saving fell. This negative relationship, while sometimes cited by opponents of such plans as evidence of their failure, is not well understood. None of the careful studies of the offset between contributions to targeted retirement saving accounts and other saving suggest a *negative* net effect on personal saving, and many studies suggest substantial positive effects. Understanding the relationship between household-level data on saving trends and aggregate information is therefore a research priority.

Withdrawal Behavior

A third important issue concerning the saving effects of targeted retirement saving accounts, but one that has received little research attention to date, concerns the pattern of withdrawals from these accounts after households become eligible for penalty-free withdrawals at age 59-1/2. Preliminary evidence on the flow of withdrawals and the age and income pattern of their receipt is presented in Andrews (1991), Fernandez (1992), Yakoboski (1994), and Poterba, Venti, and Wise (1995b), but none of these studies develops a formal model of what determines withdrawals.

In analyzing withdrawals, it is important to consider the disposition of assets in targeted retirement saving accounts when households reach retirement, as well as pre-retirement withdrawals. A married couple in which the husband is 65 and the wife is 62 can expect to need retirement income for nearly 25 years. Yet we do not know whether households tend to draw down these accounts relatively rapidly, in which case these assets may not have a substantial effect on the wealth position of the oldest old, or whether such assets remain in targeted retirement saving accounts until age 70-1/2, the age at which withdrawals must begin. In the latter case, the growing accumulation of targeted retirement saving account assets may affect the financial status of the oldest old.

HOUSING WEALTH AND OTHER PRIVATE SAVING

For the typical household reaching retirement age in the early 1990s, home equity is the second most important component of net worth, after Social Security wealth. Housing wealth is typically much greater than net holdings of financial assets. Prospective patterns of both the accumulation of housing wealth before retirement and the decumulation after retirement therefore play an important role in defining the financial status of future retirees.

Decisions made in youth and middle age, such as whether and when to buy a home, how rapidly to repay its mortgage, and whether to borrow against accumulating home equity, are critical determinants of the net housing wealth of prospective retirees. In addition, the rate of house price appreciation is a key factor in determining net housing wealth at retirement, just as the rate of return on financial assets plays a central role in determining financial net worth at retirement.

Although one widely cited study, Mankiw and Weil (1989), suggests that real house prices may decline substantially over the next several decades, a number of other studies, cited, for example, in Poterba (1991), call this conclusion into question. Further work both on housing consumption decisions in middle age and on the link between population aging and real house prices is therefore likely to yield important information that bears on the future financial status of elderly households.

The popular perception that many elderly households are "house rich but cash poor" has stimulated research on two aspects of housing behavior: the extent to which elderly homeowners downsize their homes, thereby enabling them to use some of their wealth for other purposes, and the potential demand for reverse-annuity mortgages among elderly homeowners who for various reasons are not able to downsize.

A number of research studies have analyzed housing consumption and mo-bility decisions of elderly households, examining in part the interaction between housing wealth and other portfolio components. For elderly homeowners in their sixties and early seventies, Feinstein and McFadden (1989) and Venti and Wise (1989, 1990a) estimate annual mobility rates of approximately 4 percent, with relatively little reduction of housing wealth conditional on moving. This is the result of two types of behavior whose relative importance is not known. First, some elderly homeowners sell their homes and reinvest the proceeds to buy new homes that are not substantially less expensive than their original homes. Sec-ond, some elderly homeowners sell their homes, buy less expensive replacement homes, and either spend part of the proceeds or transfer some of the proceeds off their balance sheets, for example, with gifts to children. The pattern of housing wealth accumulation among elderly households may be very sensitive to overall patterns of house price movements. For example, Merrill (1984) found evidence that net housing wealth increased with age among respondents to the Retirement History Survey, but this may reflect the secular rise in house prices during the data sample.

The pattern of housing decumulation among the older old appears to be different from that for the younger old. Sheiner and Weil (1992) analyze data from the Current Population Survey, which includes a larger sample of older old households than the data sets used in previous studies. They find substantially greater rates of homeowner mobility than in earlier studies, particularly surround-ing times of other shocks such as the death of a spouse, and they find a much greater incidence of homeowner-to-renter transitions among this group than among the younger elderly.

The second issue that has attracted research attention concerns the demand for reverse annuity mortgages among elderly households. Capozza and Megbolugbe (1994) survey a number of recent studies on this issue and outline the key economic considerations in the demand for reverse annuity mortgages. Venti and Wise (1989) cast doubt on the stylized view of cash-poor, house-rich elderly by showing that there is a positive correlation between cash income and net housing wealth. The elderly households with substantial housing assets to borrow against are much less likely to be cash constrained than elderly households with limited housing assets. Mayer and Simons (1994) present more recent evidence on the potential demand for reverse annuity mortgages, based on information in the 1984 and 1990 SIPPs. Their results suggest that at most one-quarter of households aged 65 or above would be strong candidates for reverse annuity mortgages, but they do not disaggregate the elderly to compare the young and old old. There is some evidence that elderly households in California and some parts of the Northeast, regions that have experienced rapid house price appreciation over the last two decades, would be particularly likely to raise their income if they participated in reverse annuity mortgage programs.

The households that retired during the last two decades lived through a period of substantial increase in real house prices. Between 1974 and 1980, for example, real house prices rose nearly 30 percent (see Poterba, 1991). The associated capital gains on housing were probably unanticipated, so the value of net housing equity at retirement was probably greater than what these retirees would have predicted 10 or 20 years before retirement. Even if real house prices do not decline during the next 30 years, there is no strong basis for projecting a repetition of the real house price growth of the recent past. This suggests that future elderly households are likely to have a smaller relative stock of net housing wealth than their predecessors. Analyzing how this will affect saving behavior as households approach retirement, and asset profiles after retirement, is an important research issue.

CONCLUSION AND FUTURE RESEARCH NEEDS

This background survey suggests that for many of the important questions of interest with respect to private saving and the future financial status of the elderly, the existing research base does not provide detailed and convincing information on crucial parameter values and behavioral elasticities. In some cases, this is the result of data limitations that will be partly remedied by the HRS. The HRS will combine detailed projections of Social Security and private pension benefits once an individual retires with data on wealth holdings before and after retirement, and will permit new estimates of the effect of retirement income streams on other asset accumulation. It will also replace a number of data sets such as the Retirement History Survey that provide a dated indication of the financial status and saving behavior of elderly households.

With respect to a number of issues, however, even the HRS will not resolve the research controversy. This is because existing empirical work on saving is hamstrung by the absence of exogenous shocks to saving opportunities. Past and potential future work is therefore limited to focusing on potentially contaminated sources of information on the relationship between Social Security wealth, pension wealth, and other personal financial saving. A key direction for future work should be modeling and evaluating the potential biases that result from individual heterogeneity in saving behavior and from the possibly endogenous choice by individuals of what types of saving to do (IRAs, 401(k)s, etc.) and even what firms to work for.

The difficulty of resolving some perennial questions about saving behavior should not deflect research attention from assessing a number of the emerging trends in the saving and financial behavior of future retirees. Among the central issues that warrant study are the rise of defined contribution as opposed to defined benefit pension plans, the growing popularity of targeted retirement saving accounts as vehicles for personal saving, and the impact of growing numbers of two-earner couples who will reach retirement with multiple sources of income.

REFERENCES

Aaron, H.J.
   1982   *Economic Effects of Social Security*. Washington, D.C.: Brookings Institution.
Andreoni, J.
   1989   Giving with impure altruism: Applications to charity and Ricardian equivalence. *Journal of Political Economy* 97:1447-1458.
Andrews, E.S.
   1991   Retirement savings and lump sum distributions. *Benefits Quarterly* 2:47-58.
Attanasio, O.
   1992   An Analysis of Life-Cycle Accumulation of Financial Assets. Unpublished manuscript. Stanford University.
   1993   *A Cohort Analysis of Saving Behavior by U.S. Households*. NBER Working Paper #4454. Cambridge, Mass.: National Bureau of Economic Research.
Attanasio, O., and G. Weber
   1995   Is consumption growth consistent with intertemporal optimization? Evidence from the Consumer Expenditure Survey. *Journal of Political Economy* 103:1121-1157.
Auerbach, A.J., and L.J. Kotlikoff
   1983   An examination of empirical tests of Social Security and savings. Pp. 161-174 in E. Helpman, ed., *Social Policy Evaluation: An Economic Perspective*. New York: Academic Press.
Auerbach, A.J., L.J. Kotlikoff, and D.N. Weil
   1992   The Increasing Annuitization of the Elderly: Estimates and Implications. Unpublished manuscript. University of Pennsylvania.
Barro, R.J.
   1974   Are government bonds net wealth? *Journal of Political Economy* 82(6):1095-1117.
   1978   *The Impact of Social Security on Private Saving: Evidence from the United States Time Series*. Washington, D.C.: American Enterprise Institute.
Barro, R.J., and G.M. MacDonald
   1979   Social Security and consumer spending in an international cross-section. *Journal of Public Economics* 11:275-289.
Beller, D.J., and H.H. Lawrence
   1992   Trends in private pension plan coverage. Pp. 59-96 in J.A. Turner and D.J. Beller, eds., *Trends in Pensions 1992*. Washington, D.C.: U.S. Department of Labor, Pension and Welfare Benefits Administration.

Bernheim, B.D.
   1987a Dissaving after retirement: Testing the pure lifecycle hypothesis. Pp. 237-274 in Z. Bodie, J. Shoven, and D. Wise, eds., *Issues in Pension Economics.* Chicago, Ill.: University of Chicago Press.
   1987b The economic effects of Social Security: Toward a reconciliation of theory and measurement. *Journal of Public Economics* 33:273-304.
   1993 *Is the Baby Boom Generation Preparing Adequately for Retirement? Summary Report.* Princeton, N.J.: Merrill Lynch.
   1994 Do Households Appreciate Their Financial Vulnerabilities? An Analysis of Actions, Perceptions, and Public Policy. Unpublished manuscript. Department of Economics, Stanford University.
Bernheim, B.D., and J.K. Scholz
   1993 Private saving and public policy. Pp. 73-110 in J. Poterba, ed., *Tax Policy and the Economy* Vol. 7. Cambridge, Mass.: MIT Press.
Bernheim, B.D., A. Shleifer, and L.H. Summers
   1985 The strategic bequest motive. *Journal of Political Economy* 93:1045-1076.
Blanchard, O.J.
   1993 Movements in the equity premium. *Brookings Papers on Economic Activity* 2:75-138.
Blinder, A.S., R.H. Gordon, and D.E. Wise
   1983 Social Security, bequests, and the life cycle theory of saving: Cross-sectional tests. Pp. 89-122 in F. Modigliani and R. Hemming, eds., *The Determinants of National Saving and Wealth.* New York: St. Martin's Press.
Bosworth, B., G. Burtless, and J. Sabelhaus
   1991 The decline in saving: Evidence from household surveys. *Brookings Papers on Economic Activity* 1:183-256.
Cagan, P.
   1965 *The Effect of Pension Plans on Aggregate Saving: Evidence from a Sample Survey.* National Bureau of Economic Research Occasional Paper 95. New York: Columbia University Press.
Capozza, D., and I. Megbolugbe
   1994 Introduction [to special issue on housing finance for the elderly]. *Journal of the American Real Estate and Urban Economics Association* 22:197-203.
Carroll, C.D.
   1992 The buffer-stock theory of saving: Some macroeconomic evidence. *Brookings Papers on Economic Activity* 2:61-135.
Carroll, C.D., and A.A. Samwick
   1993 The Nature and Magnitude of Precautionary Wealth. Unpublished manuscript. Federal Reserve Board of Governors, Washington, D.C.
Congressional Budget Office
   1993 *Baby Boomers in Retirement: An Early Perspective.* Washington, D.C.: U.S. Government Printing Office.
Diamond, P.A., and J.A. Hausman
   1984 Individual retirement and saving behavior. *Journal of Public Economics* 23:81-114.
Edlin, A.S.
   1993 Is college financial aid equitable and efficient? *Journal of Economic Perspectives* 7:143-158.
Engen, E.M., W.G. Gale, and J.K. Scholz
   1994 Do savings incentives work. *Brookings Papers on Economic Activity* 1994(1):85-180.
Feinstein, J., and D. McFadden
   1989 The dynamics of housing demand by the elderly: Wealth, cash flow and demographic effects. Pp. 55-86 in D.A. Wise, ed., *The Economics of Aging.* Chicago, Ill.: University of Chicago Press.

Feldstein, M.S.
  1974   Social Security, induced retirement, and aggregate capital accumulation. *Journal of Political Economy* 82(5):905-926.
  1982   Social Security and private saving: Reply. *Journal of Political Economy* 90:630-641.
  1995   College scholarship rules and private saving. *American Economic Review* 85(June):552-566.
Feldstein, M.S., and A. Pellechio
  1979   Social Security and household wealth accumulation: New microeconometric evidence. *Review of Economics and Statistics* 61(3):361-368.
Fernandez, P.A.
  1992   Preretirement lump sum distributions. Pp. 285-318 in J.A. Turner and D.J. Beller, eds., *Trends in Pensions 1992*. Washington, D.C., U.S. Department of Labor, Pension and Welfare Benefits Administration.
Gale, W.G.
  1995   The Effects of Pensions on Wealth: A Re-evaluation of Theory and Evidence. Unpublished paper. Brookings Institution, Washington, D.C.
Gale, W.G., and E. Engen
  1995   Debt, Taxes, and the Effects of 401(k) Plans on Household Wealth Accumulation. Unpublished manuscript. Brookings Institution, Washington, DC.
Gale, W.G., and J.K. Scholz
  1994   IRAs and household saving. *American Economic Review* 84(5):1233-1260.
Hall, R.E.
  1988   Intertemporal substitution in consumption. *Journal of Political Economy* 96:339-357.
Hubbard, R.G.
  1986   Pension wealth and individual saving. *Journal of Money, Credit, and Banking* 18:167-178.
Hubbard, R.G., J. Skinner, and S.P. Zeldes
  1994   The importance of precautionary motives in explaining individual and aggregate saving. *Carnegie-Rochester Conference Series on Public Policy* 40(June):59-126.
Hurd, M.
  1987   Savings of the elderly and desired bequests. *American Economic Review* 77(3):298-312.
  1990a Research on the elderly: Economic status, retirement and consumption and saving. *Journal of Economic Literature* 28(2):565-637.
  1990b *Wealth Depletion and Life Cycle Consumption by the Elderly.* NBER Working Paper #3472. Cambridge, Mass.: National Bureau of Economic Research.
  1992   Forecasting the Consumption, Income, and Wealth of the Elderly. Unpublished manuscript. Department of Economics, The State University of New York, Stoney Brook.
Juster, F.T., and J.P. Smith
  1994   Improving the Quality of Economic Data: Lessons From the HRS. Unpublished manuscript. Institute for Social Research, University of Michigan.
King, M.A., and L. Dicks-Mireaux
  1982   Asset holdings and the life cycle. *Economic Journal* 92:247-267.
Kotlikoff, L.J.
  1984   Taxation and savings: A neoclassical perspective. *Journal of Economic Literature* 22:1576-1629.
  1988   Intergenerational transfers and savings. *The Journal of Economic Perspectives* 2(2):41-58.
Krueger, A., and J.S. Pischke
  1992   The effect of Social Security on labor supply: A cohort analysis of the notch generation. *Journal of Labor Economics* 10:412-437.

Laibson, D.
  1994   Golden Eggs and Hyperbolic Discounting. Unpublished manuscript. Harvard University.
Leimer, D.R., and S. Lesnoy
  1982   Social Security and private saving: New time series evidence. *Journal of Political Economy* 90:606-629.
Leimer, D.R., and D.H. Richardson
  1992   Social Security, uncertainty adjustments, and the consumption decision. *Economica* 59(235):311-335.
Mankiw, N.G., and D. Weil
  1989   The baby boom, the baby bust, and the housing market. *Regional Science and Urban Economics* 19:235-258.
Mayer, C.J., and K.V. Simons
  1994   A new look at reverse mortgages: Potential market and institutional constraints. *New England Economic Review* March/April:15-26.
Merrill, S.
  1984   Home equity and the elderly. Pp. 197-227 in H. Aaron and G. Burtless, eds., *Retirement and Economic Behavior*. Washington, D.C.: Brookings Institution.
Mirer, T.W.
  1979   The wealth-age relationship among the aged. *American Economic Review* 69:435-443.
Modigliani, F.
  1988   The role of intergenerational transfers and life cycle saving in the accumulation of wealth. *The Journal of Economic Perspectives* 2(2):15-40.
Munnell, A.
  1982   *The Effect of Social Security on Private Saving*. Washington, D.C.: Brookings Institution.
Organization for Economic Cooperation and Development
  1994   *Taxation and Household Saving*. Working Paper No. 2 on Tax Analysis and Tax Statistics. Paris.
Papke, L., M. Petersen, and J.M. Poterba
  1996   Did 401(k) replace other employer-provided pensions? In D. Wise, ed., *Further Studies in the Economics of Aging*. Chicago, Ill.: University of Chicago Press.
Poterba, J.M.
  1991   House price dynamics. *Brookings Papers on Economic Activity* 2:143-203.
  1996   401(k) plans and personal saving in the United States. In S. Schieber and J. Shoven, eds., *Public Policy Toward Pensions*. Washington, D.C.: Twentieth Century Fund.
Poterba, J.M., ed.
  1994   *International Comparison of Household Saving*. Chicago, Ill.: University of Chicago Press.
Poterba. J.M., S.F. Venti, and D.A. Wise
  1994a Targeted retirement saving and the net worth of elderly Americans. *American Economic Review* 84(2):180-185.
  1994b 401(k) plans and tax-deferred saving. Pp. 105-138 in D. Wise, ed., *Studies in the Economics of Aging*. Chicago, Ill.: University of Chicago Press.
  1995a Do 401(k) contributions crowd out other personal saving? *Journal of Public Economics* 58:1-32.
  1995b *Lump Sum Distributions from Retirement Savings Plans: Receipt and Utilization*. NBER Working Paper #5298. Cambridge, Mass.: National Bureau of Economic Research.
  1996   Do retirement saving programs increase saving? *Journal of Economic Perspectives* (forthcoming).

Salisbury, D.
    1993   Policy implications of changes in employer pension protection. In Employee Benefit
            Research Institute, *Pensions in a Changing Economy*. Washington, D.C.: Employee
            Benefit Research Institute.
Samwick, A.A.
    1994   The Limited Offset Between Pension Wealth and Other Private Wealth: Implications of
            Buffer Stock Saving. Unpublished manuscript. Dartmouth College.
Schieber, S., and J.B. Shoven
    1994   *The Consequences of Population Aging on Private Pension Fund Saving and Asset Mar-
            kets*. NBER Working Paper #4665. Cambridge, Mass.: National Bureau of Economic
            Research.
Sheffrin, H.M., and R. Thaler
    1988   The behavioral life-cycle hypothesis. *Economic Inquiry* 26:609-643.
Sheiner, L., and D.N. Weil
    1992   *The Housing Wealth of the Aged*. NBER Working Paper #4115. Cambridge, Mass.:
            National Bureau of Economic Research.
Shorrocks, A.F.
    1975   The age-wealth relationship: A cross-section and cohort analysis. *Review of Economics
            and Statistics* 57:155-163.
Siegel, J.J.
    1994   *Stocks for the Long Run: A Guide to Selecting Markets for Long Term Growth*.
            Homewood, Ill.: Irwin.
Summers, L.H.
    1981   Capital taxation and capital accumulation in a life cycle growth model. *American Eco-
            nomic Review* 71:533-544.
Thaler, R.H.
    1994   Psychology and savings policies. *American Economic Review* 84(2):186-192.
VanDerhei, J.
    1992   New evidence that employees choose conservative investments for their retirement funds.
            Employee Benefit Notes 13(February):1-3.
Venti, S.F., and D.A. Wise
    1987   IRAs and saving. Pp. 7-52 in M. Feldstein, ed., *The Effects of Taxation on Capital
            Accumulation*. Chicago, Ill.: University of Chicago Press.
    1989   Aging, moving and housing wealth. Pp. 9-48 in D.A. Wise, ed., *The Economics of Aging*.
            Chicago, Ill.: University of Chicago Press.
    1990a   But they don't want to reduce housing equity. Pp. 13-29 in D.A. Wise, ed., *Issues in the
            Economics of Aging*. Chicago, Ill.: University of Chicago Press.
    1990b   Have IRAs increased U.S. saving? *Quarterly Journal of Economics* 105:661-698.
    1996   The wealth of cohorts: Retirement saving and the changing assets of older Americans. In
            S. Schieber and J. Shoven, eds., *Public Policy Toward Pensions*. Washington, D.C.:
            Twentieth Century Fund.
Yakoboski, P.
    1994   Retirement program lump-sum distributions: Hundreds of billions in hidden pension
            income. *EBRI Issue Brief* Number 146(February). Washington, D.C.: Employee
            Benefit Research Institute.
Yakoboski, P., and A. Reilly
    1994   Salary reduction plans and individual saving for retirement. *EBRI Issue Brief* Number
            155(November). Washington, D.C.: Employee Benefit Research Institute.

5

Retirement Age and Retirement Income: The Role of the Firm

Donald O. Parsons

Understanding the retirement behavior of American workers and their income security in retirement requires knowledge of the motivations of employers as well as workers and the government.[1] For example, the federal government has implemented a wide range of laws to permit or encourage later retirement in the private sector. Legal restrictions were imposed on maximum age-of-hire rules and on mandatory retirement before age 70 in the Age Discrimination in Employment Act of 1967 (ADEA); both practices have since been effectively abolished. Other legislation has outlawed pension plans that stop pension accrual at age 65 or deny older new hires the right to participate in company pensions. In a different direction, the 1983 Amendments to the Social Security Act set up a time schedule for the raising of normal retirement under Social Security to age 67. At the same time, however, private employers are increasingly including special early retirement incentives in pension benefit formulas (Mitchell, 1992). Whether this trend is a passive response by employers to greater demands by workers for early retirement or an active attempt by employers to reduce the number of older workers is not clear, although one must at least entertain the second possibility.[2]

Firms contribute in two important ways to the income security of older

The comments of participants at the panel conference on retirement modeling, especially those of Dallas Salisbury and Eugene Steuerle, are gratefully acknowledged. I have also benefited from the suggestions of Robert Clark and Richard Ippolito and from the detailed comments of members of the panel.

individuals: by providing jobs to those who want to work and by providing pension income to those who do not. The ability and willingness of private employers to offer jobs and pensions has been changing in the last two decades. Large changes have occurred, not only in age-based legislation, but in the economy's industrial base, the economic platform that provides both work opportunities and post-retirement income. Among other changes are the widely noted decline in the relative share of the large-firm, highly unionized sector and the expansion of the service sector.

This sectoral shift offers both opportunities and dangers to older individuals. On the one hand, employment in the service sector appears to be much more open to older Americans (Ruhm, 1990; Quinn, Burkhauser, and Myers, 1990), so that older individuals should have greater access to jobs in the future. On the other hand, they may need to work for more years if the expanding sectors remain relatively ungenerous in their pension offerings. Indeed recent evidence indicates that pension coverage in the United States declined in the 1980s, driven in part by relative employment declines in high-pension-coverage sectors (Woods, 1989; Parsons, 1991b, 1994; Bloom and Freeman, 1992; and Even and Macpherson, 1994a), although preliminary evidence from the May 1993 pension supplement indicates that coverage rates have stabilized in the 1990s (Woods, 1993; U.S. Department of Labor et al., 1994). At the same time, there has been a shift in the composition of pension coverage away from the traditional final-salary-based, retirement annuity programs (defined benefit plans) and toward savings-like, lump-sum programs (defined contribution plans) with payouts dependent on the returns-to-plan assets.[3] These compositional shifts can also be partly explained by the relative decline in industries that traditionally offered defined benefit plans, although both the general decline in pensions and the shift toward defined contribution plans are evident within industrial sectors as well. The trend toward defined contribution plans introduces an unwelcome element of uncertainty into policy planning because we lack broad experience with such plans.

What are the strategies underlying employers' retirement and pension policies? How and, of equal importance, why do these strategies vary across firms, workers, and market structures?[4] Although one can occasionally uncover direct evidence on employer intentions (Gratton, 1990), usually this information must be gleaned indirectly from observations of the age-related elements of employment conditions, including maximum age-of-hire restrictions, compulsory retirement rules, actuarially unfair pensions, age-restricted eligibility for retirement plans, and special retirement incentive programs or "windows." The motivations for age-based policies are often ambiguous. With pensions, for example, the firm has two plausible objectives: (1) to serve as an efficient conduit for fringe benefits that its workers value, for example, as a mechanism for securing tax-deferred retirement income, and (2) to structure compensation in a way that induces desirable behavior from workers at least cost, shaping compensation profiles and bonding worker mobility and on-the-job performance. Evidence for each of these two objectives, which are not mutually exclusive, can be found in the literature, but the quantitative importance of each in molding the firm's behavior toward the aged remains unknown.

Throughout this review, special attention is paid to the impact of firm size on retirement policies. To anticipate later conclusions, retirement age and pension coverage are strongly shaped by firm size and union status, and a substantial part of recent trends in pension coverage and type (defined benefit and defined contribution) can be explained by shifts in industrial structure away from the large-firm, unionized sector. The effects of firm size and union status on retirement age and retirement income can themselves be explained by transactions costs, especially firm size differences in (1) the administrative costs of sorting and reassigning older workers as their productive attributes evolve and (2) the administrative costs of providing retirement income to separated workers. Recent trends in pension structure can be explained by changes in these same administrative costs, especially those changes induced by shifting government regulations, although permissive legislation that has expanded the range of tax-favored pension vehicles to include 401(k) plans has also had a major impact on recent pension developments. Alternative hypotheses, notably broader transactions-cost hypotheses that stress agency problems and/or contract reliability, can explain many of the same behaviors, and more detailed data and more carefully developed implications are required to assess the relative importance of these competing, but not mutually exclusive, hypotheses.

This paper proceeds in the following way. I begin in the next section by summarizing the "aging problem" as the firm might view it and then review aspects of the firm's employment contracting behavior that are of special relevance to aging policies. The function of this section is to gather together in one place a set of worker and firm behavioral characteristics that can explain the retirement and pension policies of the firm and the variation in these policies across firm size. In the section on "The Employment of Older Workers," I begin the review of what is known about the role of the firm in retirement behavior and retirement income, turning first to the employment question: what determines the firm's propensity to employ older workers? I examine the mechanisms firms use to alter the extent of employment of older workers—the age profile of compensation, mandatory retirement, and maximum age-of-hire. In the section "Employer-Provided Pensions," I then consider the closely related question of firm pension policies, again focusing on why firms establish the plans that they do. The answers to this question are then used to explain recent pension trends, in aggregate and by type of pension plan. I then conclude in the final section with a discussion of the data collection and research needed to develop more reliable retirement-age and pension policy models.

THE AGING WORKER AND THE FIRM

The Aging Worker

The aging worker faces a variety of problems that potentially affect his or her productivity. (That these effects exist does not mean that firms correctly estimate their magnitudes; I return to the question of age bias below.) At the most basic level, mortality rates increase with age. This reality may limit the worker's usefulness to the firm, especially if substantial training is involved. Two additional dimensions of the aging process may be important: (1) that physical and mental attributes, especially physical attributes, decline on average with age and (2) that the decline is not uniform across individuals—some workers suffer declines and others do not.[5]

Self-reported health data from the National Center for Health Statistics illustrate the age profile of depreciation of the human "machinery" along several dimensions; see Table 5-1.[6] As the table indicates, certain physical problems arise early. In the age interval 55 to 65, about 16 percent of both men and women report difficulty walking a quarter of a mile, while 5 percent of men and 8 percent of women report difficulty lifting a 10-pound weight. In the oldest category, those 85 years of age or more, 50 percent of men and 60 percent of women report difficulty walking a quarter mile. On average, mental skills decline later in life.

TABLE 5-1   Health Statistics for Persons Ages 55 and Over in the United States, 1984, in Percentages

| | | Have Difficulty | | |
	Annual Death Rate	Walking 1/4 Mile	Lifting 10 lbs.	Managing Money
Ages				
Males				
55-64	1.7	15.5	5.2	1.0
65-74	3.8	21.9	6.6	2.8
75-84	8.4	29.1	9.9	5.4
85+	18.1	48.3	19.9	19.0
Females				
55-64	0.9	16.3	8.8	1.0
65-74	2.1	24.5	12.6	1.8
75-84	5.2	39.4	23.7	6.8
85+	14.1	61.5	40.8	26.2

SOURCE: National Center for Health Statistics (1987): column 1, p. 7; column 2, p. 45; column 3, p. 46; column 4, p. 54. The activity data are based on the National Health Interview Survey 1984 Supplement on Aging.

Self-reported difficulty managing money is almost nonexistent between 55 and 64.[7] Even in the 75-to-84 age interval, only 5 percent of men report trouble "managing money," a proportion that increases to 19 percent by age 85 and over (for women the corresponding statistics are similar—7% and 26%, respectively). The data also make clear that the onset of self-reported impairments is not uniform across the population. Most older individuals do not have a problem with these basic physical and mental skills. Among the men 85 or older, 50 percent report that they do not have difficulty walking one-quarter mile, 80 percent that they do not have difficulty lifting a 10-pound weight or managing their money.

It is reasonable to assume that work productivity is related to the individual's physical abilities and to his or her mental ones, with the relative importance of each dependent on the worker's job, so that work productivity in the population declines with age. Less clear, and in many ways less relevant, is whether the attributes of older workers decline with age. See Levine (1988) and Hurd (1993) for sympathetic reviews of the age/productivity literature. One could imagine a work environment sufficiently rigid in requirements and pace that all who continue working are of the same productivity; the overall decline in capabilities with age would be reflected in a reduced work rate. Certainly employers act as if abilities decline with age; the internal assessments of line managers in the Pennsylvania Railway Company, when that company first adopted a modern retirement and pension system at the turn of the century, reveal this to be the case, Gratton (1990). In a broader sample much more recently, Medoff and Abraham (1981) find evidence that productivity (as reported by supervisors) declines among older workers while pay increases. Kotlikoff and Gokhale (1992) use a novel methodology on data from a single large firm's personnel records to estimate employer perceptions of the productivity profiles for male managers, male and female office workers, and male and female salespeople. The basic proposition is that the present value of productivity and compensation should be equal at the time of hire. From wage histories and exit probabilities for workers with different ages of hire, they can estimate age profiles of productivity. There is persuasive evidence of declining productivity with age and also of large wage/productivity gaps at older ages for all but male salespeople and, somewhat more ambiguously, female salespeople, both of whom work on commission. Recall, however, that these estimates are based on employer beliefs of worker productivity. For a skeptical summary of employer beliefs in this area, see Levine (1988, chap. 8).

A caveat is that employer perceptions may not reflect reality. It is unambiguous that individuals fall prey to various physical and mental impairments at an increasing rate with age and that employers design employment contracts to moderate the effect of the aging phenomenon on firm profitability. At a minimum, these firm policies are a form of statistical discrimination—workers are treated as a class, old—that legislators have in many cases chosen to prohibit.[8] A deeper question is whether employers systematically overestimate the magnitude of this decline (Levine, 1988). Hurd (1993) provides a review of early efforts to deal with this difficult measurement issue. I suspect that empirical validation will be difficult. In situations in which objective productivity measures are available to the researcher, they are also likely to be available to the employer, but the greatest potential for bias occurs in situations in which productivity measures are the most ambiguous. In the remainder of this review, I assume that employers are reacting to what they believe to be the life-cycle productivity trend.

Obviously aging is a problem for the worker as well as the firm; of special importance to the worker is insuring himself or herself against earnings losses following the onset of a disabling condition. Such protection can take one of two forms, disability insurance or "self-insurance," accumulating sufficient assets to provide adequate consumption for a terminal period of low or no earnings. Private disability insurance coverage is notoriously incomplete and Social Security disability benefits are subject to a stringent but error-prone disability screen, placing much of the burden of income maintenance in old age on retirement programs. Of course, not all workers are equally concerned about this danger, or indeed about the future at all. Of importance to the firm's incentive to provide a pension plan, workers with high rates of time preference will place little value on pension plans, especially when they are young. As a summary, I offer the following propositions about workers and aging:

• Physical and mental attributes, especially physical attributes, decline on average with age, but the decline is not uniform across individuals—some workers suffer declines and others do not (W1).
• Workers are underinsured, especially against the early onset of health conditions that reduce work productivity (W2).
• Workers differ in the weights they place on the future; that is, they are heterogeneous in discount rates (W3).

One additional aspect of worker preferences deserves special mention because of its unusual importance in the design of retirement and retirement income plans: downward adjustments in pay and responsibility are, on average, resented by the worker, the more so the more direct and obvious the adjustment and the more individual-specific it is (W4).

The claim that workers resent negative job actions is consistent with empirical evidence in a wide set of situations, including employer design of wage and layoff policies (Bewley, 1993).[9] For a more general statement of this proposition, see Kahneman, Knetsch, and Thaler (1986). Of special importance here, workers seem to more readily accept compensation cuts in the form of actuarially unfair adjustments in pension accrual than cuts in cash payments.

The Firm

Firm retirement policies and retirement income policies are largely a function of workplace characteristics, not individual ones (Slavick, 1966; Parsons, 1992). Although there is a major exception to this rule for part-time workers, age-based contract terms vary little within a given workplace for full-time workers.[10] This workplace homogeneity is partly the result of government actions, such as nondiscrimination rules for qualified pension plans, but it is also the result of the firm's own decision calculus; when legal, one or two mandatory retirement rules have typically covered the whole workplace (Slavick, 1966).

The firm's relationship with its workers can be conceptualized as a "contract."[11] At the extremes, the employment relationship may be a spot-market transaction, with the firm's purchasing services from the worker for a relatively brief, well-defined interval, or a long-term contract, explicit or implicit, with the firm and workers' agreeing to an exchange of resources and services over a much more extended period. The primary economic factors that determine the length of the "contract" governing the employment relationship are the same as those that foster any sort of long-run contract, a relationship-specific investment on one or both parts (Williamson, 1975). In the employment contract, hiring costs and job training are believed to be investments of this type.[12] The high correlation of general and firm-specific training (Mincer, 1988) implies that, other things being equal, high-skilled workplaces will have more enduring relationships than will low-skilled ones; the returns to these investments accrue over time and a significant part may be lost if the employer/employee pair separate. In general, workers and firms find it advantageous to have long-term relationships. The worker is spared the costs and uncertainties of finding another job; the firm is able to train its workers, assess them over a longer period of time, and assign each one to an appropriate position. The volatility of demand or complementary factors may make such relationships infeasible, however, and the net returns to such relationships are likely to vary, so that some types of firms will find it optimal to have short-term relationships with their workers. To summarize: high hiring and training costs and stable demand and supply conditions foster long-term contracts (F1).

Beyond these real considerations, information processes are believed to play a major role in the determination of contract form. When compared with smaller firms, large firms appear to have two attributes important to these contracts:

- The costs of routine transactions are less in large firms (F2).
- The costs of individual, idiosyncratic decisions (in this case the assignment and monitoring of workers) are greater (F3).

Economies of scale are almost invariably large when the same activities are repeated. Setting up a payroll system or a pension plan requires a significant fixed cost. As the scale of a single operation increases, however, important information is less and less likely to reach the appropriate decision maker, or to be fully comprehended if it does (Williamson, 1967). As a consequence, the idiosyncratic aspects of a particular circumstance are likely to be lost, and decisions are likely to depend more heavily on broad rules (Oi, 1983a, 1983b, 1991). In particular, large firms are likely to perform very poorly at assessing individual attributes and appropriately assigning individuals to tasks (Garen, 1985). As Oi (1983a:79) remarked about the product market, "Large firms specialize in the production of standardized goods, while small firms supply customized goods that are produced in small quantity." It is plausible that firm personnel policies follow a similar pattern.

One can find ample support for propositions F2 and F3 in the retirement and retirement income literature.

Scale Economies in Pension Administration

Proposition F2 finds strong support in the administration costs of employer-provided pensions.[13] Pension provision ultimately involves resource collection, management, and disbursement. Each of these activities has significant fixed-cost components, so that considerable cost savings result if the worker can costlessly pool his or her pension efforts with others; for example, searching for a portfolio manager need be undertaken once, not once for each worker.

The administrative costs of a pension plan potentially include a variety of expenses incurred in the setup and maintenance of the plan and of individual accounts, including the collection of pension contributions, the tracking of workers until retirement, the financial handling of accumulated contributions, and the disbursement of funds at retirement. The cost functions of each of these various administrative activities—collection, portfolio management, disbursement, and others—may vary in form, but the total cost function seems well fitted by a log linear function (Caswell, 1976; Mitchell and Andrews, 1981).

Consider then the following model which captures the major elements of past studies:

$$\log C = \beta_0 + \beta_1 \log P + \beta_2 \log (A/P) + \beta_3 \log (P/F) + X\beta_4 + \epsilon, \qquad (1)$$

where C denotes total administrative costs, P denotes number of plan participants, A denotes total plan assets, F denotes the number of firms participating in the plan, X is a vector of other plan characteristics, and ϵ is a random element, assumed to be iid normal (independently and identically distributed). This model asserts that plan costs are a function of the number of plan participants, the assets per participant, the number of participants per firm (a measure of internal coordination costs), and possibly other factors. The crucial scale parameter is β_1, which indicates economies of scale in pension administration if less than one ($\beta_1 < 1$).

Caswell (1976), using this model to estimate the administrative cost structure of multiemployer pension plans in the construction industry, found strong evidence of large-scale economies. Drawing his data from informational forms submitted on collectively bargained pension plans to the Department of Labor in 1970, Caswell reported pension administrative costs per participant of approximately 4 percent of total contributions. Holding firm size (P/F) constant, Caswell estimated that a doubling of pension plan size yielded about a 20 percent reduction in administrative costs: $\hat{\beta}_1 - 1 = -0.202$.

Mitchell and Andrews (1981) estimated a log linear cost model similar to that of Caswell on a broader sample of multiemployer pension plans. Their data was drawn from 5500 Forms filed in 1975 in accordance with the Employment Retirement Income Security Act (ERISA) regulations. They considered only defined benefit trust plans, but did not limit their study to collectively bargained plans. In a multivariate analysis similar in form to Equation (1), they found evidence of scale economies in pension administration that were strikingly similar to Caswell's results for the construction industry. With assets per participant (A/P) held constant, a doubling of pension plan size yielded about a 20 percent reduction in administrative costs: $\hat{\beta}_1 - 1 = -0.170$.[14]

Also using data from Form 5500 filings, Turner and Beller (1989:438) report pension administrative costs per participant by plan size for (multiemployer) benefit plans in 1985. Although the Turner-Beller tables provide no data on many of the controls in the Caswell and the Mitchell-Andrews studies, estimation of the log linear model for defined benefit plans yielded estimates of scale economies similar to the earlier studies:[15]

$$\hat{\beta}_1 - 1 = -0.185 \tag{2}$$

Evidence on administrative scale economies in single-employer plans is less abundant, because it is difficult to isolate pension administrative costs within the firm. An accounting cost study of single-employer plans by Hay/Huggins (1990) reveals, however, that scale economies in single employer plans are large as well. Hay/Huggins employs a task-pricing approach, estimating the cost of activities required to maintain a defined benefit pension plan for several different plan sizes. The study appears to emphasize accountancy costs—the purchase of actuarial services to design the plan, the accounting time required to prepare the annual report, and so forth. The cost estimates for the day-to-day functioning of management, record keeping, and disbursement are probably less reliable. The estimated economies of scale for ongoing administrative costs in a defined benefit plan is (absolutely) greater than in the statistical cost studies reported above: $\hat{\beta}_1 - 1 = -0.324$. Given the potential bias in the study toward accountancy costs with their large fixed-cost component, this figure does not appear inconsistent with the 20 percent estimates of the multiemployer plans.

Given the magnitude of the scale economies in pension plan cost, a surprising finding is that small pension plans exist; indeed they exist in great number. In 1985 there were 800,000 single-employer plans covering 65 million participants, and 3,000 multiemployer plans covering 9 million workers (Turner and Beller, 1989:350). Apparently cross-firm pooling is expensive. Caswell's analysis indicates that the number of employers in multiemployer plans affects internal plan costs, perhaps owing to higher negotiation, coordination, and collection costs. Caswell's estimate of the effect on log costs of the log of (active) plan participants per firm (P/F) or β_3 is -0.153, which implies that a doubling of the number of *employers*, holding constant the total participant size of the pension plan, *increases* total administrative costs by 15 percent.

These costs no doubt rise with heterogeneity, and it is not surprising that many existing multiemployer plans are industry-specific. Indeed many are the result of collective bargaining with a single union, a situation that is likely to provide a variety of cost savings. Union effects on pension coverage are most substantial in workplaces that would otherwise not naturally support them, for example, small firm industries in which interfirm mobility is high (Slavick, 1966; Freeman, 1985). Skolnik (1976) concludes his historical review on a similar note; multiemployer pension plans supported by unions in small-firm industries were apparently a major factor in the expansion of pension coverage in the 1950s and 1960s.

Diseconomies of Scale in Idiosyncratic Decisions

The evidence that large firms use rules rather than discretion is pervasive. Although more elaborate models of mandatory retirement can be developed (see below), mandatory retirement can be viewed as no more than the wholesale substitution of rules for discretion in the separation decision. Consistent with diseconomies of scale in idiosyncratic decisions, mandatory retirement rules were almost universal in very large workplaces and much less common in small ones (Slavick, 1966; see also Parsons, 1983). Slavick undertook an ambitious mail survey of establishments to ascertain their pension and retirement policies in 1961. The sample was "a random sample, stratified by size, of all business and industrial units with 50 or more employees reporting to the Bureau of Old-Age and Survivors Insurance in March 1956" (Slavick, 1966:8). In the first wave of the survey, 466 usable returns were obtained. The relationships of retirement policy by company size is reported in Table 5-2. The strong effect of company size on retirement policy is clear; in firms of size 50 to 249, 63 percent of all plants responding reported flexible retirement plans; in firms of 10,000 or more, 10 percent reported flexible plans. Only a modest number of establishments, under 20 percent in all firm size categories, reported mixed plans such as a flexible one for some workers, a mandatory one for others.

Additional evidence that the pattern of mandatory retirement reflects the higher costs of sorting in large firms can be found in Table 5-3, in which differ-

TABLE 5-2 Distribution of Local Plants by Company Size and Compulsory Retirement Status, 1961, in Percentages (Parentheses show number of local plants)

| Size of Company | Retirement Policy | | | | |
	Flexible	Mandatory Late	Mandatory Normal	Mixed	Total
50-249	63.3%	6.7%	30.0%	—	100.0%
	(19)	(2)	(9)		(30)
250-499	40.0	11.4	42.8	5.7	100.0
	(14)	(4)	(15)	(2)	(35)
500-999	33.3	13.3	36.7	16.7	100.0
	(10)	(4)	(11)	(5)	(30)
1000-9999	14.2	17.0	53.8	15.1	100.0
	(15)	(18)	(57)	(16)	(106)
10,000+	10.3	37.9	32.8	19.0	100.0
	(6)	(22)	(19)	(11)	(58)

SOURCE: Slavick (1966:77). Copyright © 1966 by Cornell University. Used by permission of the publisher, ILR Press, an imprint of Cornell University Press.

TABLE 5-3 Distribution of Local Plants by Company Size and the "Percentage of Employees Reaching the Compulsory Retirement Age Who Were Excepted From Compulsory Retirement Policies," 1961 (Parentheses show number of local plants)

| Size of Company | Percent of Employees Excepted | | | | | |
	0%	1% - 9%	10% - 29%	30% - 49%	50%+	Total
50-249	—	20.0%	40.0%	20.0%	20.0%	100.0%
		(1)	(2)	(1)	(1)	(5)
250-449	36.4	—	63.6	—	—	100.0
	(4)		(7)			(11)
500-999	44.4	—	11.1	33.3	11.1	100.0
	(4)		(1)	(3)	(1)	(9)
(50-999)	32.0	4.0	40.0	16.0	8.0	100.0
	(8)	(1)	(10)	(4)	(2)	(25)
1000-9999	71.8	10.3	12.8	—	5.1	100.0
	(28)	(4)	(5)		(2)	(39)
10,000+	80.0	20.0	—	—	—	100.0
	(12)	(3)				(15)

SOURCE: Slavick (1966:114). Copyright © 1966 by Cornell University. Used by permission of the publisher, ILR Press, an imprint of Cornell University Press.

ences are reported by firm size in the extent to which mandatory retirement rules were "excepted." In the smallest firm category (50 to 249), all plants reported making some exceptions to the mandatory retirement age; in the largest, 80 percent report zero exceptions to the rule. Clearly, not only are large firms more likely to impose mandatory retirement rules; those that do are more likely to enforce them strictly.

An additional factor is important in forming long-term relationships, namely the reliability of the contracting partners. The following transactions costs regularity has emerged (from, e.g., Oi, 1983a): large firms are more reliable long-term contracting partners (F4). Reasons for this are not hard to enumerate. Reputational enforcement of implicit contracts is likely to be stronger in large firms (Parsons, 1986). A potential new hire is less likely to know of the reliability of a small firm than of a large one from casual hearsay. The new hire's odds of encountering a disaffected worker or a friend or relative of one from a small firm becomes vanishingly small in large labor markets. Small firms are also more likely to fail than are large ones and therefore they make less attractive contracting partners, even if much is known about their prior relationships with workers; a failed firm is a poor debtor.

Evidence for the greater contract reliability of large firms can be found in the pension literature. To the extent that employers are more reliable, they can offer a greater number of "insurance" features in the pensions they provide. Inflation protection would seem an important feature of a pension plan, one that would be valuable to most workers. A potentially valuable inflation insurance attribute of a pension is the inflation adjustment of retiree benefits after retirement. If not an explicit part of a collective bargaining agreement, such a process relies heavily on reputation mechanisms for enforcement. The presence of such post-retirement pension income protection is, therefore, an indicator of reliable implicit contracting between the organization and the worker.

Clark, Allen, and Sumner (1986) report on the post-retirement adjustment of pensions during the high (and unexpected) inflation period of the 1970s; between 1973 and 1979, the consumer price index increased by 63.3 percent. In the pension sample they analyzed, the change in benefits as a percentage of the change in the consumer price index over the 1973-1979 period among pre-1972 retirees was 37.9 percent (1986:185).[16] The relative adjustment was 45.2 percent among union plans, only 29.2 percent among nonunion ones. Much of this difference, however, appears to be due to the disproportionate union representation in large firms. Consider the reported variation in post-retirement adjustments in benefits by collective bargaining status and plan size in Table 5-4. It would appear that post-retirement adjustments within pension plans of equal size are largely unaffected by collective bargaining status within plans of similar size.

Evidence from a wide variety of sources indicates that the implicit contract is a surprisingly strong one. Allen, Clark, and McDermed (1995) report that the incidence of post-retirement benefit adjustments in the 1980s, although propor-

TABLE 5-4   The Change in Mean Pension Benefits
between 1973 and 1979 as a Percentage of the Change
in the Consumer Price Index Among Pre-1973 Retirees,
by Plan Size (1979) and Collective Bargaining Status,
in Percentages

Size of Firm	With Collective Bargaining	Without Collective Bargaining
1-99	6.3	5.2
100-499	18.8	26.7
500-999	17.9	25.0
1000-4999	13.3	15.8
5000-9999	33.3	32.5
10,000+	66.7	42.8

SOURCE: Clark, Allen, and Sumner (1986:Tables 13 and 14).

tionately less generous than in the high inflation 1970s, were independent of the financial performance of the pension plan, a result that suggests that firms did not renege on expected inflation adjustments simply because plan performance was poor. (They provide weak evidence that the magnitude of the inflation adjustment was affected by plan performance.) Cornwell, Dorsey, and Mehrzad (1991) find no evidence that firms strategically lay off workers prior to retirement when inflation rates are unusually high so that the "quit" value of the pension is much less than the "stay value." (These terms are more carefully defined below.) Curme and Kahn (1990) find only weak evidence that the likelihood of business failure affects the incidence of pensions (only among nonunion, nonmanufacturing workers is the industry failure rate significantly and positively related to pension coverage rates), suggesting that workers are in general not concerned about this contingency. The data, it should be noted, are drawn from the post-ERISA period (1983).

In a somewhat different direction, Ippolito (1986:Chap. 13) reports that "reversions" of overfunded pension plans—terminating the program and capturing the value of the plan above the level required by ERISA (the pension's quit value), was relatively rare and was frequently accompanied by the establishment of a new plan. Moreover, the probability of a voluntary reversion was not significantly affected by the recent prosperity of the industry. In a more exhaustive study, Petersen (1992) does find modest evidence of strategic reversions that might have breached the implicit contract between firm and workers, at least before a federal excise tax was placed on the activity in 1986. (Ippolito's data were also from the pre-1986 period.) "Firms that are experiencing income shortfalls and that are least able to obtain additional funding in the financial markets are most likely to revert their pensions" (Petersen, 1992:1047). As Ippolito

(1986) stresses, it is impossible to know with current data whether this is a loan or a breach of contract. However, Pontiff, Schleifer, and Weisbach (1990) report that reversions are more frequent after takeovers and especially after hostile takeovers, when a breach of the implicit contract would seem most plausible, but the effects are not large: 15 percent of hostile acquirers revert within 2 years of the takeover; only 8 percent of friendly acquirers do so.

THE EMPLOYMENT OF OLDER WORKERS[17]

Firms differ greatly in their propensity to employ older workers. Before I explore that statement more carefully, it will be useful to decompose the universe of jobs by partitioning firm/worker matches into those expected to be short term and those expected to be long term. In the discussion below, these will be labeled short-term contracts and long-term contracts, although the contract may be an implicit one. For short-term contracts, the duration of the job is by definition limited and the firm can vary the age distribution of its employees only through age-of-hire restrictions. Moreover, short job tenure discourages pension coverage because, in the absence of unions or other trade group organizations, short tenure translates into small pension accounts, which are more expensive per dollar to administer than large ones. Short-term contract jobs are more likely to be part time, and part-time jobs are more likely to be short term, but the linkage is not a tight one. Full-year, part-week jobs are often quite stable over time (Blank, 1989), although even stable part-time jobs are typically associated with relatively low pension coverage.

In long-term relationships, the policy options multiply. As workers age, the firm can maintain them in their long-term jobs, with or without pay cuts; it can reassign them, typically reducing their responsibilities, again with or without pay cuts; or it can release them, with or without pensions. In the absence of legal restrictions, a firm can implement its age policies by rule, across broad classes of workers, or selectively, perhaps screening older workers more intensively than younger ones. Although job reassignment by rule at a given age is not unknown, most rules trigger separation from the firm (mandatory retirement). In another direction, long-term contracts make the provision of pensions less costly. In the dual labor market framework, short-term jobs are more likely to be "bad" jobs and bad jobs are more likely to be short term, but again the association is far from perfect; from jobs in construction to those in economic consulting, job duration may be limited yet the job very lucrative.

Consider now the measurement of employment propensity by age. A plausible, but simple measure of employment propensity by age is the share of the firm's work force that is over x years of age, say 55:

$$S55 = \frac{\text{Number of Workers 55 or Older}}{\text{Number of Workers in Total}}$$

In a stationary world, this measure would appear to capture unambiguously the sense of the firm's age policy on employment, although it is less appealing in a nonstationary one. Because new hires are drawn disproportionately from new entrants, the proportion of new hires that is older will be lower (or higher) in a rapidly growing (or declining) firm than in the steady state. For example, the fact that workers in the farm sector are disproportionately older may say less about the intrinsic employment prospects of older workers in that sector than about the fact that employment in the farm sector has been in secular decline. Conversely a rapidly growing industry will, other things being equal, have fewer older workers.

The S55 measure is strongly and negatively related to both firm size and unionism (Parsons, 1983). The larger the firm size, the lower the fraction of the work force that is composed of older workers. The similarity of the large-firm effect and the union effect on the employment share of older workers suggests that the large-firm effect may be no more than a pension income effect, signifying nothing about firm demand—workers with pensions retire earlier than do those without pensions. If large firms serve as relatively cost-effective financial intermediaries, then by providing pensions they may make early retirement relatively more attractive to the worker. Similarly, if Internal Revenue Service (IRS) nondiscrimination clauses force firms to "oversave" on behalf of some workers, most plausibly low-income workers, then again workers might retire earlier than they otherwise would. Conversely, older workers may retire disproportionately because large firms find older workers especially unproductive, perhaps because of high sorting and reassignment costs. In short, the relative absence of older workers in some workplaces may be driven by supply or demand considerations.

To explore the demand factors that influence the older worker employment share, it is useful to look at the policies that the firm can use to manipulate the fraction of older workers in its work force: (1) the age profile of compensation, which influences voluntary job-departure decisions, and (2) quantity constraints on the employment of older workers, including more or less formal policies on maximum age of hire and/or compulsory retirement. Because of the negative responses of workers to direct wage cuts (W4), firms seem to focus on pension structure and direct age-based hiring and retention practices to alter the worker's employment structure.

Compensation Profiles

In standard labor supply models of retirement, firms monitor the worker's productivity and, in competitive markets, pass on that value to the worker in the form of a compensation offer. The worker then calculates his or her optimal work strategy based on current compensation and the expected lifetime wage profile. The shape of the compensation profile reflects the firm's estimate of the worker's productivity profile, which in turn is presumably a function of the worker's occupation and education. It may also be a function of the characteristics of the firm. For example, if firms of a particular type are very poor at reassigning workers as the worker's talents and physical and mental attributes change, the worker's wage offer in those firms will decline more precipitously than otherwise, perhaps inducing earlier departure from these firms. The standard argument is that large firms have greater difficulty making idiosyncratic decisions (F3) and may therefore be less efficient at transferring older workers to new positions that maximize their productivities. If this is true, workers in large firms should have greater declines in total compensation with age than do workers in other firms.

There is substantial evidence that long-term-contract firms historically reduced the compensation levels of workers as they aged, almost exclusively through actuarially unfair adjustments to pension benefits that are now illegal. There is also good evidence that these accrual strategies have the expected effects on retirement behaviors (see below and the reviews in Kotlikoff and Wise, 1989, and Quinn, Burkhauser, and Myers, 1990).

The standard wage model is, of course, only one of many, and other models imply quite different firm motivations. An alternative model of actuarially unfair pension structures derives the terminal provisions of employment contracts as an employer-employee response to the incompleteness of the disability-insurance market (see Nalebuff and Zeckhauser, 1985, and Merton, 1985).[18] In this environment, actuarially unfair pensions arise in the optimal employment contract as implicit disability insurance: resources are shifted to early job leavers who are disproportionately individuals unable to work because of the early onset of a severe disability. There may be moral hazard problems; workers retire earlier under this incentive system, but that is an unwanted side effect rather than an objective of the firm.

Age-based quantity constraints suffer from no such ambiguity of interpretation. These constraints may restrict hiring practices and/or retention practices, both of which are important in the determination of the share of older individuals in the work force. The two mechanisms are potentially related in an important way; if firms retain workers because of heavy specific human capital investments, they are likely to prefer hiring younger workers to maximize the returns to training. (There is a limit, of course, to this process—very young workers with high intrinsic turnover rates would also be avoided.) In the spot market, of course, only hiring practices are important because, by definition, jobs are of limited duration.

At one level, the crucial policy issue is the share of older workers employed by the firm; whether a firm employs large numbers of older workers because it hires many older new hires or because it retains many previously employed workers is not important. The openness of the firm to new hires of older workers is crucial, however, to unemployed older workers, so that the analyses of retention and new-hire behaviors hold a policy interest beyond their implications for employment levels. These two quantity constraints are considered in the remainder of this section.

Mandatory Retirement Rules

Because of recent legislation to make mandatory retirement rules illegal, such rules have been the subject of considerable study by economists and others. Most intensely studied has been the motivation for mandatory retirement rules (e.g., Lazear, 1979; Blinder, 1982; see also the literature reviews in Parsons, 1986; Leigh, 1984; and Lang, 1989). Although currently illegal in most circumstances in the United States, mandatory retirement rules surely reflect underlying employer demand considerations that are perhaps only imperfectly legislated away and therefore remain of policy interest. For example, one would conjecture that most "bridge" jobs between career jobs and complete withdrawal from the labor force are *not* characterized by rules on maximum age of hire or job retention. We return to this question below.

Why are long-term contracts so frequently characterized by fixed-age termination provisions in the absence of government regulation? The most prominent theory of mandatory retirement is that proposed by Lazear. Lazear's basic insight is that mandatory retirement is a quantity constraint, one imposed and enforced by management, so that net compensation at that point in the life cycle must exceed the value of product. This is a special case of the general result of Akerlof and Miyazaki (1980); employment contracts in which wages optimally deviate from productivity will typically require quantity specifications as well as wage specifications. The fundamental issue then is why wage premiums are being paid to workers near the mandatory retirement age and why the restriction on these wage premiums takes the form of an age limitation.

Lazear's discussion of mandatory retirement is diffuse and includes the implausible argument that pensions are deferred payments with the property that they can be altered after retirement to adjust for late-arriving information on worker productivity. More appealing is the proposition that can perhaps be summarized as follows:

(1) Compensation grows faster over the life cycle than does productivity because of lifelong monitoring problems: at some point wages exceed productivity as a consequence.

(2) The deviation between wage and productivity may lead to a deviation away from the worker's (unconstrained) choice of retirement age.

Under this argument, mandatory retirement rules simply induce workers to retire at the age they would choose if they faced a compensation scheme that reflected their productivity rather than their age.

Blinder (1982) has proposed a variant on argument (2), that the divergence of wages from productivity may be the consequence of specific human capital. The existence of specific human capital, however, does not itself generate over-payment in the final period: as in the Lazear model, additional assumptions on the age profiles of wages and productivity are required. In both cases the models are "completed" with an appeal to the notion that a continuing, indeed growing, gap between wages and productivity requires a well-specified terminal point for the contract to "balance" as it must for a profit-maximizing firm in a competitive market. This argument does not hold in a model that recognizes the existence of disability and death. Even without mandatory retirement, work is not forever. If able to contract freely, employers and workers appear to prefer a fixed-end-point contract, but that is a choice, not a requirement.

In one direct attempt to assess the validity of the Lazear hypothesis, Hutchens (1987) estimates the impact of detailed job characteristics, including an index of work repetitiveness and of firm-specific human capital, on firm personnel poli-cies, including pensions, mandatory retirement, long tenure, and wage rates.[19] First introducing work repetitiveness, he concludes, "Within this population of older workers, jobs with repetitive tasks tend to be characterized by low wages, short job tenures, lack of pensions, and absence of mandatory retirement, ceteris paribus" (1987:S163). As Hutchens notes, this pattern of results is consistent with virtually all theories, but he takes special note of the fact that it is consistent with Lazear's "delayed payment" theory of pensions; if the work activity is simple, the malfeasance detection lag should be short. Subsequent analyses by Hutchens in the same paper reveal that the job repetitiveness finding may simply reflect its (negative) correlation with the training and education requirements of the job; when a general educational development index is included, the repetition measure is insignificant and indeed of the wrong sign.

The fact that mandatory retirement rules are disproportionately found in large, unionized firms could be the result of the agency problems laid out by Lazear or Blinder. Alternatively it could be no more than a reflection of the fact that large, unionized firms have more formal rules of all types, itself a reflection of the high cost of dealing with idiosyncratic decisions in large firms. There is strong evidence that large firms have high transactions costs in such matters, including the lack of exceptions to the mandatory retirement rules (see "The Aging Worker and the Firm" above). The number of mandatory retirement plans in the typical firm is one or two (Slavick, 1966), with little or no distinction made across workers in different occupations. A broad distinction is occasionally made across blue collar and white collar workers, with the blue collar workers typically having the later compulsory retirement age.

Other evidence also casts doubt on the Lazear and Blinder hypotheses, at least in the simple form in which they were originally presented. For example, when the minimum legal mandatory retirement age was pushed to 70, a number of researchers predicted that the legislation would have little effect on retirement behavior because the rules were binding on the decisions of a relatively few workers. Most workers covered by mandatory retirement provisions planned to retire by the age at which the original rules would become effective (Barker and Clark, 1980; Burkhauser and Quinn, 1983; Parnes and Nestel, 1981). This prediction seems to have been validated by subsequent events.

The fact that mandatory retirement rules do not appear to be targeted on the average worker suggests, however, that the answer to the question of why mandatory retirement rules exist must be sought somewhere other than the representative-worker models of Lazear or Blinder; the best evidence is that employers can move older workers out of their work places with appropriate uses of the pension carrot if they are long tenured in the firm; the stick is not needed. For excellent reviews, see Quinn, Burkhauser, and Myers (1990) and Kotlikoff and Wise (1989). I argue that the rationale for mandatory retirement lies instead in the age-of-hire heterogeneity of the work force (Parsons, 1991a). The rules are binding, not on the standard case of those with long tenure and comfortable prospective pension incomes, but on those who entered the pension-covered job later in life and therefore carry with them more limited pension rights.[20] These rules provide a mechanism for limiting the wage premiums captured by these late arrivals (who will have accumulated less generous pension rights at the traditional retirement age and will therefore be more likely to desire continued employment into their less productive older years).

New-Hire Policies

Before I turn to the review of firm new-hire policies and what they imply about the firm's demand for older workers, consider the measurement question. One measure of the firm's desire to hire older workers is the share of older workers who are recent hires, that is, the ratio of new hires of older workers (say hires within the last 5 years) to the total employment of older workers in the firm or industry (Hutchens, 1986, 1987, 1993):

$$SN55a = \frac{\text{Number of Workers 55+ Hired in Last 5 Years}}{\text{Total Number of Workers 55+}}$$

This measure is sensitive to hiring trends in the industry. Firms tend to reduce hiring before they begin laying off workers so that a declining firm or industry will, other things being equal, have a low SN55a measure. An alternative measure that is more robust to recent demand fluctuations would be the following:

$$\text{SN55b} = \frac{\text{Number of Workers 55+ Hired in Last 5 Years}}{\text{Number of Workers of All Ages Hired in Last 5 Years}}$$

This measure norms new hires of older workers by the number of new hires of all workers. Both measures are perhaps best interpreted as an index of the prevalence of long-term contracting in the industry. SN55a, for example, is simply an indicator of how the older worker came to be employed in the industry, as a new hire or a retention, and is silent on the question of how good a provider of jobs for older workers the firm may be.

In a series of studies, Hutchens (1986, 1987, 1993) examines the distribution of new hires of older workers across industries and occupations. Hutchens (1986) creates an index of older three-digit industry and occupation changers as a fraction of all older workers (a variant of SN55a) using data from the 1970 1-in-1,000 census data file. In the 28,000 occupational and industrial cells he created, the index ranged from 0.329 to 1.11.

> Examples of jobs with low values of the index are lawyers in legal services and welders in miscellaneous fabricated metals. Jobs with high values include de- livery- and route-men in miscellaneous wholesale trade and janitors in medical and other health services (Hutchens, 1986:453).

Hutchens reports that the share of older workers that have been recently hired is highly and inversely correlated with other indexes of long-term contracting, such as tenure, premium earnings, pension coverage, and the presence of mandatory retirement rules. Hutchens specifically notes that this constellation of results is consistent with agency-induced upward-sloping wage profiles of Lazear (1979, 1983), but again it is also consistent with any other long-term contract motivation—it is in fact a measure of long-term contracting. Using both SN55a and SN55b measures, he demonstrates that the new hires of older workers are much more concentrated by occupation and industry cell than the employment of older workers in general or new hires of younger workers (Hutchens, 1987).

In a subsequent paper, Hutchens (1993) creates the same SN55a index, using CPS data in the 1980s, and merges it into the 1988 Survey of Displaced Workers. He then examines various relationships on the merged data, including the impact of age on an index of post-displacement job quality and the impact of pre-displacement job tenure on the size of the decline in the index and compensation between pre- and post-displacement separation. Surprisingly, in a sample of married, male high school graduates, there was no relationship between the post-displacement job index and age. Or as Hutchens (1993:99) remarks, "There is no support for the hypothesis that older workers tend to obtain jobs in industries and occupations characterized by short job tenures." Indeed older workers were more likely to find jobs in their old industry and occupation, though they were also more likely to be not employed. The negative finding on short tenure is somewhat puzzling and appears to be inconsistent with findings in the bridge-job literature.

Given the prevalence of long-term contracting in large, unionized firms, it should not be surprising to find that, when legal, large and unionized firms hire relatively few older workers and indeed have formal age-of-hire restrictions. If the system is structured to encourage career jobs, then firms may avoid hiring older workers as an indirect result of their hiring/training system. The bridge-job literature suggests that job openings for older workers are found primarily in low wage/part-time jobs. Unfortunately the focus of this literature has been on the stability of occupation and industry between career jobs and bridge jobs rather than on the size and union status of the job as is the case in the pension literature. As Ruhm (1990:488) summarizes his findings based on data from the Retirement History Survey:

> Despite the high financial costs of changing employment sectors, bridge jobs are rarely located in the same one-digit industry and occupation as career employment. Fewer than a quarter (23.9%) of respondents remain in their career industry and occupation in their first subsequent position, and barely half (51.6%) stay in either the same one-digit industry or occupation.

For those who consider themselves partially retired, the percentage who take bridge jobs in the same industry and occupation is only 11.4 percent (Ruhm, 1990:489). "Workers almost never partially retire on their career jobs" Ruhm, 1990:490). Using an alternative definition of career job, Quinn, Burkhauser, and Myers (1990:177) report that only 5 percent of male wage and salary earners in the Retirement History Survey who leave full-time career jobs move to part time status on the career job, less than half the fraction that are part-time on new jobs.[21] See Hurd (1993) and Hurd and McGarry (1993) for reviews of this and related research.

A more interesting, but more empirically delicate question is whether large, unionized firms hire fewer older workers, given the firm's contracting status (long term or short). For example, if older job applicants are more heterogeneous, making assessment of their capabilities more difficult, larger firms may be more reluctant than small ones to hire or retain them (Parsons, 1983).

EMPLOYER-PROVIDED PENSIONS

Employers are a major supplier of retirement annuities in the United States. Below I first review what is known about the forces that determine the distribution of employer-provided pensions across sectors.[22] I then turn to consideration of recent pension trends. Not all pensions are the same, and discussions of both the point-in-time equilibrium and secular trends would be incomplete without partitioning pensions by type. It is useful to distinguish three types of pension plans: defined benefit plans, traditional defined contribution plans, and 401(k) plans. Defined benefit plans typically offer the retiree an annuity based on years of service and age, in contrast to defined contribution plans, which are essentially savings plans with investment risk on the worker's shoulders rather than the firm's.[23] The employer may not even commit to contributing to the plan on a regular basis; in the recent past almost two-thirds of all defined contribution plans were deferred profit-sharing plans, with employer contributions specified in a variety of ways, including employer discretion, Kruse (1993). Although 401(k) plans have characteristics in common with traditional defined contribution plans, they have unique features that warrant separate consideration. The typical 401(k) plan involves voluntary employee participation in the plan through employee contributions and, in most cases, with employer matching. The 401(k) plans are popular as secondary plans, although our main interest will be in their use as primary plans.

The Locus of Pension Coverage

Consider first the locus of pension coverage without distinguishing specific types. As with age-based hiring provisions, pension coverage is a workplace phenomenon, not an individual one (Slavick, 1966; Parsons, 1992). IRS nondiscrimination rules reinforce the scale and transaction-cost economies that make coverage of employment rules so broad; employer-provided pensions qualify for favorable tax treatment only if they are available to a broad cross section of workers in the workplace.

Although it is not immediately relevant to the discussion, I should note that this workplace-wide characteristic makes problematic the usual interpretation of parameters in pension studies. Treating the estimated parameters in individual-pension-status regressions as individual-demand equations or reduced-form (demand and supply) equations just because the data are individual observations is incorrect in a heterogeneous workplace. For example, as a demand-driven phenomenon, individual pension coverage is the convolution of two processes: the firm's response to the aggregate characteristics of its workers and the worker's choice of firm. In a world of positive mobility costs and varying wage premiums across workplaces, the choice of employer will be driven by a wide range of forces other than pension status. Indeed, at the age many workers settle into lifetime contract jobs, there is little reason to imagine that pension coverage status is a crucial factor. The young are often ignorant of the nature of their pensions (Mitchell, 1988; Gustman and Steinmeier, 1989), an observation consistent with the finding that young workers do not pay compensating differentials for pension coverage (see below). Pension coverage is a function of the distribution of worker characteristics, not of individual ones.

The industrial locus of employer-provided pensions can be explained reasonably well by two factors: the tax advantages that tax deferral offers high-income workers and the economies of scale in pension administration costs that make pension provisions cheaper the larger the pension pool (the firm or union) (Parsons, 1992). For example, pension coverage is much more prevalent in workplaces characterized by high average earnings and in large, unionized workplaces (Slavick, 1966; Lazear, 1979; Parsons, 1983; Freeman, 1985; Dorsey, 1982, 1987). For additional evidence on the responsiveness of pension provision to tax policies, see Woodbury and Huang (1991) and Reagan and Turner (1995); for a discussion of scale economies in pension provision, see section on "The Aging Worker and the Firm" above.

That these two factors are sufficient to explain the industrial locus of pension status does not mean that other factors are not important, but that the other factors either are collinear with scale and income or are not of the same magnitude of effect. Chief among the set of alternative hypotheses is the agency argument, most systematically developed by Ippolito (1985, 1986, 1987). Nonvested pensions provide a form of mobility and performance bond.[24] Historically, employer-provided pensions were overwhelmingly defined benefit plans, with the firm promising longtime, "loyal" workers the equivalent of an annuity upon retirement, but offering nothing if the worker left without employer approval. Pension bonding of this sort could have a number of objectives, including the following: (1) bonding against union activity (Latimer, 1932; Williamson, 1992; Gratton, 1990; and a variant on this argument by Ippolito, 1985);[25] (2) bonding against voluntary job turnover; and (3) bonding against poor job performance.[26] Gratton's review of internal deliberations at the Pennsylvania Railroad suggests that the first two objectives may have been especially important in the early development of employer-provided pensions (see also Williamson, 1992).

The importance of private pensions as voluntary job-mobility bonds is currently the focus of debate (e.g., Gustman and Steinmeier, 1995; Allen, Clark, and McDermed, 1993). Before summarizing the elements of this debate, it is useful to recall that pensions as a mobility bond have been severely constrained by legislation in the past two decades. In particular, ERISA has greatly restricted the firm's vesting options, thereby limiting the firm's ability to backload the contract. Prior to ERISA, 40 percent of all pensions were never vested. Now all pensions must be vested in a relatively short time; under recent amendments to ERISA, a firm using cliff vesting, for example, must vest its workers' pensions within 5 years. If the pension is vested, the penalty for quitting a job is more modest, the difference between the quit value of the pension and the stay value (Ippolito, 1986).[27] This difference is largely driven by the incomplete inflation protection afforded benefits to those who separate from the firm long before retirement. In the typical defined benefit plan, benefits are payable only after a specified age, with payments based on a measure of final years' earnings. The final years' earnings base provides implicit inflation protection to employed workers, but the nominal earnings of job leavers are frozen in time. Although this quit penalty may be of serious concern to a potential job leaver, the penalty is less than the total loss of pension rights associated with an unauthorized job departure in an unvested plan.

Accurate measurement of causal influences becomes correspondingly more important, but measurement is a problem here, especially the separation of the mobility-disincentive effect of the quit-stay differential from the pay premium effect of the pension. The existence of a pension plan is correlated with reduced early and midlife mobility (Schiller and Weiss, 1979; Mitchell, 1982). What is less clear is whether this effect is due to a compensation premium or to a specific pension effect. Allen, Clark, and McDermed (1993) believe they have separated these effects successfully and estimate a large disincentive effect. Gustman and Steinmeier (1995) question this finding on a number of grounds, including their own estimates, which suggest a much smaller role for the capital loss effect. They also argue that the losses implied by the quit-stay differential are rather small compared with even a modest raise, the end result, presumably, of a quit. Perhaps most compelling is their finding that the mobility-reducing effect of defined contribution plans, which have no significant quit penalty, is almost identical to that of defined benefit plans, which do (see also Even and Macpherson, 1992). Unfortunately the identification of pension type (defined benefit versus defined contribution) is subject to large errors in these data sets, so the power of this finding is correspondingly diminished.[28]

Measurement of the pay premium is especially difficult, involving as it does the question of whether the worker is paying for his or her pension through a compensating differential (reduced wages). Although economists are generally willing to assume the existence of compensating differentials, there is little solid empirical evidence of this phenomenon. The majority of the compensating differential studies report small and imprecise effects of pension coverage on earnings, although at least one recent effort finds stronger evidence for such an effect (Montgomery, Shaw, and Benedict, 1992). Because earnings affect pension coverage and pension coverage affects earnings, the empirical analysis inevitably involves instrumental variables and inclusion restrictions that would fail rather modest plausibility standards.

Defined benefit plans can also be used to "gracefully" sculpt the age profile of compensation without inducing serious worker morale problems (W4), and indeed economists have accumulated a great deal of evidence that the structure of defined benefit plans can be used to induce exit from the firm (e.g., Burkhauser, 1979, 1980; Lazear, 1983; Lazear and Moore, 1988; Ippolito, 1986; Kotlikoff and Wise, 1989; and Stock and Wise, 1990. For important surveys, see Fields and Mitchell, 1984; Ippolito, 1986; Kotlikoff and Wise, 1989; and Quinn, Burkhauser, and Myers, 1990). The basic notion is that the age profile of earnings tends to be stable but that variations in the accumulation of pension benefit rights by age can be structured to reduce effective compensation, providing firms with a graceful way to reduce a worker's compensation. For example, it was once common to stop pension accruals at age 65, so that future benefits would not increase with continued work after 65. The actuarial value of compensation is reduced because pension income is postponed a year, which not only reduces the present value of the benefit flow, but also reduces its actuarial value because of positive mortality rates. With pension benefits of reasonable size, these effects can be very large relative to annual earnings although it should be again noted that the options available to the firm in constructing an age-based benefit are now severely restricted by government regulation.

Kotlikoff and Wise (1989:Chap. 4) present the beginnings of an analysis of how pension accrual rates vary with attributes of the firm and worker although confidentiality restrictions on their data, the Bureau of Labor Statistics' 1979 Level of Benefits Survey, limit firm characteristics to an industry identifier. Kotlikoff and Wise report that pension accrual rates are quite similar across industries (and occupations) for plans with the same early and normal retirement ages. They report large differences across industries in normal retirement age, however, including an especially low "normal age of retirement" in the transportation sector (55 years). The reasons for this differential are not explored. Clearly much remains to be done in this area. A critical question is the economic importance to the firm of this mechanism for reducing worker compensation.

Although defined benefit plans have historically been the predominant form of coverage in the United States, defined contribution plans, often equated with savings plans, have grown rapidly in the last decade. Before a discussion of these trends, it will be useful to consider the factors that determine the industrial locus of pensions by type. In defined contribution plans, the firm's contributions typically vest immediately and lump-sum settlements at the time of job separation are common. Administrative costs are low, even for small plans, much less than those in a defined benefit plan. For plans with 50 to 99 participants, the absolute administrative cost differential between defined benefit and defined contribution plans was equal to $100 in 1985, approximately the same as the total cost of supplying a defined contribution plan. The absolute cost differential is only $39 for plans with 20,000 to 49,999 participants. Defined contribution plans are also more easily transportable across firms, an appealing attribute when firm mobility is intrinsically high as in seasonal work.[29]

Other factors may also explain the concentration of defined benefit plans in large workplaces. These plans have a number of agency properties that are likely to be more highly valued in large firms; for example, the various bonding and wage-sculpting attributes of pensions discussed in the last section are in fact characteristics of defined benefit plans. However, defined contribution plans may also have agency functions. The great majority of defined contribution plans are deferred profit-sharing plans, with employer contributions based on profits, wages, and simple "employer discretion" (Kruse, 1993). Economists are prone to assume that worker payments contingent on the success of the firm serve to align worker motivations with those of the firm and therefore increase productivity, although Kruse's efforts to measure the productivity effect of profit-sharing plans

are disappointing from that perspective. Estimated productivity effects are positive on average, but the dispersion is large and the magnitude of effect small.
Surprisingly, strict profit-sharing plans (employer contributions based on a pre-
specified profit share) are less productive than those in which employer contributions are at the firm's discretion (Kruse, 1993). Andrews (1992) argues that
profit-sharing plans are attractive to employers for a quite different reason, the
flexibility of contributions. In a bad year, firms can contribute less to the pension
plan, in good years more. This literature has not been integrated with the bonding
literature discussed above.

The average 401(k) plan is surely more costly to administer than is a traditional defined contribution plan, simply because the element of employee volun-
teerism adds an idiosyncratic element to the program, but it also has important
cost-saving properties—the employer contributes only to workers who themselves contribute. The targeting effect endows this program with a tremendous
total cost advantage over universal plans despite the higher administrative costs.
Ippolito (1992, 1994) argues that 401(k) plans have agency effects as well. Specifically, they selectively encourage high discounters, possibly less reliable
workers, to choose other employers, both by providing greater compensation to
workers who choose to save and by effectively offering cash bonuses to workers
who choose to separate now—the bulk of such plans offer lump-sum payment
options at the time of job separation. The empirical importance of these effects
has not yet been established; disentangling these effects from the targeting effect
of 401(k) plans will not be easy.

Primary 401(k) plans are more prevalent in small firms, although perhaps too
much can be made of this fact. IRS guidelines for tax-exempt status for this type
of pension were not circulated until 1982, and historicity appears to be a major
factor in the choice of pension plans. Primary pension plans were already well
established in larger firms, and replacing these plans with 401(k) plans would be
expensive, certainly more expensive than the adoption of such a plan by a firm
that had no plan. That said, 401(k)-type plans appear to be the pension plan of
choice for firms adopting pension plans for the first time, superior to both defined
benefit and traditional defined contribution plans.

Trends in Pension Coverage

Much of the recent literature has explored the determinants of two basic
trends, a decline in the 1980s in male pension coverage rates and household
pension coverage rates and a shift in coverage from defined benefit plans to
defined contribution plans. Research in both areas suggests that responsibility
for these trends is more or less evenly divided between (1) a structural effect,
resulting from changes in industrial structure, and (2) a behavioral effect—
changes in firm behavior, given workplace characteristics. The latter may be
induced by regulatory changes, of which there have been many in this period, and

by nonstructural changes in the workplace, for example, the squeeze on profits by more intense international competition in the heavy manufacturing sector.

Regulatory changes with direct effects on pension coverage have been both negative and positive. The most obvious trend has been a negative one, the ever-tightening regulatory restrictions on the form of defined benefit plans. Not only have these regulatory shifts limited the usefulness of defined benefit plans to the firm, but the constant flow of regulatory changes has meant that firms with such plans have faced several decades of "one-time" transactions costs in order to bring their programs in line with changing regulations. A positive change has been the innovation in a whole new class of pension instruments, 401(k) plans, which offer important targeting advantages, as was noted earlier. Certainly these regulatory changes are consistent with the almost continuous decline in defined benefit plans as a fraction of all primary plans and the explosion of 401(k) plans, both primary and secondary. Indeed one could conjecture that the permissive legislation on 401(k) plans was a response to the increasing regulatory burden on defined benefit plans.

The 1980s were characterized by a more or less continuous decline in pension coverage rates for males and for households as a whole and a modest increase in coverage for females. A large fraction of the decreasing coverage rates for males in the 1980s (Woods, 1989; Parsons, 1991b, 1994; Bloom and Freeman, 1992; Even and Macpherson, 1994a) and for households (Parsons, 1991b) can be explained by changes in the industrial composition of the workplace. Indeed in explaining the coverage decline, each of these studies notes the importance of structural shifts, especially the shift out of the large-firm, highly unionized sectors that have traditionally supported pension plans. More specific hypotheses are difficult to distinguish. The importance of administrative cost increases in explaining the residual decline has been proposed by Parsons (1992, 1994) and Even and Macpherson (1992), but is difficult to test persuasively because of the same collinearity of alternatives that has plagued the analysis of the determinants of the locus of pension coverage. For example, the coverage decline in the 1980s is also consistent with the reduced agency value of defined benefit pensions due to legislative restrictions (Ippolito, 1986, 1987). Indeed Logue (1979) made just such a prediction shortly after the passage of ERISA, based on the argument that ERISA vesting requirements limit the usefulness of pensions as a bonding device. Later restrictions on age-based actuarial reductions have limited the usefulness of pension accruals to sculpt wages.

The early 1990s appear to have witnessed a moderating of this trend, with coverage rates more or less flat.[30] The reasons for this shift in trend have not yet been carefully examined, but would appear to have much to do with the introduction of 401(k) plans. The transformation of pension coverage to defined contribution plans and particularly to 401(k) plans has been dramatic. According to the U.S. Department of Labor et al. (1994:7):

In 1983, only 3% of full-time workers received coverage under a 401(k) plan compared to 47% under other types of plans. By 1993, the coverage rate for full-time workers under 401(k) plans had increased to 27%, while coverage under other types of plans had fallen to 33%.

About 10 percent had coverage under both 401(k) and another type of plan. The timing of this expansion is easily explained, since it was not until the early 1980s that the IRS clarified the conditions under which such a plan could qualify for tax deferral.

A number of researchers have explored the causes of the shift toward defined contribution plans as a fraction of all pension plans, in most cases lumping together 401(k) plans and traditional defined contribution plans. How much of the shift toward defined contribution plans can be attributed to changes to job structure, and how much to behavioral changes within firm types? One might expect a priori that the structural effect has been substantial. As Table 5-5 shows, for administrative cost reasons alone, defined contribution plans are especially popular in small firms. The industrial shift toward smaller, nonunion workplaces obviously increases the likelihood that a workplace will offer a defined contribution pension or no pension at all.

Estimates of the magnitude of the industrial-shift effect on pension type are sensitive to precisely how the question is posed. Using a variety of data sources, Clark and McDermed (1990) find that less than 20 percent of the change in the share of all *plans* that are defined benefit can be attributed to structural change.

TABLE 5-5 Pension Plan Administrative Costs per Participant in Multiemployer Plans, by Plan Type, 1985, in Dollars

Number of Participants	Program Type		
	Defined Benefit	Defined Contribution	Cost Differential
Total	83.24	40.06	43.18
50-99	212.86	102.80	100.06
100-249	214.45	103.10	111.35
250-499	167.85	69.01	98.84
500-999	132.16	53.25	78.91
1000-2,499	127.57	48.51	79.06
2,500-4,999	107.76	32.71	75.05
5,000-9,999	98.62	22.24	76.38
10,000-19,999	82.56	37.18	45.38
20,000-49,999	72.12	33.12	39.00
50,000 or more	59.02	—	—

SOURCE: Turner and Beller (1989:Table G2, p. 438).

They replicate their findings over a longer interval in Clark, McDermed, and White (1992). Changes in firm size and industry appear to provide little explanation of why defined benefit plans have fallen as a share of all pension plans. Gustman and Steinmeier (1992), using a similar partitioning methodology, find that the job structure effect is quite substantial, certainly more than half the story if one considers the change in *participant* share. Ippolito (1992), following Gustman and Steinmeier's approach, obtains a similar result, as does Kruse (1995).

The different results when measuring plans and when measuring participants arise in part because a large share of the overall decline in defined benefit coverage rates is the result of shrinking workplaces rather than of firms switching from one type of plan to another (Kruse, 1995; Papke, Petersen, and Poterba, 1993). As mentioned above, there is strong historicity in a firm's choice of plan type, presumably because the costs of switching from one system to another are quite high; Cheadle (1989) stresses this point. Much of the growth in defined contribution plans comes from smaller firms' adopting a plan for the first time. From a social welfare viewpoint, perhaps the participant-weighted results are the more relevant.

However one measures the effect of job restructuring on plan type, a substantial residual effect exists and requires explanation. The rising popularity of defined contribution plans has been attributed to a number of factors:

(1) regulation-induced increases in administrative costs that are especially adverse to defined benefit plans (Hay-Huggins, 1990; Ippolito, 1992);

(2) regulatory restrictions that limit agency attributes of defined benefit plans, especially bonding and wage-sculpting attributes (Clark and McDermed, 1990; Clark, McDermed, and White, 1992);

(3) innovations in tax-deferred defined contribution plans, especially 401(k)-type plans. The innovations are of two types: (a) targeting efficiencies (Ippolito, 1994), and (b) agency effects (Ippolito, 1994).

The rough coincidence of policy changes—the rapid increase in administrative costs for defined benefit plans, partly fueled by a constant flow of "one-time" changes in ERISA regulations; the growing restrictions on vesting and pension accruals; and the introduction of new 401(k) plans in 1978 followed by an IRS interpretation of the practical applicability of this type of plan several years later—makes difficult any reliable disentangling of the competing effects of these changes.

The administrative cost argument would seem sufficient, however. Certainly administrative costs can explain the popularity of defined contribution plans in small firms (Table 5-5; see also Ippolito, 1992). As noted above, in very small firms, the administrative costs of defined benefit plans are twice those of defined contribution plans. Moreover, the cost study by Hay/Huggins (1990) indicates that regulatory changes have *increased* the administrative costs of defined benefit plans much more sharply than defined contribution plans. Still Ippolito (1992, 1994) argues persuasively that the absolute magnitude of the differential between defined benefit and defined defined contribution plans, is small in medium and large workplaces and would seem too modest to induce the observed shifts in these workplaces. Whether the remaining, unexplained shift toward defined contribution plans is due to the regulatory stifling of the bonding and wage-sculpting features of defined benefit plans or to the regulatory encouragement of 401(k) plans is much harder to determine with existing data. The mushrooming of 401(k) plans between 1983 and 1993 would seem to tip the scales toward the third hypothesis, the desirability of 401(k) plans because of the obvious targeting efficiencies and perhaps because of agency value as well.

A Pension Puzzle

In the introduction to this section, it was noted that there were two obvious reasons why a firm might provide workers with a pension: (1) to serve as an efficient conduit for fringe benefits that its workers value, that is, as a mechanism for securing tax-deferred retirement income, and (2) to structure compensation in a way that induces desirable behavior from workers at least cost, shaping compensation profiles and bonding worker mobility and on-the-job performance. Although the industrial locus of pensions can be explained in large measure by either or both of these considerations, there is little direct evidence that either motivation in fact moves firms to provide pensions.

As mentioned above, the evidence in support of compensating differentials (lower wages where the firm offers its workers a pension) is weak, but is essential to the hypothesis that the firm is a least cost conduit of this fringe benefit. The best one can offer is that measurement difficulties make the claim hard to prove. Efforts to demonstrate that pensions increase worker productivity, essential to the agency hypothesis, have been similarly unsuccessful. In one such study, Allen and Clark (1987) report that other things being equal, productivity is lower if the firm offers a pension. The productivity impact of traditional defined contribution pensions has been more intensively examined because these plans are largely profit-sharing plans. In a review of this literature, Kruse (1993) reports that profit sharing is associated with greater productivity in a majority of the several hundred estimates from 26 studies that Kruse surveyed. The variation in estimates is quite large, however; 10 percent of all studies report negative results and another 30 percent positive, but insignificant results. Of special relevance to the present paper, he finds that deferred profit-sharing plans are less productive than immediate payout plans. In short, the returns to the firm offering a pension plan have not been isolated.

CONCLUSIONS

A summary of a review, especially of a literature as extensive and diffuse as this one, is either unnecessary or essential. I will take the latter position and give my personal impression of the literature. Without question, retirement age and pension coverage are strongly shaped by firm size and union status. Not surprisingly, then, a substantial part of recent trends in pension coverage and type (defined benefit and defined contribution) can be explained by shifts in industrial structure away from the large-firm, unionized sector. (Corresponding employment effects have been limited by the fact that industrial shifts have their greatest impact on new entrants, who are disproportionately young.) The effects of firm size and union status on retirement age and retirement income can themselves be explained by transactions costs, especially firm size differences in (1) the administrative costs of sorting and reassigning older workers as their productive attributes evolve and (2) the administrative costs of providing retirement income to separated workers. The effect of sorting and reassignment costs on the firm's demand for older workers is most clearly revealed in new-hire restrictions and in compulsory retirement rules when these practices were legal. The effect of pension administration costs in pension coverage and pension type. Recent trends in pension structure as well as levels can be explained by changes in administrative costs, especially by changes induced by shifting government regulations, although permissive legislation that has expanded the range of tax-favored pension vehicles to include 401(k) plans has also had a major impact on recent pension developments. Alternative hypotheses, notably broader transactions-cost hypotheses that stress agency problems and/or contract reliability, can explain many of the same observations, and more detailed data and more carefully developed implications are required to assess the relative importance of these alternatives.

Clearly an integrated research program on the firm's age-based employment practices is required if we are to predict with confidence the behavior of the firm in response to government actions. On the basis of what we know today, we could not predict the impact on firm employment and pension policies of the scheduled increase in the age of normal retirement under Social Security. Will firms encourage longer "career" life by increasing the normal age of retirement in defined benefit plans, as I suspect government planners imagine? Will they simply buy out reluctant job leavers without changing their employment policies as they appear to have done after the various regulatory changes favoring later retirement in the last two decades—for example, the abolition of mandatory retirement and (unfavorable) age-based pension accrual rules. How will firms adjust their employment and pension practices to the changing pension environment of retirees in the leaner world of 401(k)s? We are not close to having the level of understanding that would permit us to make quantitative estimates on employer behavior. A great deal of basic and applied research is required before we can seriously confront these questions.

In this section I first describe what I feel to be the ideal data set for the study of this issue; the survey would be an extension of current survey instruments that link worker survey responses with employer descriptions of the worker's pension participation. I then proceed to less ambitious goals, describing smaller, but useful data collection efforts, followed by suggestions for basic and applied research activities.

Basic Data Needs

The Ideal: Matched Worker/Firm Surveys of Workplaces

The fundamental data need is clear and has been forcefully spelled out by Gustman and Mitchell (1992:78):

> A nationally representative data set, preferably longitudinal and centered around the firm, is needed. It should match information on employee characteristics with the employer-side data pension plans as well as other characteristics of the firms, their inputs, and their financial structure. Pension plan descriptions would best be accompanied by information on the distribution of wages of . . . workers, their numbers, and other characteristics.

It is important to stress that this data set must include information on (1) the firm's production technologies and organizational structure (most obviously firm size and collective bargaining status), (2) explicit employer policies on the employment of older workers and on pensions, and (3) worker data, including the usual socioeconomic and demographic characteristics.

The review above suggests that because of the workplace-wide nature of employment and pension plans, the worker data must be linked not only with employer characteristics and policies, but with the characteristics of other workers in the same workplace. This would require workplace sampling of workers, so that aggregate characteristics of the workplace could be computed.[31] The matching of employer-provided pension data only with the individual responses of *older* workers, as in the National Longitudinal Survey of Mature Women and in the Health and Retirement Survey, although valuable for labor supply studies, is of little use in the study of firm behavior.

The longitudinal element of the survey design is useful, of course, if the investigator is to exploit statistical procedures to deal with unobservable, permanent heterogeneity. It has a more substantive motivation as well, namely to estimate the responsiveness of firms to regulatory change. Pension provisions do change (Mitchell, 1992; Mitchell and Luzadis, 1988; Luzadis and Mitchell, 1991) but not rapidly, suggesting that firms face major transactions costs in changing systems (see the discussion above of firm adoption patterns of 401(k) plans). We know little about these transactions costs; as a result we have only the vaguest idea what the long-run distribution of pension types will look like following the introduction of a new tax-favored pension instrument such as 401(k) plans. If the study is not longitudinal in design, appropriate retrospective data should be asked, for example, when a particular pension plan was adopted and firm and worker characteristics at that time. Such a retrospective design has obvious deficiencies.

Second Best: Employer Surveys with Estimates of Worker Characteristics

In the absence of the ideal, a second-best approach is to survey employers and ask them the usual sorts of questions on pension coverage and type, age-related employment policies, and other areas, but also ask them questions designed to characterize the firm's work force, including age and occupational mix. See, for example, the Small Business Administration's (SBA) U.S. Establishment and Enterprise Microdata set (described in Scott, Berger and Garen, 1995), in which firms were asked to estimate the age distributions of workplaces. (A more detailed description of this database can be found in Jack Faucett Associates, 1990.) Careful thought will be required if we are to ask questions of worker characteristics that the employer could reasonably be expected to know (without a large investment of firm resources).

Case Studies

In the absence of the ideal matched worker-employer data set across many workplaces, the more grueling approach of multiple individual case studies may be needed. Given the importance of characterizing the workplace, such studies may serve as pilot studies for a more ambitious survey approach. As the review above suggests, we are still somewhat unclear on what factors are crucial for understanding the firm's retirement and retirement income policies.

Administrative Cost Surveys

Administrative costs are crucially important in forming employer responses to both employment decisions (monitoring and reassignment costs) and pensions (pension administrative costs), but remain relatively unstudied. A broad attack on this issue would, I think, be worthwhile. An important first step might involve an expansion of the Labor Department's Form 5500 to include greater information on the pension plan itself, including whether it is a primary or secondary plan for the employer and the number of other employers in the pension plan. The current instrument is not designed for research purposes, so that attempting to determine whether a plan is primary or secondary in the workplace is a matter of conjecture. Analysts using the Form 5500 data, for example, failed to pick up one of the major pension trends of the 1980s, the decline in male pension coverage. See Beller (1989) and Beller and Lawrence (1992). Additional information on characteristics of the firm and its workers would be desirable, but unlikely, at least in this government-mandated vehicle.

Other direct information on worker monitoring and reassignment costs are theoretically conceivable, but will require more imaginative collection techniques. The firm itself is not likely to have high-quality data on specific administrative functions; especially in smaller firms, monitoring and reassignment costs are likely to be buried in general overhead. Cruder measures of these activities may be obtainable, perhaps modeled after employer surveys of job-training activities, such as the Employment Opportunity Pilot Project-National Center for Vocational Education (EOPP-NCRVE) data set or the more recent Small Business Administration replication of the EOPP-NCRVE survey. One reassuring note: the crudely measured estimates of worker and employer training activities in these data sets appear to be broadly valid.

Historical Analyses of Firm Behavior

Even with strong assurances, firms are likely to be wary of providing too much candid information on the policies that directly affect their older workers. In any case certain behaviors are likely to be repressed by law. Work by economic and business historians might be especially valuable in this situation. For example, we know little about age-of-hire strategies, given the limitations on age-of-hire restrictions in ADEA. Did ADEA affect age-of-hire practices or only public advertising of age-of-hire practices? How was hiring behavior transformed by outlawing these practices? What evidence exists from less litigious times of the motivations for various employment practices (e.g., Gratton, 1990; Williamson, 1992; Ransom and Sutch, 1986)?

Basic Research

The Determinants of Industry Structure

The evidence suggests that large changes in retirement and pension policies derive primarily from two sources: (1) changes in the underlying structure of the production enterprise such as the size of plants and firms and their union status and (2) government changes in Social Security and aging policies. Pension coverage is strongly affected by plant and firm size and the declines in average firm size and union density have apparently contributed substantially to recent declines in defined benefit coverage. Very recent data support the belief that the firm size trend has reversed itself since 1991 (*The Economist*, 1995). Although ad hoc arguments are possible to explain these trends, we have little ability to predict these trends. Perhaps they are unpredictable, but perhaps not; support for fundamental theoretical and empirical research in this area seems warranted if we are to make reasonable *projections* of the work activity rates of older individuals and of their pension rights.

The Firm, Information, and Control

If the efforts recommended in the last section are successful, then we will have a reasonable idea of the industrial structure within which employment policy decisions are made. Basic research on how and why firms of a given type make the decisions they do would also be worthwhile. The terminal conditions of the employment "contract" are just one element in a complex system, and fundamental research on the employment relationship should be encouraged. How is information on workers transmitted within and between organizations. This should be an empirical as well as a theoretical undertaking.

An issue that deserves special note is the psychological basis of employment contracting. The psychological component of the employment relationship is poorly understood. What workers perceive as appropriate behavior is crucial in forming the terminal conditions of the employment contract, but does not appear to be the quite the same as what an economist might imagine to be fair. To take an obvious example, a reduction in compensation with age through unfavorable pension accrual appears to serve quite adequately as a "graceful" way to cut wages; direct reductions in wages are much more likely to lead to reduced morale (see, e.g., Bewley, 1993). Economists find the distinction hard to fathom.

The relationship between firm managers and firm owners, especially the informational relationship, may have important implications for firm behavior. Managers may bury personnel costs in unfunded retirement promises that inflate current profit measures. Apparently this is not a problem among large firms in the private sector—the stock market seems to reflect underfunded pensions in a reasonable way. Smaller firms and public ones are a different matter as are less obvious liabilities, such as retiree health insurance promises. When accounting rules were revised to include estimates of these costs as a liability, a significant number of firms adjusted by reducing the generosity of these promises.

Aging and the Firm: Unfinished Business

Priority Topics

Age Profiles of Productivity More systematic development of lifetime productivity profiles would be valuable, especially the uncovering of environmental factors that influence the magnitude of productivity declines late in the work life.

The "Ideal" Workplace Age Distribution Age accounting is becoming more prevalent in large firms, suggesting that firms may have preferences over the age-experience distribution of their work forces. Firm efforts to balance their work force by age and experience when downsizing would suggest such an objective. For example, the military officer corps have target rank distributions that may provide insights into the nature of an ideal age distribution. Recent work on the theory of hierarchies (Demougin and Siow, 1994) might be useful here.

Employment Practices in Small Firms Because employment practices in smaller firms are generally more informal, age-related practices in these firms remain largely unstudied. Andrews (1989) provides an important exception. The dismissal-demotion decision and the related pension/pay decision are no doubt less systematic in small workplaces. Age-related behaviors in high-skilled small firms are likely to be quite different than those in low-skilled firms. The growth of employment in these sectors and their importance to the aged as bridge jobs would argue for more detailed study.

Pension Design Firm strategies behind many features of pension plans remain unconsidered. To take one example, there is, to my knowledge, no well-developed theory of the separate age and service criteria in pension benefit formulas. Early retirement provisions have become more common and early retirement benefits more generous in the 1980s (Mitchell, 1992). The reasons for these trends are not well understood. Oddly, Mitchell also notes that disability benefit provisions have become more stringent, increasingly requiring workers to qualify for long-term disability insurance. (The implications of early retirement for retirement income late in retirement is, to my knowledge, unstudied.)

Pension Coverage and Pension "Receipt" Empirical studies of the linkage between pension coverage during the work life and pension receipt in retirement, focusing perhaps on the environmental factors that alter the linkage, would be useful. ERISA was passed in 1974 in part to tighten this link—vesting requirements were restricted and pension promises partly guaranteed. Nonetheless pension receipt remains linked to job mobility; vesting is imperfect (Sahin, 1989, 1989; Hay/Huggins, 1988; Turner, 1993); and inflation may diminish the value of pension rights that link past earnings with future benefits (Allen, Clark, and Sumner, 1986; Allen, Clark, and McDermed, 1992, 1995). The transition from defined benefit plans to defined contribution plans, which are much more likely to offer lump-sum payouts at job separations, raises the same basic issue in a slightly different way, will pension resources be available to support the consumption of older individuals?

Emerging Issues

Early Retirement Incentive Plans We know very little about early retirement incentive plans. Under one interpretation, they are the logical outcome of recent legislation to protect the jobs of older Americans—firms are forced to buy out workers whom they might otherwise force out. Some idea of the "price" of such buyouts would be useful: What percentage of the target group will accept a buyout of given size? How is the buyout function affected by worker characteristics? By the size of Social Security payments? Once these characteristics are better understood, we will be in a better position to understand why firms implement the policies. Lumsdaine, Stock, and Wise (1990) and Hackett (1995) offer a start on this research program.[32] Unfortunately the temporary nature of these offers makes data collection difficult; at any single point in time, few firms have recently completed a buyout. Some choice-based samples will no doubt have to be constructed.

Employer-Provided Health Insurance for Retirees The mushrooming of health care costs and accountant concerns about these liabilities has brought the issue of employer-provided health insurance for retirees to the fore. Scott, Berger, and Garen (1995) provide evidence that the indirect effect on the new-hire rate of older workers of providing this perquisite is negative and large in absolute value. Macpherson (1992) reports, from data drawn from the August 1988 Current Population Survey, that retirement health benefits are most prevalent in the same types of workplaces that offer defined benefit pensions—large, unionized firms with highly paid, full-time workers. Barron and Fraedrich (1994) confirm Macpherson's firm size results and also find a robust relationship between the firm's provision of retirement health insurance and the extent to which it trains new hires. They attribute this correlation to the self-screening properties of retirement health insurance, although the motivational attribution is not compelling. The issue of how coverage will evolve as costs continue to rise and the structure of pensions change is of obvious policy importance.

NOTES

1. The government, of course, is also a major employer. In the review to follow, I focus on private employers, though government employers face many of the same employment problems and in many cases adopt similar policies toward older workers.

2. In his conference comments, Dallas Salisbury argued convincingly that it is important to separate equilibrium from disequilibrium situations. "The strongest unions have been the most successful in negotiation of early retirement ages. Employers in the public and private sector regularly attempt to negotiate these ages up, suggesting that it is primarily demand in the first instance, possibly turning to a reduction mode at points when an employer wishes to downsize (recent federal government buyouts support this pattern).

3. In his conference comments, Dallas Salisbury stressed the diversity of defined benefit plans, noting that 45 percent of defined benefit plans offer lump-sum payouts.

4. I introduce government actions only when they are designed to manage aspects of the employment relationship, and I consider the *motivations* for the government's actions only in passing.

5. The data clearly indicate that morbidity or sickness rates increase with age. In an interesting study of track and field performance by age, Fair (1991:Abstract) reports: "For most of the running

events (400 meters through the half marathon), the slowdown rate per year [in maximum perfor-mance] is estimated to be 0.80 percent between 35 and 51. At age 51 the rate begins to increase. It is 1.04 percent at age 60, 1.46 percent at age 75, and 2.01 percent at age 95." It is important to distinguish these *point-in-time* results from *trends* in fitness by age, over which there is considerable controversy (Lee and Skinner, in this volume).

6. Although the data are worker estimates, not firm estimates, they may still reflect social prejudices, ones accepted by the individuals themselves.

7. Again it is important to point out that this pattern of reporting may be subject to social biases—admitting that one is having difficulty managing money is more socially acceptable at older ages.

8. Straka (1992) provides a thoughtful review of the distinction between statistical discrimina-tion and prejudicial discrimination.

9. Blinder (1988) supports the inverse of this argument, that a worker would prefer to be the only one in an organization to receive a raise. He estimates that he would be equally happy with a 10 percent raise for himself alone and a 15 percent across-the-board increase to the entire Princeton University faculty.

10. Preliminary estimates from the May 1993 pension supplement indicate that the coverage rate of full-time workers was 56 percent, that of part-time workers 15 percent (U.S. Department of Labor, 1994:50).

11. For a review of the contract approach to the employment relationship, see Parsons (1986).

12. For recent discussions of this proposition, see Oi (1983a, 1983b, 1991) and Parsons (1986, 1990).

13. Beyond the studies summarized in detail below, see Andrews (1992).

14. Mitchell and Andrews found much larger scale economies in assets per participant: $\hat{\beta}_2 - 1 = -0.730$.

15. The dependent variable in this model was the log of average benefits rather than the log of total benefits and the estimated coefficient on participant numbers adjusted to correspond with the earlier estimates. The midpoint of the interval was used as the estimate of plan size in each category except that of the largest plans, which was unbounded. This category was omitted.

16. This indexation rate dropped sharply in the 1980s; it was 22 percent over the 1980-1984 period and 10 percent from 1984 to 1988 (Allen, Clark, and McDermed, 1992:333).

17. For related reviews of the material in this section, see Allen and Clark (1987) and Straka (1992).

18. For a survey of earlier work on insurance aspects of long-term employment contracting, see Parsons (1986).

19. Hutchens ignores the fact that mandatory retirement rules are typically uniform across the workplace and implicitly assumes that each worker is individually assigned mandatory retirement status at an appropriate age. This misspecification of the actual choice process is standard practice in the pension literature as well. See the next section.

20. The nature of past jobs, particularly of the pension rights of those jobs, will affect the extent of underinsurance. In this discussion it is assumed that all past jobs have been in the sector not covered by private pensions.

21. Ruhm defines a career job as the longest job the individual holds in his work life; Quinn, Burkhauser, and Myers define it as the last job held for 10 or more years.

22. There are a number of excellent reviews of the pension literature. For a recent one, see Gustman, Mitchell, and Steinmeier (1994).

23. As noted earlier, defined benefit plans are quite diverse in structure. Salisbury reports that 45 percent of all defined benefit plans offer lump-sum payouts.

24. For recent discussions of worker bonding in a more general framework, see Parsons (1986), Carmichael (1989), and Akerlof and Katz (1989).

25. Ippolito (1985) provides a modern variant on this old story, claiming that firms strategically

underfunded pensions as a bonding device against extreme union demands—any threat to the firm's economic viability was a threat to the workers' pensions.

26. For a review of the literature on the latter two processes, see Parsons (1986).

27. For a somewhat different approach to the same problem, see Lazear and Moore (1988) and Stock and Wise (1990).

28. Turner (1993) notes that defined contribution plans can and do contain length-of-service rewards, for example, increasing employer contributions with tenure, although these features do not appear to be sufficiently common to overturn Gustman and Steinmeier's point.

29. For a more complete discussion of the mobility attributes of alternative pension schemes, see Turner (1993).

30. Even and Macpherson (1994b) note, however, that the negative coverage trend has continued for less educated male workers.

31. For those workplaces with multiple "contracts," most commonly collectively bargained and not, multiple worker aggregations would presumably be useful—within contract groups and within the firm as a whole.

32. Lumsdaine, Stock, and Wise (1990) estimate the magnitude of the acceptance response to a single large firm's early retirement incentive offer, and then assess whether the plan is optimal under alternative assumptions about the firm's objective. They argue that, if the objective is simply to downsize the workforce, they could do the job more cheaply using the information generated in their study to target the program to the most response segments of the work force. Hackett (1995) assesses data on the response of U.S. Navy officers to a series of early retirement incentive plans. He has data on internal promotion prospects—which are known to both the officers and the Navy and finds that the acceptance rate of the plan is inversely related to the officer's likelihood of promotion. From the firm's perspective, the plan had desirable self-screening properties.

REFERENCES

Akerlof, G.A., and L.F. Katz
    1989   Workers' trust funds and the logic of wage profiles. *Quarterly Review of Economics* August:525-536.

Akerlof, G.A., and H. Miyazaki
    1980   The implicit contract theory of unemployment meets the wage bill argument. *Review of Economic Studies* 47(January):321-338.

Allen, S.G., and R.L. Clark
    1987   Pensions and firm performance. In *Human Resources and the Performance of the Firm.* Industrial Relations Research Association Series. Madison, Wisc.: Industrial Relations Research Association.

Allen, S.G., R.L. Clark, and A.A. McDermed
    1992   Post-retirement benefit increases in the 1980s. Pp. 319-339 in J.A. Turner and D.J. Beller, eds., *Trends in Pensions 1992.* Washington, D.C.: U.S. Department of Labor, Pension and Welfare Benefits Administration.
    1993   Pension bonding and lifetime jobs. *Journal of Human Resources* 28:463-481.
    1995   Post-retirement increases in pensions in the 1980s: Did plan finances matter? *Research on Aging* 17(June):190-208.

Allen, S.G., R.L. Clark, and D. Sumner
    1986   Post-retirement adjustments of pensions. *Journal of Human Resources* 21:118-137.

Andrews, E.S.
    1989   *Pension Policy and Small Employers: At What Price Coverage?* Washington, D.C.: Employee Benefit Research Institute.

1992   The growth and distribution of 401(k) plans. Pp. 149-176 in J.A. Turner and D.J. Beller, eds., *Trends in Pensions 1992*. Washington, D.C.: U.S. Department of Labor, Pension and Welfare Benefits Administration.

Barker, D.T., and R.L. Clark
1980   Mandatory retirement and labor-force participation of respondents in the Retirement History Study. *Social Security Bulletin* 43(November):20-29.

Barron, J.M., and A. Fraedrich
1994   The implications of job matching for retirement health insurance and leave benefits. *Applied Economics* 26:425-435.

Beller, D.J.
1989   Coverage and vesting patterns in private pension plans, 1975-1985. Pp. 39-68 in J.A. Turner and D.J. Beller, eds., *Trends in Pensions*. Washington, D.C.: U.S. Department of Labor, Pension and Welfare Benefits Administration.

Beller, D.J., and H.H. Lawrence
1992   Trends in private pension plan coverage. Pp. 59-96 in J.A. Turner and D.J. Beller, eds., *Trends in Pensions 1992*. Washington, D.C.: U.S. Department of Labor, Pension and Welfare Benefits Administration.

Bewley, T.
1993   A Depressed Labor Market as Explained by Participants. Unpublished manuscript. Department of Economics, Yale University.

Blank, R.M.
1989   The role of part-time work in women's labor market choices over time. *American Economic Review* 79(May):295-299.

Blinder, A.S.
1982   *Private Pensions and Public Pensions: Theory and Fact*. NBER Working Paper #902. Cambridge, Mass.: National Bureau of Economic Research.
1988   Richard T. Ely lecture: The challenge of high unemployment. *American Economic Review* 78(May):1-15.

Bloom, D.E., and R.B. Freeman
1992   The fall in private pension coverage in the United States *American Economic Review, Papers and Proceedings* 82(2):539-545.

Burkhauser, R.V.
1979   The pension acceptance decision of older workers. *Journal of Human Resources* 14(1):63-75.
1980   The early acceptance of Social Security: An asset maximization approach. *Industrial and Labor Relations Review* 33(July):484-492.

Burkhauser, R.V., and J.F. Quinn
1983   Is mandatory retirement overrated? Evidence from the 1970s. *Journal of Human Resources* 18(Summer):337-358.

Carmichael, H.L.
1989   Self-enforcing contracts, shirking, and life cycle incentives. *The Journal of Economic Perspectives* 3(Fall):65-84.

Caswell, J.W.
1976   Economic efficiency in pension plan administration: A study of the construction industry. *Journal of Risk and Insurance* 43(2):257-273.

Cheadle, A.
1989   Explaining patterns of profit sharing activity. *Industrial Relations* 28:387-400.

Clark, R.L., S.C. Allen, and D. Sumner
1986   Inflation and pension benefits. Pp. 177-250 in R.A. Ippolito and W.W. Kolodrubetz, eds., *Handbook of Pension Statistics 1985*. Chicago, Ill.: Commerce Clearing House, Inc.

Clark, R.L., and A.A. McDermed
  1990 *The Choice of Pension Plans in a Changing Regulatory Environment.* Washington, D.C.: American Enterprise Institute.
Clark, R.L., A.A. McDermed, and M. White
  1992 Firm Choice of Type of Pension Plan: Trends and Determinants. Presented at Future of Pensions in America, a conference sponsored by the Pension Research Council, Philadelphia, Pa.
Cornwell, C., S. Dorsey, and N. Mehrzad
  1991 Opportunistic behavior by firms in implicit pension contracts. *Journal of Human Resources* 26:704-725.
Curme, M., and L.M. Kahn
  1990 The impact of the threat of bankruptcy on the structure of compensation. *Journal of Labor Economics* 8:419-447.
Demougin, D., and A. Siow
  1994 Careers in ongoing hierarchies. *American Economic Review* 84:1261-1277.
Dorsey, S.
  1982 A model and empirical estimates of worker pension coverage in the U.S. *Southern Economic Journal* 49:506-520.
  1987 The economic functions of private pensions: An empirical analysis. *Journal of Labor Economics* 5:S171-S189.
The Economist
  1995 The puzzling infirmity of America's small firms. *The Economist* 18(February):63-64.
Even, W.E., and D.A. Macpherson
  1992 Pensions, Labor Turnover, and Employer Size. Unpublished manuscript. (WP 92-09-2) Department of Economics, Florida State University, Tallahassee, Fla.
  1994a Why did male pension coverage decline in the 1980s? *Industrial and Labor Relations Review* 47:439-453.
  1994b Why Has the Decline in Pension Coverage Accelerated Among Less Educated Workers? Unpublished manuscript. Department of Economics, Miami University, Oxford, Ohio.
Fair, R.C.
  1991 *How Fast Do Old Men Slow Down?* NBER Working Paper #3757. Cambridge, Mass.: National Bureau of Economic Research.
Fields, G.S., and O.S. Mitchell
  1984 *Retirement, Pensions and Social Security.* Cambridge, Mass.: MIT Press.
Freeman, R.B.
  1985 Unions, pensions, and union pension funds. Pp. 123-156 in D.A. Wise, ed., *Pensions, Labor, and Individual Choice.* Chicago, Ill.: University of Chicago Press.
Garen, J.E.
  1985 Worker heterogeneity, job screening, and firm size. *Journal of Political Economy* 93:715-739.
Gratton, B.
  1990 A triumph in modern philanthropy: Age criteria in labor management at the Pennsylvania Railroad, 1875-1930. *Business History Review* 64:630-656.
Gustman, A.L., and O.S. Mitchell
  1992 Pensions and labor market activity: Behavior and data requirements. Pp. 39-87 in Z. Bodie and A.H. Munnell, eds., *Pensions and the Economy: Sources, Uses, and Limitations of Data.* Philadelphia, Pa.: Pension Research Council Publications and University of Pennsylvania Press.
Gustman, A.L., O.S. Mitchell, and T.L. Steinmeier
  1994 The role of pensions in the labor market. *Industrial and Labor Relations Review* 47(3):417-438.

Gustman, A.L., and T.L. Steinmeier
   1989   An analysis of pension benefit formulas, pension wealth and incentives from pensions. Pp. 53-106 in R.G. Ehrenberg, ed., *Research in Labor Economics* 10.
   1992   The stampede towards defined contribution pension plans: Fact or fiction? *Industrial Relations* 31(2):361-369.
   1995   *Pension Incentives and Job Mobility.* Kalamazoo, Mich.: W.E. Upjohn Institute for Employment Research.
Hackett, J.M.
   1995   A Cost-of-Leaving Model of the Response to Buyout Plans: Quality Effects of Downsizing in the Naval Officer Corps. Unpublished Ph.D. dissertation (in progress). Department of Econmics, Ohio State University.
Hay/Huggins Company, Inc.
   1988   The Effect of Job Mobility on Pension Benefits. Unpublished manuscript. Hay/Huggins Company, Inc., Washington, D.C.
   1990   Pension Plan Expense Study for the Pension Benefit Guarantee Corporation. Unpublished manuscript. Hay/Huggins Company, Inc., Washington, D.C.
Hurd, M.
   1993   *The Effect of Labor Market Rigidities on the Labor Force Behavior of Older Workers.* NBER Working Paper #4462. Cambridge, Mass.: National Bureau of Economic Research.
Hurd, M., and K. McGarry
   1993   *The Relationship Between Job Characteristics and Retirement.* NBER Working Paper #4558. Cambridge, Mass.: National Bureau of Economic Research.
Hutchens, R.
   1986   Delayed payment contracts and a firm's propensity to hire older workers. *Journal of Labor Economics* 4(4):439-457.
   1987   A test of Lazear's theory of delayed payment contract. *Journal of Labor Economics* 5(4)Part 2:S153-S170.
   1993   Restricted job opportunities and the older worker. Pp. 81-102 in O.S. Mitchell, ed., *As the Workforce Ages.* Ithaca, N.Y.: ILR Press.
Ippolito, R.A.
   1985   The economic function of underfunded pension plans. *The Journal of Law and Economics* 28(3):611-651.
   1986   *Pensions, Economics and Public Policy.* Homewood, Ill.: Dow Jones-Irwin.
   1987   The implicit pension contract: Developments and new directions. *Journal of Human Resources* 22(3):441-467.
   1992   The Proliferation of Defined Contribution Plans. Unpublished manuscript. Pension Benefit Guaranty Corporation, Washington, D.C.
   1994   A Sorting Theory of Defined Contribution Pensions. Unpublished manuscript. Pension Benefit Guaranty Corporation, Washington, D.C.
Jack Faucett Associates
   1990   *The 1988 U.S. Establishment and Enterprise Microdata (USEEM) and the 1984-1988 Weighted Linked U.S. Establishment Longitudinal Microdata (USELM).* NTIS #PB91-150987. Washington, D.C.: Small Business Administration.
Kahneman, D., J.L. Knetsch, and R. Thaler
   1986   Fairness as a constraint on profit-seeking: Entitlements in the market. *American Economic Review* 76:728-741.
Kotlikoff, L.J., and J. Gokhale
   1992   Estimating a firm's age-productivity profile using the present value of workers' earnings. *Quarterly Journal of Economics* (November):1215-1242.

Kotlikoff, L.J., and D.A. Wise
  1989 *The Wage Carrot and the Pension Stick: Retirement Benefits and Labor Force Participation.* Kalamazoo, Mich.: W.E. Upjohn Institute for Employment Research.
Kruse, D.L.
  1993 *Profit Sharing: Does It Make a Difference?* Kalamazoo, Mich.: W.E. Upjohn Institute for Employment Research.
  1995 Pension substitution in the 1980's: Why the shift toward defined contribution pension plans? *Industrial Relations* 34(2):218-241.
Lang, K.
  1989 Why was there mandatory retirement? *Journal of Public Economics* 39:127-136.
Latimer, M.W.
  1932 *Industrial Pension Systems.* New York: Industrial Relations Counselors.
Lazear, E.P.
  1979 Why is there mandatory retirement? *Journal of Political Economy* 87(6):1261-1284.
  1983 Pensions as severance pay. Pp. 57-89 in Z. Bodie and J.B. Shoven, eds., *Financial Aspects of the United States Pension System.* Chicago, Ill.: University of Chicago Press.
Lazear, E.P., and R.L. Moore
  1988 Pensions and turnover. Pp. 163-188 in Z. Bodie, J.B. Shoven, and D.A. Wise, eds., *Pensions in the U.S. Economy.* Chicago, Ill.: University of Chicago Press.
Leigh, D.E.
  1984 Why is there mandatory retirement? An empirical reexamination. *Journal of Human Resources* 19:512 531.
Levine, M.L.
  1988 *Age Discrimination and the Mandatory Retirement Controversy.* Balitmore, Md.: Johns Hopkins University.
Logue, D.E.
  1979 *Legislative Influence on Corporate Pension Plans.* Washington, D.C.: American Enterprise Institute.
Lumsdaine, R., J. Stock, and D.A. Wise
  1990 Efficient windows and labor force reduction. *Journal of Public Economics* 43:131-159.
Luzadis, R.A., and O.S. Mitchell
  1991 Explaining pension dynamics. *Journal of Human Resources* 26(4):679-703.
Macpherson, D.A.
  1992 Employer-provided retiree health insurance: Who is covered? *Economics Letters* 39:95-99.
Medoff, J.L., and K.G. Abraham
  1981 Are those paid more really more productive? The case of experience. *Journal of Human Resources* 16:186-216.
Merton, R.C.
  1985 Comment. Pp. 343-356 in D.A. Wise, ed., *Pensions, Labor, and Individual Choice.* Chicago, Ill.: University of Chicago Press.
Mincer, J.
  1988 *Job Training, Wage Growth, and Labor Turnover.* NBER Working Paper #2690. Cambridge, Mass.: National Bureau of Economic Research.
Mitchell, O.S.
  1982 Fringe benefits and labor mobility. *The Journal of Human Resources* 17:286-298.
  1988 Worker knowledge of pension provisions. *Journal of Labor Economics* 6(1):28-39.
  1992 Trends in pension benefit formulas and retirement provisions. Pp. 177-216 in J.A. Turner and D.J. Beller, eds., *Trends in Pensions 1992.* Washington, D.C.: U.S. Department of Labor, Pension and Welfare Benefits Administration.

Mitchell, O.S., and E.S. Andrews
 1981 Scale economies in private multi-employer pension systems. *Industrial and Labor Relations Review* 34:522-530.
Mitchell, O.S., and R.A. Luzadis
 1988 Changes in pension incentives through time. *Industrial and Labor Relations Review* 42(1):100-108.
Montgomery, E., K. Shaw, and M.E. Benedict
 1992 Pensions and wages: An hedonic price theory approach. *International Economic Review* 33:111-128.
Nalebuff, B., and R.J. Zeckhauser
 1985 Pensions and the retirement decision. Pp. 283-316 in D.A. Wise, ed., *Pensions, Labor, and Individual Choice.* Chicago, Ill.: University of Chicago Press.
National Center for Health Statistics
 1987 *Health Statistics on Older Persons: United States, 1986.* Analytical and Epidemiological Studies, Series 3, No. 25. (PHS)87-1409. Washington, D.C.: U.S. Department of Health and Human Services.
Oi, W.Y.
 1983a The fixed employment costs of specialized labor. Pp. 63-116 in J.E. Triplett, ed., *The Measurement of Labor Cost.* Chicago, Ill.: University of Chicago Press.
 1983b Heterogenous firms and the organization of production. *Economic Inquiry* 21:147-171.
 1991 Low wages and small firms. Pp. 1-39 in R. Ehrenberg, ed., *Research in Labor Economics.* Vol. 12. Greenwich, Conn.: JAI Press.
Papke, L., M. Petersen, and J.M. Poterba
 1993 *Did 401(k) Plans Replace Other Employer Provided Pensions?* NBER Working Paper #4501. Cambridge, Mass.: National Bureau of Economic Research.
Parnes, H.S., and G. Nestel
 1981 The retirement experience. Pp. 155-197 in H. Parnes, ed., *Work and Retirement.* Cambridge, Mass.: MIT Press.
Parsons, D.O.
 1983 *The Industrial Demand for Older Workers.* Working Paper 84-9. Department of Economics, Ohio State University.
 1986 The employment relationship: Job attachment, work effort, and the nature of contracts. Pp. 789-848 in O. Ashenfelter and R. Layard, eds., *Handbook of Labor Economics.* Vol. II. Amsterdam: North Holland.
 1990 The firm's decision to train. Pp. 53-75 in L.J. Bassi and D.L. Crawford, eds., *Research in Labor Economics.* Vol. 11. Greenwich, Conn.: JAI Press.
 1991a Aging and the Employment Contract. Unpublished manuscript. Department of Economics, Ohio State University.
 1991b The decline in private pension coverage in the United States. *Economics Letters* 36:419-423.
 1992 A Work Place Model of Private Pension Coverage. Unpublished manuscript. Department of Economics, Ohio State University.
 1994 Recent trends in pension coverage rates. Pp. 39-52 in R.P. Hinz, J.A. Turner, and P.A. Fernandez, eds., *Pension Coverage Issues for the '90s.* Washington, D.C.: U.S. Department of Labor, Pension and Welfare Benefits Administration.
Petersen, M.A.
 1992 Pension reversion and worker-stockholder wealth transfers. *Quarterly Journal of Economics* 107(3):1033-1056.
Pontiff, J., A. Schleifer, and M.S. Weisbach
 1990 Reversion of excess pension assets after takeover. *RAND Journal of Economics* 21(Winter):600-613.

Quinn, J.F., R.V. Burkhauser, and D.A. Myers
    1990   *Passing the Torch: The Influence of Economic Incentives on Work and Retirement.*
            Kalamazoo, Mich.: W.E. Upjohn Institute for Employment Research.
Ransom, R.L., and R. Sutch
    1986   The labor of older Americans: Retirement of men on and off the job, 1870-1937. *Journal
            of Economic History* 46(March):1-30.
Reagan, P.B., and J.A. Turner
    1995   Did the Decline in Marginal Tax Rates During the 1980s Reduce Pension Coverage?
            Unpublished manuscript. Department of Economics, Ohio State University.
Ruhm, C.J.
    1990   Bridge jobs and partial retirement. *Journal of Labor Economics* 8(4):482-501.
Sahin, I.
    1989   *Private Pensions and Employee Mobility.* New York: Quorum Books.
Schiller, B.R., and R.D. Weiss
    1979   The impact of private pensions on firm attachment. *Review of Economics and Statistics*
            61(August):369-380.
Scott, F.A., M.C. Berger, and J.E. Garen
    1995   Do health insurance and pension costs reduce the job opportunities of older workers?
            Industrial and Labor Relations Review 48(July):775-791.
Skolnik, A.M.
    1976   Private pension plans, 1950-74. *Social Security Bulletin* June:3-17.
Slavick, F.
    1966   *Flexible Retirement in the American Economy.* Ithaca, N.Y.: New York State School of
            Industrial and Labor Relations.
Stock, J.H., and D.A. Wise
    1990   The pension inducement to retire: An option value analysis. Pp. 205-224 in D.A. Wise,
            ed., *Issues in the Economics of Aging.* Chicago, Ill.: University of Chicago Press.
Straka, J.W.
    1992   *The Demand for Older Workers: The Neglected Side of a Labor Market.* Studies in
            Income Distribution No. 15. Office of Research and Statistics, Social Security Adminis-
            tration. Washington, D.C.: U.S. Department of Health and Human Services.
Turner, J.A.
    1993   *Pension Policy for a Mobile Labor Force.* Kalamazoo, Mich.: W.E. Upjohn Institute for
            Employment Research.
Turner, J.A., and D.J. Beller, eds.
    1989   *Trends in Pensions.* Washington, D.C.: U.S. Department of Labor, Pension and Welfare
            Benefits Administration.
U.S. Department of Labor, Social Security Administration, U.S. Small Business Administration, and
Pension Benefit Guaranty Corporation
    1994   *Pension and Health Benefits of American Workers: New Findings From the April 1993
            Current Population Survey.* Washington, D.C.: U.S. Department of Labor.
Williamson, O.
    1967   Hierarchical control and optimum firm size. *Journal of Political Economy* 75:123-138.
    1975   *Markets and Hierarchies—Analysis and Antitrust Implications: A Study in the Econom-
            ics of Internal Organization.* New York: The Free Press.
Williamson, S.H.
    1992   U.S. and Canadian pensions before 1930: A historical perspective. Pp. 35-58 in J.A.
            Turner and D.J. Beller, eds., *Trends in Pensions 1992.* Washington, D.C.: U.S. Depart-
            ment of Labor, Pension and Welfare Benefits Administration.

Woodbury, S.A., and W. Huang
   1991   *The Tax Treatment of Fringe Benefits.* Kalamazoo, Mich.: W.E. Upjohn Institute for
          Employment Research.
Woods, J.R.
   1989   Pension coverage among private wage and salary workers: Preliminary findings from the
          1988 survey of employee benefits. *Social Security Bulletin* 52(October):2-19.
   1993   Pension coverage among the baby boomers: Initial findings from a 1993 survey. *Social
          Security Bulletin* 57(Fall):12-25.

6
Assessing Forecasts of Mortality, Health Status, and Health Costs During Baby Boomers' Retirement

Ronald D. Lee and Jonathan Skinner

The U.S. economy may soon stagger under the weight of the elderly baby boomers, who are expected both to live much longer than earlier cohorts of the elderly and to fuel continued growth in health care costs. Recent projections of life expectancy suggest that the Social Security Administration may be under considerable strain to support the nearly threefold growth by 2040 in the number of people over age 65 (Lee and Carter, 1992). Many of these elderly will be in nursing homes; Schneider and Guralnik (1990) predict "there may be two to three times as many individuals aged 85 years and above in nursing homes in 2040 as there are individuals aged 65 years and above in nursing homes today!" Combined with projected increases in the population of disabled elderly is the rapid growth in health expenses per elderly person. The Health Care Financing Administration (HCFA) forecasts that nearly one-third of gross domestic product will be spent on health care by 2030 (Burner, Waldo, and McKusick, 1992). Auerbach and Kotlikoff (1994) predict that future generations will be required to pay in taxes *82 cents* per dollar of income to support currently legislated Social Security and Medicare benefits. It is possible, of course, that the elderly might be expected to pay more out of pocket. But calculations by Bernheim (1994) suggest that, if anything, most baby boom families are saving too little for their retirement.

Ronald Lee's research for this paper was supported by National Institute on Aging grant AG11761-01A1. The authors are grateful to David Cutler, John Bound, Alan Garber, Bert Kestenbaum, Nancy Maritato, S. Jay Olshansky, Joshua Wiener, and panel members for helpful suggestions.

An alternative view is much more optimistic about retirement prospects for the baby boom generation. Disability and morbidity will continue to become more compressed, leading to healthier years later in life (Manton, Stallard, and Liu, 1993a; Manton, Corder, and Stallard, 1993) as well as to a secular increase in the average retirement age. The Social Security tax base may be buoyed by immigration and increased fertility rates. The economic demands of higher health care costs will be offset by productivity gains and higher income levels; projections from the ICF-Brookings model, for example, anticipate the percentage of elderly (65+) requiring Medicaid coverage for long-term care to decline by 2018 (Wiener, Illston, and Hanley, 1994). Another projection of long-term health care costs predicts that nursing home expenses, as a fraction of median income, will actually decline by the year 2030 (Zedlewski and McBride, 1992). As a recent *Business Week* cover story concluded, "The elderly are more vital than before. Americans can afford to grow old. And they will grow old gracefully" (Farrell, 1994, p. 68).

Figuring out which of these two scenarios is correct is clearly crucial for forming policies to prepare for the next century. If the retiring baby boom generation will drag down the American economy by 2020, then government policies designed to smooth the projected health and Social Security costs are likely to be most effective now, while the baby boomers are nearing the peak of their earning capacity. Conversely, a government program designed to save against a nonexistent crisis can disrupt the saving and retirement plans of the generation it was designed to help.

In this paper, we attempt to identify the major factors that account for these very different predictions, and we suggest how these discrepancies can be reconciled. We focus on data requirements that may be useful, or even necessary, to piece together the puzzle of how health and mortality trends will affect retirement income security in 2020. We also stress, however, that much of the work that remains to be done is not simply gathering or linking more data. Instead, the task of reconciling the two divergent views of baby boom retirement must involve more consensus about the interpretation of the data or more generally developing modeling strategies that are more likely to hold long-term predictive power. For example, as we show below, a large part of the difference in projections of health costs depends on alternative assumptions about the extent to which the relative price of health care will rise over the next 40 years. Projections of this type are based on past data, but it is not clear whether the past 25 years reflect a long-term trend or a transition to a new steady state in which medical care prices are stabilized. Improvements in mortality do not result from the passage of time, but rather from the influence on biological processes of changes in health care interventions, lifestyle choices, medical technology, epidemiological processes, and so on, and the evolution of these is not well understood (see Warner, 1993). Similarly, changes in income and health care costs depend on many influences, including policy decisions to be taken in the future, that are difficult to predict over the long run. In other words, many of the problems to be surmounted involve the modeling or interpretation of the existing data, rather than shortfalls in the data themselves. These problems are more intractable (and divisive) than simply collecting better data and relate fundamentally to the intrinsic difficulties in forecasting very complex economic systems.

We focus on four issues related to projecting how mortality, health status, and health costs will affect retirement income over the next 30 to 50 years. The first general issue is how rapidly mortality will decline. There are a wide range of mortality projections. Which statistical approaches hold the greatest promise for long-term projections necessary to maintain the financial viability of the Social Security system? We suggest a number of research approaches, using existing data, that may improve our ability to assess the predictive power of competing models of mortality. Finally, we discuss how mortality projections of specific ethnic groups, or of the very elderly, can be improved.

The second issue is, what will be the health-disability status of the elderly in the next 30 to 50 years? There is considerable debate about the growth in the number of disabled or frail elderly as the consequence of many more people living past age 85. This is a crucial question both for baby boomers setting aside resources for future illness and for future Medicare and Medicaid expenditures. Despite the controversy over the future progress of morbidity and disability, there is surprising agreement in projections of the nursing home population in 2020. Since a consensus doesn't necessarily mean that these predictions are correct, we also consider some possible strategies for better measuring long-term changes in patterns of disability.

The third issue is a related question: given the predicted health-disability levels, how will per-person costs for a given health-disability level evolve in the next 30 years? Will health care costs continue to grow at historical rates, or will they converge to a rate commensurate with wage growth? Determining which of these scenarios is correct is crucial in deciding whether baby boomers will enjoy a plentiful or a strapped retirement. The answer is not likely to be found solely by extrapolating the past 30 years of information. We argue that structural predictions require better information about whether changes in health care costs are the consequence of economic and political policies or are generated by a residual called "technological progress." This question cannot be resolved simply by collecting more data, but must come through improved modeling strategies.

Finally, we consider how these various factors might be expected to affect retirement income—after Social Security payments are received and after health costs are spent—for the baby boom generation in the coming 40 years. For example, how might extended life span affect the ability of the Social Security Administration to pay benefits? Such a question requires information not just about the elderly population, but about the working population in 2020 as well. If disability does decline over time, would retirement ages be extended, providing more earned income and placing less strain on households' nest eggs? Finally, most of the projections relate to aggregate or per capita spending or utilization. But it is very likely that different socioeconomic groups would fare differently under predicted changes in income and in health spending. We know that people with lower socioeconomic status have substantially higher rates of disability. We also know that income growth for this group has been lagging behind aggregate growth rates (or even declining). Yet the nexus of disability, income, and wealth accumulation, especially for lower income households, is not well understood.

HOW RAPIDLY WILL MORTALITY DECLINE?

To determine whether the Social Security and private pension funds held by the baby boom generation are actuarially sound, it is necessary to have good forecasts of mortality so that one knows how long participants in a plan are likely to draw benefits. A distinct but related problem for a pay-as-you-go pension program is that one also needs forecasts of the population in the ages that qualify for benefits. Forecasting the elderly population decades ahead requires forecasting the mortality not only of the elderly but also of the younger adults who, if they survive, will become elderly. For long-term forecasts, one must deal with the entire age distribution of mortality, from infancy on up. We consider both problems here. Population forecasts for the age group 65+ over a time horizon of 65 years evidently depend primarily on forecasts of mortality, and fertility does not enter in. However, to some degree they depend on forecasts of the rate and age distribution of immigration as well: in 1990, 8.6 percent of the elderly population was foreign born, according to the Census bureau. In this paper, we will largely ignore the immigration issue and focus on forecasts of mortality. The reader is also referred to a critical review of the topic by an interdisciplinary group convened by the National Academy of Sciences/Institute of Medicine whose views are summarized in Stoto and Durch, 1993.

Mortality Decline in the United States During the 20th Century

The pace of mortality decline in the United States during the 20th century has varied, as shown by Table 6-1, and there is one subperiod, 1954-1968, in which the age-standardized male death rate actually rose.[1] Overall, the figures in the table do not give a strong impression of either an accelerating or a decelerating rate of decline. However, it is useful to consider a hypothetical population in which each age-specific death rate declines at its own constant exponential rate. Life expectancy would rise at a slowing pace because death rates at younger ages would approach zero, and increasingly the deaths averted would be those of the elderly, who would not live many more years in any case. Thus there is a built-in tendency for life-expectancy gains to decelerate even if each age-specific rate continues to decline steadily. Nothing, of course, says that death rates cannot begin to decline more rapidly at older ages, but unless there is a break with

TABLE 6-1   Annual Rate of Decline in
Age-Adjusted U.S. Death Rates, by Sex for
Selected Periods

Period	Males	Females
1900-1936	0.8	0.9
1936-1954	1.6	2.5
1954-1968	−0.2	0.8
1968-1990	1.5	1.4

NOTE: This is the rate at which the crude death rate would
have declined for a population with the age distribution of
the 1990 U.S. population subject to the age-specific death
rates of each period.

SOURCE: Social Security Administration (1992).

historical trends, life-expectancy gains are bound to slow. Indeed, life expectancy
increased by about 18 years from 1900 to 1944, but by only about 10 years from
1944 to 1988; Lee and Carter (1992) forecast it to rise by only 6.5 years in the 44
years from 1988 to 2032.

Comparisons of Forecasts

Many people rely on mortality projections by the Bureau of the Census and/
or the Office of the Actuary of the Social Security Administration (SSA). These
agencies generally forecast less rapid declines in mortality, and smaller gains in
life expectancy, than do other recent mortality forecasts available today. Their
forecasts are roughly consistent with the views of some authors, such as Fries
(1980, 1989) and Olshansky, Carnes, and Cassel (1990), who argue that future
life expectancy is bounded at around 85 years for the general population (sexes
combined).

Other authors argue that life expectancy as high as 100 years may be obtainable in the not too distant future. For example, Manton, Stallard, and Tolley
(1991) calculate a lower bound to attainable future life expectancy of 95 or 100
years, if people were to adopt optimal lifestyles, and also claim that such levels
are already exhibited by some special subpopulations with particularly healthy
lifestyles, such as Mormon high priests. Ahlburg and Vaupel (1990) foresee the
possibility of such high life expectancies by 2080 by extrapolating the rapid rates
of mortality decline that obtained in the United States in the 1970s. Obviously a
U.S. life expectancy of 95 or 100 years would have important implications for
pension systems of all kinds.

In work described more fully below, Lee and Carter (1992) use extrapolative time series methods combined with a simple model of the age distribution of mortality to forecast that life expectancy will rise to about 86 years by 2065 (with a 95% probability interval of 81 to 90 years), or to 84.3 by 2050. These forecasts implied a life-expectancy gain that was twice that forecast by the Census Bureau and SSA at the time, and is still twice as great as the SSA forecasts and substantially higher than those of the Census Bureau.

These large differences in forecasted levels of mortality lead, of course, to correspondingly large differences in forecasts of the number of elderly. For example, point forecasts for the number of people over age 85 in 2050 vary from 18 million in the Census projections to 41 million by Manton, Stallard, and Tolley. Furthermore, the forecast by Manton, Stallard, and Tolley lies far outside the high-low bracket given by Census.

The SSA forecasts consider trends in 10 groups of causes of death. At the start of the forecast period, the death rates from each cause are assumed to continue to decline at the exponential rate observed during a 20-year base period. These initial rates of decline are then merged into ultimate rates of decline that are assumed for each of the cause groups based on an assessment of various factors believed to influence the rate of decline for each cause in the long run. The ultimate rates of decline are fully in effect about 25 years into the forecast. (This discussion is based on Social Security Administration, 1992.)

The forecasts that result from this approach imply a sharp slowing of the rates of decline of mortality at all ages, relative both to the previous two decades and to longer run historical trends, measuring from the start of almost any decade back to 1900. Table 6-2 shows the difference between long-run historical trends and the rates of decline assumed in the SSA forecast. These differences are great at the youngest ages, where they imply that the SSA death-rate forecasts would be about five times as high as the simple trend-extrapolated rates. The differences diminish with age and are least for rates at 65+. For men in these ages, the difference is negligible, but for women it is considerable. More detailed calculations show that at the younger old ages, in the 60s and 70s, the SSA forecasts rates for females that are 60 percent to 70 percent higher than simple trend extrapolation would suggest. If instead we compare the forecasts to the average rate of decline from 1968 to 1988 for the total age-adjusted death rate, 1.49 percent per year for males and 1.56 for females, the contrast with the SSA forecasts is even greater. There is nothing intrinsically wrong with forecasting that mortality will decline more slowly in the future than it has in the past, and SSA evidently believes it is right to do so, based on its cause-specific analysis.

Other Methods of Forecasting Mortality Change

From a demographic point of view, the problem of forecasting mortality has two aspects that may be usefully separated conceptually, and which are in fact often separated procedurally. First, one must deal with the complexity of the age

TABLE 6-2   Average Annual Rate of Decline in Mortality for Base Period Versus SSA Forecast, by Age and Sex, Percent per Year

Age Group	1900-1988 (base period)	1988-2066 (forecast period)	Forecast Rate – Base Rate	Ratio of Forecast to Trend Extrapolation in 2068
Male				
0-14	3.25	1.21	-2.04	4.9
15-24	1.54	0.65	-0.89	2.0
25-64	1.09	0.71	-0.38	1.3
65 +	0.52	0.54	0.02	1.0
Total	0.95	0.60	-0.35	1.3
Female				
0-14	3.39	1.24	-2.15	5.3
15-24	2.52	0.61	-1.91	4.4
25-64	1.59	0.61	-0.98	2.1
65 +	0.95	0.55	-0.40	1.4

SOURCE: The first two columns of data are taken directly from Table 4 in Social Security Administration (1992:9). The third column is the second minus the first. The last column is calculated as exp(-78*entry from previous column). It represents the ratio of the SSA forecast of mortality levels in 2068 to the death rate in 2068 that would result from extrapolating the historical trend from the period 1900-1988.

distribution of mortality, somehow reducing the dimensionality of the problem so that it is not necessary to forecast the many age-specific rates separately and independently. Second, one must forecast the level of mortality and decide how the level is to be characterized and measured. For example, *Statistics Canada* first prepares a forecast of life expectancy at birth, taking this as the measure of level, and then determines how to allocate death rates by age in a manner consistent with the prior forecast of life expectancy. For other approaches, such as modeling health status as the outcome of dynamic disease processes and changing risk factors, this distinction is less useful. We will first discuss the problem of age distribution and then that of level.

In recent work, there have been two approaches to dealing with age distribution. In the functional parametric approach, a complicated nonlinear function of age with up to nine parameters is fit to the age profile of mortality for a given year or series of years. Changes in the level of mortality then come from changes in the parameters. In practice it may be desirable to hold most of the parameters fixed and capture changes over time through variations in just three key parameters (see McNown and Rogers, 1989, 1992). Forecasts of level and age distribution are obtained by modeling the sample period variations in these key parameters and then forecasting them.

A different approach uses so-called relational methods. In this approach, a standard age profile of mortality is established, representing a central tendency in the shape of the age distribution. New mortality schedules representing different levels of mortality are then generated by some transformation of the standard, where the transformation may be characterized by one or two parameters. The Lee-Carter (1992) method is of this form. In it, the model:

$$\ln(m_{x,t}) = a_x + k_t b_x + e_{x,t}$$

is fit to the sample period age-time-specific mortality rates, $m_{x,t}$. Here $\exp(a_x)$ can be viewed as the standard schedule, and the coefficient b_x describes how this standard is transformed to generate new age schedules of rates when k_t, the index of mortality level, varies. Time series methods can be used to model the sample period variation in k_t, and the estimated model can then be used to forecast k_t. From these forecasts, forecasts of $m_{x,t}$ can be recovered using the equation. In most applications of this model, k_t is well modeled as random walk with drift. Gomez de Leon (1990), using exploratory data analysis on Norway's extensive historical mortality data, selected this model from among a variety of simple models to represent patterns of change, based on a variety of criteria including goodness of fit.

This model makes some strong assumptions. If the model fit perfectly in the sense that all errors $e_{x,t}$ were zero, then any age-specific death rate could be expressed as a linear function of any other, and the correlations among them would all be unity. Autocorrelations for each rate would equal the autocorrelation of k_t. Lee and Carter construct probability intervals for the mortality forecasts generated in this way, and for forecasts of period life expectancy. Figure 6-1 plots base period estimates and forecasts for k_t, while Figure 6-2 plots life expectancy since 1900 and its forecast derived from that of k. It is notable that whereas the time path of historical life expectancy is decelerating (the gains in the first half of the period were twice as great as those in the second half of the period), the trend in k is roughly linear, and the gains in the two subperiods were equal. Also note that while rates of mortality decline reported in Table 6-1 were quite variable across subperiods, the decline in k, which indexes the log of the level of mortality, appears quite regular.

The Lee-Carter forecasts foresee substantially larger gains in life expectancy than do the SSA forecasts: about 10 years versus about 5 years. We have seen that the SSA forecasts assume a substantial slowing of mortality decline. The Lee-Carter forecasts come close to assuming that historical trends will continue, although this is more nearly true for some age groups than for others. For ages over 60, for complicated reasons, the forecasts published in Lee and Carter (1992) are for more rapid decline than the average rates for 1900 to 1987 and come closer to the average rates of decline for 1930 to 1987.

Both the Lee-Carter and Rogers-McNown approaches draw on time series analysis and ARIMA type models for forecasting the level of mortality. Another

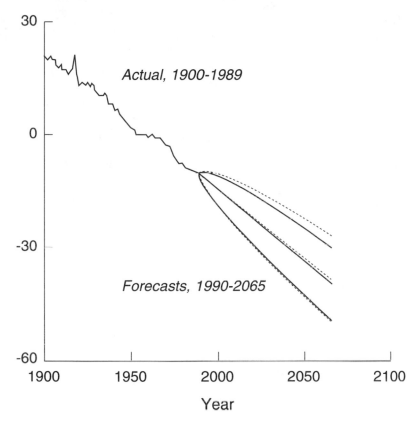

FIGURE 6-1 Comparison of mortality forecasts to 2065, based on data from 1900-1989 (dots) and from 1933-1989 (solid), with 95 percent confidence bands. NOTE: Both forecasts are (0,1,0). The forecast from 1900 has a dummy for the influenza epidemic; see text.

approach has been to develop a standard trajectory for life expectancy based on the historical record for many populations and to incorporate the pronounced tendency for life expectancy to rise more slowly when it is at high levels than when it is at low levels. This approach has often been used quite successfully by international agencies.

While there is certainly room for further work on extrapolative models (see, e.g., suggestions made below), current work appears to be pursuing logical directions, and there is no reason to expect that major new initiatives in this area would have a high payoff. The real question, we believe, is whether these extrapolative methods currently yield the best possible forecasts, or whether other models, incorporating more structural information about the complicated biological processes leading to disease and death, might yield superior forecasts. One possibil-

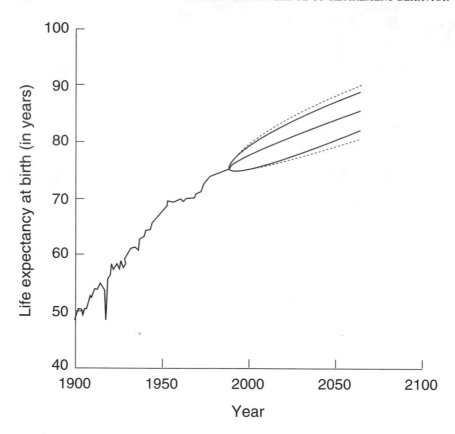

FIGURE 6-2 U.S. life expectancy and forecasts (95 percent confidence intervals with and without uncertainty from trend term). NOTE: The forecasts employ a (0,1,0) model with an influenza dummy estimated on mortality data from 1900 to 1989. The 95 percent confidence intervals are shown with and without uncertainty from drift.

ity is to apply extrapolative methods to cause-specific data, which permits relevant medical and biological outside information to be introduced to some degree, as is done by SSA. The development and estimation of explicit statistical models relating disease, disability, and mortality to individual behaviors and risk factors, as will be further discussed later, is another possibility drawing on deeper information. Still another approach is to consider the history of mortality change in terms of epochs of progress against particular kinds of diseases and, in so doing, to identify the likely future direction and pace of progress.

David Cutler has suggested the following illustrative periodization for U.S. mortality since 1850: (1) 1850-1880: Primitive medical knowledge and poor sanitary conditions yield high mortality, particularly for children. (2) 1880-1920: Rapid mortality declines reflect improvements in water supplies and general sanitary conditions. (3) 1920 to 1950: Continuing dramatic progress against infectious diseases result from the development of antibiotics and other effective treatments. (4) 1950-1970: The end of dramatic gains against communicable diseases and slow progress against chronic and degenerative diseases result in more slowly declining mortality. (5) 1970-present: Reductions in cardiovascular mortality result from lifstyle improvements and more effective treatment.

What does this approach suggest for future mortality trends? There are a number of possibilities: (1) Ever more money is spent on limited-applicability major surgery for cardiovascular diseases, and modest reductions occur in mortality largely owing to lower levels of smoking. (2) Expensive treatments are curtailed with little effect on mortality, and cost growth slows. (3) The genetic revolution leads to earlier diagnosis and treatment of disease, leading to substantial mortality improvements and slower growth in health costs. (4) Dramatic progress is made against chronic and degenerative diseases through behavioral lifestyle changes, through new genetic interventions, and through progress in treating cancer, with uncertain implications for costs. (5) Newly emerging infectious diseases such as AIDS, new antibiotic-resistant strains of old diseases, and diseases caused by worsening environmental conditions lead to rising mortality, with uncertain effects on costs.

This range of possible future scenarios shows the difficulty with the approach. A case could be made for each. How is the forecaster to choose among them? The record since 1900, as summarized by the mortality index plotted in Figure 6-1, shows a surprisingly regular pattern of decline, despite such major breakthroughs as the development of antibiotics. Forecasts using exactly the same method, but with starting dates ranging from 1900 to 1960, yield virtually identical forecasts of mortality and probability bounds for the United States (see Lee and Carter, 1992); a starting date of 1970 yields forecasts of more rapid mortality decline, but starting in 1980 gives results quite similar to those from earlier starting dates. This consistency suggests that historical periods of relative progress and stagnation tend to average out and do not lead to turning points in the underlying trend of mortality.

Evaluating the Uncertainty of Mortality Forecasts

Considerable progress has been made in describing the uncertainty of mortality forecasts in recent years. In a notable paper, Alho and Spencer (1990) develop probability intervals for the SSA mortality forecasts. They find that below age 20, the SSA high-low bounds are narrower than empirical 95 percent probability intervals; from 40 to 64, they are wider; and for other ages, they are about equal to the empirical bounds. In interpreting these results, it is important to keep in mind that these bounds refer to the probability distribution for mortality in any given single year, not for the general level of mortality over the forecast horizon. Lee and Carter (1992) provide probability intervals describing the uncertainty arising in their extrapolative method. The difficulty is that these quantifications, based on time series analysis, do not allow for specification error or for the possibility of larger breaks in patterns than have occurred in the historical past. Some may find this approach to assessing uncertainty persuasive, and indeed it is common in statistical forecasting. Others, however, believe that because of genetic research or lifestyle modification, such structural breaks may be imminent and that therefore the probability intervals based on time series models are too narrow (see Stoto and Durch, 1993).

We do not know how to attach a probability to attaining a life expectancy of 100 by 2030. The Lee-Carter model assigns this outcome a positive probability, but one that is vanishingly small. However, the mere fact that reputable and well-informed scientists believe that such an outcome is a real possibility, and one that should be contemplated in formulating policy, suggests that it does not have negligible probability (Stoto and Durch, 1993). It is very important that this probability be better assessed. Unfortunately, we do not have any concrete suggestions to make on how to do it.

It is also possible, of course, that the extrapolative methods may greatly overstate future mortality declines. If these methods were used to extrapolate backwards before 1900, the result would imply that during the 19th century mortality declined rapidly from impossibly high levels at its beginning. In reality, however, mortality levels were fairly stable throughout the 19th century (see Haines, 1994). In other words, there was an abrupt acceleration of the pace of mortality decline some time around the beginning of the 20th century, and the Lee-Carter model was fit only to the years after the acceleration took place. It therefore overstates the support for a constant rate of mortality decline and understates the variance in rate of decline. In sum, it is best to view the Lee-Carter probability intervals on mortality forecasts as lower bounds on the uncertainty of the forecasts.

One possible reason for slower mortality decline in the future is the emergence of new diseases such as AIDS. The current impact of AIDS mortality on life expectancy at birth is not large on average, although it is substantial for some subpopulations. Census has incorporated AIDS mortality explicitly into the 1992 projections. In the middle projection assumption for mortality, "the incidence of AIDS is projected to increase linearly until the turn of the century. After 2000, mortality from AIDS will slowly decrease, returning to the 1990 level of AIDS mortality by 2050" (Bureau of the Census, 1993:xxvi; see Campbell, 1991, for the analysis underlying these assumptions). Under the Census scenario for low gains in life expectancy, which incorporates somewhat more pessimistic AIDS projections, AIDS mortality would reduce life expectancy for males by 0.9 years, and for females by 0.2 years, for an average reduction of about 0.5 years, where these figures apply to the year 2005 and later.[2] For an alternative analysis that is critical of these methods but that leads to lower projected increases in AIDS mortality, see Bloom and Glied (1992).

We will make three kinds of suggestions for advancing work in the area of mortality forecasts: straightforward research using existing data and established methods; data collection; and modeling.

Some Specific Research Suggestions Using Existing Data and Established Methods

It would be useful to reexamine the studies of life expectancy in special subpopulations such as Mormon high priests, as reviewed by Manton, Stallard, and Tolley (1991). The data on the subpopulations do not actually contain much information about death rates at very old ages. Mortality rates are imputed at old ages by multiplying a standard mortality schedule (which does cover mortality at very old ages) by the standard mortality ratios estimated in each study. It is possible that the use of U.S. mortality rates at old ages as a standard has led to questionable results. It would be a simple matter to recompute these using as the standard either a reliable mortality schedule, such as that for Sweden, or the Kestenbaum (1992) rates for the United States. We would then learn whether the apparently very high life expectancies for these subpopulations were artifacts of the estimation method.

By analyzing the past record of the United Nations and the Census Bureau in forecasting population size, Stoto (1983) derived a measure of the standard error of the implied forecasts of growth rates. These ex post standard errors have been widely used to attach prospective probability intervals to population forecasts, although some strong assumptions are evidently required to do so. The Stoto intervals have been compared with those arising from Lee and Tuljapurkar's (1994) stochastic population forecasts (to be discussed below) and found to be similar. We believe it would be useful to apply the Stoto method more broadly to variables produced in demographic forecasts other than average population growth rates or equivalently future population sizes. In particular, the method could be applied to the following:

• Assessing the performance in forecasting mortality: by the United Nations for individual countries, and by the U.S. Census Bureau and Social Security actuary. Standard errors based on some evaluation metric could then be compared with probability intervals from Lee and Carter (1992) and Alho and Spencer (1985, 1990), and perhaps to McNown, Rogers, and Little (1995).

• Assessing the performance of forecasts of dependency ratios and comparing these with high-low brackets from official forecasts and with the Lee and Tuljapurkar (1994) intervals.

A last suggestion is that the McNown-Rogers and the Lee-Carter models be fitted and tested on data from populations with high-quality data at older ages, such as Sweden, France, and Japan (see recommendations in Stoto and Durch,

1993). In sum, there are various dimensions along which demographic forecasts can be assessed using existing data. These assessment approaches may allow researchers to better reach a consensus on future mortality trends.

Recommended Improvements in Data

Mortality data for older ages in the United States are believed by many to be seriously deficient, to the extent that analyses based on them are thought to be flawed. For example, Kannisto (1994:14-16) reports on old-age mortality data for 32 populations, almost all of developed countries. Based on diagnostic tests on the data, he ranks the U.S. data as "weak" along with those from Canada, Chile, and New Zealand (for the Maoris), and rejects them as too unreliable for further analysis. Others believe the U.S. data to be usable for many purposes. It is important that the quality of these data be more convincingly established (Coale and Kisker, 1990; Bennett and Olshansky, 1994; Kestenbaum, 1992; Himes, 1994). Ideally, of course, one would want to have accurate measures of mortality at very old ages.

SSA prepares estimates and forecasts of the mortality of the U.S. population. It uses registration and census data for death rates up to age 64, but for ages 65 to 95, it uses Medicare records. These have two advantages: first, documentation of age is required at enrollment, and second, the numerators and denominators come from the same very large data set and are therefore less vulnerable to errors arising from age misreporting. Above age 95 a mathematical formula is used to impute mortality rates because the problem of phantom Medicare enrollees becomes increasingly severe. Kestenbaum (1992) reviews these procedures and data sources, and shows that the HCFA Medicare data files that are generally used contain many errors not present in the master-beneficiary-role files of the SSA. He tracks down the sources of errors, and confirms through a matching analysis that the master-beneficiary-role file data for Medicare Plan B enrollees (excluding the railroad-retirement subpopulation) are highly consistent with death certificate data for Texas and Massachusetts. His analysis, and new estimates of mortality rates in extreme old age, are for 1987 only. He finds that rates based on the HCFA data files are reasonably accurate until age 97 or so, but that after that they increasingly understate death rates calculated more carefully from the master-beneficiary-role files. Kestenbaum's work shows that it should be possible to construct improved estimates of mortality at older ages, at least for the last two decades or so.

Despite the fact that SSA does not use the NCHS data for older ages, a recent paper (Bennett and Olshansky, 1994) finds that employing adjustments suggested by Coale and Kisker (1990) together with adjusted rates calculated by Kestenbaum (1992) would reduce current estimated life expectancy at age 65 by 0.5 years, reduce the projected population over age 65 in 2050 by 3.3 million relative to the SSA forecasts (and by far more relative to the Census forecasts), and "significantly influence the projected solvency of the trust funds of the United States" (Bennett and Olshansky, 1994). This study used the standard SSA assumptions, while simply adjusting the initial levels of mortality.

Medicare data, analyzed along the lines pioneered by Kestenbaum (1992), appear to offer the best route to developing satisfactory measures of oldest old mortality for the United States, possibly as far back as the late 1960s (but see a cautionary note in Elo and Preston, 1994:13, on the quality of age reporting in these data and other problems with them). Establishing this data set merits high priority and should be relatively inexpensive. The following specific steps would be likely to yield significant benefits in more accurate measures of old-age mortality:[3]

• Kestenbaum's (1992) procedures should be used to estimate death rates for the older population back to the earliest date feasible, possibly to the late 1960s. These death rates should routinely be calculated on an annual basis. Care should be taken with records originating earlier in the history of the system, when documentation of age for enrollees was less stringent.
• There should be systematic reconciliation and balancing of the Medicare records at HCFA and in SSA's master-beneficiary-role files. HCFA misses many death records that these files have. Some reconciliation is now done for ages over 95; this should be done for other ages as well.
• SSA should make better use of outside information, such as death certificates, which are now often discarded if they do not prove to be administratively useful, even if they might have valuable statistical uses.
• Algorithms could be developed to impute deaths in some cases, based on such information as age and years elapsed since last use of Medicare.
• The master-beneficiary-role files should be checked to ensure that there is no more than one record per person enrolled, although this is not expected to be a major problem.

One might wonder why it is necessary to be so concerned with the mortality of the oldest old or the extremely old. Currently, only about 32 percent survive from birth to age 85 in period life tables, and only 6 percent survive from birth to 95. But according to the Lee-Carter forecasts, by 2030 half of births will be surviving to 85 (in period life tables), and 16 percent will be surviving to 95. By 2060, these figures will be 60 percent and 25 percent. Our current annual life tables from NCHS lump all deaths at ages over 85 together into the open-ended category. Clearly, pension and Social Security liabilities will be strongly affected by what happens to mortality after age 85.

Even after the Kestenbaum adjustments, the United States exhibits lower mortality at older ages than is observed in other populations of Europe and Japan with high-quality data. Canada, with data that are somewhat better than those of the United States, shares this deviant pattern. Is there a special North American age pattern of mortality? If so, why? Or are there further defects in the U.S. mortality data even for death rates at ages 70 to 79? These are important questions, since researchers seeking results applicable to the United States, and frustrated by the poor quality of U.S. data, frequently turn to international data of higher quality. This research area deserves attention (see Himes, 1994; Himes, Preston, and Condran, 1994; and Bennett and Olshansky, 1994).

Mortality data for the period before 1933 in the United States are available, but of uncertain quality (Alter, 1990). Some problems arise from the usual source of age exaggeration at old ages; others arise from the limited number of states reporting registered deaths during this period. These data are useful for statistical studies of mortality change in the United States and for extrapolative methods. It would be worth using systematic methods to inflate the rates for death-registration states to national totals (it is not clear how this is now done in available data sets), and to assess the reliability of these data carefully, particularly for mortality at older ages, building on Alter's work.

Mortality data by race/ethnic group are of suspect quality. Some studies have found that high proportions, on the order of 30 percent, of the deaths of members of some ethnic groups are misclassified as occurring to non-Hispanic whites, based on the classification of these deceased individuals in the census that provides the denominators for calculating death rates. The Bureau of the Census (1993:ix) did special calculations of mortality by race/ethnicity, estimating the life expectancies reported in Table 6-3.

Many people would be surprised to learn that estimated life expectancy is 1.8 years greater for Hispanics than for non-Hispanic whites; and 1.6 years greater for American Indians than for non-Hispanic whites. Observable health conditions and access to medical care seem inconsistent with these data. It is also very striking that the life expectancy for Asians is fully 7 years greater than for white non-Hispanics; this is an enormous difference, and the Asian life expectancy might be the highest observed anywhere in the world for a subpopulation this

TABLE 6-3   Census Estimates of Life Expectancy by Race/Ethnicity, 1993

Ethnic Group	Life Expectancy at Birth
Hispanic	79.0
White, not Hispanic	76.6
Black, not Hispanic	70.2
American Indian, not Hispanic	76.3
Asian, not Hispanic	82.9

SOURCE: U.S. Bureau of the Census (1993).

large. So there are reasons to doubt the accuracy of these estimates, and the misclassification of ethnicity on death certificates is a plausible source of error.

Yet it is far from clear that these estimates are wrong. Elo and Preston (1994) have conducted a careful review of recent estimates derived from a variety of kinds of data sources, including longitudinal survey data in which race/ethnicity is held fixed, Social Security data linked to death records, and conventional census and vital registration data. They conclude that Asian-Pacific Islander mortality is substantially below that of non-Hispanic whites and that Hispanic mortality is also lower than that of non-Hispanic whites. They thus confirm the direction of the differentials found by the Census Bureau.

It is possible that the Medicare data discussed earlier could be useful in this context. Unfortunately, in the past the only race/ethnic information gathered was white, black and other, and this was for the primary beneficiary rather than for the actual person (who might, for example, be a surviving widow of a different race/ethnicity). The data are now being reclassified according to own race/ethnicity. Beginning in 1980-1982, information was gathered along the now-standard lines (white, black, Asian, North American Indian, Hispanic), but only new applicants for Social Security cards or those applying for replacement cards supplied the information. There is soon to be a mailing to about 2.5 million beneficiaries to elicit more detailed race/ethnic information on a voluntary basis. It appears, therefore, that in a couple of years it may be possible to calculate much-improved race/ethnic mortality rates for the elderly. This would be a major advance, and it is important that the data analysis actually be carried out. It is also important that other approaches be pursued, such as the revealing analysis by Preston, et al. (1994) of black-white mortality differentials based on attempted linkage of data from the Census Bureau, Vital Registration, and Social Security.

Finally, it is not clear that forecasting by cause of death is preferable to forecasting overall mortality. However, if forecasting by cause of death is to be done, then it is necessary to improve the cause-of-death data, particularly at older ages, and to take into account multiple causes of death (see Stoto and Durch, 1993).

Recommended Research on Modeling and Methods

In principle, it should be possible to improve extrapolative forecasts by bringing to bear knowledge about medical progress in specific areas. Experience to date, largely from the use by Social Security of experts on specific causes of death, has not been encouraging. One might be tempted to carry out a mortality forecast disaggregated by cause of death using other means. Whenever this is done in an extrapolative mode, one is likely to get a lower forecast of life expectancy gains since the more rapidly declining causes of death necessarily come to claim a smaller and smaller share of total mortality while the share of the slowly declining causes of death grows. Not infrequently, mortality from some causes is increasing absolutely, for example, death rates for some cancers. In this case, the effect is even more pronounced. The decline of the aggregate, being a weighted average of cause-specific rate, slows (Wilmoth and Preston, 1994), and if any cause-specific rate is actually increasing, then in the very long run the aggregate forecast will be for rising mortality overall. To point out that this is so is not to say that it is wrong. Furthermore, extrapolative forecasts need not extrapolate constant exponential rates of change for cause-specific death rates forever: asymptotes could be imposed, or shares could be forecast rather than levels.

An alternative approach is to explicitly model and estimate the disease processes (at least in general terms) leading to disability, recovery, or death. This is the approach taken by Manton and his collaborators. Their variables include risk factors, such as lifestyle behaviors like smoking, drinking, and exercise. By exogenously varying these risk factors, they can simulate the effects of policies or behavioral changes on mortality and disability. In addition to such analytic simulations, mortality projections can be generated by forecasting each of the risk factors, perhaps by extrapolating observed trends from longitudinal data sets. Such an approach is attractive in many respects. At the same time, it suffers from difficulty in obtaining long time series of the relevant variables, perhaps from some instability in the forecasts and perhaps from some difficulty in obtaining probability intervals. Another problem is that uncertainty about long-term trends in mortality is simply pushed back onto uncertainty about the underlying risk factors. There may be new patterns of behavior, for example, that could worsen long-term survival trends.

HEALTH STATUS PROJECTIONS AND THE COMPRESSION OF DISABILITY

The burden of the baby boom retirement cohort will depend not just on their total number, but also on their health. In this section, we consider the difficulties in forecasting whether people in the next century can look forward to an active, healthy retirement or a relatively frail and inactive one.

The Compression Debate

The original Fries (1980) article hypothesized a biological limit to average human life expectancy at around 85 years in a population.[4] Declining prevalence rates of morbidity and disability would lead to a gradual "compression" of morbidity and disability, which would in turn reduce the costs of providing health care and ancillary services for large numbers of chronically ill elderly people. The previous section discussed more recent evidence strongly suggesting that the "old-old," those over age 85, are expected to be among the fastest growing segments of the population for the foreseeable future. Even if there is a compression of morbidity over the individual life cycle, there may be a rapid expansion of the numbers of elderly frail people in the population requiring outpatient or institutional care, given the extremely rapid growth that is forecast for the population age 85 and over (e.g., Schneider and Guralnik, 1990).

One problem with predicting how disability will evolve over the next 40 years is the difficulty in establishing trends from historical data. The reason is that there is no unique definition of disability; objective medical measures such as blood pressure are imperfectly correlated with functional ability, while more subjective self-reported measures of disability may be functions of economic factors such as disability insurance benefits or may evolve over time according to changing social norms. Below, we consider the empirical evidence on secular changes in four types of measurement for disability, ranging from objective (blood pressure, body mass index) to subjective, self-reported disability.

Objective health measures have the advantage of being comparable over time, although they are only imperfectly correlated with a more inclusive definition of disability. Waidmann, Bound, and Schoenbaum (1995), for example, compare the incidence of men and women with systolic blood pressure at or above 140 mmHg between 1971-1975 and 1976-1980 using successive waves of the National Health and Nutrition Examination Surveys (NHANES I and NHANES II). They found a decline in the prevalence of high blood pressure of 14 percent for men and 19 percent for women. (The decline was less pronounced when they included people taking medical treatment for hypertension as part of their "high blood pressure" group.) During this same time period, however, self-reported hypertension increased by about 5 percent. These data illustrate one important pitfall with self-reported disability measures. Better medical treatment is likely to identify or categorize more types of disability, leading to higher self-reported levels of disability even if the average level of severity is declining in the population due to treatment. Extrapolating such self-reported trends is problematic.

Another easily measured indicator of health status is the body mass index, the ratio of weight to height. Costa (1994) compared the pension medical records of Civil War veterans in 1900 with data for men of a similar age from the National Health Interview Survey (NHIS) in 1985-1991. She found first that the body mass index was a surprisingly stable predictor of labor force participation across the two data sources. Second, she found a substantial increase in the average body mass index between 1900 and the 1980s. Using labor force participation as an indicator of functional health, her estimates suggest that had the Civil War veterans enjoyed the same distribution of body mass index as men of similar ages in the 1980s, their labor force participation would have been 6 percentage points higher. These objective measures of disability point towards a secular improvement in at least a limited measurement of health status.

The second general classification of disability relies on the incidence of specific diseases. For example, comparing the medical records of the same Civil War veterans early in the 20th century with medical records of World War II veterans in 1983 suggests dramatic declines in the prevalence of musculoskeletal, digestive, and circulatory diseases (Fogel, Costa, and Kim, 1993). These results imply a long-term secular compression of disability, at least among the "young-old" male veterans in their sample.

Liebson et al. (1992), however, caution that many of the studies of morbidity compression suffer from systematic data problems. There may be changes in the designation of the disease or in the likelihood of a physician's diagnosing a particular problem prior to death. Most studies do not include autopsy information that could inform whether the individual had a particular disease that was never diagnosed and hence did not appear in a retrospective study of health care records. Liebson et al. (1992) relied on a community-based sample of people living near Rochester, Minnesota, with comprehensive standardized data going back to 1907 that provided better medical information than most studies of this type. Examining specific disease categories, they found little evidence favoring long-term (20-year) compression for stroke or coronary heart disease.[5]

A third approach to measuring disability is to measure changes in functional ability, typically measured by activities of daily living, such as eating, dressing, or bathing, and instrumental activities of daily living, such as light housework, meal preparation, or money management. Manton, Stallard, and Liu (1993a, 1993b), and Manton, Corder, and Stallard (1993) for example, used longitudinal data, the National Long Term Care Survey (NLTCS) in 1982, 1984, and 1989 to estimate transition matrices among different levels of disability, where the levels of disability depended on how many activities of daily living the respondent reported difficulty in performing. Using a variety of statistical approaches, they found a secular decline in age-adjusted disability during the period of analysis.

Their model is quite general and allows transitions both into and out of disabled states over time. By using changes over a short period of time in a consistent longitudinal data set, they avoid many of the problems with changing definitions of morbidity and mortality noted by Liebson et al. (1992). However, the disadvantage is that their data are relatively short term, and the transition matrices may not accurately capture the "low frequency" trends in disability that are required for long-term projections. For example, Manton, Stallard, and Liu (1993b) forecast disability levels in the year 2020 based on the transition matrix estimated using 1982 and 1984 data.

The final approach to measuring disability is to use self-reported health assessments. Even though these are is in some respects the most direct way to measure the state of disability, they exhibit dramatic short-term fluctuations. For example, Wolfe and Haveman (1990) show that predicted disability rates for a male older white widower changed from 9.3 percent in 1962 (based on unweighted data) to 33.4 percent in 1973, down to 23.6 percent in 1980, and back up to 32.6 percent in 1984. Waidmann, Bound, and Schoenbaum (1995) used Census Bureau data to show that the percentage of men aged 45 to 64 reporting they were unable to work rose from 6.3 percent in 1970 to 9.7 percent in 1980 and fell back to 8.8 percent in 1990. For women in the same age group, the corresponding percentages were 8.8 percent in 1970, 11.1 percent in 1980, and 9.4 percent in 1990. Given the evidence discussed above on more objective measures of underlying health, it seems likely that such changes are the consequence of more than just shifts in the underlying level of health status.

One possibility for the rising levels of disability during the 1970s was that as life expectancy was improving, those who in earlier decades would have died were now surviving but in a frail and disabled state. However, Waidmann, Bound, and Schoenbaum (1995) find little evidence to support this view. They find the magnitude of the changes in disability levels too large to be accounted for by the rise in the population of the people who are now surviving to later ages. A more plausible explanation for the variation in self-reported disability is shifts in the eligibility and generosity of the federal disability insurance program.

The federal government expanded eligibility and benefits from the early 1960s through the mid-1970s, and the number of workers receiving disability insurance grew from 0.5 million in 1960 to 2.9 million in 1980 (U.S. Congress, House, 1994:61). However, by the late 1970s and early 1980s, eligibility was curtailed sharply; the percentage of successful applications dropped from 46 percent in 1977 to only 29 percent in 1982 (U.S. Congress, House, 1994:60). Since the early 1980s, both the percentage of successful applications and the total number of those receiving disability insurance have risen, so that in 1993, 3.7 million disabled workers received benefits. Clearly, the pattern in self-reported disability, the rise during the 1970s and the dip during the 1980s, matches the secular path of disability benefits (e.g., Wolfe and Haveman, 1990), and there is a close correspondence between the magnitudes of changes in disability-insurance beneficiaries and patterns of self-reported disability (Waidmann, Bound, and Schoenbaum, 1995).

In sum, there are a wide range of variables that measure different aspects of disability. While objective measures, such as the body mass index and the presence of hypertension, allow for accurate comparisons over time, they may also be imperfectly correlated with the "true" level of disability. On the other hand, self-reported assessments of difficulty in daily functions and in the ability to work provide a clearer picture of who in the population is disabled, but the social norm of disability may itself evolve over time, making secular comparisons, and long-term *predictions* more problematic. Finally, it is possible that in the longer term, improvements in infrastructure, technology, travel, or job flexibility could affect what society construes as "disability," or even the link between underlying morbidity and activities of daily living. While the debate over the compression of disability is still not entirely resolved, the existing evidence suggests a trend towards lower levels of disability among the elderly population.

If the debate over compression is not entirely resolved, most forecasts of nursing home patients—the most obvious symptom of endemic disability in the elderly population—do not exhibit a great deal of variation, even for projections going out 30 years. Manton, Stallard, and Liu (1993b) predict 3.2 million people over age 65 in nursing homes in 2020, Wiener, Illston, and Hanley (1994) predict 3.6 million by 2018, while Schneider and Guralnik (1990) suggest about 2.6 million for the middle Census Bureau projection for 2020 or about 3.2 million for the high Census projection.[6]

The close similarity of these predictions does not mean that they are accurate. Even to the extent that more sophisticated prediction models account for trends in levels of disability, there may also be changes in the demand for nursing home patients if the underlying health status is held constant. A large fraction of the elderly disabled are cared for in the community, often by their children. And as Soldo and Freedman (1994) emphasize, there is a great potential for substitution among different sources of care for the disabled elderly, ranging from care by their children, to community-based assistance programs to institutionalization in, for example, nursing homes. Of the estimated 5.5 million elderly people who are disabled, only 24 percent are in institutions, with the remaining three-quarters cared for by family members or public programs (Soldo and Freedman, 1994).[7] As the baby boom generation retires, there may be fewer potential family caregivers for this group, given the smaller average size of families (through both fewer children and a greater proportion of divorced households). Alternatively, there may be changes in the financing of outpatient home care services for the disabled. Relatively modest *proportional* changes in the composition of care for the 76 percent of disabled elderly who are noninstitutionalized will have a much larger proportional impact on the size of the institutionalized population. By the same token, changes in medical conditions deemed "appropriate" for nursing home care (e.g., Berg et al., 1970) can shift, leading to further variation in nursing home bed demand.

Strategies to Modeling Disability

There are different strategies to modeling how changes in the distribution of disability levels will evolve over the next 40 years. As noted above, the easiest approach is simply to take the current fraction of disabled among those, say, between ages 85 and 90, and multiply it by the number of people predicted to be alive in the same age group. In some cases, one simply uses these projections to predict the number of people who will need hip replacements, or the population of nursing homes (e.g., Schneider and Guralnik, 1990). Overall cost forecasts can also be calculated by appropriate multiplication of the disabled population base times the average cost for this group. This approach ignores potential changes in the incidence of disability or in the age composition of disability.[8]

A more complicated approach is to focus on the underlying level of activities of daily living or instrumental activities of daily living as the disability "state" and predict these underlying levels without tracking the actual type of disease (e.g., Manton, Stallard, and Liu, 1993a, 1993b). This method is still nonstructural in that it makes the assumption that transition probabilities into and out of disability states is a function solely of a person's current disability and not of the underlying disease. By allowing for a transition matrix among different levels of disability, however, this method provides a very general model of disability that can be used for predicted trends in overall disability levels.

A more structural approach is to focus on specific diseases that are associated with differing periods of morbidity and disability (National Research Council, 1988:102). For example, Alzheimer's disease is generally associated with longer periods of disability. Cancer has a lengthy morbidity, but a relatively short period during which the patient is disabled. One might expect that if the incidence of Alzheimer's disease and cancer were to change over the next 20 years, the transition probabilities of the type estimated by Manton, Stallard, and Liu (1993b) might change as well. To the extent that we have information on changes in the relative shares of each disease category, this approach yields a more accurate prediction of future *average* levels of morbidity and disability. It also requires more structural knowledge about the subsequent morbidity or disability experiences of people who would have been afflicted by heart disease.

This approach holds promise in allowing more detailed disease-specific information about trends to be used in generating overall levels of morbidity and disability. However, the modeling requirements are also substantially larger because they require making inferences about transitions among disability levels for, say, the individual who avoided having a stroke in 1995 because of improvements in medical treatment or lifestyle. Is this person systematically different from the average individual in the same age group? Multidimensional models that allow for interactions among various levels of disability have large data requirements, but also allow for a great deal of flexibility (see Manton and Stallard, 1994).

Recommendations for Improving Modeling and Data Collection

Data requirements expand with the complexity of the model of disability. To make any inferences about changes over time in the prevalence of disability, one requires a representative sample of initial respondents and careful follow-up to document transitions both into and out of disability states. The NLTCS, for example, began with screening calls to 35,790 people based on Medicare records; these people included a group with disabilities, an institutionalized group, and a control of noninstitutionalized nondisabled. Because the initial sample was representative of the underlying population, valid transition probabilities between 1982 and 1984 (and subsequent years) could be made after correcting for nonresponse bias. The Health and Retirement Survey (HRS), currently in its second wave, will also provide detailed information about disability transitions over the next 15 years, as will the Asset and Health Dynamics Among the Oldest Old (AHEAD) survey, which focuses on older people.[9]

One shortcoming of existing studies, such as the NLTCS or the Longitudinal Study on Aging is that even when the sample is drawn from a representative population, the number of people in the sample who enter a nursing home is small. Of that group, the percentage who remain for more than 1 year is fewer still. While the number of people who remain in nursing homes for long periods is relatively small, they account for a large fraction of costs, so that accurately forecasting this group is crucial.

Some surveys attempt to overcome this problem by oversampling those with chronic health problems. For example, the National Long Term Care Channeling Evaluation sampled on the basis of observed risk of being institutionalized. The problem with this approach is that the sample is not representative of the population, so that inferences cannot be made for the purpose of forecasts. The National Nursing Home Survey provides no information about people who aren't admitted to nursing homes and provides only a cross-sectional snapshot of nursing home admissions.[10]

The second potential problem with existing data sets is nonresponse. We have argued above that long-term longitudinal panels are necessary to elicit low-frequency changes in the compression of disability over time. Yet even a low nonresponse rate of 3 percent to 4 percent annually can translate into losing 35 percent to 40 percent of the sample after 15 years. It therefore seems clear that cross-sectional samples of health, such as the NHIS, will still be of value in providing benchmarks of long-term trends in disability given that the questions asked are comparable over long periods of time.

Third, the HRS will provide detailed information for the next 15 years on a cohort of people initially in their 50s. By 2010, we should have a good handle on the retirement and disability experiences of this group (as well as older cohorts surveyed in AHEAD study). To assess long-term trends among the "young-old," however, requires detailed information about later cohorts, such as the group now aged 41 to 50. In other words, just knowing how a particular cohort fares does not in itself provide information for assessing long-term trends in disability and health needs; one requires survey information on a comparison cohort group. Comparing people in their 70s from the first AHEAD wave, with the HRS waves in the 2010, when those sampled will also be in their 70s, would provide a good measure of changes over time in disability. A survey that follows cohorts now in their 40s, to be fielded beginning in 2002, would improve long-term estimates of secular trends in disability.

In sum, the major problem with estimating long-term trends in disability is likely to be getting transition matrices that are sufficiently long term to reflect the low-frequency variation in rates and levels of disability. Coupled with the data requirements, however, is the problem of interpretation: will the notion of disability in the year 2020 be similar to that today? These issues will be partially resolved as some of the newer data sources, such as the HRS and AHEAD, continue to provide information on the retirement and disability experiences of their samples.

PREDICTING HEALTH CARE COSTS

Predicting the overall level of health care costs in 2020 and beyond is a daunting task. Total costs can be separated into two parts, prices and quantities. The quantity of "real" health care services in the future will depend on the size and age composition of the population, the underlying health status (or disability levels) of the age categories, the utilization of health services for a given level of health status or disability, and the intensity of such health services. The price of this service will depend on the general inflation rate over the next 25 years and the change in the relative price of health care.

The previous sections have focused on the size and composition of the population and the underlying health status or disability level of that population. We are not particularly concerned with the inflation rate for the next 25 years. So in this section, we focus on the remaining unknown variables: the level of health services (for a given underlying health status and age composition) and the relative price of health care in terms of other (nonmedical) goods.

Predicting Real Health Care Services by Demographic Group

The first step is to use current data to get a benchmark of how real quantities of health care services might be expected to evolve over time with changes in the age composition and in disability levels.[11] In general, health care expenditures rise by age and by disability or health status (e.g., Manton, Stallard, and Liu, 1993a; Chulis et al., 1993). To the extent that expenditures in a given year are valid measures of health care *services*, we can make inferences about the use of health care services by examining the evidence on health care expenditures.[12]

Empirical evidence suggests that it is important to distinguish between the real health services of those who survive to a given age and those who do not. Health costs are much higher in the months prior to death (Lubitz and Prihoda, 1984). Consequently, some of the measured increase of average health costs with age is actually due to the fact that in older age groups, death rates are higher, and therefore the mix of those surviving and those dying is increasingly tilted towards those dying (i.e., those requiring higher average levels of health services). Falling mortality may reduce *unconditional* per capita health service use at every age by reducing the age-specific proportion who are near death, and hence reducing the proportion of those with high demand for health services.

There is some controversy over how health care services near death vary by age or disability state. One study shows that among a group of retired workers in their 60s, median health expenditures for people who died between 1982 and 1984 was $8,012 for people with some functional limitations, but $11,846 for those without limitations (McCoy et al., 1992). In other words, health care services near death were *higher* among the healthier population than for the less healthy. Of course, we observe only Medicare claims in this study, and not the full range of health expenses for the two groups. Determining how changes in the prevalence of disability among the population affect health services utilization requires better information about differences in health care services over the life cycle by level and type of disability. There is some evidence that Medicare expenditures on older people (i.e., ages 85+) near death are below those for younger people (e.g., Temkin-Greener et al., 1992), but there is potential for newer studies, such as the HRS linked with Medicare data, or the Medicare 20 percent sample, to provide a better picture of the dynamics of health care use among these different groups.

Predicting Health Care Quantities and Prices for the Next Century

Even if we know how the level of health care services varies by different attributes of the population, a much harder problem is to predict how real health services and prices will evolve over the next 30 to 40 years. Official predictions by HCFA of national health expenditures, expressed as a ratio of gross domestic product, to the year 2030 are presented in Figure 6-3. Predicted growth is substantial, with overall national health spending reaching 26.5 percent of gross domestic product by 2020 and 32 percent by 2030. While spending nearly one-third of gross domestic product on health care may at first appear implausible, the

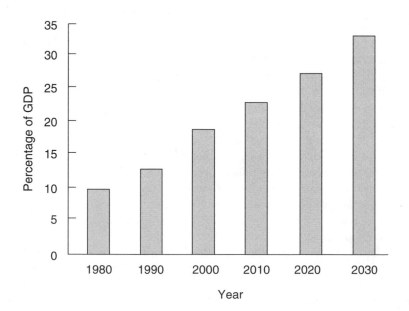

FIGURE 6-3 National health expenditures as a percent of gross domestic product, 1980-2030. SOURCE: Burner, Waldo, and McKusick (1992).

TABLE 6-4   Accounting for Increases in Real per Capita Health Spending, 1980-2030

| Category | Annual Real Growth | Share of Annual Real Growth Due to | | |
		Utilization	Intensity	Change in Relative Prices
Physician Services				
1980-1990	4.6	7.3	40.0	52.7
1990-2000	6.5	12.3	35.1	52.6
2000-2030	3.6	9.9	28.8	61.3
Inpatient Hospital				
1980-1990	6.4	−91.0	138.1	52.9
1990-2000	6.5	−7.4	59.9	47.6
2000-2030	4.1	34.2	24.4	41.4
Nursing Homes[a]				
1980-1990	5.2	2.4	70.0	27.6
1990-2000	6.6	18.7	54.2	27.1
2000-2030	3.8	37.5	44.6	17.9

NOTE: Column 1 shows the annualized real change in total health spending for each decade (or decades). This column reports real changes in total hospital expenditures (rather than just inpatient expenditures). Columns 2 to 4 calculate the contribution of the particular factor (utilization per capita, intensity, or relative price) as a percent of total real per capita change. For the three decades 2000 to 2030, the proportional changes are averaged for the purpose of this table.

[a]Excludes intermediate care facilities for the mentally retarded.

SOURCE: Burner, Waldo, and McKusick (1992).

forecast is based conservatively on the trend of real health care spending that stretches back 30 years.

What part of this overall increase is caused by changes in quantities, and what part by changes in relative prices? Burner, Waldo, and McKusick (1992) break down their estimates further; some of their results are shown in Table 6-4. In this table, we exclude changes owing to population growth and general price level changes, and focus on the relative importance of the three factors mentioned above—utilization, intensity, and changes in relative health care prices—in explaining the overall costs of real per capital health care expenses.

Real per capita expenditures on each category of health care selected above (physician, inpatient hospital, and nursing home) are expected to rise at a roughly 6-1/2 percent annual rate through the rest of this century before stabilizing at roughly 4 percent annually from 2000 to 2030. Of that increase, approximately half is attributed to a change in the relative price of health care for physician and inpatient care, and less than one-third to nursing homes. Although inpatient hospital services experienced a large relative decline in utilization rates, with a corresponding increase in intensity, during the 1980s, utilization growth is predicted to rebound and to account for about one-third of hospital cost growth during the first 30 years of the next century. By contrast, growth in nursing home costs is predicted to arise largely from an increase in the age composition of the population and changes in intensity of care.[13]

Predicting changes in relative prices and real quantities is a difficult task. In the estimates presented above, the positive increases in both the real quantity of health services and the real price are suggestive of increasing demand for health services, with a corresponding movement along the supply curve. If there is an error in the prediction of health care utilization, for example, it will tend to be magnified in the prediction of total costs. If demand for health care is less than predicted, then the implied increase in the real price of health care will also be less than predicted, leading to even greater cost savings. Alternatively, if there is a movement along the demand curve for health (i.e., higher prices lead to lower quantity consumed), the growth in health care costs will be attenuated.

One component of the increase in predicted real health services, particularly for nursing home care, is the increased total demand for medical care as the baby boom generation ages.[14] Do countries with more rapidly growing elderly populations experience more rapid health care costs? To test this proposition, Getzen (1992) compared a cross section of countries that belong to the Organization for Economic Cooperation and Development (OECD) since 1960. He found little evidence that the fraction of the population over age 65 was correlated with health spending as a share of gross domestic product, or that the *change* in the share of the population over age 65 was correlated with the *change* in the share of health spending in gross domestic product. In other words, his results suggest that the predicted impact on health care costs of the aging baby boom generation is likely to be overstated because increased demand will be offset by an "adjustment to budget realities" through a reduction in utilization (for a given age group), intensity, or prices.[15]

A less sanguine prediction for future fiscal burdens comes from Auerbach and Kotlikoff (1994). They use HCFA predictions to suggest that under current policies, current fiscal policies "may require a net lifetime tax rate of *82 percent* on future generations of Americans." And as they note, the assumption of rising health care costs through 2030 contributes greatly to their striking result. When they assume that health care costs are stabilized at their 1994 levels, so that health spending changes only because of demographic shifts, the lifetime tax burden increases only from 37 cents per dollar for a person born in 1960 to 45 cents per dollar for future generations (Auerbach and Kotlikoff, 1994:34).[16] In other words, the increasing relative price of health care is responsible for increasing the future generations' tax burden from 45 to 82 cents.

One may still wonder how an increase in Medicare and Medicaid payments by the government can account for raising the lifetime tax from 45 cents per dollar to 82 cents per dollar, given that total government spending on health care is predicted to rise by only about 17 percent of gross domestic product through 2030 (Burner, Waldo, and McKusick, 1992). The magnitude of the Auerbach-Kotlikoff result can be explained partially by the structure of the policy experiment. In their model, people born in 1992 are locked in to the current tax policies, so they pay just 36 cents per dollar of lifetime income, even though they spend most of their life in a regime in which health care is extremely costly (recall that this generation is only 38 by the time health care costs stabilize at 32% of gross domestic product in 2030). Hence the unfortunate babies born in 1993, and in subsequent years, are handed an enormous debt burden made even worse by the fact that debt has been accumulating at the real rate of interest assumed equal to 6 percent.

The Wiener, Illston, and Hanley (1994) projections relate solely to long-term care, but their assumptions are quite different. Instead of a long-term trend growth rate relative to gross domestic product, as in the HCFA projections, they assume that nursing home reimbursement rates simply keep pace with wage growth. What difference does this assumption make? According to the HCFA projections, annual nursing home plus home health care expenditures are projected to increase by $181.5 billion by 2020, in 1993 dollars. By contrast, Wiener, Illston, and Hanley project an increase of only $93 billion (to the year 2018). For evaluating the retirement prospects of the baby boom generation, it matters crucially whether one views the 30-year trend in health spending as a transition to a new steady state or as a trend destined to continue (until gross domestic product is exhausted!).

Conceptual Issues in Modeling Health Care Cost Projections

The problem of forecasting the general price of health care costs cannot be resolved simply with more historical data on prices. The relative price of health care is determined by market, institutional, and government forces, and the fact that many factors have contributed to its rise in the past does not mean that these factors won't be stabilized, or even reversed, in the future. The problem is that we do not have a good model of how health care costs are determined.

For example, it is likely that the evolution of government health costs is quite different from that of private health costs. So far, the U.S. government has provided health entitlements such as Medicare and Medicaid, which have expanded rapidly in recent decades despite various attempts to contain health care costs. It will be difficult to know a priori whether the government will continue to provide health care assistance as an entitlement or switch to global budgeting, as have most OECD countries (see Wolfe and Moran, 1993). In the HCFA projections, for example, there are only modest shifts in the composition of health care spending between the private and the public sector. But should the government switch to global expenditure caps, for example, both the price of health care and the real quantity of health care services would be strongly affected. To make informed predictions about the expected value of future health care expenditures therefore requires some knowledge of the *probability* that the federal government will impose global expenditure caps, but such a prediction presupposes that we have a model for the likelihood of the government's legislating comprehensive health care reform with expenditure caps.

Private costs are determined at a substantially more decentralized level and depend on the preferences of employees and their employers, as well as on tax and regulatory considerations affecting the design of health care benefits. The evolution of such factors is also hard to envision. Whether the shift toward managed care will continue and, if so, in what form (and with what cost saving) is difficult to predict based on current information (see Employee Benefit Research Institute, 1995). Generating a prediction for the trend in the composition of employee-provided health care is problematic; placing confidence intervals on such a prediction would be nearly impossible.

One might also expect substantial interaction between private and public spending. For example, cutbacks in Medicaid or Medicare reimbursements could be partly passed along by hospitals and health care providers to the private sector. Alternatively, U.S. government legislation of health care reform along the lines of the Clinton plan would change the balance between private and public spending on health as well as blur the distinction between the two sectors.

Below, we discuss some recent studies that have focused on the determination of government-financed health service and price determination. As noted above, government programs such as Medicare and Medicaid directly affect just one part of the health care sector. However, the centralized and more comprehensive sources of data from the federal government make such programs easier to evaluate for research purposes.

Some recent efforts to account for changes in overall Medicare spending have focused on cross-sectional variation in physician density and practice patterns (e.g., Holahan, Dor, and Zuckerman, 1990). Other analysts view the increase in health costs as reflecting the taste of consumers for more technologically complex health care (Newhouse, 1992). The view that technology is driving health care costs certainly receives some support from the evidence on continued growth in costs, despite cost-cutting programs such as the prospective payment system. However, McClellan (1994) suggests that the prospective payment system did little to stem the tide of health care costs and may actually have contributed to continued growth in hospital costs. He argued that diagnostic related groups are related not to a particular diagnosis, but to a means of treatment. In other words, a heart attack treated by coronary artery bypass graft falls into a different diagnostic related group than a heart attack treated nonsurgically. He showed that within 5 years of the start of the prospective payment system, nonsurgical (and less costly) diagnostic related group admissions dropped by 50 percent, while surgical diagnostic related group admissions grew by roughly 50 percent. In other words, the growth in the overall price index, at least for the 1980s, may be affected by government reimbursement policies, which are, of course, policy variables subject to change. This approach, which stresses analysis on a relatively micro scale to elicit dynamic trends in health costs, holds promise for understanding the determination of health care costs.

A related issue is, under what scenario would "the populace" more generally allow the projected continued growth in health care spending? Auerbach and Kotlikoff (1994) predict that between 1992 and 2029, health care costs for a 65-year-old will rise from 13 percent to 29 percent of income, leaving average nonmedical consumption essentially unchanged. As was shown in Table 6-4, much of the increase in spending is the consequence of increased utilization and intensity of services, not simply a change in the relative price of a given medical procedure. But it would seem unlikely that health costs would be allowed to claim an additional 16 percent of income without yielding anything of value to these future retirees. That is, if health costs continue to claim a larger fraction of gross domestic product, it could be that technological progress would provide sufficient improvement in health status that people would be willing to spend the additional resources on health care (rather than on non-health-care goods). Looking just at consumption net of medical expenses might not provide an accurate assessment of overall welfare.

In sum, typical forecasting approaches that project forward trends in individual price series are unlikely to predict future price trends successfully. Understanding the factors that determine health care costs (and quantities) will improve the accuracy of price predictions. Unfortunately, much work remains to be done in understanding what factors are important in determining health care costs and how they might be expected to evolve over the next 30 years.

HOW WILL CHANGING MORTALITY, HEALTH, AND HEALTH COSTS AFFECT RETIREMENT INCOME SECURITY?

One of the primary issues facing policy makers is how changes in mortality and health status and health costs might be expected to affect the income security of baby boom retirees. We have not yet considered the feedback effects of how such demographic and health changes might affect retirement income. In the subsections below, we look at a number of factors that are important in piecing together the puzzle of how the long-term trends discussed above affect retirement security.

The Effect of Changes in the Demographic Structure on Income Security for the Elderly

It is important for policy makers to know the degree of uncertainty that is associated with the forecasts that they use. Important decisions to raise both payroll tax rates and retirement age have been taken based on very long-term forecasts of the old age dependency ratios. But how seriously should these forecasts be taken? How uncertain are they?

Traditional Approaches

The traditional method for formulating population forecasts is scenario-based. The forecaster chooses what are believed to be the most likely or perhaps the statistically "expected" trajectories for fertility, mortality, and migration, including age distributions, and then generates forecasts by using well-known accounting identities. In choosing vital rate trajectories, the forecaster could certainly use any of the extrapolative methods just described. This method is quite straightforward, except for the relatively minor point that the population projection based on the expected values of stochastic rates does not equal the expected value of the population forecast based on stochastic vital rates; in practice the difference appears to be small enough to ignore (Lee and Tuljapurkar, 1994).

The real difficulty with the scenario-based approach comes when it is used to convey information about the degree of uncertainty associated with a population forecast. This is done by constructing two alternative trajectories for each rate, one above and one below the medium or preferred trajectory. The forecaster then combines these trajectories into high, medium, and low scenarios in ways that depend on the purpose of the forecast. For example, the Census Bureau combines high fertility and low mortality into a high scenario, and low fertility and high mortality into a low scenario. This gives the greatest range for the population growth rate and the future population size. However, since high fertility tends to make the population young, while low mortality tends to make the population old, the high and low scenarios do not cover a correspondingly broad range for the old age dependency ratio. Furthermore, because the scenarios assume that fertility is always high or low and mortality is always high or low, the Census Bureau's approach ignores all possible trajectories in which there is fluctuation. Yet strong fluctuations like the baby boom and baby bust have occurred in the past, and they lead to more extreme outcomes than the scenarios. Also, a little thought will verify that a scenario-based forecast cannot possibly yield probability intervals that are consistent among the different items that are forecast since variations in annual numbers or single age groups tend to be offsetting when the numbers or groups are summed to form larger population aggregates—broader age groups, or total population size, for example. So the basic method used by virtually all official forecasts to convey information about uncertainty is deeply flawed and largely incapable of informing policy.

Stochastic Population Forecasts

Because plans for Social Security are made with an extremely long lead time, and because policy changes might have major effects on both the macro-economy and the life-cycle planning of individuals, it is particularly important to take into account the degree of certainty with which long-term forecasts should be viewed. Considerable progress has been made in recent years in producing stochastic population forecasts with consistent and meaningful probability intervals for all items forecast (Alho and Spencer, 1985; Davis, 1988; Alho, 1992; Pflaumer, 1988; McNown and Rogers, 1992; Lee and Tuljapurkar, 1994). The approach of Lee and Tuljapurkar (1994) is to formulate models of age-specific fertility (see Lee, 1993) and age-specific mortality (Lee and Carter, 1992), with fertility and mortality each driven by a single time-varying parameter that is modeled and estimated using standard techniques of time series analysis. Migration could in principle be handled in exactly the same way, but was actually taken as deterministic at the level assumed in Census Bureau forecasts. These fitted models of stochastically varying rates are then taken as inputs to the population renewal process, and the propagation of error is carefully tracked, with all variances and covariances taken into account. Drawing on results in Tuljapurkar (1990), Lee and Carter derive and calculate analytic results for a quartic approximation to find both the expected value of the forecast and the probability intervals. Similar results can be obtained using Monte Carlo methods (repeated stochastic simulations) based on the stochastic models of vital rates.

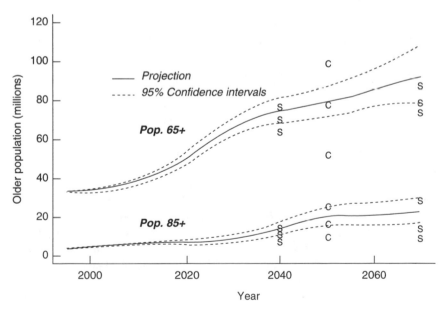

FIGURE 6-4 Projections of the population aged 65 and over and aged 85 and over from Lee and Tuljapurkar (1994) (solid lines), the Social Security Administration (S), and the Bureau of the Census (C).

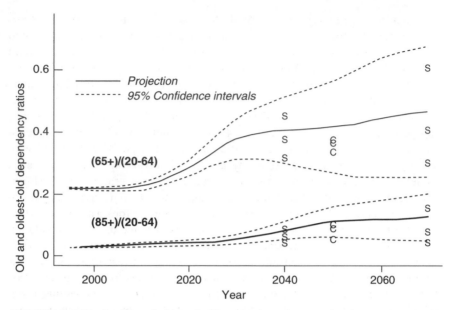

FIGURE 6-5 Projections of old and oldest-old dependency ratios from Lee and Tul-japurkar (1994) (solid lines), the Social Security Administration (S), and the Bureau of the Census (C).

Figure 6-4 shows forecasts derived in this way for the population 65+ and 85+, with 95 percent probability intervals. The figure also shows SSA forecasts for the same quantities in 2040 and 2070, and Census Bureau forecasts for 2050, including high, medium and low variants for both. Note the very different indications of uncertainty given by the Census Bureau and SSA in each case. Figure 6-5 shows forecasts of the old age dependency ratio, that is (population 65+)/(population 20-65), and the oldest old dependency ratio in a similar format. Note that whereas before, the Census brackets were substantially wider than the SSA brackets, in this case they have become substantially narrower, and very implausibly so. That is because the Census Bureau arrays low mortality with high fertility in their high scenario, for example. The Census forecasters are very aware of this problem, but it is inescapable. One could choose different scenarios from among the large set offered by the Census Bureau to get a different contrast, but there is no consistent or logical way to do this. Nor, it is important to add, is there any way to attach any kind of probability to these brackets, or to those of SSA.[17]

To a first approximation, and other things equal, payroll tax rates for Old Age, Survivors and Disability Insurance benefits must vary in proportion to the old age dependency ratio. It is because of the projected increases in this ratio that in the 1980s it was decided to begin to raise payroll taxes in order to accumulate a substantial reserve before the retirement of the baby boom generation, and to slowly raise above 65 the age at which full retirement benefits could be received. According to the point forecasts in Lee and Tuljapurkar (1994), the old age dependency ratio will increase by 34 percent by 2020 and by 98 percent, a virtual doubling, by 2050 (see Figure 6-5). These figures are only slightly higher than those of the Census Bureau and SSA, and they are daunting. But is it appropriate to make long-term policy decisions based on such expected increases in old age dependency? According again to Lee and Tuljapurkar, the 95 percent probability interval is bounded below in 2020 by a 22 percent increase, and in 2050 by a 28 percent increase—very different from the expected doubling. The intervals are bounded above by a 46 percent increase in 2020 and a 167 percent increase in 2050, suggesting heavy pressure indeed on payroll taxes and the Trust Fund. Yet this range of possibilities most likely understates the width of the range with 95 percent probability coverage, since some kinds of uncertainty were not taken into account.

Figure 6-6 shows the corresponding forecasts for the total dependency ratio, or (population ≤20 + population ≥65)/(population 20 to 65). Now it is the turn of the SSA forecasts to have an implausibly tiny bracket, particularly in 2040. This is because the SSA obtains its low or "optimistic" forecast by combining high mortality with high fertility, thus getting the lowest old age dependency ratio. But

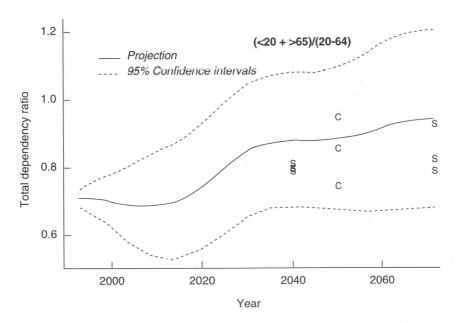

FIGURE 6-6 Projections of the total dependency ratio from Lee and Tuljapurkar (1994) (solid lines), the Social Security Administration (S), and the Bureau of the Census (C).

the high fertility also produces many child dependents, which raises the total dependency ratio.

If we consider the Lee-Tuljapurkar intervals for the total dependency ratio, the uncertainty is still very large. However, because child dependency and old age dependency generally move in opposite directions, the possibilities are muted and the bracket is narrowed. For example, in 2050 the upper bound of the old age dependency ratio was 2.1 times as great as the lower bound. For the total dependency ratio, however, it was only 1.6 times as great. Any sort of weighting of the age groups for tax yield and for program costs is easily incorporated into the analysis, and corresponding probability intervals can be derived.

The Lee-Tuljapurkar probability intervals do not reflect all sources of uncertainty. In particular, they do not reflect uncertainty arising from measurement error (data quality) or from the possibility of model misspecification and structural change beyond the range occurring historically during the base period. Nonetheless, these probabilistic forecasts represent an important step forward in conveying to policy makers the degree of uncertainty associated with demographic forecasts.

The stochastic population forecasts shown in Figures 6-4 to 6-6 do not simply produce new scenarios based on upper and lower probabilistic forecasts of the vital rates. Some researchers have made population forecasts of this kind (McNown and Rogers, 1992). However, such an approach suffers from most of the problems of the traditional scenario-based forecast, and no probabilistic interpretation is possible for the results. For example, the high population size forecast produced in this way would be based on fertility adhering to the upper bound of every individual percent probability bound (p), which for a horizon of T years would only have probability $1- (1-p)^T$. The stochastic population forecasts shown in Figures 6-4 and 6-6 instead treat fertility and mortality as random variables at every iteration of the forecast, keeping track of all the numerous variances and covariances. Similar results can also be obtained by Monte Carlo procedures, based on many hundreds of stochastic simulations of population trajectories, where the vital rates at each iteration are based on the estimated models, plus random shocks with appropriate covariance structures.

It is important to realize that the probability bounds consequently mean something very different in Figures 6-4 to 6-6 than do the scenario-based high, medium, and low bounds of traditional projections. This is not simply because a probability is attached to the former and not to the latter. The probability bounds indicate estimates of the range in which the quantity is 95 percent likely to be found *in the specific period in question*—here an average over a 5-year interval.[18] The upper bound on the scenario projection does not indicate a bound for a single year or for a 5-year average, unless vital rates are thought to be perfectly correlated over time. It is, in fact, difficult to give any interpretation to their bounds in this context. No one would suggest that fertility would exactly and consistently follow the high trajectory and mortality the low trajectory over the entire span of the forecast, yet that is the scenario underlying the high projection of the Census Bureau, for example.

Consider the important problem of calculating the probability that the Social Security reserve fund will fall to zero before a given date, under a given deterministic set of tax and benefit schedules and a set of deterministic economic assumptions. This calculation could not be done in any meaningful sense using the scenario-based projection, but can be carried out using the stochastic population forecast. To do this one would *not* derive the implications of following the upper and lower 95 percent bounds for the relevant quantities, which would be inappropriate. The correct calculation requires taking into account the full structure of covariances from year to year and across ages in all the relevant demographic quantities. One way to do this would be to use the Monte Carlo approach sketched above and simply to calculate the reserve fund for each year under each simulation and then, from these results for hundreds of simulations, calculate the distribution of the levels of the reserve fund in each year. This kind of calculation has not previously been possible. It illustrates how stochastic population forecasts can support a quantum increase in information for planning in the face of demographic uncertainty.

There are no new recommendations for data under this heading. Data are needed to model the vital rate processes, but once this is done, population totals are generated by recursive accounting identities. It would take us too far afield to consider the adequacy of data as a basis for forecasting fertility and migration.

So far as methods and models are concerned, however, research is badly needed on how to use these increasingly available stochastic demographic forecasts in policy formation (Tuljapurkar, 1992). How can the probability intervals for demographic quantities be combined with estimates of uncertainty for forecasts of economic variables? Health care costs? When can independence be assumed? If it cannot, what then? What should loss functions be?

Finally, we would like to call attention here to an earlier recommendation for Stoto-like analyses of past performance in forecasting dependency ratios and other measures, so that standard errors can be compared with those from the stochastic forecasts.

The Impact of Improving Patterns of Disability on Delaying Retirement

If the incidence of disability declines during ages associated with retirement (60 to 70), we might expect that retirement will be delayed, increasing the financial security of people planning their retirement. Health and disability, and particularly the transition from good health to a disabled state, have been well established in the literature as important determinants of retirement. The estimate from one structural model (Gustman and Steinmeier, 1986) suggests that the magnitude of the disability coefficient is equivalent to an increase of 4 years in age. In other words, a person who is not disabled would be predicted to retire 4 years later than an equivalent person with a disability. If the proportion of the working population with a disability were to decline by 10 percentage points—a substantial decline—the average retirement age would increase by less than 5 months. In other words, estimates from cross-sectional data on retirement behavior do not suggest large changes in retirement patterns, and hence in retirement income security, as the consequence of lower projected disability rates in the future.

It is well established, however, that cross-sectional estimates of variables may not provide good predictions of time series changes. For example, employers may be more willing to employ (or re-employ) older workers if the employers expect that a smaller fraction of their elderly workers will become disabled while working at their firm. As noted earlier, the self-reported perception of disability may be subject to variation as the consequence of government or social policy towards older workers (e.g., Waidmann, Bound, and Schoenbaum, 1995; Wolfe and Haveman, 1990).

Uncovering how work and retirement will evolve in the long term is a difficult problem. The current trend appears to be towards earlier retirement, not later retirement, suggesting that the secular changes in underlying health status that might be expected to delay retirement in the future are currently being offset by other factors, perhaps related to disability insurance among others. To detect the evolution of retirement decisions requires a long-term panel of people nearing retirement, coupled with detailed information on activities of daily living and instrumental activities of daily living measured in a consistent way over time. The Retirement History Survey (RHS) is a reasonably long-term panel, but it occurred during dramatic changes in social insurance policy towards the elderly, such as an increase in real Social Security benefits. The HRS again shows great promise in shedding light on this important issue, because it begins with families nearing retirement. Nevertheless, one would also like to have a comparison cohort with objective questions that could be matched with the HRS or an earlier survey.

The Distribution of Health Expenses Among Out-of-Pocket, Private Insurance, and Public Insurance

Out-of-pocket health expenditures are an important component of financial security at retirement. These out-of-pocket expenditures are determined both by the general level of health care expenditures and by the fraction of total expenditures paid out of pocket by the household. Of course, someone must pay for even the health expenses not paid out of pocket, so changes in the financing of government (or perhaps private) health insurance may also affect the financial security of retirees. In this section, we first document recent secular trends in the fraction of total expenditures paid out of pocket. Second, we consider how changes in the share of health spending accounted for by out-of-pocket costs (including private insurance premiums) might affect the indirect as well as the direct costs of health care for baby boom retirees. Finally, we consider data issues in measuring out-of-pocket expenditures.

Most projections of health costs assume a relatively stable fraction of government and private cost sharing. For example, Wiener, Illston, and Hanley (1994) predict an increase in the number of nursing home patients who spend more than 40 percent of income and assets on nursing home care, from 36 percent in 1993 to 39 percent in 2018 assuming current Medicaid policy. This predicted amount is quite modest, especially given the 25-year horizon. While not directly comparable, recent evidence on overall out-of-pocket expenses suggests that the burden of health care costs for the elderly has been rising substantially in the past several decades. Between 1977 and 1987, the percentage of elderly households (age 65+) who spent at least 20 percent of their income on out-of-pocket expenses rose from 7.0 percent to 10.6 percent (Taylor and Banthin, 1994). These figures, based on the National Medical Expenditure Surveys (NMES) in 1977 and 1987, do not even include nursing home expenses, which are likely to be substantial for a small fraction of the population.

The mix between out-of-pocket and government or private insurance payments affects the share of retiree health benefits that are actually paid by the cohort of retirees. Suppose, for example, that the out-of-pocket expenditure share declines, with the government picking up the shortfall. As a consequence, tax revenue needs to be larger to pay for the additional government share of health expenditures.[19] The increased share of government spending and taxation would then transfer resources from younger taxpayers (who foot the higher government share through their tax payments) to older generations (who benefit from the increased government spending for their medical bills).

By contrast, increases in private health care spending would be more likely to be borne by the recipients, either directly through out-of-pocket expenses or indirectly through higher insurance premiums. Of course, health insurance provided by employers for their retired employees may entail some redistribution across cohorts, as rising health care costs of retired employers are implicitly paid through higher insurance costs of current workers. Still, the prospects for intergenerational transfers are much more pronounced in the public than in the private sector.

Despite the importance of out-of-pocket expenditures for assessing prospects for retirement security, we know surprisingly little about their characteristics from current data sources. Covinsky et al. (1994), for example, reported that of 2,661 seriously ill patients who survived their hospital stay, 31 percent lost all or most of their savings as a consequence of their illness. However, this is a very specific sample of ill patients, which makes inferences about the prevalence of catastrophic expenses difficult. The NMES is cross-sectional, and cannot provide a good picture of how these costs evolve over time. For example, one might expect that out-of-pocket health expenses would pose a greater problem to future retiring baby boomers if catastrophic costs tended to be persistent. In other words, if households are randomly struck with out-of-pocket expenses equal to 20 percent of income, they can smooth consumption by drawing down assets or other contingencies. However, if only a few households are subject to 20 percent health expenses in every year, then these families would be subject to considerable financial distress. But there are few if any longitudinal studies of out-of-pocket health expenses. Feenberg and Skinner (1994) did use truncated panel tax data to infer the time series properties of out-of-pocket expenses in 1968-1973, but their study was limited to people who itemized in each year. More recent longitudinal data with detailed out-of-pocket expenses would be extremely useful.

Another problem with existing data is the weak link between nursing home and noninstitutionalized cost data. Both the 1977 and 1987 surveys, for example, exclude all nursing home costs from their measure of out-of-pocket expenses (although the 1987 study did make some efforts to statistically link the nursing home data with the noninstitutionalized data). Hence there is no data source that provides a general picture of the overall risk in out-of-pocket health care costs.

The Distribution of Retirement Income

Most of the estimates for future health status and health costs have focused on aggregate or average levels. Few have accounted for the fraction of people who would be deemed disadvantaged because of poor health and low levels of income and wealth. Wiener, Illston, and Hanley (1994) are notable for providing measures of the number of nursing home patients expected to be receiving Medicaid or the percentage incurring very high costs relative to income. They can provide these projections because their model simulates a large number of "people" through disability and income generators, allowing a detailed description of the *distribution* of health and income realizations.

Some additional factors may be necessary to capture changes in the distribution of retirement income security. Projections typically assume a homogeneous growth in wage rates among all individuals. Yet wage growth rates of lower educated people are falling behind the average growth rates, and in many cases are even negative in real terms (see Levy and Murnane, 1992). It is likely that this group would face a very difficult retirement in the face of rising health care costs. The government Medicaid burden might also be substantially larger than forecast, given the likelihood of many households falling short of a sufficient level of income and wealth to support nursing home costs.

Similarly, socioeconomic status tends to be strongly correlated with levels of disability. For example, Figure 6-7, taken from House et al. (1990), shows the number of chronic conditions as a function of age for the lowest and highest socioeconomic class. At ages 55 to 64, for example, the average number of

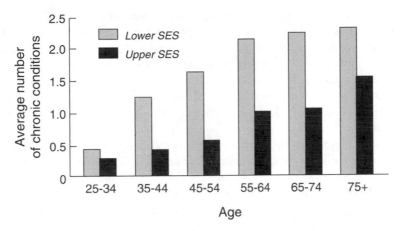

FIGURE 6-7 Average number of chronic conditions by socioeconomic status and age.
SOURCE: House et al. (1990:App. A).

chronic conditions for the upper socioeconomic status group is less than half the
number of conditions for the lower socioeconomic group. Of course, some part
of this correlation may be the consequence of poor health conditions reducing
earning capacity (Preston and Taubman, 1994). The authors attempted to partially correct for this by requiring both low income and low education attainment
for the lowest socioeconomic status, and both high income and high education for
the highest socioeconomic status. Still, disentangling the correlation between
poor health levels and income is an important research topic that can be potentially addressed with longitudinal data on past earnings and current disability
patterns.

Lower income households tend to face substantially higher levels of disability, laggard growth in income, and low levels of wealth relative to their income
(Hubbard, Skinner, and Zeldes, 1995). This is the group most likely at risk from
higher levels of out-of-pocket health care costs or cutbacks in Social Security
payments. However, there are no projections for this group that account for the
correlation among lower wages, poor health, lower wealth levels, and lower life
expectancy (Preston and Taubman, 1994).

Another shortcoming of most projections involving health care costs is that
either assets are assumed to grow exogenously (Wiener, Illston, and Hanley,
1994) or saving rates are assumed to be held constant (Auerbach and Kotlikoff,
1994). Yet changes in the composition and magnitude of health care costs (particularly those out of pocket) may be expected to affect the accumulation behavior of households. For example, in Hubbard, Skinner, and Zeldes (1994, 1995),
uncertainty about out-of-pocket health costs causes most people to save more in
response to additional risk. In their model, however, those with a reasonable

chance of becoming eligible for Medicaid in the event of a bad health shock (or Aid to Families with Dependent Children [AFDC] in the event of a bad shock to earnings) save less because of asset-based means testing. Because welfare programs typically restrict eligibility to people with less than $3,000 in assets, any personal saving above that amount is effectively taxed at a 100 percent rate in the event an individual requires long-term Medicaid or AFDC assistance. In their simulation model, such asset-based means testing programs reduce saving for lower income households.

In sum, projections about retirement security often focus on average levels of health care expenditures within quite broad demographic groups. However, the design of appropriate public policy is probably more concerned with the retirement outcomes of a specified group of people, perhaps those in the bottom quintile or quartile of the income distribution. Hence developing methods for predicting the financial security of specific demographic groups may be beneficial for policy purposes.

It may be possible to learn more about the correlation among saving, income growth, disability, and health care use with the ongoing project to match up data from the Panel Study of Income Dynamics with Medicare data. HRS and AHEAD, with their linked data of health, assets, and income, can provide a better picture of the group of elderly who are likely to receive the lowest levels of income and assets, and experience (perhaps) the greatest levels of disability.

CONCLUSION

The economic well-being of the baby boom generation during retirement will depend crucially on the evolution of mortality rates, disability, and health care costs. Whether longer life expectancy will strain Social Security and private pensions, or whether rising health care costs and many frail elderly will place a large burden on the economy, would be useful to know now, when there is still time to prepare for potentially large government and private expenses in the future. In this paper, we have examined a number of issues related to predicting health and mortality in the next century and have identified why different approaches to prediction or estimation have sometimes yielded such different estimates. In some cases, the controversies about predictions can be addressed by better use of existing data sources or by additional data collection.

An underlying theme of this paper is that many of the real questions about retirement income security cannot be answered simply by collecting more data or by running more complex estimation procedures. In the case of mortality, the crucial question is whether the observed trend in mortality rate reductions will be sustained for the next 50 years. By the same token, the fundamental question about health care costs is whether cost increases from the past 30 years might be expected to persist until the year 2030. Determining the answers to these questions is difficult and requires conceptual and theoretical advances as well as more and better data.

NOTES

1. However, these dates were presumably chosen not randomly but to maximize the variation, and so the marked contrasts in rates should be interpreted with caution.

2. In the forecast for low gains in life expectancy, basic death rates are assumed to stay constant at their 1990 levels, and these are increased by AIDS death rates, which are assumed to increase linearly to 2005 and then to remain constant throughout the forecast period (Bureau of the Census, 1993:xi). Therefore the impact of pessimistically projected future increases in AIDS mortality on life expectancy can be calculated by comparing this projected life expectancy with that in 1990.

3. These are based on personal communication with Bert Kestenbaum.

4. Individuals, of course, might live longer but the average across individuals would be bounded in this way.

5. Kaplan (1991), in a study of Alameda County, concluded that age-specific prevalences of some chronic conditions might be expected to rise over time.

6. Zedlewski and McBride (1992) predict 3 million nursing home residents in 2010 and 4.3 million in 2030, so a midpoint of about 3.6 million in 2020 would be roughly consistent with the estimates in the text.

7. Obviously, average levels of disability in nursing homes are higher than levels among the disabled in the community. Still, there is a 35 percent chance that a widow with two children and 5 to 6 activities-of-daily-living limitations will have as her primary caregiver one of her children (Soldo and Freedman, 1994).

8. Guralnik (1991) shows that people tend to be more impaired in the 2 or 3 years before death and that the costs of such impairment of those about to die increase with age. Therefore, as mortality declines and deaths are increasingly shifted toward older ages, the costs arising from this impairment prior to death will also tend to rise. Note, however, that in the transition from one mortality regime to another, there will be a countervailing tendency for deaths to drop below their steady-state value and therefore for costs to diminish.

9. Also see National Research Council (1988) for a detailed discussion of data sources and limitations.

10. Research by Alan Garber and Thomas MaCurdy has focused on combining data from the NLTCS and the National Nursing Home Survey, although the units of observation in the two samples are obviously different.

11. We focus here on direct medical costs. A more general definition of costs would include the indirect costs of lost work and informal caregiving.

12. Since expenditures are price multiplied by quantity, one can make inferences about the average use of health care services among demographic groups from cost data if one is willing to assume that the price "indexes" facing the different demographic groups are similar. In other words, when we use cost data to make inferences about relative health services use, we are making the assumption that if people aged 65 and above have expenditures that are twice those of people under age 65, this older group is receiving twice the real quantity of health care services.

13. Utilization per capita apparently comprises both changes in visits per person in a given age group and changes in the overall distribution of different ages.

14. Some part of the increase in relative prices can also be traced to the increased demand for real health services as the age composition of the population changes.

15. As Getzen notes, variation in increases in health care costs across countries may have swamped the effects that were due to population changes alone.

16. Of course, even an increase of 8 cents per dollar of lifetime income (37 cents versus 45 cents)

is a substantial increase in the tax burden of future generations and is caused largely by the pay-as-you-go nature of the current Social Security and Medicare programs (see Kotlikoff, 1992).

17. Analysis by the Census Bureau of the past performance of its forecasts, along lines pioneered by Stoto (1983), does give some idea of the probability coverage to assign to the forecasts of population size, but these cannot be applied to any other demographic measure except population growth rates, and certainly not to dependency ratios.

18. Because some cancellation of variations will occur over the 5-year interval, this probability interval will be narrower in percentage terms than the corresponding interval for a single year or for a point in time.

19. Of course, other government spending could be cut to pay for the higher share of government health spending. But were the share of government health spending lower, taxes could also be lower, if other government spending programs were held constant.

REFERENCES

Ahlburg, D., and J. Vaupel
  1990   Alternative projections of the U.S. population. *Demography* 27(4):639-652.
Alho, J.M.
  1992   The magnitude of error due to different vital processes in population forecasts. Pp. 301-314 in D. Ahlburg and K. Land, eds., *Population Forecasting*, a special issue of *The International Journal of Forecasting* 8(3).
Alho, J.M., and B.D. Spencer
  1985   Uncertain population forecasting. *Journal of the American Statistical Association* 80(390):306-314.
  1990   Error models for official mortality forecasts. *Journal of the American Statistical Association* 85:609-616.
Alter, G.
  1990   Old Age Mortality and Age Misreporting in the United States, 1900-1940. Paper presented at the annual meetings of the Population Association of America, Toronto, Ontario.
Auerbach, A.J. and L.J. Kotlikoff
  1994   *The United States' Fiscal and Saving Crises and Their Implications for the Baby Boom Generation.* Report to Merrill Lynch & Co. (February).
Bennett, N.G., and S.J. Olshansky
  1994   The Impact of Adjustments to Official Mortality Schedules on Projected Age Structure and the Future of Age-Entitlement Programs in the United States. Unpublished manuscript. Department of Sociology, Yale University, New Haven, Conn.
Berg, R.L., F.E. Browning, J.G. Hill, and W. Wenkert
  1970   Assessing the health needs of the aged. *Health Services Research* 5(Spring):327-331.
Bernheim, B.D.
  1994   *The Merrill Lynch Baby Boom Retirement Index.* Merrill Lynch & Co.
Bloom, D., and S. Glied
  1992   Projecting the number of new AIDS cases in the United States. Pp. 339-366 in D. Ahlburg and K. Land, eds., *Population Forecasting, A Special Issue of the International Journal of Forecasting* 8(3).
Bureau of the Census
  1993   *Population Projections of the United States, by Age, Sex, Race, and Hispanic Origin: 1993-2050.* Current Population Reports, P-25-1104, by Jennifer Cheeseman Day. Washington, D.C.: U.S. Department of Commerce.
Burner, S.T., D.R. Waldo, and D.R. McKusick
  1992   National health expenditures projections through 2030. *Health Care Financing Review* 14(1):1-29.

Campbell, P.R.
  1991 Projected AIDS-Age-Sex-Race/Ethnicity Specific Death Rates for the Period 1990 to
        2005. Unpublished paper. The Population Projection Branch, U.S. Bureau of the Census,
        Washington, D.C.
Chulis, G.S., F.J. Eppig, M.O. Hogan, D.R. Waldo, and R.H. Arnett
  1993 Health insurance and the elderly: Data from MCBS. *Health Care Financing Review*
        14(3):163-181.
Coale, A.J., and E.E. Kisker
  1990 Defects in data on old-age mortality in the United States: New procedures for calculating
        mortality schedules and life tables at the highest ages. *Asian and Pacific Population
        Forum* 4(1):1-32.
Costa, D.L.
  1994 *Health and Labor Force Participation of Older Men, 1900-1991.* NBER Working Paper
        #4929. Cambridge, Mass.: National Bureau of Economic Research.
Covinsky, K.E., L. Goldman, E.F. Cook, R. Oye, N. Desbiens, D. Reding, W. Fulkerson, A.F.
        Connors, Jr., J. Lynn, and R.S. Phillips
  1994 The impact of serious illness on patients' families. SUPPORT investigators. Study to
        understand prognoses and preferences for outcomes and risks of treatment. *JAMA*
        272(23):1839-1844.
Davis, W.
  1988 *Calculation of the Variance of Population Forecasts.* Bureau of the Census, Statistical
        Research Division Report Series, SRD Research Report Number: Census/SRD/RR-88/
        20. Washington, D.C.: U.S. Department of Commerce.
Elo, I.T., and S.H. Preston
  1994 Racial and Ethnic Differences in American Mortality at Older Ages. Paper prepared for
        the Workshop on Racial and Ethnic Differences in Late Life in the United States, Com-
        mittee on Population, National Research Council.
Employee Benefit Research Institute
  1995 *The Future of Employment-Based Health Benefits.* Special Report and Issue Brief No.
        161. Washington, D.C.: Employee Benefit Research Institute.
Farrell, C.
  1994 The economics of aging: Why the growing number of elderly won't bankrupt America.
        Business Week (September 12):60-68.
Feenberg, D., and J. Skinner
  1994 The risk and duration of catastrophic health care expenditures. *Review of Economics and
        Statistics* 76(November):633-647.
Fogel, R.W., D.L. Costa, and J.M. Kim
  1993 Secular Trends in the Distribution of Chronic Conditions and Disabilities at Young Adult
        and Late Ages, 1860-1988: Some Preliminary Findings. Unpublished manuscript. Uni-
        versity of Chicago.
Fries, J.F.
  1980 Aging, natural death, and the compression of morbidity. *New England Journal of Medi-
        cine* 303:130-136.
  1989 The compression of morbidity: Near or far? *The Milbank Quarterly* 67:208-232.
Getzen, T.E.
  1992 Population aging and the growth of health expenditures. *Journal of Gerontology: Social
        Sciences* 47(3):S98-S104.
Gomez de Leon, J.
  1990 Empirical DEA Models to Fit and Project Time Series of Age-Specific Mortality Rates.
        Unpublished manuscript. National Council on Population (CONAPO), Mexico, D.F.,
        Mexico.

Guralnik, J.M.
    1991   Prospects for the compression of morbidity: The challenge posed by increasing disability
            in the years prior to death. *Journal of Aging and Health* 3(2):138-154.
Gustman, A.L., and T.L. Steinmeier
    1986   A structural retirement model. *Econometrica* 54(3):555-584.
Haines, M.
    1994   *The Population of the United States, 1790-1920.* Working Paper No. 56, Historical Fac-
            tors in Long Run Growth. Cambridge, Mass.: National Bureau of Economic Research.
Himes, C.L.
    1994   Modern patterns of mortality in Sweden, Japan, and the United States. *Demography*
            31(4):633-650.
Himes, C.L., S.H. Preston, and G.A. Condran
    1994   A relational model of mortality at older ages in low mortality countries. *Population
            Studies* 48(2):269-292.
Holahan, J., A. Dor, and S. Zuckerman
    1990   Understanding the recent growth in Medicare physician expenditures. *Journal of the
            American Medical Association* 263(12):1658-1661.
House, J.S., R.C. Kessler, A.R. Herzog, R.P. Mero, A.M. Kinney, and M.J. Breslow
    1990   Age, socioeconomic status, and health. *The Milbank Quarterly* 68(3):383-411.
Hubbard, R.G., J. Skinner, and S.P. Zeldes
    1994   The importance of precautionary motives in explaining individual and aggregate saving.
            Carnegie-Rochester Conference Series on Public Policy 40(June):59-126.
    1995   Social insurance and precautionary saving. *Journal of Political Economy* 103(2):360-
            399.
Kannisto, V.
    1994   *Development of Oldest-Old Mortality, 1950-1990: Evidence From 28 Developed Coun-
            tries.* Odense Monographs on Population Aging 1. Odense University Press.
Kaplan, G.A.
    1991   Epidemiologic observations on the compression of morbidity. *Journal of Aging and
            Health* 3(2):155-171.
Kestenbaum, B.
    1992   A description of the extreme aged population based on improved Medicare enrollment
            data. *Demography* 29(4):565-580.
Kotlikoff, L.J.
    1992   *Generational Accounting.* New York: The Free Press.
Lee, R.D.
    1993   Modeling and forecasting the time series of U.S. fertility: Age distribution, range and
            ultimate level. *International Journal of Forecasting* 9(2):187-202.
Lee, R.D., and L. Carter
    1992   Modeling and forecasting the time series of U.S. mortality. *Journal of the American
            Statistical Association* 87(419):659-671.
Lee, R.D., and S. Tuljapurkar
    1994   Stochastic population forecasts for the U.S.: Beyond high, medium and low. *Journal of
            the American Statistical Association* 89(428):1175-1189.
Levy, F., and R.J. Murnane
    1992   U.S. earnings levels and earnings inequality: A review of recent trends and proposed
            explanations. *Journal of Economic Literature* 30(3):1333-1381.
Liebson, C.L., D.J. Ballard, J.P. Whisnant, and L.J. Melton
    1992   The compression of morbidity hypothesis: Promise and pitfalls of using record-linked
            data bases to assess secular trends in morbidity and mortality. *The Milbank Quarterly*
            70(1):127-154.

Lubitz, J., and R. Prihoda
    1984   The use and costs of Medicare services in the last 2 years of life. *Health Care Financing Review* 5(3):117-131.

Manton, K.G., L.S. Corder, and E. Stallard
    1993   Estimates of change in chronic disability and institutional incidence and prevalence rates in the U.S. elderly population from the 1982, 1984, and 1989 National Long Term Care Survey. *Journals of Gerontology* 48(4):S153-S166.

Manton, K.G., and E. Stallard
    1994   Medical demography: Interaction of disability dynamics and mortality. Pp. 217-278 in L.G. Martin and S.H. Preston, eds., *Demography of Aging*. Washington, D.C.: National Academy Press.

Manton, K.G., E. Stallard, and K. Liu
    1993a Forecasts of active life expectancy: Policy and fiscal implications. *The Journals of Gerontology* 48(Special Issue):11-26.
    1993b Frailty and forecasts of active life expectancy in the United States. In K.G. Manton, B.H. Singer, and R.M. Suzman, eds., *Forecasting the Health of Elderly Populations*. New York: Springer-Verlag.

Manton, K.G., E. Stallard, and H.D. Tolley
    1991   Limits to human life expectancy: Evidence, prospects, and implications. *Population and Development Review* 17(4):603-638.

McClellan, M.
    1994   Why Do Hospital Costs Keep Rising? Hospital Reimbursement, Hospital Production, and the Puzzles of Medicare's Prospective Payment System. Unpublished manuscript.

McCoy, J.L., H.M. Iams, M.D. Packard, and J. Shapiro
    1992   Health of retired workers: Survival status and Medicare service use. *Health Care Financing Review* 13(3):65-76.

McNown, R., and A. Rogers
    1989   Forecasting mortality: A parameterized time series approach. *Demography* 26(4):645-660.
    1992   Forecasting cause-specific mortality using time series methods. *International Journal of Forecasting* 8(3)413-432.

McNown, R., A. Rogers, and J. Little
    1995   Simplicity and complexity in extrapolative population forecasting models. *Mathematical Population Studies* 5(3):235-257.

National Research Council
    1988   *The Aging Population in the Twenty-First Century: Statistics for Health Policy*. Washington, D.C.: National Academy of Sciences.

Newhouse, J.
    1992   Medical care costs: How much welfare loss? *Journal of Economic Perspectives* 6(3):3-22.

Olshansky, S.J., B.A. Carnes, and C. Cassel
    1990   In search of Methuselah: Estimating the upper limits to human longevity. *Science* 250:634-640.

Pflaumer, P.
    1988   Confidence intervals for population projections based on Monte Carlo methods. *International Journal of Forecasting* 4:135-142.

Preston, S.H., I.T. Elo, I. Rosenwaike, and M. Hill
    1994   African American Mortality at Older Ages: Results of a Matching Study. Unpublished manuscript. Population Studies Center, University of Pennsylvania.

Preston, S.H., and P. Taubman
    1994   Socioeconomic differences in adult mortality and health status. Pp. 279-318 in L.G.
            Martin and S.H. Preston, eds., *Demography of Aging*. Washington, D.C.: National Acad-
            emy Press.
Schneider, E.L., and J.M Guralnik
    1990   The aging of America: Impact on health care costs. *Journal of the American Medical
            Association* 263(17).
Social Security Administration
    1992   *Life Tables for the United States Social Security Area, 1990-2080*. Actuarial Study No.
            107, SSA Pub. No. 11-11536. Washington, D.C.: U.S. Department of Health and Human
            Services.
Soldo, B.J., and V.A. Freedman
    1994   Care of the elderly: Division of labor among the family, market, and state. Pp. 195-216
            in L.G. Martin and S.H. Preston, eds., *Demography of Aging*. Washington, D.C.: Na-
            tional Academy of Press.
Stoto, M.
    1983   The accuracy of population projections. *Journal of the American Statistical Association*
            78(381):13-20.
Stoto, M.A., and J.S. Durch
    1993   Forecasting survival, health, and disability: Report on a workshop. *Population and
            Development Review* 19(3):557-581.
Taylor, A., and J. Banthin
    1994   *Changes in Out-of-Pocket Expenditures for Personal Health Services: 1977 and 1987*.
            AHCPR No. 94-0065, National Medical Expenditure Survey Research Findings 21.
            Agency for Health Care Policy and Research, Public Health Service. Rockville, Md.:
            U.S. Department of Health and Human Services.
Temkin-Greener, H., M.A. Meiners, E.A. Petty, and J.S. Szydlowski
    1992   The use and cost of health services prior to death: A comparison of the Medicare-only
            and the Medicare-Medicaid elderly population. *The Milbank Quarterly* 70(4):679-701.
Tuljapurkar, S.
    1990   Population dynamics in variable environments. Lecture notes in *Biomathematics* (85)
            Springer-Verlag.
    1992   Stochastic population forecasts and their uses. Pp. 385-392 in D. Ahlburg and K. Land.,
            eds., *Population Forecasting, A Special Issue of the International Journal of Forecasting*
            8(3).
U.S. Congress, House
    1994   *1994 Green Book: Overview of Entitlement Programs*. Committee on Ways and Means,
            WMCP 103-27. Washington, D.C.: U.S. Government Printing Office.
Waidmann, T., J. Bound, and M. Schoenbaum
    1995   *The Illusion of Failure: Trends in the Self-Reported Health of the U.S. Elderly*. NBER
            Working Paper #5017. Cambridge, Mass.: National Bureau of Economic Research.
Warner, H.R.
    1993   Molecular biological approaches to understanding aging and senescence. Pp. 307-365 in
            K.G. Manton, B.H. Singer, and R.M. Suzman, eds., *Forecasting the Health of Elderly
            Populations*. New York: Springer-Verlag.
Wiener, J.M., L.H. Illston, and R.J. Hanley
    1994   *Sharing the Burden: Strategies for Public and Private Long-Term Care Insurance*. Wash-
            ington, D.C.: The Brookings Institution.
Wilmoth, J.R., and S. Preston
    1994   Are Mortality Projections Always More Pessimistic When Disaggregated by Cause of
            Death? Paper presented at the 1994 Annual Meetings of the Population Association of
            America, Miami, Fla.

Wolfe, B.L., and R. Haveman
   1990   Trends in the prevalence of work disability from 1962 to 1984, and their correlates. *The
           Milbank Quarterly* 68(1):53-80.
Wolfe, P.R., and D.W. Moran
   1993   Global budgeting in the OECD countries. *Health Care Financing Review* 14(3):55-76.
Zedlewski, S.R., and T.D. McBride
   1992   The changing profile of the elderly: Effects on future long-term care needs and financing.
           The Milbank Quarterly 70(2):247-275.

7

A Framework for Analyzing Future Retirement Income Security

Gary Burtless

Over the past couple of decades Americans have become increasingly anxious about their prospects for enjoying a comfortable income in old age. Until recently this concern focused mainly on the Social Security system, which had a highly publicized brush with insolvency in the early 1980s. Most young workers now lack confidence that they will receive Social Security pensions as generous as those received by the current generation of retirees. Indeed, many claim skepticism they will collect any Social Security benefits at all.

Distrust by younger workers has been fueled by popular and academic analyses that claim currently promised benefits are too high to be financed under the present tax schedule. Even though the Social Security program has enjoyed comfortable and growing surpluses since the mid-1980s, the retirement of the huge baby boom generation after 2010 may force the system into insolvency unless benefits are cut or payroll taxes increased. If survey respondents' views are accepted at face value, many young workers apparently believe benefits will be slashed or eliminated entirely.

More recently analysts have begun to consider the risks facing other components of the U.S. retirement income system. A popular image to describe that system is the three-legged stool, consisting of Social Security benefits, employer pensions, and private retirement saving. The financial risks facing employer pensions have recently been analyzed by Sylvester Schieber and John Shoven

I am grateful to John Hambor, Eric Hanushek, Marvin Kosters, and Alicia Munnell for helpful comments on an earlier version of the paper.

(1994). Douglas Bernheim (1993) has examined the adequacy of private saving among prime-age workers. Both sets of authors demonstrate that the retirement income stool could be quite wobbly by the time the baby boom generation reaches retirement. Schieber and Shoven point out that the value of pension assets may fall sharply when a large generation of new retirees attempts to convert financial market assets into retirement consumption. Bernheim argues that, even if asset values were to be secure, the current saving rate of baby boom workers would be grossly inadequate to ensure them a comfortable standard of living after they retire.

All three pillars of the retirement income system are influenced by public policy. Social Security is a creation of the federal government. Private pension plans are heavily regulated by federal legislation and regulatory agencies. Public employee pension plans have been established and continue to be maintained by federal, state, and local government officials. Nonpension household saving is influenced by tax policy as well as by public regulation of the institutions that hold the bulk of nonpension financial assets. If the future income flows from these retirement income sources seem less secure than they once did, part of the explanation may be that defective laws or poor public regulation have undermined the safety of the system. A simpler explanation, of course, is that the long-term economic outlook has worsened, leaving Americans with less confidence in the future than they had 20 years ago. Even if public policies were optimal, young and middle-aged workers would feel greater anxiety about their prospects for enjoying a comfortable retirement.

How realistic are the fears of current workers? Is it likely that the Social Security system will default on promised benefits within the life spans of people who are now contributing to the system? Will private pensions and nonpension savings be adequate to finance comfortable retirement consumption in the next century? The federal government regularly publishes a document that helps answer these questions—the *Annual Report* of the Social Security trustees (see Social Security Administration, 1994). This report offers detailed forecasts of the future financial operations of the Social Security Trust Fund under alternative assumptions about trends in the economy and the future size and age distribution of the population. Though the reports contain clear evidence that Social Security and Medicare are not sustainable under current law and using plausible assumptions about the future, they provide little guidance about the size or timing of the benefit cuts that would be needed to protect the solvency of the programs. In addition, they shed no light on the financial prospects of the employer pension system, nor do they evaluate current saving patterns of active workers in relation to sensible retirement income goals. Readers of the reports are correct to feel anxious about the sustainability of Social Security and Medicare under present law. But they are given little information to decide how the programs should be changed or whether greater reliance on private retirement income would improve workers' prospects for a safe income in old age.

The goal of this paper is to offer a framework for analyzing retirement income security over the next several generations. I suggest a procedure to assess the risks facing each of the main sources of retirement income and summarize the overall income prospects of future generations of retired workers.[1] The proposed analysis extends the methodology currently used by the Social Security actuary to evaluate Old Age, Survivors and Disability Insurance (OASDI) solvency. In essence I urge that private pension solvency and future benefit levels be assessed using methods similar to those now used by the Social Security actuary. In addition, private saving accumulations of successive generations of workers should be predicted using alternative models of household saving behavior. Finally, the results of the separate analyses of the three major legs of the retirement income stool should be combined in a macroeconomic model that makes explicit the relationship between aggregate saving and investment in one period and output, saving, and investment in subsequent periods. As we shall see, this last step requires a fundamental revision in the methods currently used by the Social Security actuary, for it involves development of an explicit model of national income, investment, and saving. The OASDI trustees' *Annual Report* now treats future national income as fixed and traces out the implications for Social Security of the assumed path of future gross domestic product. In the proposed framework, the net savings accumulated through Social Security, the employer pension system, and nonpension household saving would affect potential national income (and hence retirement consumption) in future periods through its effect on the capital stock and the net foreign assets owned by U.S. residents.

The ultimate goal of retirement income forecasting is to improve decision making in the near term. A good forecasting model can inform voters and policy makers in two ways. It can suggest reforms in the current legal or regulatory environment that might improve the effectiveness of the retirement system or one of its major components. A good set of forecasts can also help individuals decide how much to save privately in light of the uncertainty surrounding public and private pension promises. The forecasting model should therefore yield explicit measures of the uncertainty of model forecasts, reflecting uncertainty arising because basic parameters are estimated with wide confidence bounds and because analysts do not agree about the correct model to describe the determination of income and saving.

The main concern about retirement income security is the fear that future retirees will be left with too little income from Social Security, employer pensions, and nonpension saving to enjoy consumption levels in retirement as high as those they enjoyed while working. Of equal concern to many observers is the situation of future workers. Will heavy payroll tax burdens reduce workers' earnings so much that their living standards could fall below current levels? A good forecasting model should produce estimates of net real earnings and retirement income replacement rates for successive generations of active and retired workers.

In setting retirement policy, a goal of the social planner might be to minimize the risk that future workers will suffer reductions in after-tax real wages in comparison with current wage levels. Another objective might be to avoid situations in which future retiree cohorts receive combined retirement incomes below, say, 70 percent of their net earned incomes while they were at work. These suggested "objectives" of retirement income policy might strike some readers as odd. A more natural objective is to maximize the expected present value of future welfare, subject perhaps to a minimum income guarantee for old or disabled persons. I suspect, however, that avoiding steep reductions in consumption during retirement and sharp increases in payroll tax burdens while actively employed are the main concerns most people have in mind when they express anxiety about the future of Social Security or private pensions. The proposed model would allow these concerns to be examined in a systematic way.

The remainder of the paper focuses narrowly on the provision of cash income in retirement. It ignores the large fraction of retirement consumption that is financed with public insurance and in-kind programs, including Medicare, public housing, and food stamps. The analytical framework could be extended to cover these consumption subsidies, but the extension will be left to future analysts.

In the next section I describe the current methods used by the Social Security actuary to evaluate OASDI solvency and show how they can be extended to analyze private pensions and nonpension household saving. The extension will require development of simple or more elaborate models of pension accrual and household saving. The approach to modeling recommended in this paper is dynamic microsimulation. The information requirements for this kind of model are also described. Since microsimulation is a costly and somewhat controversial approach to forecasting, the subsequent section considers alternatives to microsimulation and weighs the pros and cons of the alternative approaches. The section titled "Macroeconomic Policy" introduces a straightforward model of aggregate output, investment, and saving and shows how such a model can be used to combine the results from detailed models of the determinants of Social Security solvency, employer pension accruals, and nonpension saving. Combining the models for the separate components of retirement income into a larger model of the economy has several advantages. It permits the analyst to impose sensible cross-restrictions on equations that determine the individual components of private and public saving. It offers a macroeconomic framework for determining prices and rates of return on financial assets held by pension plans and private savers. Most important, it specifies the link between saving decisions that are made in one period and the wages, potential consumption levels, and investment opportunities available in later periods. Of course, economists do not agree on the model that best describes the relationship among these variables. As a result, any sensible forecasting model must permit analysts to show the effects on the forecast of using an alternative set of assumptions about saving behavior and income determination.

The section called "Cycles" considers the effect of cycles in economic variables that are crucial to the solvency of Social Security and private pensions. Although business cycles are not particularly important to the long-term solvency of Social Security, they play a larger role for private pensions and can have an enormous effect on the private retirement incomes of particular worker cohorts. The paper concludes with a brief summary.

MICRO MODELS OF RETIREMENT INCOME

The starting point for analyzing future retirement income flows is an accurate representation of the Social Security and employer pension entitlements for which workers will become eligible over the next two or three generations. A reasonable baseline assumption is that these entitlements will be accumulated for the foreseeable future under current laws and private pension fund practice. This is the assumption used by the Social Security actuary in evaluating the current financial status of the OASDI Trust Funds, for example. Although the assumption leads to some clear internal inconsistencies, it is useful for showing the implications of current law and administrative practices if they are left unchanged. The most straightforward and probably most accurate method of predicting the trend in employer pension and private saving accumulation is to impute earnings and pension and saving accruals to representative workers from successive cohorts. This method also has the advantage of permitting analysts to examine the distribution of retirement income flows within a generation. The approach to forecasting just described is commonly called dynamic microsimulation.

Social Security Forecasts

The *Annual Report* of the Social Security Trustees contains detailed financial information on the current and future status of the OASDI programs. In recent years the report has offered an evaluation of the trust funds under three sets of assumptions, labeled low-cost, intermediate, and high-cost, corresponding to optimistic, moderate, and pessimistic projections of the future solvency of Social Security. The forecast period extends over the next 75 years. The Social Security actuary's predictions are derived from a cell-based model that projects the number of people with given characteristics who are expected to contribute to the Social Security program as well as the number who will be eligible for and collect benefits. Each projection is painstakingly derived based on an extensive set of detailed assumptions about future economic and demographic trends. The most important assumptions can be summarized in terms of the long-run values of a handful of critical variables. The crucial demographic assumptions define future birth rates, mortality rates by gender at each age, age-specific disability rates, and net immigration into the United States. The critical economic assumptions describe the long-run trend in output per worker, annual price change, real interest rates, changes in labor force participation by age and gender, and the trend in untaxed fringe benefits as a percentage of labor compensation. Figures 7-1 and 7-2 show forecasts of future income, outgo, and Trust Fund operating surpluses (excluding interest payments) under the three sets of assumptions used in the *1994 Annual Report* (Board of Trustees).

When embodied in an actuarial model, the trustees' assumptions can be used to build up a picture in each future year of the age and gender distribution of all active workers, of workers who contribute to the Social Security system, and of recipients of OASDI pensions. In addition, the actuarial model yields a forecast in each future year of average labor compensation and the average covered wage and taxable earnings of U.S. workers, the average benefit received by new claimants in a variety of categories, and the change in the average nominal value of benefits in force, taking into account price inflation and the mortality experience of people who were previously collecting benefits. Although the Trustees' *Annual Report* does not include estimates of the average replacement rate received by successive cohorts of Social Security claimants, such estimates could be produced using information generated by the actuarial model. The report also includes no estimates of the future increases in payroll taxes or reductions in Social Security benefits that would be needed to restore the program to long-term solvency. Such estimates, however, could be derived in a straightforward manner based on statistics contained in the report (see Aaron and Burtless, 1989).

One reason the trustees' *Annual Report* does not include estimates of the adjustments in taxes and benefits that would be necessary to keep Social Security out of bankruptcy is the maintained assumption that future taxes and benefits will be determined under the law in effect when the reports are prepared. This is a reasonable basis for evaluating the solvency of the system under current law, but it is not very helpful to pensioners who wonder whether they will be able to collect full benefits over their entire retirement. Nor does it provide much guidance to young workers who would like estimates of the tax rate they will face in 20 years and the benefits they can expect to collect in retirement. Yet the evidence in the *1994 Annual Report* clearly shows that some modification in contribution rates or benefits will be needed if the pessimistic or intermediate assumptions in the report turn out to be correct (see Figures 7-1 and 7-2).

No one can offer a reliable prediction of future policy changes, of course, but the *Annual Reports* could offer simple descriptions of specific changes that would restore long-term solvency under the low-cost, intermediate, and high-cost assumptions.[2] For example, what is the amount of the payroll tax increase in 2010 that would eliminate the long-run imbalance under the pessimistic and intermediate assumptions? If the normal retirement age were raised in 2-month increments every calendar year starting in 2027, how much would the retirement age have to rise to eliminate the long-term imbalance?[3]

To reliably analyze the fortunes of different cohorts under Social Security, the current actuarial model should be supplemented with a dynamic microsimu-

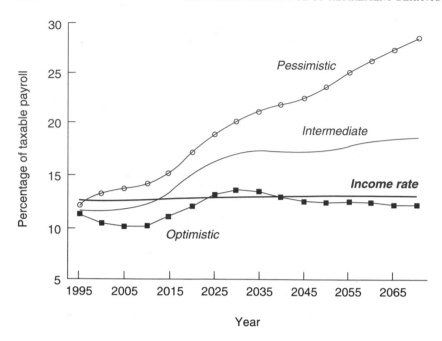

FIGURE 7-1 OASDI cost rates under alternative assumptions, 1995-2070. SOURCE: Social Security Administration (1994).

lation model that depicts the lifetime experiences of a representative sample of workers from successive cohorts. The justification for this strategy is described under "Rationale for Dynamic Microsimulation" below. One example of a dynamic microsimulation model is the Dynamic Simulation of Income Model (DYNASIM) maintained by the Urban Institute (see Orcutt et al., 1976; Johnson, Wertheimer, and Zedlewski, 1983; Johnson and Zedlewski, 1983). Although a dynamic simulation model can be far less elaborate than DYNASIM, the general approach would be similar. For representative members of each cohort, the model would predict marriage, births, divorce and remarriage, education, disability, labor force participation, annual earnings, Social Security contributions, self-employment, job turnover, retirement, OASDI entitlements, and death. Birth, marriage, divorce, remarriage, employment, and mortality rates would be identical to those assumed in the Social Security forecast. Annual employment and earnings totals, by gender and age, would correspond to detailed projections now prepared by the Social Security actuary for each year in the projection period. Social Security benefits would be calculated for insured workers when they are predicted to retire or become disabled. The main output of the simulation model is a set of demographic, labor force, and Social Security benefits histories for each member of the sample. The Social Security Administration is in an unusual

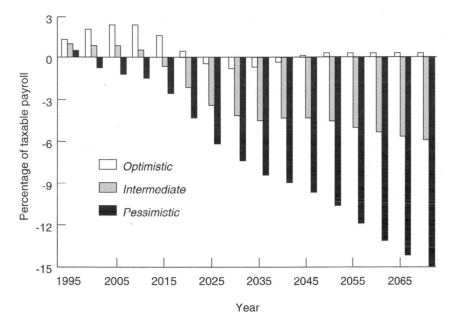

FIGURE 7-2   OASDI cash surpluses under alternative assumptions, 1995-2070.
SOURCE: Social Security Administration (1994).

position to create representative and accurate earnings histories, for its administrative files contain the lifetime earnings records of millions of current and past
contributors to Social Security. Moreover, the Social Security benefit records
often contain some relevant information about family composition and relationships. In many cases, these records provide data about the child and spouse
dependents of retired and deceased workers.

An advantage of the microsimulation strategy is that it allows straightforward calculation of the average Social Security replacement rate and rate of
internal return on contributions for successive cohorts of retirees. More important, microsimulation allows analysts to examine the distribution of replacement
rates within cohorts. While this exercise might seem uninteresting under the
maintained assumption that current OASDI law remains unchanged, it is more
interesting when analysts attempt to measure the effects of reforms that will be
needed to restore actuarial balance in the Social Security system. How many
individuals or families would face extraordinarily low earnings-replacement rates
in old age? The most important advantage of the strategy, however, is that it can
be extended in a straightforward way to predict the accumulation of employer-
sponsored pension credits and nonpension personal saving. This extension is
nearly impossible to achieve using the cell-based modeling strategy currently

used by the Social Security actuary. Cell-based modeling strategies are especially unsuited to predicting private pension entitlements and their relationship with Social Security retirement benefits.

Employer-Sponsored Pensions

The microsimulation strategy must be extended if it is to be applied to calculation of employer pension saving. Unlike the Social Security system, which is a uniform, compulsory program covering nearly all active workers, the employer pension system consists of over 700,000 individual plans covering a little over half the work force (Paine, 1993). Some employer-sponsored plans are compulsory for all workers on the employer's payroll, whereas others are voluntary and do not allow workers to participate unless they make contributions to the plan. There are two basic types of plans, defined benefit and defined contribution; these have fundamentally different patterns of accumulation of fund assets and worker entitlements. Many workers are covered by both types of plans. While it is possible to forecast the accumulation of fund assets under employer pension plans without reference to the accumulations of individual workers, it is essentially impossible to predict future retirement income flows for future cohorts without detailed predictions of the entitlements of representative workers in the cohort.

This overview suggests it is much more difficult to accurately predict employer pension accruals than Social Security accruals in a dynamic microsimulation model. In addition to the information needed to forecast Social Security benefits, the analyst requires information on each worker's industrial attachment, tenure with a particular employer, pension plan coverage on each job, decision to be covered by the plan if it is voluntary, choice of contribution level (if applicable), accrual of benefit entitlements under the plan, and lump-sum withdrawals from pension plans (if these are permitted). Since employers have increasingly preferred to offer defined contribution rather than (or in addition to) defined benefit plans, the analyst must also define a baseline assumption on whether and how rapidly this trend will continue. Although formidable, these analytical obstacles are not insurmountable. Sheila Zedlewski (1984) has used the DYNASIM model to describe the pattern of individual pension accrual and retiree income through 2020.[4]

Existing microsimulation models must be broadened if they are to provide an accurate representation of the pattern of aggregate fund accumulation and de-accumulation that will occur over the next few generations. Schieber and Shoven (1994) recently estimated the 75-year outlook for pension fund reserves using assumptions similar to those in the Social Security trustees' intermediate projection. Figure 7-3 shows their forecast of net inflows and outflows for employer pension funds under the assumption that current employer and employee contribution rates are maintained and the benefit structure of defined benefit plans

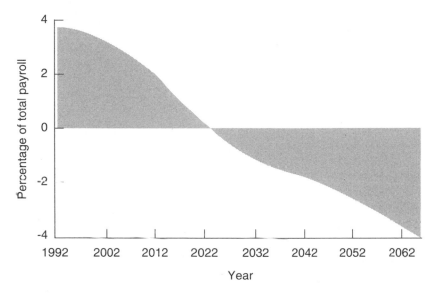

FIGURE 7-3 Net pension saving divided by total payroll, 1992-2065. SOURCE: Schieber and Shoven (1994)

remains unchanged. Notice that the pattern of asset accumulation and de-accumulation is similar to that for Social Security under the intermediate demographic and economic assumptions (Figure 7-2). Assets will be added to the funds over the next two decades and then drawn down after the baby boom generation retires.

To duplicate Schieber and Shoven's estimates in a microsimulation model, the analyst must calculate and then sum the worker and employer contributions to individual plans, calculate fund earnings on previous asset holdings, and subtract lump-sum withdrawals to active workers and pension payments to current retirees. If simple assumptions are used about the returns on fund assets, these calculations are straightforward for defined contribution plans. The calculations are more complicated for defined benefit plans since the amount of contribution is dependent on the actuarial rule the employer uses in funding its plan, changes in the value of the assets held in the fund, the amount of past underfunding or overfunding, and tax regulations that may produce a discrepancy between the economic value of a pension promise and the amount the firm is permitted to contribute to the fund. It is practically impossible to accurately impute the exact distribution of fund contributions for representative workers covered by over 100,000 defined benefit plans, where each fund is faced with a unique funding obligation. So long as the sum of defined benefit contributions across workers is close to a sensible total and so long as pension credits are accurately assigned to individual workers, this shortcoming of the microsimulation approach is not serious.

For each *worker* included in the microsimulation, the suggested approach generates a work history, an estimate of retirement benefits earned under employer defined benefit plans, an estimate of assets and pension annuities earned under defined contribution plans, and an estimate of Social Security monthly benefits at disability or retirement, including spousal or dependent benefits. The sum of these income flows represents the total annuity income available to most retirees. (Because it is hard for individuals to purchase fair annuities, few Americans convert other private savings into annuities after they retire.) The worker's replacement rate is calculated as the real after-tax value of annuity income in some year of retirement divided by average real after-tax wages during some period of his or her active career.

For each *year* in the forecast period, the proposed simulation yields estimates of aggregate contributions of workers and employers to private pension plans and Social Security, earnings on the assets held by the funds and the Social Security Trust Fund, and disbursements to pensioners and workers who withdraw assets from retirement plans before retirement.

To implement this strategy, analysts will need to make predictions of the returns earned by pension funds on their assets. The Social Security projections are straightforward because they require a prediction of only one interest rate, the average rate on U.S. Treasury securities. Since nearly all of the assets held by the Social Security Trust Fund can be sold at par, the fund does not face any capital risk from movement in asset prices. Pension funds hold a much wider variety of assets, and most of them are exposed to capital market risk. For Treasury and corporate bonds in pension fund portfolios, the risk might be small since funds can time the maturity of their bonds to match their anticipated liabilities. Bonds are therefore held to maturity, and the capital risk from early redemption is minimal. If pension fund portfolios include equities, the funds will be exposed to stock market risk. The risk seems particularly high after 2010 when many funds will be liquidating assets to pay pensions to their baby boom retirees (see Figure 7-3).

Schieber and Shoven (1994) assume a relatively fixed rate of return over their forecast period, but as they point out, this assumption is questionable unless we can identify a large and affluent group of investors who want to buy assets when the pension funds will attempt to sell them. For the purpose of creating a baseline simulation, Schieber and Shoven have nonetheless selected a reasonable assumption—average rates of return on different classes of assets will be stable and similar to those enjoyed by investors in the past. To perform simulations corresponding to the Social Security's optimistic and pessimistic forecasts, this assumption could be scaled up or down as appropriate. The basic procedure is useful for evaluating the returns earned in defined benefit plans and the *average* return in defined contribution plans. It is incomplete, however, for evaluating the benefits workers can expect to receive under defined contribution plans. On average, these plans will probably earn the market rate of return. But individual workers can earn substantially more or less depending on the investment success of their plan. The microsimulation model must reflect this diversity of actual experience by imputing a distribution of returns to workers enrolled in different defined contribution plans.

In any event, private pension fund modeling requires the analyst to make more extensive and detailed assumptions about returns and asset prices than are required in the Social Security forecast. More important, these assumptions are crucial in assessing the retirement income flows workers can expect in retirement. Most future income of the Social Security system is derived from taxes imposed on wages; relatively little is derived from returns on its asset portfolio. (In the intermediate and pessimistic forecasts, net interest received by the Trust Fund over the full 75-year projection period is negative.) Workers enrolled in defined contribution plans derive much more of their retirement income from returns on their investments. If these investments perform poorly, for an individual or an entire cohort, retirement income will be depressed. If they perform well, private pension income could exceed Social Security benefits for a majority of future retirees. A notable advantage of microsimulation is that it permits the analyst to examine the distribution of individual outcomes for retirement income. Some individuals will enjoy exceptionally high private retirement incomes; others will obtain meager pensions. This diversity of experience is difficult to analyze using aggregate or cell-based prediction strategies.

Household Saving

The imputation of personal saving is very easy if the analyst accepts a simple model of saving. It is notoriously difficult if the analyst believes that most consumers follow a life-cycle rule and recalibrate their consumption path every time they receive new information about economic variables that affect expected future earnings, asset prices, or real returns. The more complex the saving rule followed by consumers, the greater the advantage of using dynamic microsimulation to predict future saving levels.

Under a simple model of saving, persons save a fixed proportion of their current net income in a savings account that earns the average rate of return on financial assets typically held by households (i.e., on household savings outside of pension plans). Saving rates may vary by age and family circumstances. The saving rate by age and household type can be estimated for a cross section of the population using a variety of surveys, including the Consumer Expenditure Survey, the Survey of Consumer Finances, and the Survey of Income and Program Participation. Individuals accumulate assets (including their homes and businesses) according to a fixed assumption about the rate of personal, nonpension saving at each age. Though this assumption could conceivably yield reasonable estimates of *aggregate* personal saving in each year (see the section "Rationale for Dynamic Microsimulation"), it offers a poor method for imputing saving and wealth accumulation to *individual* households. The impressive fact about saving rates in a cross section is that they differ so widely among families, even among families that otherwise appear to be very similar (see Bosworth, Burtless, and Sabelhaus, 1991). Partly as a result, wealth in the United States is distributed much more unequally than income. If analysts wish to replicate the actual distribution of wealth and saving, they must impute individual asset accumulation using a sophisticated variant of the age-determined saving rule just described.[5]

Implementing a life-cycle consumption rule within a microsimulation model is a much more difficult undertaking, especially if we assume that consumers form their expectations in a fully rational way (see Auerbach and Kotlikoff, 1983, 1984). This approach is certainly worth pursuing if analysts accept the premises of the model, but it requires a large investment if it is to duplicate the observed pattern of household saving. Many economists are skeptical of the model because simple versions of it are not very successful in accounting for important aspects of personal saving. For example, many American workers enter retirement without any assets. A large percentage of workers who do have assets apparently continue to add to them after they retire. Neither fact is easy to reconcile with simple versions of the life-cycle model.

Whatever saving model is adopted, the analyst must determine whether individuals take pension saving and accrual of Social Security benefit rights into account when they decide how much to save outside of pension funds. If pension accruals are taken into account, individuals in generous pension plans will save less than similar individuals who are not covered by a pension. The evidence for this proposition at the individual level is not persuasive although that may be because workers with a high propensity to save are attracted to employers that offer generous pension plans. At any rate, it may be more natural to resolve this issue when treating the issue of aggregate saving than when imputing annual saving rates to individuals represented in the microsimulation sample (see below). Given the goals of the microsimulation, the most important objectives of the imputation procedure are to reliably predict aggregate private saving in each year of the forecast period, by age cohort, and to generate plausible estimates of the distribution of nonpension wealth around the time of each cohort's retirement. It is less important that year-by-year predictions of nonpension saving be accurate at the individual level.

DYNAMIC MICROSIMULATION

Rationale

The approach to forecasting outlined in the previous section relies heavily on dynamic microsimulation. Some baseline assumptions of the forecast, such as fertility trends, average wage growth, and labor force participation, may be based on Social Security actuarial reports. But most predictions of the model will rest on a method of forecasting that differs sharply from the one used by the Social Security actuary.

There are several alternatives to dynamic microsimulation. One alternative is the cell-based method of forecasting often used by Social Security Administration analysts. Under this approach, analysts predict program costs or outcomes for specific population groups (such as widows reaching age 60) instead of representative households. The approach is inexpensive and can be reliable when analysts are interested in forecasting only a small number of outcomes (e.g., average Social Security entitlements and labor force participation rate). It seems less useful if analysts wish to predict a large number of outcomes (average pension accumulation in a defined contribution plan, average entitlement in a defined benefit pension plan, average savings, average earnings, etc.) or if it is important to understand the distribution of outcomes within population cells. For example, the analyst or policy maker may be interested in obtaining an estimate of the percentage of households that will receive combined Social Security and private pensions that replace less than 30 percent of pre-retirement wage earnings. This kind of estimate is difficult or impossible to derive using cell-based forecasting methods, unless the cells represent very narrow groups of the population. (In that case, of course, the practical difference between microsimulation and the cell-based method is negligible.)

Another alternative to microsimulation is macroeconomic forecasting. A macroeconomic model predicts economy-wide outcomes, such as the unemployment rate, the real return on Treasury securities, and average labor compensation, based on appropriate theory and a set of simultaneously determined equations estimated with aggregate time series data. This kind of model can be effectively used to predict a wide variety of variables that determine the level and adequacy of future retirement incomes (see "Macroeconomic Policy" below). Macroeconomic models are less useful for predicting outcomes when a wide diversity of outcomes across households is likely to occur. For example, a macroeconomic model offers the most appropriate framework for estimating the average real rates of return on tangible and financial assets. It is less suitable for imputing the distribution of rates of return that will be enjoyed by different classes of investors or individual households.

While it is essential to know the economy-wide rate of return enjoyed by U.S. investors, in forecasting future retirement income flows it is also important to understand how these returns will be distributed across different pension plans and households. Dynamic microsimulation provides a suitable framework for imputing returns to individual plans and households. Of course, analysts may lack reliable information about how rates of return are distributed across classes of investors and individual households. Microsimulation estimates may therefore depend on *guesses* about the distribution of returns. While this may appear to be a less reliable basis for prediction than macroeconomic models, in fact it is not. A macroeconomic model yields a single prediction of the rate of return on a particular asset (say, corporate equities). But it is well known that some fund managers obtain higher returns than the market average while a majority achieve worse returns. Under these circumstances, it is more accurate to predict diversity in the investment return of pension funds than to assume identical returns, even if the exact distribution of returns across funds is unknown. Moreover, by clearly defining the kind of information that is needed to describe the distribution of returns across pension funds and households, construction of the dynamic micro-simulation model has helped define a research area where more empirical data are needed.

Disadvantages

The dynamic simulation approach outlined under "Micro Models of Retire-ment" has several disadvantages. Some are described in the National Research Council's survey of microsimulation modeling (Citro and Hanushek, 1991; see especially pp. 114-122). Complex simulation models require a heavy investment of time and effort from skilled researchers and programmers. The models them-selves are often unwieldy and require a highly trained staff to ensure that policy simulations are appropriately performed. Detailed information about a wide variety of human behaviors is needed if the model is to provide a realistic picture of the future labor force status and family relationships of U.S. residents. In addition to accurate baseline data covering a representative sample of house-holds, the simulation model requires plausible models of behavior for a wide range of social and economic interactions. It is unclear whether current models of behavior are accurate enough to provide a reliable guide to population dynam-ics over the next 20 years, much less over the 75-year time horizon examined by the Social Security actuary.

In spite of these difficulties, it is hard to conceive of a practical alternative approach to the analysis of future retirement income flows. The basic goal of the Social Security system and employer pension plans is to provide an adequate level of retirement income to retired and disabled workers and their dependents. The goal is not only to offer adequate retirement incomes *on average* but to offer adequate incomes to all workers who spend most of their careers in full-time jobs. To determine whether the U.S. retirement income system accomplishes that goal, it is necessary to predict retirement income flows for a sample of representative workers. Prediction of the population average replacement rate or of average replacement rates within population cells cannot reveal whether the distribution of replacement rates across individuals is accomplishing the goal of the retire-ment system. In particular, if Social Security benefits are sharply reduced and powerful incentives offered for additional private pension and retirement saving accumulation, predictions from a microsimulation model are needed to show how replacement rates may be distributed among retirees.

Analysts can take practical steps to minimize the disadvantages of microsimulation. To ensure that the results are understandable to ordinary users, the basic simulation model should be kept fairly simple. If evidence for a particular model of behavior is weak or highly controversial, analysts should use straightforward and clearly described assumptions, rather than a complex behavioral model, to predict crucial aspects of behavior, for example, job turnover, job entry, marriage, remarriage, divorce, or childbearing. The goal of the modeling exercise is to predict the distribution of retirement incomes and evaluate the impact of alternative policies on the distribution of incomes and contribution rates; the goal is *not* to test the implications of cutting-edge models of social and economic behavior. In predicting job exit, for example, the probability of exit could be assumed to be correlated with just three or four characteristics of the worker (say, age, gender, wage, and current tenure on the job). This simple assumption precludes many sophisticated models of job turnover, for example, those that link worker turnover to the pattern of private pension accrual. The sophisticated models of behavior may be correct, but there is no reason to embed these models in the basic simulation model until it is clear that they enjoy broad acceptance in the social scientific community. Since social scientists are often uncertain about the correct model of behavior, it is in fact desirable to examine in a systematic way the sensitivity of predictions to alternative behavioral assumptions or models (see below).

The disadvantages of microsimulation relative to other methods of analysis and prediction are easy to exaggerate. Microsimulation requires the analyst to spell out explicitly the relationship between individual characteristics and behavioral outcomes (e.g., between age, job tenure, and job exit). Policy makers and many analysts are uncomfortable making detailed predictions for behaviors about which empirical knowledge is weak. Aggregate and cell-based prediction methods do not seem to require this kind of detailed modeling. Yet these methods implicitly rest on assumptions about detailed behavioral relationships that are explicitly treated in dynamic microsimulation modeling. For example, a cell-based prediction methodology may yield the prediction that 55 percent of 60- to 64-year-old retirees in 2020 will qualify for private pensions that have an average value of one-third of the economy-wide wage. Even though the cell-based prediction strategy may appear to embody no explicit assumption about the relationship between age, job tenure, and the probability of job exit, the fact is that some such assumption is implicit in the prediction that the average pension will amount to one-third—rather than one-quarter or one-half—of the economy-wide monthly wage. An important difference between dynamic microsimulation and other prediction strategies is that the microsimulation analyst is forced to be more explicit and detailed in selecting behavioral assumptions. This represents a strength rather than a weakness of the approach. Analysts can plainly see which behavioral relationships are crucial for purposes of predicting future retirement benefits and retirement income burdens. Government agencies can focus their research budgets on understanding these relationships rather than on topical areas that are less critical to evaluating retirement income policy.

MACROECONOMIC MODELING

The results from the microsimulation models of Social Security, private pensions, and nonpension household saving can be combined in a natural way in a macroeconomic model. In fact, the macroeconomic model represents a crucial advance over current Social Security actuarial forecasts for the purposes of policy evaluation. It permits analysts to predict the change in national saving, and hence in future output, that the Social Security system and other retirement programs cause. In addition, it allows analysts to model explicitly the relationship between different components of public and private saving.

The Social Security projections are based on the premise that future taxes and benefits will be determined under current law. As we have seen, this yields an internal inconsistency, because two of the three projections suggest that the Trust Fund will be exhausted long before the end of the 75-year planning horizon. The probable effect of this imbalance is that taxes will be raised or benefits reduced sometime before the Trust Fund is depleted.

In addition to this policy inconsistency, there is an economic inconsistency in the forecast. Under the intermediate assumptions of the 1994 trustees' report (Social Security Administration, 1994), OASDI tax revenue will exceed benefit outlays by 0.2 percent of gross domestic product in 2010; in 2065, predicted tax revenue will *fall short* of benefit payments by 2.0 percent of gross domestic product. Over the same period, the predicted cash deficit of Medicare-Part A will climb from 1.0 percent of gross domestic product to 3.4 percent of gross domestic product (Social Security Administration, 1994, p. 185). Over a 55-year period, the combined cash operating deficit of Social Security and Medicare-Part A is predicted to climb by 4.6 percent of gross domestic product. (Under the high-cost assumptions in the report, the combined deficit will grow by nearly 10 percent of gross domestic product.) Unless other federal taxes rise by a third or non-OASDI government outlays fall sharply, the intermediate forecast implies that the federal deficit will more than double. Aggregate saving and net domestic investment may fall, limiting the rise in national income and real wages. This effect is ignored in the trustees' forecast, because future growth rates are generated by growth in the labor force and the assumed steady growth in average labor productivity. If productivity growth is affected by domestic investment and saving, as most economists believe, an important channel of effect is missed.

Determination of Aggregate Output

In a standard growth model, national output is produced by combining the factors of production. In the Cobb-Douglas production function, capital (K) and labor (L) are combined in period t to produce total output (Y),

(1) $Y_t = A(t)K_t^\alpha L_t^{1-\alpha}$,

where $A(t)$ is an efficiency parameter that rises from year to year as a result of technical progress. Labor supply in period t is assumed to be fixed and can be taken either from the Social Security actuary's forecast or directly from the dynamic microsimulation model. The capital stock is not mentioned in the Social Security forecast. It must be calculated in a base year using information published by the Department of Commerce and then projected in future years as the capital stock in the base period plus the cumulative sum of domestic investment, I, over the projection period, with a constant geometric rate of depreciation, δ:

(2) $K_t = (1-\delta) K_{t-1} + I_t$.

The compensation rate for labor, w, and the gross rate of return on capital, r, are determined by the marginal conditions

(3) $w = \partial Y/\partial L = (1 - \alpha)(Y/L)$,

and

(4) $r = \partial Y/\partial K = \alpha(Y/K)$.

The rate of interest on financial assets, as well as the gross profitability of businesses, is tied to movements in r.[6]

Aggregate U.S. saving (S) is divided between domestic investment and net foreign investment, I_F:

(5) $I + I_F \equiv S$.

If the United States were a closed economy, I_F would be zero by definition. Annual additions to the capital stock could be calculated simply from knowing S. Since the United States is an open economy, I_F can be positive or negative depending on whether the nation runs a surplus or deficit in its trade account.

National saving consists of government saving (S_G) and private saving (S_P)

(6) $S = S_G + S_P$,

where

$$(7) \quad S_G = T - G = (T_{SS} - B_{SS}) + (T_O - G_O),$$

and

$$(8) \quad S_P = S_{Pen} + S_{HH} + S_O.$$

Government saving is the difference between taxes (T) and spending (G). It is convenient to divide public saving into the Social Security operating surplus (Social Security taxes less benefit payments) and the surplus or deficit in the remainder of government operations $(T_O - G_O)$.[7] Private saving consists of pension saving (S_{Pen}), nonpension household saving (S_{HH}), and other private saving (S_O), primarily retained corporate earnings.

The model described in equations (1) through (8) can be solved after specifying the relationships that determine public and private saving and the division of national saving between domestic and foreign investment.[8] As a starting hypothesis, we might assume that net foreign investment is zero or is a constant but modest fraction of national output. Domestic investment will then vary directly with movements in national saving. If gross saving is a fixed percentage of gross domestic product—say, 18 percent of Y—then equations (1), (2), (3), and (5) can be used to solve for the technical efficiency factors in (1) that would exactly reproduce the Social Security actuary's 75-year forecast of future gross domestic product and average worker compensation. Deviations from this baseline assumption about the determinants of national saving will produce deviations in the future path of investment, national output, wages, pension accruals, and Social Security surpluses and deficits (see Aaron, Bosworth, and Burtless, 1989, pp. 55-82, 131-33).

Alternative Saving Models

Many analysts will be dissatisfied with the assumptions underlying the Social Security forecast and with the saving assumptions described in the previous paragraph. An alternative approach is to specify the rate of growth of $A(t)$ a priori and then prepare a baseline forecast using the analyst's preferred public and private saving functions. For example, suppose the analyst believes that government dissaving will average 3 percent of gross domestic product for the foreseeable future while S_O will average 3 percent of gross domestic product. Since S_G and S_O always sum to zero under these assumptions, future saving will be determined solely by pension saving and nonpension household saving. Estimates from the microsimulation model yield predictions of the sum of S_{Pen} and S_{HH} for each year of the forecast period.[9] Note that variations in national saving under these assumptions occur solely because of the predicted aging of the U.S. population, which is the main factor causing pension saving and nonpension household saving to vary over time.

Several theories of saving can be expressed as restrictions on the saving equations, (6) through (8). For example, the Ricardian equivalence theorem implies that any deviation of S_G from its baseline path will be offset by an equal and opposite deviation in S_P; S will be left unchanged.[10] This hypothesis is not very helpful for establishing a baseline path of S_G or S_P, but it does imply that a variety of policies intended to boost public saving will have little if any effect on national saving or future output. Suggestions that federal deficits be slashed or Social Security surpluses increased are futile under this interpretation, since private savers will reduce their saving by an offsetting amount.

A similar though less sweeping theory is sometimes advanced to explain worker reactions to employer pension plans. Well-informed workers recognize that their employers set aside part of compensation in a retirement saving plan. When saving in the pension plan is increased but remains less than the amount workers would otherwise save for retirement, they will promptly reduce their household saving to offset the increased pension plan saving. If saving in the plan *exceeds* the amount the workers would otherwise save, they reduce their savings to zero and borrow from lenders up to their borrowing limit. The pension plan will affect overall personal saving only to the extent that workers are prevented from borrowing as much as they would like. According to this theory, the simulation model should attempt to explain $S_{Pen}+S_{HH}$. The division of private saving into separate pension and nonpension components is meaningless. Moreover, federal tax or regulatory policies that attempt to restrict contributions into pension plans or to encourage employers to establish new plans will have only a limited influence on saving. Workers will offset the effect of the changes in pension contributions by adjusting S_{HH}.[11]

The most popular theory to explain saving is the life-cycle/permanent income model. In principle, this theory should explain *all* saving by households, including saving in and out of pension plans. Martin Feldstein (1974) extended the theory to explain workers' reactions to Social Security pensions. Since these pensions substitute for retirement saving that workers would otherwise have been forced to do on their own, Feldstein reasoned that Social Security could reduce workers' incentive to save. His evidence persuaded him that it did, though many economists remain skeptical of this evidence. Feldstein's extension of the basic life-cycle model is not easy to describe in terms of equations (6) through (8). However, future reductions in the generosity of Social Security pensions would certainly be expected to increase the amount of private saving, either in employer pension plans or in other household accounts.

If the life-cycle/permanent income model is correct, households will be induced to change their saving behavior by changes in their earnings prospects and movements in the real after-tax interest rate. Unfortunately, economists do not know whether an increase in the rate of return increases or decreases the amount consumers will choose to save. At different points in the life cycle, the effect of an interest rate increase is likely to differ. A dynamic microsimulation model thus offers a suitable context for implementing the life-cycle model in a sensible way. No two economists would agree, however, on the best way to implement the life-cycle theory in a realistic model of household decision making. One reason, mentioned earlier, is that the theory has a hard time explaining the behavior of a large percentage of Americans. Theorists are thus forced to modify the basic theory to account for obvious empirical contradictions.[12] Different theorists have proposed different modifications to rescue the basic theory.

One implication of nondynastic versions of the life-cycle model is that consumers will have different reactions to a change in the expected real rate of return depending on their position in the life cycle. (This begs the question of how consumers decide whether a change in the *observed* rate of return can be interpreted as a change in the permanent rate.) In response to an increase in real returns, young consumers without any assets may raise their saving. Older consumers can reduce their saving, assuming increased rates have not caused them to experience capital losses. The effect on aggregate saving may be ambiguous and may depend on the distribution of income and wealth across age groups; even for a population with a fixed age structure, it may cycle over time. The best way to investigate these issues is with a dynamic microsimulation model that realistically reflects the age distribution of the population over a very long time horizon. The fact remains, however, that economists have proven more adept at designing simulation models than achieving consensus on the crucial parameters of the individual life-cycle consumption function.

CYCLES

The discussion so far has rested on the assumption that many crucial variables attain a stable steady-state path. Predicted cycles in some variables depend mainly on the demographic cycle: predicted labor force growth will slow and eventually stop; after a period of relative stability through 2010, the fraction of the population over 65 will climb rapidly and then rise more slowly. Except in their most pessimistic forecast, the Social Security trustees ignore the possibility that the economy will ever enter a recession. In their most pessimistic projection, the trustees assume two recessions will occur within the next 10 years. Over the following 65 years, the pessimistic forecast assumes steady unemployment and productivity growth.

Because the trustees assume that critical economic and demographic variables will eventually attain stable values, their forecast omits uncertainty arising from sudden and unexpected swings in important variables—real interest rates, productivity growth, birth rates, and price inflation. Equation (4) in the macroeconomic model allows the possibility that saving-induced swings in the investment rate can produce changes in the real rate of return. But the model essentially accepts the trustees' forecast that productivity, births, and prices will follow steady and predictable paths over the forecasting horizon.

This assumption may have little practical significance for the Social Security forecast. So long as the interest rate and inflation achieve the predicted *average* levels over the projection period, the long-term actuarial balance of Social Security will probably be little affected. It would be interesting, however, to systematically investigate whether this is true. If real interest rates are low when the Trust Funds have a large balance but then rise as the funds are depleted, the Social Security program will obviously be in a worse position than if the same average rate of return were sustained over the 75-year planning period. Moreover, if productivity improvement is rapid in the years immediately before the baby boom generation retires and then slows down after 2015, the Trust Fund may be in worse financial shape than if productivity improves smoothly over 75 years.[13]

Cycles in critical economic variables can have an even larger impact on employer pensions and private saving. Few defined benefit employer pensions are indexed to inflation, for example, so their real value drops sharply if inflation climbs by, say, 4 percent. Even if the average 75-year inflation rate is 4 percent, as assumed in the intermediate Social Security projection, this will be small comfort to workers who happen to retire during a period when inflation averages 8 percent. For Social Security pensions, the rise in inflation has a small effect on expected real pensions during retirement; higher inflation reduces the real value of pensions slightly. For most employer-sponsored pensions, the effect will be much more dramatic. As noted earlier, swings in the real interest rate can also produce large effects on the fortunes of private pension funds and private savers. They will have much smaller effects on the financial status of Social Security.

To systematically analyze the risks facing future retiree income, it seems essential to take cycles seriously. Even if cycles make little difference in the long run, they can have large and devastating consequences for particular cohorts of workers and retirees. At a minimum, analysts should investigate the impact of irregular cycles on some of the critical variables, notably, the rate of improvement in technical efficiency ($A(t)$), price inflation, unemployment, market rates of return on different categories of assets, births, and mortality improvement. One lesson that recent history has taught is that each of these variables *has* an important cyclical component. Even if we cannot describe a completely convincing theory to explain this cyclical variation, it is important to evaluate its impact on each major component of retirement income. I suspect that plausible cyclical variability in certain variables will have a larger influence on some sources of retirement income than on others. When weighing reforms in different elements of the retirement income system, analysts and policy makers should understand how cycles can affect each leg of the income stool.

CONCLUSION

This paper suggests a modeling strategy to evaluate retirement income security over the next two or three generations. The strategy combines dynamic microsimulation with a simple macroeconomic growth model. Microsimulation is needed to accurately predict the retirement income sources of successive worker cohorts. It offers a natural way to implement the most popular theory of household saving, the life-cycle/permanent income model. Analysts who prefer simpler models can easily implement them using either the microeconomic or the macroeconomic component of the model. The macroeconomic model is essential to understanding the feedback effects of higher or lower retirement saving on future output, wages, and rates of return, all of which help determine the living standards of successive cohorts of workers and retirees.

The proposed strategy can be implemented in discrete steps. An initial step requires the creation of a straightforward dynamic microsimulation model predicting labor force status, job tenure and turnover, private pension and Social Security accrual, and household saving behavior for a representative sample of U.S. workers. This model can be based on existing dynamic simulation models or it can be derived from reanalysis of good cross-sectional or longitudinal files, including the Survey of Income and Program Participation and the Panel Study of Income Dynamics. A second step is to ensure that aggregate predictions from the microsimulation model duplicate predictions of the Social Security actuarial model (e.g., predictions of the age distribution of the population, of the number of persons eligible for and receiving OASDI, of the average Social Security benefit, of Social Security contributions, and of average compensation and taxable wages). At this point the microsimulation component of the model can be utilized in practical policy analysis. The model can be used, for example, to analyze the impact of growing inequality in the distribution of money wages and fringe benefits (see Levy and Murnane, 1992) and the implications of growing earnings inequality for Social Security replacement rates and financial obligations. Earnings inequality and its implications for pension entitlements are much harder to examine using the cell-based forecasting methods of the Social Security actuarial model.

The next step in implementing the model is to develop a macroeconomic model in which aggregate savings are divided into domestic uses and foreign investment. The model may be either simple or complex although for purposes of long-run simulation it probably makes sense to keep the model straightforward and understandable. (Elaborate models of the aggregate economy are typically used to forecast over fairly short periods, usually less than 5 years and almost always less than 10 years. The models are usually elaborate because they are used to forecast many more variables than analysts will be interested in here.) The macroeconomic model must not only explain how savings is divided across alternative uses; it must also account for growth in the capital stock, worker productivity, and wages, and it must explain market rates of return on different classes of assets. As a first approximation, the predictions of the model should be consistent with the productivity, wage, and interest rate forecasts in the Social Security trustees' report. After completion of this step, the model can be used to analyze the realism of the forecasts in the trustees' report. Do the trustees' predictions of interest rates and productivity make sense in view of the likely availability of future savings? What kind of assumptions about future public and private saving are needed to make the trustees' predictions plausible? The model can also be used for practical policy simulation. If Social Security taxes were immediately increased to reduce the long-term imbalance in the Trust Funds, would the resulting increase in public saving adversely affect private pension returns? If so, would private pensions fall? By how much?

The first implementation of the microsimulation and macroeconomic models will probably be simple and almost certainly unrealistic. The realism of the model can eventually be improved by introducing more elaborate and accurate behavioral modeling. A long-run goal of the exercise is to improve the reliability of the forecasts through improvement in basic knowledge available to simulation designers. Model development can help in selecting topics for empirical research by highlighting the behavioral relationships that are critical for the purpose of reliable forecasting. Even where economists remain divided about the correct representation of economic behavior, the simulation approach is helpful in showing the sensitivity of forecasts to changes in assumptions about critical behavioral relationships.

Actuaries and economists do not have good enough models or information to forecast reliably. It is important under these circumstances to alert users of forecasts to the uncertainty in the forecast. The current *Annual Report* of the OASDI Trustees (Social Security Administration, 1994) already contains information that can help users understand the uncertainty behind the intermediate projections. In particular, it contains estimates of future national income and Social Security solvency using more pessimistic and more optimistic assumptions than those used to make the intermediate projection. This information can and should be improved, not only in the trustees' report but also in any comprehensive forecast of future retirement income flows. As a first step, analysts should attempt to describe the likelihood of the pessimistic and optimistic assumptions about critical economic and demographic variables. This analysis should be based on evidence from as far back in the historical record as it is possible to go; the forecast should not be dominated by experience of the very recent past. In defining the pessimistic and optimistic assumptions used in any long-term forecast, analysts should attempt to select optimistic and pessimistic assumptions that are about equally likely (or unlikely) to occur. Even if the analyst does not choose an intermediate set of assumptions that is exactly midway between the optimistic and pessimistic assumptions, it still makes sense to select the extreme assumptions so that they bound the likely experience in a symmetrical way.

In selecting the optimistic and pessimistic assumptions, analysts should also consider the historical experience to see whether favorable outcomes in some of the critical variables have been systematically correlated with unfavorable outcomes in other critical variables. If such correlation exists, optimistic and pessimistic assumptions should be selected to reflect this fact.

Broad interest in retirement issues has been spurred by growing awareness among specialists and ordinary citizens that Social Security may not be able to pay promised benefits. Voter anxiety is understandable. The population is aging, and the proportion of Americans older than 65 will climb rapidly after 2010 under almost any reasonable assumption about future births and deaths. The predictable aging of the U.S. population has led analysts to investigate whether there are predictable consequences of population aging. Many potential consequences have been identified, including effects on Social Security reserves and payroll tax rates, saving patterns, and living standards in retirement.

The focus on predictable demographic variables is somewhat ironic. The outlook for Social Security solvency and future living standards has worsened for a variety of reasons, but the predictable aging of the population is far from the most important. A more salient reason for increased pessimism about the future is the decline in productivity improvement, that is, in the annual growth of $A(t)$ in

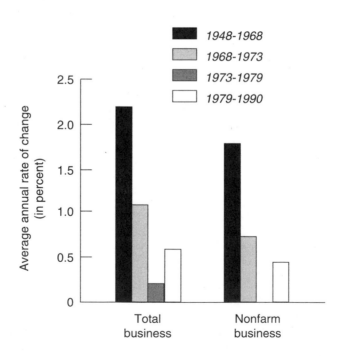

FIGURE 7-4 Multifactor productivity growth, selected periods, 1948-1990. SOURCE: Baily, Burtless, and Litan (1993).

equation (1). Figure 7-4 shows changes in the rate of improvement in multifactor productivity from 1948 through 1990. These estimates represent our best guess of the rate of improvement in pure technical efficiency. Estimates are shown separately for the nonfarm business economy and the entire business economy. With either measure, the rate of improvement in technical efficiency has slowed sharply over the postwar period. Slower multifactor productivity growth has a much more dramatic effect on future retiree or worker living standards than expected changes in the age distribution of the population. If technical efficiency in production were to improve as fast between 1994 and 2034 as it did between 1948 and 1968, future workers would enjoy far higher living standards than today's workers, even if the payroll tax doubles between 1994 and 2034.[14]

One goal of the alternative forecasts in the Social Security trustees' report is to alert readers to the influence of differences in underlying assumptions. This paper argues that the effects of differing assumptions should be evaluated for employer pensions and private savings as they are for Social Security solvency. As a starting point, analysts should examine the implications for future pensions and private household saving of the optimistic, intermediate, and pessimistic assumptions currently used in the trustees' report.

In addition, we should systematically examine the consequences of alternative assumptions about the determination of aggregate saving and the allocation of saving between domestic and foreign investment. Not only are analysts uncertain about the future path of fundamental technical and demographic variables, such as productivity growth, birth rates, and mortality improvement; they are also uncertain about the correct model to use in predicting private and aggregate saving. As it happens, aggregate saving crucially affects the future income available to be divided between workers and retirees. A prudent policy maker would demand some information about the implications of this model uncertainty.

Finally, current methods of the Social Security actuary could be extended in a logical way to assess the consequences of cyclical variation in economic and demographic variables. Because the current forecasts do not consider the effects of cycles that occur more than 10 years from now, they can miss significant threats to the solvency of Social Security and to replacement rates available to future workers. The omission is likely to be even more important for private sources of retirement income, including both private pensions and financial assets held by retirees. An interesting topic for future research is the optimal design of public policy in light of the different risks that face the three legs of the retirement income stool.

NOTES

1. The motivation for a research program along these lines was described in Burtless (1994).
2. In fact, the *Annual Reports* contain enough information so that readers can estimate the tax

increases needed to restore long-term actuarial balance under two different scenarios. In future years when the predicted annual cost rate of OASDI exceeds the predicted income rate, the difference between the two rates is approximately equivalent to the payroll tax increase that would be necessary to keep Social Security solvent under a pay-as-you-go system (see Social Security Administration, 1994:106-107). Alternatively, long-term actuarial balance could be restored if taxes are immediately and permanently raised by the difference between the summarized 75-year cost rate and 75-year income rate. In the *1994 Annual Report* the long-run cost rate under the intermediate assumptions was 15.37 percent of taxable payroll while the income rate was 13.24 percent of payroll, yielding a required payroll tax increase of approximately 2.13 percentage points (Social Security Administration, 1994:191).

3. To calculate the size of the required tax rate changes or retirement age adjustments that would be needed in the long run, analysts must look beyond the 75-year time horizon covered in the current trustees' reports. Both the pessimistic and the intermediate forecasts suggest that the annual cost rate continues to rise above the income rate in the last years of the forecast period. By implication, even if action is taken to restore actuarial balance within the 75-year period from 1994 through 2068, it is likely that OASDI will fall out of actuarial balance in some 75-year period that begins before 2068 but after 1994. A further tax rate increase or retirement age adjustment would then be needed. See Aaron, Bosworth, and Burtless (1989), pp. 44-48.

4. For an alternative approach and a description of the Pension and Retirement Income simulation Model (PRISM), see Kennell and Sheils (1990). Haveman and Lacker (1984) offer a useful comparison of the two pension-simulation models. The DYNASIM model was updated in 1983 (and renamed DYNASIM2). Ross (1991) provides a brief description and comparison of the PRISM and DYNASIM2 models.

5. For example, each household head could be assigned a preferred saving rate that is *permanently* higher or lower than that of the average person of the same age. The individual's saving rate in a particular year could be calculated as a sum of the age-specific saving rate, the permanent difference from the average rate, and a random error term, possibly one that is correlated with the disturbance in the household's labor earnings.

6. A more realistic model of interest rate determination and asset returns would be needed in a complete model.

7. Interest on the Social Security Trust Fund is ignored in this formulation. Interest payments earned by the fund are an expense for the remainder of the government, so the interest payments have no net effect on government saving. In order to be consistent with the microsimulation model, net saving in government employee pension plans should be treated as part of household saving rather than government saving. Contributions and withdrawals from these plans should be treated in exactly the same way as contributions and withdrawals from private pension funds.

8. A realistic model would divide the national economy into several sectors, including agriculture, nonfarm business, housing services, and nonprofit and government entities. Each sector uses inputs and produces a flow of goods and services under a unique production function. The analyst must specify rules for allocating investment and workers across these sectors.

9. Under the assumptions of this saving model, the microsimulation can be performed only one year at a time. Since the capital stock and wages in period $t+1$ are determined by saving and investment in period t, it follows that some microsimulation calculations for period $t+1$ cannot be performed until a complete solution is found for saving and investment in the previous period. Of course, if the worker's employment and job turnover are assumed independent of real wages and unearned income changes, some calculations in the microsimulation model could be performed without any prediction of investment in previous periods.

10. For a defense of the empirical relevance of Ricardian equivalence, see Seater (1993). For a critique, see Bernheim (1987) and Gramlich (1989). Unlike Seater, I do not find the evidence for full Ricardian equivalence very compelling. The simultaneous and sharp decline in both public and private U.S. saving in the 1980s seems hard to reconcile with any plausible version of the theory.

11. The same theory is sometimes offered to explain why S_O should be included directly in household saving. This saving consists mainly of retained earnings in U.S. corporations. Since the corporations are owned primarily by U.S. households or their agents (pension funds, insurance companies, etc.), well-informed households should see through the corporate veil and take account of corporate saving behavior when deciding how much to save out of dividends, interest payments, and labor earnings. I do not find this theory very convincing unless corporate saving is directly and consistently reflected in equity prices.

12. For example, Hubbard, Skinner, and Zeldes (1994) rescue the model by theorizing that income uncertainty and asset-tested transfer programs can erode the incentive to save for a minority of households.

13. Real benefits received by baby boom retirees are determined by the average real wage in the year they reach age 60. The real tax base out of which those benefits will be paid depends on economy-wide wages in the years after baby boomers retire. The burden of paying for Social Security pensions will therefore be larger as the rate of productivity improvement after baby boomers retire declines.

14. For an illustration, see Aaron, Bosworth, and Burtless (1989), pp. 91-96.

REFERENCES

Aaron, H.J., B. Bosworth, and G. Burtless
    1989   *Can America Afford to Grow Old?* Washington, D.C.: Brookings Institution.
Aaron, H.J., and G. Burtless
    1989   Fiscal policy and the dynamic inconsistency of Social Security forecasts. *The American Economic Review, Papers and Proceedings* 79(2):91-96.
Auerbach, A.J., and L.J. Kotlikoff
    1983   National savings, economic welfare, and the structure of taxation. Pp. 459-493 in M. Feldstein, ed., *Behavioral Simulation Methods in Tax Policy Analysis.* Chicago, Ill.: Univeristy of Chicago Press.
    1984   Social Security and the economics of the demographic transition. Pp. 255-275 in H.J. Aaron and G. Burtless, eds., *Retirement and Economic Behavior.* Washington, D.C.: Brookings Institution.
Baily, M.N., G. Burtless, and R.E. Litan
    1993   *Growth with Equity: Economic Policymaking for the Next Century.* Washington, D.C.: Brookings Institution.
Bernheim, B.D.
    1987   Ricardian equivalence: An evaluation of theory and evidence. Pp. 263-304 in *NBER Macroeconomics Annual.* Cambridge, Mass.: MIT Press.
    1993   *Is the Baby Boom Generation Preparing Adequately for Retirement?* New York: Merrill Lynch.
Bosworth, B., G. Burtless, and J. Sabelhaus
    1991   The decline in saving: Evidence from household surveys. *Brookings Papers on Economic Activity* 1:183-256.
Burtless, G.
    1994   The uncertainty of Social Security forecasts in policy analysis and planning. Pp. 1-20 in Public Trustees, Social Security and Medicare Boards of Trustees, *Future Income and Health Care Needs and Resources for the Aged.* Baltimore, Md.: Social Security Administration.
Citro, C.F., and E.A. Hanushek, eds.
    1991   *Improving Information for Social Policy Decisions: The Uses of Microsimulation Modeling. Vol. I, Review and Recommendations.* Washington, D.C.: National Academy Press.

Feldstein, M.S.
    1974   Social Security, induced retirement, and aggregate capital accumulation. *Journal of Political Economy* 82(5):905-926.
Gramlich, E.M.
    1989   Budget deficits and national saving: Are politicians exogenous? *Journal of Economic Perspectives* 3(2):23-36.
Haveman, R.H., and J. Lacker
    1984   *Discrepancies in Projecting Future Public and Private Pension Benefits: A Comparison and Critique of Two Micro-Data Simulation Models.* Research on Poverty Special Report 36. Madison, Wisc.: University of Wisconsin.
Hubbard, R.G., J. Skinner, and S.P. Zeldes
    1994   Expanding the life-cycle model: Precautionary saving and public policy. *The American Economic Review, Papers and Proceedings* 84(2):174-179.
Johnson, J., R. Wertheimer, and S.R. Zedlewski
    1983   *The Family and Earnings History Model.* Urban Institute Project Report 1434-03. Washington, D.C.: Urban Institute.
Johnson, J., and S.R. Zedlewski
    1983   The Jobs and Benefits History Model. Unpublished manuscript. Urban Institute, Washington, D.C.
Kennell, D.L., and J.F. Sheils
    1990   PRISM: Dynamic simulation of pension and retirement income. Pp. 137-172 in G.H. Lewis and R.C. Michel, eds., *Microsimulation Techniques for Tax and Transfer Analysis.* Washington, D.C.: Urban Institute Press.
Levy, F., and R.J. Murnane
    1992   U.S. earnings levels and earnings inequality: A review of recent trends and proposed explanations. *Journal of Economic Literature* 30(3):1333-1381.
Orcutt, G., S. Caldwell, R. Wertheimer II, S. Franklin, G. Hendricks, G. Peabody, J. Smith, and S. Zedlewski
    1976   *Policy Exploration Through Microanalytic Simulation.* Washington, D.C.: Urban Institute Press.
Paine, T.H.
    1993   The changing character of pensions: Where employers are headed. Pp. 33-40 in R.V. Burkhauser and D.L. Salisbury, eds., *Pensions in a Changing Economy.* Washington, D.C.: Employee Benefit Research Institute.
Ross, C.M.
    1991   DYNASIM2 and PRISM: Examples of dynamic modeling. Pp. 121-140 in C.F. Citro and E.A. Hanushek, eds., *Improving Information for Social Policy Decisions: The Uses of Microsimulation Modeling. Vol. II, Technical Papers.* Washington, D.C.: National Academy Press.
Schieber, S., and J.B. Shoven
    1994   *The Consequences of Population Aging on Private Pension Fund Saving and Asset Markets.* NBER Working Paper #4665. Cambridge, Mass.: National Bureau of Economic Research.
Seater, J.J.
    1993   Ricardian equivalence. *Journal of Economic Literature* 31(1):142-190.
Social Security Administration
    1994   *1994 Annual Report of the Board of Trustees, Federal OASI and DI Trust Funds.* Washington, D.C.: U.S. Social Security Administration.
Zedlewski, S.R.
    1984   The private pension system to the year 2020. Pp. 315-341 in H.J. Aaron and G. Burtless, eds., *Retirement and Economic Behavior.* Washington, D.C.: Brookings Institution.

Biographical Sketches

ERIC A. HANUSHEK (*Chair*) is professor of economics and public policy and director of the W. Allen Wallis Institute of Political Economy at the University of Rochester. Formerly, he was deputy director of the Congressional Budget Office, and he has held academic appointments at Yale University and the U.S. Air Force Academy. His research involves applied public finance and public policy analysis, with special reference to schooling and aspects of income determination. He is a past president of the Association for Public Policy Analysis and Management, and he has had governmental appointments at the Cost of Living Council and the Council of Economic Advisers. He received a Ph.D. degree in economics from the Massachusetts Institute of Technology.

GARY BURTLESS is a senior fellow in the economic studies program at the Brookings Institution in Washington, D.C. Previously, he served as an economist in the Office of the Secretary of the U.S. Department of Labor and at the U.S. Department of Health, Education, and Welfare. His research focuses on issues connected with public finance, aging, saving, labor markets, income distribution, social insurance, and the behavioral effects of government tax and transfer policy. He is the author of numerous articles on the effects of Social Security, welfare, unemployment insurance, and taxes. He received a Ph.D. degree in economics from the Massachusetts Institute of Technology.

ALAN L. GUSTMAN is Loren M. Berry professor of economics at Dartmouth College and a research associate at the National Bureau of Economic Research. Formerly, he was a Special Assistant for Economic Affairs at the U.S. Department of Labor. His research has involved labor and public economics, with strong emphasis on the economics of retirement, pensions, and Social Security. He serves on the Steering Committee of the Health and Retirement Survey and on the Technical Advisory Panel of the National Longitudinal Survey. He received a Ph.D. degree in economics from the University of Michigan.

F. THOMAS JUSTER is a research scientist at the Survey Research Center and professor of economics at the University of Michigan, Ann Arbor. His research includes the design of economic and social accounting systems, the analysis of saving and wealth accumulation patterns among U.S. households, the analysis of time allocation among households, and the development of measures of economic well-being. He has served on a number of National Research Council committees and chaired the Committee on the Supply and Demand for Mathematics and Science Teachers. He is a fellow of the American Statistical Association and chaired its Committee on the Quality of Economic Data. He is also a fellow of the National Association of Business Economists. He received a B.S. degree in education from Rutgers University and a Ph.D. degree in economics from Columbia University.

RONALD D. LEE is professor of demography and economics and chair of the Department of Demography at the University of California, Berkeley. He also currently serves as the director of the Center for the Demography and Economics of Aging and as a member of the neuroscience, behavior, and sociology of aging subcommittee of the National Institute on Aging of the National Institutes of Health. His research focuses on demography and population studies, particularly from an economic point of view. A member of the National Academy of Sciences and chair of the Committee on Population, he has worked on many panels, currently serving on the Panel on Demographic and Economic Impacts of Immigration. He is a past president of the Population Association of America. He received a master's degree in demography from the University of California at Berkeley and a Ph.D. degree in economics from Harvard University.

ROBIN L. LUMSDAINE is an assistant professor of economics at Princeton University and a faculty research fellow at the National Bureau of Economic Research. Her research is in the areas of time-series econometrics and the economics of aging. In 1996-1997 she will be a national fellow at the Hoover Institution at Stanford University. Previously, she was a visiting scholar at Northwestern University, the Federal Reserve Board of Governors, and the International Monetary Fund. She is an associate editor for *The Journal of Business and Economic Statistics*. She received a Ph.D. degree in economics from Harvard University.

NANCY L. MARITATO is a member of the staff of the Committee on National Statistics and the Committee on Population. Previously, she worked as an economist in the Office of the Assistant Secretary for Planning and Evaluation at the U.S. Department of Health and Human Services, at the Institute for Research on Poverty at the University of Wisconsin, and with the President's Council of Economic Advisers. Her interests focus on poverty and welfare policy analysis. She received B.A. and M.A. degrees in economics from the University of Wisconsin, where she is currently working on a Ph.D. degree in economics.

DONALD O. PARSONS is professor emeritus of economics at Ohio State University. He has held the Siena Chair in economics at the University of Siena (Italy), where he received a Fulbright Scholar Distinquished Lecturing Award. He has also been the Harry Scherman Research Fellow at the National Bureau of Economic Research and a visiting scholar at the Centre for Socio-legal Studies, Wolfson College, Oxford University. His recent research has focused on labor market contracts, including pension and retirement issues, and the design of social insurance programs, with special reference to disability insurance. He received a Ph.D. degree in economics from the University of Chicago.

JAMES M. POTERBA is the Mitsui professor of economics at the Massachusetts Institute of Technology, where he has taught since 1982. He is also director of the Public Economics Research Program at the National Bureau of Economic Research, coeditor of the *Journal of Public Economics*, and a fellow of the American Academy of Arts and Sciences and of the Econometric Society. His research focuses on the economic analysis of taxation, government expenditure programs, and financial markets; his recent work has emphasized the effect of taxation on the financial behavior of households and firms and the tax treatment of employee benefits. He recently completed a term as a director of the American Finance Association. He received a D.Phil. degree in economics from Oxford University.

JONATHAN S. SKINNER is professor of economics at Dartmouth College and senior research associate at the Center for Evaluative Clinical Sciences, Dartmouth Medical School. He is also a research associate at the National Bureau of Economic Research. Prior to joining the Dartmouth faculty, he taught at the University of Virginia, the University of Washington, Stanford University, and Harvard University. His research interests are in tax policy, consumption and saving, and the economics of the Medicare program. He received a Ph.D. degree in economics from the University of California, Los Angeles.